The Low Budget Video Bible

Publisher's Cataloging in Publication
(Prepared by Quality Books Inc.)

Roth, Cliff.
  The low budget video bible : the essential do-it-yourself guide
to creating top notch video on a shoestring budget / Cliff Roth. --
2nd ed.
   p. cm.
   Includes index.
   ISBN 0-9635216-1-6

   1. Video recordings--Production and direction--Guidebooks. 2.
Video tape recorders and recording--Guidebooks.   I. Title.

PN1992.94.R68 1995   791.45'023
                                        QBI95-20322

The Low Budget Video Bible

The essential do-it-yourself guide
to making top notch video
on a shoestring budget

Cliff Roth

Desktop Video Systems

New York

Contents

Part I   Low Budget Video Basics

1   Low Budget, Big Budget   3

2   Shopping for a Camcorder   21

3   Camcorder Basics: The Camera Section   47

4   VCR and Camcorder Tape Basics   71

5   Other Camcorder Features and Frills   81

6   The Ultimate Camcorder   93

7   Camcorder Production Tips   99

8   Tripods   113

Part II   Tape and Editing

9   Low Budget Tape Formats   123

10   The VHS Family: VHS, Super-VHS, VHS-C, S-VHS-C   133

11   The 8mm Family: Hi8 and 8mm   137

12   The DV and MiniDV Format   141

13   The 3/4" U-matic Format   157

14   Erase Heads and Editing   163

15   The Language of the Moving Image   167

16   Shopping for an Editing VCR   187

17   Tape Editing Technology   199

18   Building an Editing System   231

19   Nonlinear Digital Video Editing Technology   261

20   Time Base Correctors   275

Part III   Audio, Lighting, Graphics, Travel, Etc.

21   Audio Basics 281

22   Lighting   319

23   Graphics & Optics   339

24   Producing and Directing   359

25   Travelling with a Camcorder   367

Part IV   **New Media and Opportunities**

26   Cable TV   383

27   Public Access   387

28   Finding Funding   395

29   HDTV and Wide Screen TV   403

30   Direct Broadcast Satellites   409

31   The Internet   413

32   Conclusion   419

Appendix: LowBudget Video Resources   421

Index   451

Detailed Contents

Introduction   xv
    You Can Do It!   xv
    Social-Political Introduction   xvii
    Technical Introduction   xviii
    Introduction to Second Edition   xxi
Acknowledgments   xxiii

. . . .
Part I   Low Budget Video Basics

1   **Low Budget, Big Budget   3**
    Low Budget Budgets:
    How to Spend Your Precious Money   6
    Industrial and Consumer Video Equipment   10
    "Broadcast Quality"   11
    Broadcast, Industrial, and Consumer Formats
    Comparison   12
    Camera vs. Tape Quality   16
    Nonlinear Editing   17

2   **Shopping for a Camcorder   21**
    The Gray Market   29
    The Complete Field Production Kit   32
    Which To Buy   33
    Sony CDR-VX1000   36
    Panasonic PV-DV1000 Camcorder   40

3   **Camcorder Basics: The Camera Section   47**
    The Lens   48
    Wide Angle vs. Telephoto   49
    Automatic Focus Systems   52
    "Normal" Focal Lengths   56

Automatic And Manual Iris   57
F-stop Numbers and Lens "Speed"   61
The Image Sensor   61
White Balance Color Adjustments   69

4   **VCR and Camcorder Tape Basics   71**
Helical Recording 71
Resolution   74
S/N Ratio and Generation Loss   75
Time Base Accuracy   76
S-Video Connections   77
Tape Loading And Operation   78
Flying Erase Head   80
Audio Recording   80

5   **Other Camcorder Features and Frills   81**
The Viewfinder   81
Title Systems   84
Electronic High Speed Shutters   85
Self Timer   86
Digital Special Effects   88
Image Stabilization   89

6   **The Ultimate Camcorder   93**
Everything, and Tiny   93

7   **Camcorder Production Tips   99**

8   **Tripods   113**
Good Head   114
The Steadicam JR   117

Part II   **Tape and Editing**

9   **Low Budget Tape Formats   123**
Video Format War   124
Quick Comparison of Videocassette Formats   126
Tape Brands   127

10 The VHS Family: VHS, Super-VHS, VHS-C, S-VHS-C   133
Video Track   133
Audio   133
VHS Index/Address Track   135

11 The 8mm Family: Hi8 and 8mm   137
Video Track   137
Audio   138
8mm Time Code Track (RC and Industrial)   140

12 The DV and MiniDV Format   141
The First Models   141
Editing Nirvana   142
Solid and Stable   143
Audio Flexibility   143
Firewire Connection   144
The DV Cassettes   145
The DV Tracks   146
DV's Data Compression   147
Comparison With Broadcast Digital Video   149
No Generation Loss   151
DVC and DVCPro   153
HDTV-Ready   155

13 The 3/4" U-matic Format   157
When To Consider Using 3/4"   158
The Audio Advantage   159
An Inexpensive, Intermediate Format   160
A Few Words About the Fancier Stuff   161

14 Erase Heads and Editing   163
The Flying Erase Head   164

15 The Language of the Moving Image   167
Quick Guide to Editing: 167
The Art of Editing   168
Camera Angles   171
Shooting to Edit vs. 'In-camera' Editing   179
Storyboards, Scripts, and Shot Lists   184

16 Shopping for an Editing VCR   187
    Panasonic AG-1980   189
    Sony DHR-1000   191
    Sony EVS-7000   192
    Other Consumer VCRs   193
    Special Features On Industrial Models   195
    Getting Started   197

17 Tape Editing Technology   199
    The Basic Home Editing Setup   199
    Technical Quality and the Flying Erase Head   201
    The Pro Gear   202
    Low Budget Desktop Video Editing   203
    Types of Edit Controllers   204
    On-line and Off-line Editing   205
    Remote Connections   207
    Editing Accuracy   212
    Control Track Editing   214
    Time Code: SMPTE, VITC, RC, and MiniDV   215
    Edit Decision Lists   216
    Workprints   219
    Assemble vs. Insert Editing   220
    A/V Dubs   225
    Time Code Editing vs. Control Track Editing   227
    Making Hi8 and MiniDV Window Dub Tapes
    with RC Time Code   229

18 Building an Editing System   231
    Generation Loss   232
    A/B Roll Editing   236
    The Time Base Corrector, Image Mixer,
    and Frame Synchronizer   236
    One Channel Digital Effects   237
    Utilizing the GPI as a Trigger   237
    Image Mixers: The Video Toaster   238
    Low-Cost A/V Image Mixers   243
    Videonics MX-1   245
    Panasonic WJ-AVE7   247
    Panasonic WJ-AVE5 Digital AV Mixer   249

Sony XV-D1000   252
Panasonic WJ-MX30   254
Edit Controllers: Videonics Thumbs Up   256
FutureVideo Edit Controllers   259

19   **Nonlinear Digital Video Editing Technology**   261
Digital Tape and Nonlinear Video   262
Quicktime and Computer Video   264
Digital Video is Not Inherently Better   267
The Video Flyer   269
CineWorks Nonlinear Editing   270
The Hybrid Future   274

20   **Time Base Correctors**   275
The Personal TBC   276
Multigeneration Testing   277

Part III   Audio, Lighting, Graphics, Travel, Etc.

21   **Audio Basics 281**
Sound and Perception—Psychoacoustics   282
The Audio Tracks   283
Microphones   287
Recording Sound on Location   298
Automatic Gain Control   308
Making a Music Video   310
Editing Audio   315

22   **Lighting   319**
Three Point Lighting   319
Apparent Sources Of Light   325
Electrical Considerations   330
Portable Lighting   332
White Balance   333

23   **Graphics & Optics   339**
Titles   339
Computer Graphics   342

Artwork   343
Animation   344
Lens Filters and Adapters   354

24   Producing and Directing   359
The Producer   360
The Director   360
Three Step Production Process   362
Staying Friends   366

25   Travelling with a Camcorder   367
What To Bring   367
Security   370
International Travel   371
International Video Standards   373

Part IV   **New Media and Opportunities**

26   Cable TV   383

27   Public Access   387
Public Access and the First Amendment   389
The Cable Communications Act   390
How to Get Public Access
on Your Local Cable System   392

28   Finding Funding   395
Proposals   396
Commercial Television   397
Grants   398
Investors and Limited Partnerships   400

29   HDTV and Wide Screen TV   403
16 x 9   406
HDTV Politics   406

30   Direct Broadcast Satellites   409

31   The Internet   413

Bandwidth and Modem Speed   414
Online And Off The Hook   415
Multimedia On the Net: Today and Tomorrow   416

32   Conclusion   419

Appendix: Low Budget Video Resources
A: DVS Video Editing Service   421
B: Support and Access Organizations   422
C: Manufacturers   423
D: Funding Sources   427
E: Recommended Reading   428
F: Frequently Asked Questions   429
G: Glossary   434
H: Acronym Glossary   448

Index   451

Introduction

Fantastic improvements in the quality of home video equipment have put low budget equipment almost—but not quite—on par with fancy broadcast quality gear costing ten to one hundred times as much.

This book is intended to help the low budget videomaker get the most out of the capabilities in the consumer camcorder formats—VHS, 8mm, Super-VHS, Hi8, S-VHS-C, VHS-C, and MiniDV.

This is *not* a book about how to operate a fancy TV studio, or how to get a job in the industry. Such topics are part of the "professional" video world, whereas this book is intended to address the needs of the lower-budget "semi-professional," student, artist, or serious amateur.

If you have a lot of interest in making your own video productions but don't have a lot of money to work with, this book can help you squeeze maximum quality out of relatively low cost consumer and industrial video equipment.

You Can Do It!

Make no mistake about it: Using nothing more than a modern video camcorder, you can produce superb original works with near-professional technical quality. That's the lowest budget video there is — shooting and editing in the camcorder. You edit as you go along, building the original tape as an artist layers paint on canvas.

This in-camera editing approach is not for the fainthearted, however. You must be decisive about erasing over boring parts, with no going back.

At a budget level slightly higher than editing-in-the-camcorder, there's the process that most people think of as "real" video editing: editing from one tape to another. You gain the advantages of being able to shoot out of sequence, taking maximum advantage of each camera setup, to shoot multiple takes, and to make creative decisions after the shoot.

Whichever approach you choose, this book is intended to help you understand the equipment needed for videomaking, and how to use it to maximum advantage.

You'll find a lot of overlap among the various chapters. You'll never technically understand editing, for example, unless you also have some understanding of how video recording works, and how different types of audio tracks are recorded with each format. Let me apologize in advance for any repetition you encounter wading through this stuff. For the sake of readers looking up information on a specific topic, I've tried to make each section as complete and self-contained as possible. Sprinkled throughout this book are detailed descriptions and reviews of certain products and technologies that are leading the way toward producing even higher quality video at lower cost.

This book covers a lot of technical topics, but don't be intimidated by it. This is not an engineering manual. Rather, it is an attempt to explain video technology to the millions of people who are now shooting and editing with low budget video equipment. The way a camcorder works is more complicated than frames of film clicking past a shutter mechanism, such as with old-fashioned home movie cameras, but it is still understandable.

When it comes to video technology, knowledge is power. This is especially true when working on a low budget. If you've got tons of money, you can buy every production frill you need. On a low budget, you've got to be versatile and innovative. You'll need to maximize the creative and technical capabilities of the equipment you're using. Getting the biggest bang for the buck is what this book is all about.

At the lowest budget levels you are walking through a technical mine field. Two competing Japanese manufacturing camps—Matsushita (Panasonic and JVC) and Sony—have created numerous competing video recording systems, each with advantages and disadvantages. Picking one or the other arbitrarily is a mistake that can limit your video production capabilities. This book is intended to help you understand and choose between the formats, keeping an open mind to such possibilities as shooting in Hi8 and editing onto S-VHS.

The newest camcorder tape, MiniDV, may finally put the format wars to rest – as both major camcorder camps have agreed on the same cassette. If you can afford it by all means choose MiniDV, as it's significantly better than the others. And note that even MiniDV is offered in slightly different flavors by Sony and Panasonic.

Although this book may seem to go on and on about technical details, there's one thing that every low budget producer has learned through trial and error: Focus your energies on the less expensive aspects of your production that are under your control—lighting, sound, and camera setup. Ironically, these aspects tend to be ignored most by beginning producers. While it might cost tens of thousands of dollars to upgrade from Hi8 equipment to professional formats like Digital Betacam, it costs less than two hundred dollars to buy a decent tripod with a real fluid head. Get it. Similarly, for a couple of hundred dollars you can get a good quality wireless microphone, and for even less you can get an excellent handheld wired microphone. For under fifty dollars you can get some clamp-on light reflectors, stands, and color-balanced photoflood bulbs in the 250 to 1000-watt range. For a few hundred dollars you can buy a professional light kit.

Before you start drooling over fancy industrial video gear, equip yourself with these moderately priced basic accessories.

Just owning these production tools, of course, does not guarantee professional quality results. You've got to learn to use them properly. Just because a camcorder is inexpensive doesn't mean it can't be used with the same versatile approach to camera angles as a hundred thousand dollar professional video camera. For example: do without shaky hand held panning shots when a series of well composed still shots can do the job better.

The bottom line is this: When working on a low budget, you should concentrate on those things that aren't influenced as much by budget—composition, lighting, and audio.

That, in a nutshell, is the philosophy of this whole book. Use your strengths as a low budget producer, and avoid the trap of constantly attempting shots and editing techniques that require more money.

Social-Political Introduction

Which brings us to a discussion about this book's point of view. Does low budget video represent a "movement"—politically, artistically, or otherwise? I think it does. Back in the 70s, when I cut my teeth on the precursors of today's equipment, there was a lot of hype about the "video revolution". I was involved with public access for cable television for many years, and then went into independent filmmaking and videomaking.

The political agenda of this book involves a very real and deep aspect of democracy which may seem obscured by all the technical mumbo-jumbo. Let me spell it out, briefly: Democracy is based on the free movement of ideas, literacy, and an informed electorate.

Today much of the information that citizens receive about their society is available not just in print, but as moving images and sounds. In every aspect of your life—from which brand of detergent you buy to how you behave when your car is pulled over by the police—video images have an impact. (The first "serious" film I ever made was about subliminal advertising; I also wrote several magazine articles about this fascinating phenomenon. (For some eye opening insights check out Bill Key's numerous books, including *Subliminal Seduction, Media Sexploitation, Clam Plate Orgy*, and *Age of Manipulation*—a book I contributed photos to.)

Toda's population, raised on an abundance of television, film, and video, does an excellent job of "reading" the language of the moving image. But only a relative handful are proficient at "writing" in this language; that is, in creating video or film productions. I believe that learning how to create your own video productions is democratizing, in that it takes the power to influence people's thinking with moving images, and spreads that power around among a greater number of people. It allows you to assume some responsibility for informing yourself and your peers, rather than putting all trust into the wisdom of television networks, advertisers, and the big business community that tends to underwrite practically everything you seen on TV.

Understanding how television is made, even at the low-budget level this book addresses, also makes you a far more astute viewer of professional television and film productions—including campaign commercials, news reports and many other media messages that influence the course of public affairs. The decoding of media messages has been a hot area of study on college campuses for several decades. Learning how to create such messages—to do the encoding, so to speak—provides nuts-and-bolts grounding.

Technical Introduction

Finally, before diving in, let me make one very general technical point: Underlying all the jargon and technological concepts that you are about to learn is a fundamental mystery that must be exposed.

Video technology is all based on electricity. As you probably learned in high school science, electricity is the movement of electrons through wires or electronic circuitry. In all electrical circuits—including such simple devices as the flashlight, and such complex devices as the video camcorder—subatomic particles called "electrons" are trying to make their way from the "negative" terminal of a battery to the "positive" terminal. This movement of electrons, like water flowing down a river, is what makes it all work.

But why do the electrons flow like this? Is there something good about the so-called "positive" terminal that attracts the electrons, and something evil about the "negative" terminal that they are trying to get away from? Absolutely not. In fact, the terms "positive" and "negative" are misnomers. If history were not a factor, and they had it all to do over again, scientists would name the positive negative, and the negative positive, because there's an abundance of electrons at the "negative" terminal and there's a shortage of electrons at the "positive" terminal. The point is, these names are arbitrary. The battery terminals might just as well be called yin and yang, black and white, female and male, or any other pair of names that suggest a duality.

At the heart of the electrical phenomenon, there's an attraction: Two subatomic particles, electrons and protons, are attracted to each other. Why? Nobody knows! It is a fundamental mystery of the universe.

Similarly, gravity is another mysterious force of the universe. Why do smaller objects, like people, books, pencils, cars, etc., pull toward larger objects, like the planet earth? The more mass there is, the more "gravity" something has—but what is gravity? Why is there an attraction? Nobody knows!

Top physicists—Nobel Prize winners—are still trying to unravel these mysteries. But the fact that there is an underlying mystery does not prevent us from creating practical uses for these forces. Look at how much commerce is transacted based on precise measurements of weight—precise measurements of a force that no one really understands. When you go to the store to buy apples, you do not need to know how gravity works to know that you'll pay double for a bag of apples that are pulled down twice as much by gravity.

If you think about it, you really have no better understanding of the "why" of gravity than electricity—but there's one big difference: With gravity, you have an intuitive sense of how this mysterious force behaves. You may not know why it works the way it does, but you know that a phone book weighs more than a feather.

Going through life as a low budget video producer, you'll meet all sorts of experts—video engineers, teachers, salespeople, cable system employees, etc.,—each buzzing with technical jargon and terminology so complex that you'll have no idea of what they're talking about. It's easy to get the feeling that they're in on some grand conspiracy of understanding that you just don't get. After all, they seem to know what they're talking about. Well, maybe they do, but remember, deep down, even for them, there is still an unknowable quality to it all.

Someone who understands terms like pounds and ounces and kilograms and newtons may know how to measure the effects of gravity better than someone who knows only that some things are heavy and others are light. So too someone who understands terms like volts and amps and watts and IRE units and phase and

so forth knows how to measure electronic signals better than someone who barely knows the difference between a AA-battery and a
9-volt. But knowing how to measure something and knowing why
it exists are two very different things.

Video equipment is inherently mysterious, no matter how well
you think you understand it. You'll never know it fully. It's fantas-
tically complex. Even the engineers who design the equipment
may spend years just working on one particular subsystem, without much detailed knowledge of how the other parts work.

The important thing is to develop enough understanding
about the technology you'll be using, so that a lack of know-how
won't stand between you and getting the best possible production
down on tape—at the lowest possible cost!

Introduction to Revised Second Edition

By the year 2000, one might have predicted twenty years ago, there would be low-cost, ultra compact digital video cassettes. But now that MiniDV is really here, you still can't help but marvel at how far things have come.

In the realm of audio recording, the home enthusiast for years has been able to produce works that, at least in terms of pure technical quality of the recording itself, were considered "broadcast quality" – first with open reel tape decks, and then DAT cassettes (digital audio tape).

Now, for the first time in the history of camcorders, the technical quality of a consumer format (MiniDV) actually matches and in some respects even exceeds the technical quality of professional broadcast formats (such as Beta SP, MII, one-inch). While the pros in Hollywood will always have better, far costlier gear, a certain plateau of "good enough" may finally have been reached. The next few years promise to be very interesting times for low budget producers.

In my view, the advent of the Digital Video Cassette (MiniDV) is far more important to low-budget producers than the appearance of nonlinear editing several years ago. Though nonlinear is more fun to use, the raw quality of the picture gains no advantage, compared to tape. With most nonlinear systems, except the most expensive, quality is lost when the tape original gets dumped into the hard drive, and limited disk capacity means you may not be able to have access to several hours worth of footage unless you break it into smaller blocks.

Contrast that with MiniDV: Each hour-long tape costs about $15 to $25, and holds some 11-gigabytes of data. Digital dubbing allows you to make perfect copies, with no generation loss. Before any low budget producer takes the financial plunge into nonlinear, an upgrade to MiniDV is in order. Hybrid systems, combining the best aspects of digital tape and nonlinear editing, will ultimately prevail. At least that's my prediction.

Meanwhile, although MiniDV is defined as a consumer format, at least for the time being there are plenty of consumers and enthusiasts who can't afford it. The $500 MiniDV camcorder may be available by the millennium, but it's certainly not available as this revised second edition goes to press.

Besides covering these developments, this new edition also expands coverage of the ¾" format. Sure it's a dinosaur, but there are a zillion schools and media access centers that still revolve around this quarter-century old format. With the recent wave of budget cutbacks in arts and education, one might expect the U-matic ¾" format to linger well into the next century. Though antiquated, it's still a reliable workhorse.

Finally, anyone looking at this book for the first time can ignore this, but for those who are looking at an updated edition, note that this is the "revised second edition," which includes new information, page numbers, and chapter numbers when compared with the second edition. We strive to keep this book up-to-date, and apologize for any confusion that gets caused along the way. (Educators: Please contact us to get a revised edition if you're using this for a class.)

We're very interested in your feedback. When you get a chance, please take a few moments to fill out the coupon in the back.

Acknowledgments

Special thanks to Freedom Baird for her superb help with the copy editing and organization of the manuscript. This new edition's improved look owes gratitude to Dick Hannus for the cover, Boris Ustaev, for the computer graphics, Pervaiz at Digital Output On Demand for the improved scans, and Jean LeGwin for the overall book design, layout, and typography.

Special thanks also to Matt Schlanger, video artist, for his lighting diagrams, and for his insistence that the book not merely encourage readers to mimic commercial TV, but strive for cinematic excellence. I hope it does. Mel Vapour and Paul Blake of the East Bay Media Center in Berkeley, CA get credit for similar nagging. Thanks also to John Szendeffy and Charles Hamilton, for their proofreading help.

And thanks to the many wonderful people (and organizations) that have supported my writing and teaching over the past decade, including (but not limited to) Bruce Apar, Brent Butterworth, Bob Cohen, David Elrich, Miriam Friedman, Marc Horowitz, Richard Jaccoma, Michael Goldstein, Howard Guttenplein, Reeves Lehmann, Matt York, and Bill Wolfe.

Finally, a bow of gratitude for the cooperation of the many high technology companies that make the equipment this book revolves around, including Azden, Canon, Digital Processing Systems, FutureVideo, JVC, Magnavox, Matrox, Minolta, NewTek, Panasonic, RCA, Ricoh, Sony, Toshiba, Videonics, and many others.

This book is dedicated to my son Gerry, a miracle child who has taught me to finally see home video through the eyes of the camcorder dad (and whose cuteness makes me break my own rules every time I start shooting); and to my wife Debbie, an extraordinary artist who tolerated my cursing the computer more times than any human should have to; and to the memory of my mother, who took some kind of TV production class back when she was in college, in the days of black-and-white.

The Low Budget Video Bible

PART I

Low Budget Video Basics

1   Low Budget, Big Budget

Imagine yourself as a challenger and a rebel. In the eyes of the professional television production industry, that's what you are. And that will go a long way toward explaining some of the attitudes you'll come across in your quest to be a low budget video producer.

You may not realize it at first, but by producing video using the S-VHS, Hi8, and MiniDV formats, you're ruffling some feathers. Especially if your production can actually compete in the same distribution marketplaces as professionally produced programs, such as on broadcast TV or cable TV networks.

As long as you're using low-budget video for shooting your family and friends, goofing around, or producing public access programs on cable TV, no one will mind.

But start shooting industrial documentaries, or even drama and comedy intended for sale to broadcast and cable TV, and you'll find yourself the subject of a lot of criticism and sneering — that is, if you bother to talk to anyone in "the industry."

Much of the criticism levelled against you will revolve around what sounds like techno-speak. Typical comments:

"It's not broadcast quality!"

"You don't have the signal to noise ratio needed."

"It won't hold up in editing."

This book is intended to help you understand and analyze the legitimacy (or lack thereof) of these comments.

But there's something you must understand before we dive into the technicalities of "broadcast quality": If there's a compelling enough reason to show it, any moving-image footage can be "broadcast quality."

Think about the Zapruder footage of the JFK assassination, shot on 8mm movie film (not video), and George Holiday's amateur footage of the Rodney King police beating, shot on VHS videocassette. Because these items were newsworthy, they were broadcast.

But what if you want to make TV shows that entertain and inform, like ordinary TV shows? Are low budget formats good enough to produce a 30-minute sitcom that you can sell to CBS?

The straight answer is no for S-VHS and Hi8, maybe for MiniDV.

But it's not really a question of what's "good enough." Technically, the low-budget formats are good enough in the sense that no FCC law is being violated, and audiences will not have to fiddle with their sets to get a decent picture.

As a low budget videomaker, you inevitably look at the situation from the flip side of the broadcasters' perspective — you're seeking to use the cheapest equipment that can deliver reasonably decent image and sound.

Look at it from a network's point of view: Why not use the best equipment that's commonly available?

The expense of a network quality program involves a lot more than just using fancier video equipment. In fact, the cost of the equipment may be relatively small, compared with the overall budget. Consider these other major costs a network must spend heavily on to pull off a successful show:

Star talent (recognizable names)
Producer and director with track records
Promotion (on-air and print)
Studio space
Set construction, etc.

To a network, the difference between shooting in Hi8 and shooting in Digital Betacam is negligible. From a network's point of view, Digital Betacam (explained in a few moments) is a low budget video alternative to 35-mm film!

Perhaps the clearest example of what I'm talking about here can be found in the making of TV commercials. These are the most lavish moving-image productions made — on a per-minute basis, they typically cost more than feature films. The slickest national advertising, for soft drinks, cars, beer, etc., can cost over a million dollars for a 30-second ad. Imagine making a two-hour feature film at that rate — it would cost $240 million!

Why do ads cost so much? Why shouldn't they? The cost of producing the commercial is negligible in light of other costs. A commercial is useless unless it's played. Consider what it costs to play on the air.

The most expensive time, on the annual Super-Bowl football game, can cost a million dollars for a single one-time airing of a commercial. Typical slots on network TV programs cost in the tens of thousands of dollars each.

A commercial that's part of a big campaign might typically be played hundreds of times nationwide over a period of several months, plus local insertions in desirable advertising markets. For a big, splashy campaign, fifty million dollars might be spent placing the ad on TV!

In light of such astronomical expenditures, do you think it really matters much whether the commercial cost $50,000 or $500,000 to produce?

And if you come along with your low budget video gear offering to make the commercial for $500 (hey, a couple of days' work!), can you see why you appear laughable?

But of course you can make a perfectly legitimate TV commercial for $500. It is done all the time, even at TV stations, using simple slides and announcer voice-overs instead of the lavish production found in a typical soft-drink ad.

Although this book revolves largely around the low-budget videocassette formats, keep in mind that the format is not what makes a production big budget or low budget; rather, the format chosen is a reflection of the budget involved.

So before we proceed any further, let's briefly examine the most common types of video production, and the budgets that are typically associated with them. Then we'll see how your project and production capabilities fit in. (If you're already absolutely convinced that you want to work in the Hi8 and/or S-VHS formats, and have no interest in seeing how they compare with other formats, you may wish to skip the rest of this chapter.)

For this discussion, we'll divide the world of video production into three major categories—big budget, moderate budget, and low budget. Here are typical productions, and what they might cost.

Big Budget

Feature film, theatrical (35-mm film)	$10–100 million
Made-for-TV movie (35-mm film)	$2–15 million
Network TV sitcom (Betacam or D-2)	$150,000–750,000 per episode
Commercial for national ad campaign	$50,000–1 million

Moderate Budget

A PBS documentary (like "Frontlines"), 60 min. duration	$150,000–500,000
Low-budget independent feature film	$20,000–2 million
Music video (major label)	$20,000–200,000
Industrial documentary	$2,000–100,000
Educational film/video (for schools, libraries)	$25,000–500,000

Low Budget

Wedding video, bar mitzvah	$150–1,500
Legal depositions	$100–1,000
Public access studio show	free–$100
Public access documentary, self-produced	free–$1,000
Music video (garage/small label)	$10–5,000
Video art	$10–10,000
Student film short (16-mm)	$2,000–15,000
Student video project (Hi8, S-VHS)	$10–500
Travel, vacation, family video	$2–15

This list makes no pretense of covering every possible type of production. This list is intended merely as a guide to help you see where your video production goals fit in. No doubt your production overlaps a few categories.

This book is intended for those with budgets in the $8 to $50,000 range. (George Kuchar, one of America's most talented and respected video artists, has boasted on more than one occasion that it costs him $8 to make each of his productions — the cost of the blank tape.) If, however, you're looking to spend more than $50,000 you should probably find an alternate source of information for your project.

Low Budget Budgets:
How to Spend Your Precious Money

When most low-budget video producers start thinking about a budget, they compare the cost of renting equipment with owning it. At higher budget levels, such as for network TV and film production, practically all the equipment is rented or included with the services of a specialty craftsperson/technician (such as a sound recordist whose daily rate includes the use of high performance sound recording equipment, or a cinematographer who supplies his/her own camera).

If you have a budget around $10,000, you'll have a number of choices that essentially trade off owning your own low-budet equipment against rental fees for more expensive professional gear.

If your budget is close to zero, on the other hand, your choices will be more limited. You can do quite a quite a bit with very little additional expenditure if you already own a camcorder.

Local public access TV centers and media arts centers, located in practically every major American city, are great resources for low-budget producers, and usually offer access to low budget video equipment.

Perhaps the easiest way to get a sense for how money can be spent is to look at the following examples of rough budgets for typical projects. (Note that these are ballpark numbers that don't necessarily add up perfectly. Through careful shopping you can shave down some of the numbers.)

Budget = $8

PRODUCTION EQUIPMENT:
  consumer camcorder, self-owned or from public access center
POST-PRODUCTION EQUIPMENT:
  in-camera editing, self-owned editing, or free time at public access editing center
CREW:
  you, perhaps a friend or two
OTHER:
  blank tape $8 (up to 2-hours)

Budget = $100 (already own camcorder)

PRODUCTION EQUIPMENT:
  consumer camcorder
POST-PRODUCTION EQUIPMENT:
  4-hours @ $25/hour access; or edit service
CREW:
  you, perhaps a friend or two
OTHER:
  blank tape $8

Budget = $200 (don't own camcorder)

PRODUCTION EQUIPMENT:
  consumer camcorder rental, 2-days @ $30/day
POST-PRODUCTION EQUIPMENT:
  4-hours @ $25/hour access; or edit service
CREW:
  lunch for you and two friends $40
OTHER:
  blank tape $30

Budget = $500 (already own camcorder)

PRODUCTION EQUIPMENT:
   consumer camcorder, self-owned
   lighting—rental of professional light set 3-days @ $50/day
POST-PRODUCTION:
   12-hours @ $25/hour access; or utilization of edit service
CREW:
   snacks for 2-days shooting, 4 people, $50
OTHER:
   blank tape $30

Budget = $1,000 (don't own camcorder)

PRODUCTION EQUIPMENT:
   rental of 3-chip camcorder, 1-week @ $500/week
POST-PRODUCTION:
   12-hours @ $25/hour access; or utilization of edit service
CREW:
   lunch and dinner for 4 people, 2 days, $200
OTHER:
   blank tape $30

Budget = $2,000 (don't own camcorder)

PRODUCTION EQUIPMENT:
   rental of 3-chip camcorder, 1-week @ $500/week
   rental of lights, microphones, tripod, etc. @$400/week
POST-PRODUCTION:
   20-hours @ $25/hour access; or utilization of edit service
   professional announcer, 2-hours @ $50/hr
CREW:
   lunch and dinner for 4 people, 4 days $400
OTHER:
   blank tape $60

Budget = $2,000 (want to buy camcorder)

PRODUCTION EQUIPMENT:
   purchase of one-chip camcorder, $1,200
POST-PRODUCTION:
   20-hours @ $25/hour access, or edit service
CREW:
   dinner for 4 people, $100
OTHER:
   blank tape $50
   tripod $150

Budget = $4,000 (already own camcorder)

PRODUCTION EQUIPMENT:
consumer camcorder, already owned

POST-PRODUCTION EQUIPMENT:
purchase desktop video editing system, $4,000

CREW:
you, perhaps a friend or two

OTHER:
blank tape $60

Budget = $4,000 (don't own camcorder)

PRODUCTION EQUIPMENT:
rental of 3-chip camcorder, 1-week @ $500/week
or rental of Betacam camcorder, 1-day @ $500/day

POST-PRODUCTION:
on-line editing, 10-hours @$100/hr
off-line editing, 50-hours @ $25/hour access
professional announcer, 2-hours @ $50/hr

CREW:
lunch and dinner for 4 people, 4 days $400
stipends for crew, 3 people @ $200 each

OTHER:
talent (actor/actress) $150
blank tape $60

Budget = $10,000 (don't own camcorder, but want to purchase)

PRODUCTION EQUIPMENT:
purchase top 3-chip consumer camcorder $3,500
(or purchase $1,200 1-chip camcorder, plus
rental of 3-chip camcorder, 1-week @ $500/week)
purchase tripod $200
purchase microphone $100
purchase clamp lights/ stands ($75) or pro light kit ($750)

POST-PRODUCTION EQUIPMENT:
purchase desktop editing system $6,000

CREW:
professional lighting truck, 2-days @ $500/day
meals for everyone else (volunteers) $500

OTHER:
blank tape $250

Budget = $10,000 (don't own camcorder, don't want to purchase)

PRODUCTION EQUIPMENT:
   rent 3-chip Betacam camcorder, 1-week @ $1,500/week
POST-PRODUCTION EQUIPMENT:
   on-line editing, 20 hours @ $150/hr
   off-line editing, 100 hours @ $15/hr
CREW:
   professional lighting truck, 2-days @ $500/day
   professional sound recordist, 2-days @ $250/day
   professional director of photography, 2-days $250/day
   meals for everyone $500
   editing assistant, 2-weeks @$500/week
OTHER:
   studio rental, 4-hours @ $200/hour
   music recording, 8-hours @ $25/hour
   still photography, $100
   blank tape $250

Remember, these are just typical scenarios. Every production is different. And whatever you plan, things always cost more.

In the next section, we'll examine some of the specific technical differences between various video formats.

Industrial and Consumer Video Equipment

Video camera and tape equipment tends to be broadly divided into three main categories, or markets: consumer, industrial, and broadcast. Each of the major video manufacturing companies—Sony, Panasonic, JVC—has three separate divisions to address the needs of each of these markets. After all, most people shopping for an eight-hundred dollar camcorder hardly have any interest in buying a hundred thousand dollar camera designed for use on network television.

For low-budget videomaking, we are concerned with the borderline area between the high end of the consumer equipment category and the low end of the industrial market (the industrial market encompasses schools, libraries, corporate video, etc). Some people call this high-end consumer/low-end industrial borderline area the "semiprofessional" video market; others call it "prosumer," "garage video," or "desktop video."

Whatever you call the market for it, the ability to do frame-accurate video editing using equipment that can be purchased on a

Whatever you call the market for it, the ability to do frame-accurate video editing using equipment that can be purchased on a modest budget of a few thousand dollars is opening up fantastic new creative possibilities to low budget producers. The ability to do slightly less accurate video editing using equipment that costs just a few hundred dollars (in addition to a camcorder and VCR) is letting unprecedented numbers of video enthusiasts edit together all sorts of personal and family video projects.

The camcorder itself, with its built-in editing capabilities, offers fantastic creative opportunity. But although the consumer/industrial video equipment has amazing capabilities considering the price, the big broadcast and cable TV networks, as well as most local TV stations, continue to use far more expensive equipment utilizing different videocassette and videotape formats.

Technical Comparison with Professional Equipment

Let's briefly examine how the various tape formats (broadcast, industrial, consumer) stack up against each other in quality and cost, and how they correspond with different production budgets and equipment markets. In a later section, we'll take a more in-depth look at the formats that get used most in low-budget video.

"Broadcast Quality"

The term "broadcast quality" is commonly used to distinguish top-quality video equipment that is suitable for use in network television production from the lower-cost equipment that readers of this book are primarily interested in. Two decades ago, such equipment was considered absolutely necessary for TV stations to stay within the F.C.C.'s legally allowed tolerances for over-the-air TV transmissions. But more recently, digital processing devices called "time base correctors," or TBCs, have made it possible to electronically clean up the signals from consumer quality video equipment, rendering a signal that is perfectly legal to broadcast. Indeed, popular TV programs shown on network TV commonly feature home video footage shot with so-called amateur camcorders.

Nevertheless, if you look carefully at such footage, and compare it with broadcast quality signals, you can see distinct though subtle differences in picture quality. Whether this difference is worth spending tens to hundreds of times more money for depends primarily on your budget and the anticipated size of your audience. Certainly most of the big networks, which can charge over a million dollars for a minute of advertising on top rated programs, don't

mind paying top dollar to get top quality. But smaller TV operations — like public access centers for cable television, and smaller
UHF and low power TV stations — have found the quality of S-
VHS and Hi8 equipment adequate and cost effective. MiniDV, the
newest low-budget consumer format, promises to win over even
more converts from the broadcast and professional community.

Even the biggest-budget video productions may use low-budget
desktop equipment to make editing decisions, going back to the
fancier equipment only after many of the time-consuming creative
decisions have been made. This has, until recently, been the primary use for nonlinear editing, which we'll also take a more detailed look at later. Computer-based nonlinear editing systems have
been used for years to create edit decision lists using crude-quality
computer video files; then, after the creative work is done, technicians conform the higher quality film or videotape recordings to
match the decision list.

Which format makes the most sense for your production depends on your budget, your aesthetic sense, the size of your intended audience, and lots of local/personal factors, such as finding
equipment you can conveniently borrow or rent.

Broadcast, Industrial, and Consumer Formats Comparison

Videotape formats are commonly described by the width of the
tape, similar to the way movie film is measured as 8mm, 16mm,
35mm, or 70mm. However, unlike film, where more surface area
translates directly into better image quality, with videotape systems
the issue is more complex.

All video recorders, in every format, utilize a system of helical
recording in which spinning heads record the video tracks along
slanted diagonal tracks (this process is covered in more detail later).
In addition to the width of the tape, the speed the tape travels at,
the width of each helical track, the isolation of each track from the
next, the tape formulation, and the method by which the video signals are electronically encoded all play a part in the overall quality.

The professional tape formats all record at faster speeds, and
with thicker track widths than the consumer formats. This results
in less recording time for each tape, but higher picture quality. The
more magnetic material that gets devoted to each frame of the
moving image, the better the overall quality is. Newer metal-par-
ticle tape formulations also offer higher picture quality.

Most broadcast quality video tape formats—one-inch, Betacam (which uses $^1/_2$" tape at a faster speed than consumer equipment), and M-II (also $^1/_2$" tape)—use a "component" recording process that puts the brightness (luminance) and color (chroma) information onto separate helical tracks. This method, called component recording, is more expensive and complicated but provides much better noise suppression than the composite "color under" system used in most consumer video equipment — VHS, S-VHS, VHS-C, S-VHS-C, 8mm, Hi8, and the various Betamax incarnations (but not MiniDV and DV, which are component systems). With color under, the color and chroma signals are combined onto the same helical tracks, resulting in less accuracy for each.

The newest video recording formats, including MiniDV, take this one step further by digitizing the component video signals and recording them as a series of numbers, much like the way CDs record audio digitally. The advantage of digital video recording, as with audio and text, is that there is no generation loss from one copy to the next. D-1 was the first of these formats, and has been supplanted by D-2, Digital Betacam, D-3, and D-5 for professional productions. The newest digital video format is DV (also known as MiniDV and DVC). DV, intended to be a consumer/industrial format. Switching from Hi8 or S-VHS to MiniDV can drastically improve the technical quality of a low-budget video production.

The D-2 broadcast quality format is a digital video recording system that utilizes tape approximately $^3/_4$" wide. The D-3 digital video cassette format, utilizes tape that is $^1/_2$" wide. It is somewhat less expensive than D-2, but is still prohibitively expensive for low budget applications. Ditto for Digital Betacam, which also uses $^1/_2$" wide tape, as well as D-5, the newest of the professional digital video formats.

The most expensive digital video formats – D1, D2, and D-5 – record the data "raw," while Digital Betacam and DV use data compression to reduce the amount of information that needs to be recorded. The tiny DV tapes are just $^1/_4$" wide, and use 5:1 compression (see the chapter on DV for more info).

At the other end of the video timeline is the $^3/_4$" U-matic tape format, which is probably the oldest video format still in use. This industrial videocassette format has been around for over two decades. It uses color under recording, and thus has more in common with consumer formats than professional gear, but was used extensively in the 1970s for broadcast-TV news gathering because it was the first portable videocassette format that could be run through a time base corrector (TBC—explained later) and played on TV news. Nowadays, most broadcast quality videocassette re-

Comparisons of Video Tape Formats

Format	Horiz. Resolution	Video S/N (Luminance)	Built-in TBC?	VCR Cost
BROADCAST				
1"	400-LINES	55–60dB	YES	$25,000–75,000
BETACAM SP	400-LINES	55–60dB	YES	$10,000–50,000
M-II	400-LINES	55–60dB	YES	$10,000–50,000
D-2, D-3, D-5, Digital Betacam	400-LINES	54-66dB	YES	$35,000–100,000
INDUSTRIAL				
3/4" SP	340-LINES	45–50dB	YES	$7,000–20,000
3/4" NON-SP	260-LINES	45–50dB	OPTIONAL	$4,000–7,000
S-VHS*	400-LINES	40–50dB	NO/OPTIONAL	$1,000–7,000
HI-8*	400-LINES	40–50dB	NO/OPTIONAL	$1,500–10,000
DVCPro***	500-LINES	54dB	YES	$18,000
CONSUMER				
MiniDV****	500-LINES	54dB	YES	$2,500–4,000
VHS	240-LINES	35–45dB	NO	$200–1,000
8-MM	240-LINES	40–45dB	NO	$600–2,000
ED-BETA**	500-LINES	45–50dB	NO	$2,000–5,000
SUPER-BETA**	290-LINES	40–45-dB	NO	$500–1,000
BETAMAX**	250-LINES	35–45-dB	NO	(discontinued)

*Hi8 and Super-VHS are sold as both consumer and industrial equipment.
**Betamax format equipment is no longer popular in the U.S., but is shown here for comparison.
***DVCPro and MiniDV have identical picture quality, but are only semi-compatible.
****MiniDV camcorder price.

corders (VCRs) incorporate built-in TBCs, so that perfect timing stability is an attribute of the format.

The following chart summarizes some of the technical attributes of the various videotape formats discussed thus far. It is meant as a rough guide, not as a precise comparison. Of course, within each format there are variations between makes and models.

All the references here to "decibels" and "resolution" may sound like so much mumbo-jumbo. More detailed explanations of these terms will be provided later. The chart is provided here only to show that there are indeed real, measurable technical differences between the various tape formats.

The differences in picture quality are slight, but they constitute the essence of what TV networks and professional producers are willing to pay extra for. As shown in the next set of charts, producers often have to pay double, triple, or even ten times as much money to obtain just a 10 or 20 percent improvement in performance.

Remember, consumer equipment is cheap because it is mass produced and sold through discount retail channels. Professional equipment is sold at higher markups and profits to a small elite clientele. There is no proportionality to the discrepencies in pricing between consumer and professional equipment.

Daily Rental Rates (typical) / Purchase Prices for Camera/Recorder Package or Camcorder

Format	Rental Cost Per Day	Purchase (new)
D-2, D-3, D-5, Digital Betacam	$500–$1000/day*	$50,000 +
1"	$250–$500/day*	$40,000–$60,000
Betacam SP, M-II	$200–$400/day*	$15,000–$50,000
³/₄" SP	$100–$200/day	$12,000–$30,000
³/₄"	$50–$150/day	$7,000–$15,000
MiniDV	$100–$250/day	$3,000–$15,000
Hi-8, S-VHS	$20–$150/day	$900–$10,000
8-mm, VHS	$15–$35/day	$500–$1,500

* The services of a camera person are often included in the rental package at the higher rates. Freelance camera operators often own their own equipment and don't rent it out for you to operate. You must hire them along with the equipment.

Editing System Rental Rates (typical)

Format	Rental	Purchase
D-2, D-3, D-5, Digital Betacam	$200–$500/hour	$100,000 +
1", Betacam, MII	$50–$300/hour	$50,000–$100,000
Non-linear*	$50–$200/hour	$10,000–$70,000
³/₄" SP	$35–$150/hour	$12,000–$35,000
³/₄"	$10–$75/hour	$5,000–$10,000
Hi-8, S-VHS	$8–$50/hour	$2,000–$15,000
8-mm, VHS	$5–$25/hour	$1,500–$5,000

*for pro-grade non-linear systems such as Avid, Media Logic, and Toaster Flyer. Lower cost non-linear setups, such as Adobe Premiere combined with a video board, can cost less than $3,000 including computer, but don't offer full frame rates and resolution.

In deciding which format to work in, two of the most important considerations are what it costs to rent a camera/recorder or camcorder package for a day (or week), and what it costs to edit the tape using a professional or semi-professional editing system, as shown in the following chart. Editing systems are typically rented out on an hourly basis, though discounts for booking large blocks of time are commonly available. It is also possible, of course, to set up your own editing system at home — in fact, that's the recommended solution if you're going to be doing a lot of editing. And if you're only occasionally editing, see the information in the back of this book regarding Desktop Video Systems' custom editing service.

In the consumer formats (MiniDV, S-VHS, Hi8, VHS, 8mm, S-VHS-C, VHS-C) a one-piece camcorder is most common, but with professional formats (Betacam, D-2, D-3, one-inch) a two-piece camera/recorder system is usually used (except for the cheapest Betacam units). With the more compact pro formats (Betacam, MII) the camera and recorder dock together into a one-piece shoulder-mount unit. A video camera is different from a camcorder in that it has no tape recording system built-in. The camera converts pictures into electronic signals, and the recorder encodes these electronic signals onto magnetic tape.

Professional video recorders usually incorporate built-in time code generators which mark each video frame with a unique number that becomes useful in editing. Most consumer camcorders don't have time code built-in, but as described later in this book, it is possible to record time code on an audio track. But all MiniDV models have time code, as do Canon's L-2, Sony's CCD-VX3, CCD-TR700, CCD-TR3000, and the old CCD-V801, Panasonic's industrial AG-460, AG-456 (and 455), and many top Panasonic consumer models sold in Great Britain (but not in the U.S.).

Camera vs. Tape Quality

Note that tape format is not the only determinant of picture quality. In fact, the camera with which you shoot the original footage has the greatest effect on the quality of the picture. When you rent a movie on VHS tape it has a very high quality image even though the tape has a limited resolution. The original format is 35-mm film, which is better than any video format available, including HDTV.

The quality of a video camera can be broadly expressed by the number of image sensor "chips" used. The chip is like the film surface in a video camera: it consists of hundreds of thousands of tiny light sensors (pixels). Practically all inexpensive hobbyist camcorders utilize a single chip, while practically all expensive broadcast quality cameras have three chips. There's also an in-between category of two-chip camcorders, available as both consumer and industrial models. And most recently, three-chip consumer camcorders in the MiniDV, Hi8, and S-VHS-C formats have become available, blurring distinctions between consumer and pro equipment even more.

The number of chips in the camera will actually have more effect on picture quality than the tape format you shoot in. (When you record a TV show on your VCR, it usually looks better than one-chip camcorder footage, since you're using the same consumer quality VCR. The difference is in the cameras that are used to shoot the TV show.)

Camera quality is explained in greater technical detail later, but here's the point for now: When you rent a Betacam, M-II, D-anything, or 3/4" SP package, you invariably get a three-chip camera. Hi8, S-VHS, and MiniDV are more variable — sometimes it's a one-chip camera, but better packages include a two-chip or three-chip camera. When comparing competing prices, always keep this in mind. If two different rental outfits offer $50 per day packages — but one is a one-chip camera with a 3/4" deck and the other is a three-chip Hi8 camcorder, there should be no question about which is the better deal (the three-chip Hi8).

Nonlinear Editing

Nonlinear editing is the hottest thing happening today in video production, and interest in nonlinear seems to cut across all budget categories — from Hollywood feature films down to humble low-budget independent productions. Later in this book we'll look at some specific low-budget nonlinear choices, but at this point, since we're talking about what it costs to shoot and edit, it seems appropriate to give a brief overview. With most nonlinear editing systems, the raw footage shot on videotape is transferred to a computer disk, and then edited in much the same way that desktop publishing works, using a cut-and-paste style computer interface.

Nonlinear editing can thus work with any videotape format. Many medium-budget video producers own their own nonlinear editing computers, but rent the VCR. They'll rent a professional format VCR (Betacam, D-2, D-3, etc.) for a day or two to dump the raw footage into the computer, and then rent one when the edit decisions are finished to create an edited master tape.

The advantages of nonlinear, in a nutshell, are that it's more fun to edit, you can see results more quickly, and you can change and trim edits with a minimum of fuss and no further deterioration in image quality. The big disadvantage, at least for now, is that for any given budget level under about $20,000, you can usually get better picture quality by sticking with tape editing. This will undoubtedly change as computing power gets cheaper and the cost of hard disk drives drops.

The term "nonlinear" comes from the fact that on a laser disc, magnetic computer disc, or magneto-optical disc, as with a CD audio disc, you can instantly jump from one section of the disc to another. A tape, by contrast, provides "sequential" or "linear" access — you can't get from A to E without first shuttling past B, C, and D.

The first nonlinear systems, introduced by the profesional film industry in the mid-1980s, used laser discs to hold the raw footage. A laser video disc does not record the video signal digitally, but the disc does offer non-sequential access to the material recorded on it (and offers markedly superior picture quality after repeated playings, when compared with tape). After the editing decisions were made, a film negative cutter matched the original film to the electronic editing decision list.

Today's nonlinear video editing systems, such as products from Avid, Media Logic, and the Video Toaster Flyer, all convert the "raw" video source tape(s) into compressed digital video, and store it in a bank of hard disk drives. Until recently, professional nonlinear video editing systems, like the original video disc systems, required going back to the original tapes and editing them to match the nonlinear decision list using traditional editing techniques. Today, the best nonlinear editing systems, costing upwards of $20,000, can produce video output with quality (frame rate and resolution) that matches professional tape formats. But at the top quality level each minute of video requires many megabytes of hard disk storage, so nonlinear editing is generally inappropriate for projects that involve hours and hours of raw footage, unless the footage can be broken down into smaller units, such as scenes.

Although there can be no doubt that these nonlinear systems point the way to the future of even low-budget video editing, for the time being they are more expensive than traditional tape editing. Advances in disk storage and data compression will change this—by the year 2000, nonlinear will probably replace tape even for low-budget production. But by then, HDTV may be up and running. With five times as much picture information per second as regular (NTSC) TV, HDTV will require significantly more computer power to implement nonlinear editing.

All nonlinear systems use some form of video data compression, similar to the MPEG system used in DSS satellite TV or the JPEG system used for still photographs. With the compression technology used in most low-budget nonlinear systems (under $10,000), a drop in picture quality is usually quite evident. It is possible to record a few seconds of high quality video on a hard disk; but to record half an hour or an hour or more requires compromising the quality. The worst offenders usually appear in conjunction with multimedia computer-video formats like Apple Computer's QuickTime, and Microsoft's Video for Windows. Though theoretically all these standard could encompass broadcast quality video, as implemented on most people's computers the don't – and almost always suffer from both low resolution and reduced frame rates, compared with standard video.

MiniDV looks fantastic because it records at a rate of 25 megabits per second (that's about 3 megabytes per second, since there are 8 bits in a byte). Most computer hard disk drives can't sustain that kind of rate, and even when they can, you can only record about six minutes on a 1 gigabyte (GB) drive.

Thus, for the time being, low budget video producers will generally find that tape-based systems still offer the highest quality for the lowest price.

In my view, the day when disk drives, or even solid state memory, totally replace tape will be the day when computer owners stop backing up their hard drives with tape, and start using disks or memory chips. A MiniDV tape holds some 11 gigabytes of data, and costs about $15. By contrast, an 11 gigabyte hard disk drive costs well over a thousand dollars.

In the interim, hybrid systems combining the best aspects of digital tape and nonlinear editing will become affordable. By eliminating generation loss in traditional analog tape editing, both MiniDV and nonlinear are ushering in an exciting new era of access and empowerment.

The rest of this book provides more detailed information about the equipment, formats, techniques, and distribution opportunities that are available today to low budget video producers.

2   Shopping for a Camcorder

Many low budget producers begin their videomaking adventures with the purchase of a camcorder. Although this may not necessarily be the smartest approach, the purchase of a camcorder provides numerous satisfactions: pride of ownership, status, commitment to video production, etc. Ogling new electronic equipment is a national pastime.

Nevertheless, there is a certain logic to renting or borrowing a camcorder a few times before buying one, if rental prices in your area are not prohibitively high. (Normal rates would be about $25 to $50 per day for a one-chip Hi8 or S-VHS camcorder, although prices as high as $150 per day are not uncommon.)

If you are in the market to purchase a camcorder, here are some tips to keep in mind.

• Buy New, Not Used

Technology simply advances too quickly to make used equipment a bargain. Exception: Rare camcorder models that offered unique features, and were withdrawn from the market (such as Sharp's TwinCam models with dual image sensors, or Sony's CCD-V801 with time code and semi-pro optical controls).

• Beware of Differences in Quality

Picture quality is chiefly attributable to two factors, the number of image sensor chips, and the tape format (these will be explained in more detail later). Differences among brands are minor, except that Japanese products (Sony, Panasonic, Canon, JVC, Hitachi, Sharp, Mitsubishi, Minolta, Toshiba) tend to perform a notch better than Korean and Taiwanese products (Samsung, Goldstar, Kawasho).

• Buy for Today, Not Tomorrow

The cost of equipment comes down so rapidly, and new equipment becomes obsolete so quickly that there is very little sense in buying equipment if you're not ready to use it immediately.

The Manufacturer Shell Game

Beyond the obvious task of shopping for the lowest price is the finer, more subtle art of shopping for the best value. How do you compare features, brand names, guarantees, and prices for the best mix that suits your needs?

You won't be camcorder shopping for very long before you realize that there's something fishy going on with models and brand names. If you're observant, you'll often see what appears to be the exact same camcorder selling under several different brand names, often for different prices! I'm not talking here about camcorders that are merely similar, but those that are absolutely identical — feature for feature, switch for switch.

Only a handful of factories on the entire planet are capable of manufacturing camcorders. The machine tooling and precision required for this technology are extremely intricate. There are currently no U.S. manufacturers of camcorders (although plenty of U.S. companies slap their brand names onto Japanese built products). This is not because the technology is impossible to reproduce, but because it cannot be reproduced at a competitive price.

The big Japanese consumer video manufacturers are: Sony, Matsushita, JVC (of which 50% is owned by Matsushita), Sharp, Hitachi, and Toshiba. Mitsubishi, a giant Japanese industrial conglomerate, is also active in video, and Canon, which is known mostly for optical products, has carved out a niche in prosumer and industrial video. These manufactures produce the vast majority of camcorders, though they are sold under various brand names. In some cases, such as with Canon and Minolta, Sony makes the electronic "guts" of the 8mm format camcorders, but individual companies add their own lens systems, or other features that make them unique.

Sony owns Aiwa outright. Sony's camcorders are also sold under a wide variety of brand names, including Ricoh, Nikon, Pentax, and Kyocera.

Matsushita owns Panasonic, as well as Quasar. But they also manufacture camcorders for many other brands on store shelves — including Magnavox, Sylvania, and General Electric.

Hitachi manufactures camcorders for RCA and Minolta, as well as their own brand name.

Philips and Thomson are the major non-Asian players in the consumer electronics business. Philips, a Dutch company, owns the Magnavox and Sylvania brands. Thomson is a French company that owns the RCA and GE consumer electronics brands. But as of this writing, no camcorders are actually manufactured in

Europe or the Americas—they all come from Asia, from the same eight or ten factories as all the other brands.

Thus, while it may at first appear that there are hundreds of different camcorder models, a bit of investigation will reveal that for each format (8mm, VHS, VHS-C, etc.) there are rarely more than ten or fifteen truly different models.

Consumer vs. Industrial Equipment

Each of the three most active companies in video technology—Sony, JVC, and Panasonic—also makes "industrial" video equipment which gets sold through different channels than the "consumer" equipment.

The high-end "prosumer" video consumers and "semiprofessional" videomakers have created a mild outbreak of schizophrenia among these video manufacturers. Each has two competing marketing divisions, consumer sales, and industrial sales, trying to sell video equipment to the same customers.

The method of sales and potential profit margins of these two equipment markets are completely different. Consumer video equipment is sold in an intensely competitive retail environment. Every big city has dozens if not hundreds of discount electronics stores. In New York City, nearly two pages of the Sunday New York Times are filled each week with ads from a half dozen stores listing model numbers and prices. There's absolutely no descriptive information, just model numbers and prices!

Greasing the Palms

Contrast that with the industrial market. Typically, industrial equipment is sold to TV studios and other video production businesses, as well as schools, libraries, cable-TV companies, public-access and video art centers, etc. Often an equipment package is purchased at one time, such as a complete editing system, or a three-camera studio setup. The industrial equipment dealers, who usually represent numerous brands, will make sales by bidding on a package of equipment worth anywhere from five thousand to hundreds of thousands of dollars.

In this context, there's plenty of money to be made—especially when the person making the purchasing decisions is not spending his or her own money, but is merely representing a large corporation or government institution. Three martini lunches, expense accounts, and occasional kickbacks are the order of the day here. (There are many forms of "legal kickbacks," incidentally, in which the purchase of certain equipment entitles the buyer to a variety of freebies like vacations, personal entertainment equipment, etc.)

Until recently a wide technical gulf separated the consumer and industrial video worlds. After all, the industrial buyers were interested in "serious," professional video gear—3^{1}_{4}" videocassette recorders, 3-chip cameras (and 3-tube cameras—old-fashioned vacuum tubes are still used in some top-quality video cameras), editing consoles, etc.; while the consumers just wanted junky 1^{1}_{2}" VCRs to play movies and time-shift soap opera episodes.

Along came the camcorder, and the new S-VHS and Hi8 tape formats, blurring the old category distinctions. The fanciest consumer equipment on the market now is actually superior to older industrial equipment, at least in terms of features. Sony, JVC, and Panasonic each sell low-priced camcorders, and VCRs through their industrial divisions to satisfy the needs of their industrial customers (schools, corporate video, etc.) who opt to use consumer-quality equipment. Sometimes industrial models appear to be identical to consumer versions, except they cost more and have different model numbers. Is there any real difference between such apparently identical industrial and consumer models?

This is where the nebulous area of "construction quality" becomes an issue. Call any industrial video equipment dealer in your local phone book, ask him or her to rattle off the prices for some inexpensive industrial VHS camcorders. Then ask why you shouldn't just go down to the local department store and buy a consumer model with comparable features for several hundred dollars less.

"The industrial equipment is built better," will be the retort. Is this true? Yes and no. In some cases, it's very obvious that industrial and consumer equipment are exactly the same—as obvious as the aforementioned ruse of putting different brand name labels on the exact same product. In other cases, there are differences, such as more rugged metal cases replacing plastic, or the use of different video heads intended to work only at the higher quality fast tape speed (SP only).

What is most perplexing, perhaps, even when the equipment appears to be identical, is the possibility that different quality control standards apply to consumer and industrial equipment.

Blank Tape Shell Game

I once interviewed an engineer from 3M about differences in blank video tapes, and asked what the difference was between Scotch's "EG" and "EG+" tapes. To my surprise, he explained that there was absolutely no difference in the way these two types of tape were made. All the tape is made in batches. In each batch, no matter how carefully all the factors are controlled, the tapes come out with a slight variation in quality. So after a batch is made, Scotch tests its performance. The better tapes go into the

"EG+" boxes, while the not-as-good tapes go in the "EG" boxes. He added that, more often than not, the tape is of consistently high quality, so they end up putting what they consider "EG+" quality tape into "EG" boxes.

I read once that when choosing cars for their own personal use, many Detroit auto executives prefer cars which come off the assembly line mid-week—Tuesday, Wednesday, or Thursday. The rationale is that workers are sloppier, and more lemons are made when they arrive hungover and mad at having to face another workweek on Monday; and that by Friday they're watching the clock (and not their work!) in anticipation of the weekend break.

It is indeed conceivable that in consumer electronics, equipment from the same assembly line is sorted according to performance, and then different labels are slapped on accordingly. This reasoning may convince you that it's worth paying more for a Sony than a seemingly identical Kyocera, or for an industrial camcorder rather than an identical consumer model. Unfortunately, unless you can compare technical specifications which represent guaranteed performance levels—including such factors as video signal-to-noise ratios, speed stability, linearity, etc.—there's really no way to determine if this is the case (that is, unless you wish to underwrite a full-scale scientific study of the matter, with test equipment costing hundreds of thousands of dollars to measure these subtle differences).

Despite all the techno-jargon, there's still a good deal of voodoo involved in choosing video gear.

Limiting the Consumer Market

The belief that industrial equipment is inherently superior to consumer equipment is eroding, especially with the clear superiority of MiniDV over practically all previous industrial formats. I noted earlier that equipment which used to cost tens of thousands of dollars is now selling for a couple of thousand—even though, in many cases, the industrial divisions are still selling the ten-thousand dollar machines.

The S-VHS and Hi8 formats first exacerbated this dilemma for equipment manufacturers. The 3/4" format used to draw a clear line between the "professional" video formats—which also include Betacam, MII, D-2, D-3, and 1" tapes—and the "consumer" formats—VHS, 8mm, and Betamax. There's continuing debate between video experts about which format is better, 3/4" or S-VHS or Hi8 (3/4" is generally credited with having better color rendition and timing stability, while S-VHS and Hi8 have better picture detail and hi-fi audio quality). But the fact that this debate even exists—regardless of which is better—demonstrates that several consumer formats are now in the running, and MiniDV represents a maxi monkey wrench thrown into the neat little equipment categories.

The dilemma for manufacturers is that they make both consumer and industrial equipment. They want to keep selling more and more sophisticated equipment to the expanding amateur video market, but they must take extreme care not to encourage the traditional purchasers of industrial equipment to switch over to the lower-profit consumer gear.

This could be accomplished by withholding certain professionally desirable capabilities from consumer equipment. Even though these features might only cost a few hundred dollars (or even less) to add, manufacturers require their industrial customers to spend thousands more to get them. Examples: A standard XLR microphone jack instead of the rinky dink mini-jack; separate line output jacks for the Hi-fi and linear audio tracks (thankfully, Panasonic's AG-1980 is an exception); manual audio recording control (exceptions: Sony's CDR-VX1000, CDR-VX700, Canon's L-2 and discontinued A-1 line); VITC time code on VHS-family equipment (exception: Panasonic's AG-455).

Camcorder manufacturing is an oligopoly business—just a handful of factories are capable of making them. (Then again, how many camcorder manufacturing plants can our planet support?) Manufacturers may be trying to protect the turf of their industrial divisions, but they also legitimately argue that only a small niche market of prosumers are interested in the most advanced features on consumer gear. These buyers, who might get a new camcorder every four years or more, are not a big enough market for anyone except a handful of the most established names (Sony, JVC, Panasonic, Canon).

Seasonal Variations

Any well-managed grocery store puts the freshest milk in the back of the refrigerator, and any sharp consumer knows this and checks the dates. But when it comes to buying video equipment, there's often little awareness on the part of the customer of how "fresh" the equipment is.

Nobody likes to buy day-old goods, especially if there's no commensurate discount, so manufacturers will often use confusing model numbers to prevent consumers from easily determining which merchandise is newer. Don't assume that higher model numbers represent better products. Often, a new model is introduced with a lower number just to confuse people into buying out the old stock. And don't be lured by sexy subliminal model numbers, like "SX"!

Extended Warranties

Practically everything you buy new comes with a manufacturer's warranty. (Except for so-called "gray market" goods, as explained in the next section.) At worst, the manufacturer's warranty will cover parts and labor for ninety days—that's it. Many warranties will cover parts for a year, but labor for just ninety days. The best warranties cover both for a year, or longer.

Most stores offer "extended warranty" plans which you can purchase optionally. They are almost always discussed after you've already decided to buy a camcorder or other piece of electronic merchandise. These warranties can sound appealing, but note that they are a major profit source for stores which otherwise cut margins to the bone. After shopping exhaustively for the best price, you may find yourself spending quite a bit extra on one of these plans.

The extended warranty is clearly a gamble, but in more ways than you may realize. What happens if the store you buy the warranty from goes out of business? What happens if you move to a different city? What happens if the unit breaks, you bring it in for repair, and it takes several months to get fixed?

Statistically speaking, most extended warranties are a complete rip off. The odds are worse than most games in Las Vegas. Typically, a two year extended warranty costs about ten percent of what the equipment costs. But the likelihood of having a manufacturing defect reveal itself in two years is far less than ten percent—more on the order of one or two percent for most equipment. The cost of most consumer camcorder repairs for mechanical breakdowns (the most common problem) averages around two hundred dollars. (Remember that if you drop or abuse your camcorder in any obvious way, such as cracking the lens, most extended warranties will not cover the damage.) These warranties play on the fears of consumers that they will be the unlucky ones. And there's a hefty premium to pay for the feeling of security.

Is an extended warranty plan right for you? Probably not. They're just too overpriced. An exception to this rule might be institutional organizations whose budgets must be very predictable. Such organizations should arrange for a service contract which serves as a warranty, but also includes routine maintenance.

Don't leave warranty shopping to the last minute, as most stores would prefer you do. Shop for extended warranties just as you shop for price—call around and ask what the extended warranty plan costs, and what you get. Be sure to ask what happens if the store goes out of business.

Visa and Mastercard Gold Card and American Express credit card buyers get a unique extended warranty when they buy equipment with the card—the manufacturer's warranty is doubled. At no extra charge, your 90-day warranty becomes a 180-day warranty, though you'll have to deal with the credit card company in addition to the service shop. Sometimes you have to register the equipment when you buy it (American Express requires this), and the extended period is usually limited to one year.

If nothing else, this should give you an indication of just how infrequently the equipment breaks. American Express charges merchants on a sliding scale that runs from about one to four percent of the charge—so if you charge a one-thousand dollar camcorder to your card, Amex gets around twenty or thirty dollars. With that, they're willing to double the duration of the manufacturer's warranty, while still making a good profit, because they know the statistics.

Just to see how the numbers work, let's assume a dismal five-percent failure rate for camcorders over two years, and lets assume the average repair cost is one-hundred fifty dollars (these conservative figures are purely hypothetical). A non-profit "co-op" extended warranty would need to charge just $7.50 for the two-year policy to break even (plus administrative overhead—perhaps another dollar or two). If such a plan is billed to the consumer for fifty or seventy-five dollars, the profit potential is enormous.

Extended warranty plans are so important to electronics and appliance retailing that sales people often have their success measured not by how much merchandise they've sold in a week, but by the percentage of customers that purchased extended warranties.

Price Fixing

The old-fashioned method manufacturers have used for years to jack up retail prices—price fixing—is still alive and well in the retail electronics business. In a nutshell, modern price fixing works like this: The manufacturer sets a certain "floor" price, under which retailers are not allowed to sell their products. This benefits retailers, of course, because they get higher profits, but what happens if a retailer falls out of line and drops its price to gain greater sales volume? The manufacturer can refuse to sell to that dealer, essentially stripping them of their dealership.

Several years ago, the Attorney Generals of 48 states and the District of Columbia took action against Matsushita (Panasonic) for alleged price fixing in VCRs, camcorders, telephones, and Technics brand audio equipment. According to a voluntary settlement which was reached with Panasonic, consumers who purchased the PV-400, PV-420, or PV-460 camcorders between March 1st and August 31st, 1988, were entitled to refunds of $45, $38, and $20 respectively.

Unfortunately, short of such legal action there's very little you can do to combat price fixing when you're shopping for a camcorder. If you notice a whole bunch of discount stores charging the same price for something, or when the spread is less than usual when compared with pricier department stores, then you've probably uncovered some sort of "arrangement". But individually, there's little you can do. Send a letter to your state's Attorney General and register a complaint by phone with your local Better Business Bureau for personal satisfaction. Also, buy a different brand as a pocketbook protest. (But then again, how many different brands are there, really?)

There is very rarely a "best" model. No manufacturer will throw every possible feature into one model. You must turn to professional equipment for true luxury. With consumer models, features vary so widely, and there are so many quality products, that personal preference factors like style, brand loyalty, and handling can be just as important as technical stuff. Spend a lot of time playing with a camcorder in a store before you buy it to see if it feels right. Ergonomic factors, such as where you have to reach to perform various functions, can be as important as performance factors. If you shake the camera each time you reach for the fade button, it can ruin your video more than a decrease in resolution.

The Gray Market

When shopping for video equipment, you should be aware of the "gray market." It may sound sleazy and illegal, but the gray market in America is a legitimate business, and it's thriving. Some of the best bargains in VCRs and camcorders are "gray market" goods — equipment that was originally shipped to other countries for sale there, but then diverted to the U.S. Currently the practice of selling gray market goods is perfectly legal (the Supreme Court has upheld the legality of gray market imports), though Congress has considered banning it.

Some items are available only through the gray market. High-end video equipment is regularly introduced in Japan before it comes here, contributing to a thriving gray market for state-of-the-art high-tech goodies. Similarly, there are Japanese Nintendo cartridges that can only be bought in the U.S. on the gray market.

Most Japanese electronics companies have a separate division to market products in the United States. Thus, when you buy a Sony product, the warranty card gets mailed to "Sony Corporation of America," Sony's U.S. distributor. Gray market goods bypass this U.S. distributor because they are purchased wholesale in another country.

Many goods intended for foreign markets cannot be used in the U.S. The required line voltage may be different, and TV and video products may use different scanning standards than the American "NTSC" system—called PAL and SECAM. Shoppers must watch out for these potential gray market incompatibilities.

With gray market purchases, the buyer must beware of more subtle problems, too. Although the product itself may be identical from one country to another, the printed items thrown into the box—the warranty and instruction manual—can vary. Warranties on gray market goods are often invalid, and the instruction manuals may even be printed in a foreign language.

Who Sells Gray Market Goods?

The purveyors of gray market goods tend to be the deep discount cash-and-carry stores, which often advertise super low prices in ads with nothing more than model numbers and prices. But fancier stores will occasionally deal with gray market goods, in order to bring customers products otherwise unavailable in the U.S. market. Perhaps it's a sad reflection of the U.S.'s declining importance in the global economy, but many high tech goodies are now routinely introduced in Japan and Western Europe months or years before they arrive in America.

Digital audio tape (DAT) is an excellent example of this. The official, legitimate U.S. debut of consumer DAT equipment occurred years after the equipment was already selling in both Japan and Western Europe. Threats of lawsuits from America's recording industry prevented the marketing of DA in the U.S. until a copy protection system was devised to deter amateur bootlegging. The Japanese ministry of trade had refused export licenses for consumer DAT gear bound for America. But any store with a friend overseas, or with access to a gray market wholesaler, could easily get ahold of DAT decks.

Though Japan was banning export to America, there was no legal problem in the U.S. importing gray market DAT decks, But a store's relationship with the manufacturer could become strained. If a Sony dealer sells gray market Sony goods, for instance, Sony can strip the store of its status as an "authorized dealer."

Authorized Dealers

Manufacturers claim the system of selling through authorized dealers ensures that customers have access to their full line of products, rather than just a few popular models, so they get the benefit of a better choice. The authorized dealers can also be relied upon to special order accessories and provide knowledgeable guidance to use the products properly.

But limiting who can sell a manufacturer's products to a select cartel of authorized dealers smacks of price fixing, and this issue has plagued consumer electronics retailing for many years. "Fair trade" agreements that let manufacturers set minimum retail prices were outlawed in the seventies, and consumer groups argue that current efforts to outlaw gray market goods are thinly veiled attempts to reinstitute price controls. Although manufacturers deny such allegations, it is readily apparent that authorized dealers usually charge more for products than unauthorized dealers do, since price is their only competitive edge.

How Can You Identify Gray Market Goods?

Some gray market goods are absolutely identical to their legitimate counterparts, but telltale signs sometimes identify the gray market item. Look for the serial number on the product itself, as well as the box, to see if it has been scratched off (to help conceal the transit route, and invalidate the warranty). Foreign language instruction manuals, or photocopied instruction manuals, are also dead giveaways. Missing warranty registration cards, explicit statements about a "store warranty" rather than a manufacturer's warranty, and foreign language labelling on the product itself are other sure signs of a gray market goods.

Even if none of these smoke signals appears, it doesn't hurt to simply ask a store if a product is gray market. Many stores are perfectly honest about this, and will use it to segue into a sales pitch for an extended warranty plan.

Rules Of The Gray Market Game

The biggest drawback to buying gray market goods is that the manufacturer provides no warranty protection. This can also occur when you buy regular goods (not gray market) from an unauthorized dealer; but in practice, when the goods are somehow obtained through the U.S. distribution system, manufacturers usually (but not always) honor their warranties.

Stores that make no bones about selling gray market goods often substitute their own store warranty. But with a store warranty, you run the risk that the store may go out of business, leaving you stuck with worthless paper. (When the Crazy Eddie's chain in New York went bankrupt in the late 1980s, as many as two million people were left holding worthless extended warranties!)

Also in New York, 6th Avenue Electronics' aggressive marketing of gray market goods, and brands for which they are not an authorized dealer, has not exactly endeared them with manufacturers. Close examination of their full page ads in New York newspapers reveals fine print stating that they are not an authorized dealer for Boston Acoustics speakers—in accordance with a court-approved consent decree that also requires the store to point out to customers the missing serial numbers on Boston Acoustic products.

For consumers, gray market goods are not a black and white issue. While these goods offer lower prices and sometimes higher technology than is otherwise available in this country, they are also riskier purchases and may be more difficult to use if the instruction manuals are unavailable.

For manufacturers, the issue is more clear cut: They want an end to gray market trade and have encouraged the U.S. Congress to consider passing legislation to outlaw the practice. But so far, gray market goods remain perfectly legal.

The Complete Field Production Kit

Besides the camcorder, there are a number of accessories that will really enhance your ability to create good quality video. We'll examine many of these items in more detail later, but just to get started, here's a rough list of what you'd need to include in a basic video field production kit.

- Camcorder
- Two tripods—a heavy duty fluid head model (Bogen has several at around $200) and a lightweight portable model like the Magic I or Magic II from Culman (about $140). A fluid head is crucial for smooth camera moves like tilts and pans, but weighs upwards of five pounds by itself. That's why the lightweight unit is best for travel. (Bogen and Culman tripods are sold in most professional photo stores.)
- Steadicam JR handheld camera mount ($600) in lieu of or in addition to tripods.
- Two extra batteries for camcorder (about $100 for two). Note that there are many other battery manufacturers besides the camcorder's manufacturerer; newer models may offer longer run times.
- Light kit—ideally a three-light setup like Lowell's Tota system (about $800 to $1,000), but cheap photoflood reflectors and stands make a low budget alternative (about $50).

- Portable light, rechargeable battery powered (about $50).
- Two large white reflector cards (about $5 in an art store).
- Wireless microphone system (such as Azden's or Nady's lowest cost VHF models, about $180).
- Handheld dynamic microphone (such as the Electro-Voice EV-635A, $120).
- Headphones (such as Sony MD-6, $50).
  [see the audio section of this book for a more elaborate audio kit]
- Several carrying cases for equipment ($100 to $300). I prefer using compact padded camera bags that can fit into larger knapsacks and shoulder bags.

Total cost of accessories: $800 to $2200.

Of course, most low-budget producers do not run out and buy all these things at once. To spread out the payments, each item is added as the need for it arises. To start with the absolute minimum, I'd suggest a tripod, headphones, and a portable light—in that order.

Which To Buy

The $64,000 question: Which model camcorder and/or editing VCR(s) should you buy?

New models are introduced all the time, and some camcorders don't even stay on the market for a year before the manufacturer discontinues them—so some models mentioned here may no longer be available by the time you read this.

As this edition goes to press, in 1997, the choice for top models has never been so clear: Sony's DCR-VX1000 is the winner for absolute best picture quality; while Panasonic's PV-DV1000 gets the prize for almost-as-good quality combined with in-camcorder editing features. Both are 3-chip models costing upwards of three thousand dollars.(The Sony is clearly superior for hookup to desktop editing systems, due to its firewire jack.) More detailed descriptions of these camcorders follow later.

With the advent of the MiniDV format, in my opinion it would be absurd to buy a 3-chip Hi8 or S-VHS camcorder (such as Sony's CCD-VX3), unless you've alreay got a ton of equipment in one of these older formats, or are getting a great deal on used equipment.

In the one-chip category, MiniDV's position is less clear. For best picture quality, my real advice would be to save up and buy a three-chip MiniDV model, rather than a one-chip. But for casual use, Sony's DCR-PC7 and JVC's GR-DV1 are both awfully cute, and tiny.

JVC GR-DV1 MiniDV camcorder fits in a shirt pocket.

As this book was going to press all MiniDV models cost well over two thousand dollars, so someone looking for a camcorder selling in the ballpark of one thousand to fifteen hundred dollars would still be limited to the Hi8 and Super-VHS formats. In this category, recommended Hi8 models include Sony's CCD-TR3000, and the CCD-TR700 (which may be the lowest priced camcorder you can buy with built-in time code). Canon's L-2, which also has time code, is in a class by itself due to it's interchangeable lenses, but it costs as much as many MiniDV models.

For a one-chip S-VHS camcorder, Panasonic's industrial AG-456 is the clear choice in the full-size category. For a mini-sized S-VHS-C model, JVC's GR-SZ9 packs an extraordinary amount of in-camera editing and special effects (though it gets demerits for not having a sophisticated remote control jack, as exists on all other models mentioned so far.)

Besides format, two other broad considerations are image stabilizer quality and viewfinder or viewscreen. The top of the line in image stabilization can be found in an accessory 15:1 zoom lens for Canon's L-2 and L-1 camcorders, but the lens alone costs more than most camcorders (over $2000). Many other Sony models have the optical stabilizer system – recently Sony started using the term "Super SteadyShot" to denote which models have the optical system. Canon's Hi8 ES-5000 and ES-2000 models also have the optical image stabilization, but they lack time code. (The ES-5000 has a unique and innovative eye control system that lets you start and stop the tape, or adjust focus, using movements of your eye to look at different spots in the viewfinder.)

The viewscreen style camcorders, which began with Sharp's Viewcam line, are a lot of fun to use. But beware that they're inherently unprofessional looking, the screens can be hard to see in outdoor daylight, and you lose privacy by letting others around see your viewfinder. With that said, Sharp's MiniDV format VL-D5000U is clearly the best in this category, though quite expensive. At more down to earth prices, Sony's "Vision" series camcorders (numbers beginning with CCD-TRV) offer a great combination of traditional viewfinder and viewscreen; note that the Sharp models are strictly viewscreen-only.

If you're shopping for an editing VCR, see the chapter on Editing VCRs for more detailed information. As we were going to press, the single best editing VCR ever offered to consumers was not yet on the market – Sony's long anticipated DHR-1000 MiniDV format VCR. I have gotten to play with it a bit at demonstrations, and can atest that it is truly fantastic -- an enthusiast's dream machine. It has the firewire digital dubbing jack, LANC remote control terminal, and the ability to record from analog inputs (which raises the copyright issue that delayed introduction of this model). But the estimated price of DHR-1000 was over three thousand dollars.

For a Super-VHS editing VCR, working on a more modest budget, the Panasonic AG-1980 is the hands-down Super-VHS favorite. Its predecessors, the AG-1970 and 1960, endured for over seven years as the best low-cost editing S-VHS value. The AG-1980 adds a feature that I have been crying for for over a decade – independent jacks for the linear and HiFi audio tracks. It also has a built-in time base corrector, and sells for about $1,500.

My advice to most people is not to edit onto Hi8, even if you have a Hi8 camorder, because Super-VHS offers better audio and insert-video editing capability. Nevertheless, if you need to edit onto Hi8 for a particular reason, or wish to use a VCR rather than your camcorder as the source deck in your editing system, then Sony's EVS-7000 is your likely choice. It offers time code, built-in TBC, a jog/shuttle control and tuner. If you have a computer, Sony's discontinued "V-deck" series might also be of interest. All have PCM sound.

Canon's L2 camcorder features interchangeable lenses. Courtesy of Canon USA.

For an edit controller, FutureVideo's line of computer-based standalone boxes, IBM-expansion cards and Mac/Amiga/IBM-compatible control boxes are the best choices for full-blown computer based editing systems (costing $600 to $2,000 plus the cost of the computer). On a lower budget, Videonics Thumbs Up Editor ($229) is a fantastic deal, as is the computer-based Gold Disk Video Director (about $100). As mentioned earlier, none of the current low-budget non-linear editing systems make sense, at least as far as picture quality is concerned, when compared to these tape based editing products. If you don't care about getting the best picture quality, but just want to learn about editing using your computer, get Adobe Premiere software along with just about any inexpensive video input board (or the CardCam Video-In for notebook computers).

Of course, things change rapidly. For the latest information about new models, Desktop Video Systems, the publisher of this book, offers a reasonably priced newsletter service featuring tips and advice on the latest equipment. Please refer to the information in the back of this book for more information.

Sony DCR-VX1000

Probably the single best consumer camcorder on the market as this book was going to press, Sony's DCR-VX1000 is the flagship of the Mini-DV format. Besides offering top-notch recording quality for both picture and sound, it has practically every semi-pro bell and whistle you could ask for — a three-chip image sensor system, manual everything, zebra-stripe viewfinder display, calibrated f-stops — the works. It has two advanced features that even most professional cameras lack — optical image stabilization, and digital fade from/to a freeze frame. And best of all, it has digital dubbing capability — a "firewire" connector on the back of the camcorder lets you make absolutely perfect copies, with zero generation loss, when connected to another Sony Mini-DV camcorder or DVC VCR.

The picture quality from the DCR-VX1000 is truly breathtaking. Horizontal resolution is 500-lines, and the signal-to-noise ratio of the picture is noticeably better, with much less noise in dark areas, compared with even the best Hi8 and S-VHS camcorders. The luminance and chroma S/N ratios are about 6 to 10 dB higher than the analog formats, resulting in wider contrast range and less visible noise.

Sony DCR-VX1000

The three-chip image sensor system has the inherent advantages of showing better color detail and picture subtlety, compared with one chip systems. With 410,000 pixels each, there's enough detail to spare to make the digital zoom feature — which extends the optical zoom range from 10x to 20x — palatable. The lens has a 5.9 to 59mm range, with f1.6 speed and 52mm threads (it's the same thread size as the old CCD-VX3 and CCD-TR700 Hi8 models). Focus is smoothly adjustable via a ring around the lens. Power zoom is variable speed, but there is just a hint of jerkiness as speeds shift — this is one area for improvement in the future.

The image stabilizer doesn't hurt image detail at all, because it uses the fluid-filled prism system rather than digital zooming. A rear panel flips open to reveal the battery compartment, as well as a switch that chooses between the digital zoom feature or the overlap fader (to dissolve from/to freeze frame). I always chose the latter — compared to other models with digital dissolve, the great thing about the DCR-VX1000's implementation is that it's always ready — you don't have to do anything special at the end of a shot to prepare for the dissolve-in effect.

The rear panel sports seven buttons, including program exposure, manual white balance, and self timer functions. The manual exposure override is placed on the left side of the lens, along with the focus overrides. To keep things simple, there's a full-auto mode, selectable by a switch in back. Besides allowing manual override, this switch also has a "hold" position that returns you to previous manual settings.

The camera is very comfortable to hold and use. It's compact, and one complaint that's sure to be heard from anyone who shoots professionally is that even though image quality is probably somewhere between Betacam SP and Digital Betacam, the small size means it doesn't rest on the shoulder, the way professionals are used to. That's addressed by a shoulder mount accessory that Sony sells. You can't look through the viewfinder with this shoulder mount — instead, an LCD monitor attaches to the shoulder mount. I have also mounted the DCR-VX1000 on the Steadicam JR, and achieved excellent results.

The viewfinder is a color LCD — but before semi-pro users wince (because black and white viewfinders offer finer detail for focusing), note that it has an impressive 180,000 pixels (most color viewfinders have 80 to 120,000). It is just shy of showing all the detail that you'd see on a big screen (after all, with three 410,000 pixel image sensors creating the signal, some detail must be getting lost), but it's surprisingly good. In hands-on use, I have found it more than acceptable for performing critical focus, but not superb. Occasionally I'd find a narrow range where focus didn't change, and select the center point as my best guess of best focus.

The zebra-stripe viewfinder display, available as an option in the setup menu, is extremely useful, and considered de rigueur on all professional video cameras. Whenever the brightness of the image becomes saturated — as white as it can get — instead of appearing white a diagonal black-and-white striped pattern appears. This "zebra stripe" pattern does not get recorded on tape — it just appears in the viewfinder to alert you of hot spots in the picture — such as commonly occurs with men's bald spots, foreheads, and other small bright areas of the picture. When you're using manual exposure control, the zebra-stripe display is absolutely essential for helping you determine the brightest possible exposure that doesn't saturate (which is, in a nutshell, the definition of correct exposure.)

One big improvement over the old VX3 (Hi8) is that the zebra-stripe option remains selected even when you turn the camcorder off and change batteries. In fact, all selected options remain in effect.

When shooting in low light, a calibrated pro-style video gain boost adjustment is available, incrementally selectable up to +18dB.

A crisp blue-and-white display underneath the viewfinder screen indicates elapsed tape time (with time code accuracy) and battery status. The viewfinder tilts up to 90-degrees, so you can look straight down at it. Two rubber eyecups are supplied — a normal sized one, and a large Hollywood-inspired cup that does indeed do a better job sealing light out. (The Hollywood ambience is further enhanced by the rectangular-shaped lens hood, reminiscent of Panavision lenses. Besides looking really cool, this lens hood really does a better job blocking flare than a round hood of similar length.)

By hooking up appropriate equipment to two tiny jacks you transform this camcorder into one third of a supercharged digital video editing workstation. These connections are the familiar LANC (Control-L) edit controller terminal, which assures compatibility with products from Videonics, FutureVideo, and Gold Disk (Video Director) — including time code information; and the all new DV In/Out connector. This new high-speed serial port connection has been nicknamed "firewire" in the computer industry, and enables the digital dubbing capability. (Curiously, most other brands of Mini-DV equipment don't have this connector yet — a Sony spokesperson attributed the disparity to Sony's lead time in making the necessary chips, though most observers think it has more to do with the copyright issue that has delayed introduction of DVC format VCRs.)

The single jack is both input and output, and the camcorder automatically knows whether it is supposed to send or receive a signal. Currently, by editing between two of these camcorders (or Sony's lower priced DCR-VX700, which has just one image sensor but is otherwise similar), you can achieve something which just a couple of years ago was unthinkable for under one hundred thousand dollars — the ability to edit unlimited hours of raw footage, with absolutely no generation loss, even after making copies of copies dozens of times.

Ordinary A/V and S-video output jacks are also provided. But — probably due to the copyright issue that has delayed the VCRs — there's no A/V input capability.

In the audio department, Sony included the all-important manual audio recording control — it's an ergonomic dial in the rear lower left corner. Calibrated VU meters, with peak indicator are visible on the rear panel LCD display (one obvious improvement: offer a switchable backlight for this display, which also shows exposure, and battery level.). A three level adjustable headphone volume control is also available in the setup menu — I've kept it on the loudest setting all the time, and my hearing is still good (what?).

Digital audio recording specifications, amazingly, are identical to CD and DAT quality — 16 bit samples, with 44.1-kHz sampling rate. This is the premium quality recording option for the Mini-DV format, and unlike the lower-quality four track option, you can't dub additional audio onto the original tape. You get no choice in the matter — audio recording is always 16-bit.

That's a minor complaint. The biggest one, in the audio department, is the standard-issue consumer grade mini-jack microphone input. Fortunately, the built-in microphone is very good, and mounted apart from the rest of the unit, along the top of the large pro-style carrying handle, to minimize pickup of sounds from the lens and transport motors. But if only there was a balanced-line input jack... this camcorder would then be truly pro-grade.

All kvetching aside, the DCR-VX1000 is really a fantastic camcorder that is state-of-the-art in every respect. Sony has set a new benchmark of consumer quality here, and judging by the way other manufacturers, such as JVC, have at least initially conceded this turf to Sony, it seems unlikely it will be supplanted by anything better anytime soon (possible exception: Canon). With a list price over four grand, and street prices well above three, the DCR-VX1000 is quite expensive by the standards of consumer equipment. But for the semi-pro producer, this is the bargain of the century — representing a ten-fold decrease from the price of professional digital video recording equipment such as Digital Beta-cam.

Panasonic PV-DV1000 Camcorder

Panasonic's PV-DV1000 camcorder is Panasonic's first (and only) consumer DV camcorder — a more expensive professional model (AJ-D700) is also being introduced. Like professional video cameras, the PV-DV1000 has three separate image sensor chips, for red, green and blue light. But unlike pro models, it weighs a mere two pounds, eleven ounces, fully loaded with battery and tape (which is about half the size of an 8mm cassette, holds 60-minutes, and costs about $15). That's just slightly heavier than today's run-of-the-mill camcorders, making the PV-DV1000 very suitable for travel and other everyday applications.

This camcorder has truly professional quality and features, at a semi-pro price. And, compared with the competing Sony model, the Panasonic PV-DV1000 has some interesting in-camera audio editing abilities. Its raw video (and audio) quality clearly beats any Hi8 or S-VHS camcorder by a good margin.

The PV-DV1000 is a really beautiful looking camcorder. It has an all-black finish that, combined with a very round, tubular shape, makes it reminiscent of the fancy Super-8 and 16mm amateur film cameras from the 50s and 60s. There's a touch of nightscope and bazooka mixed in. The viewfinder is the most distinctive design element — it's a big wide tube, as wide as the lens, that tilts up to 90-degrees. It has a big wide magnifying lens, and a big rubber eyecup. When tilted all the way down, the viewfinder is in-line with the lens, making pointing the camcorder very intuitive. The viewfinder itself is a bright LCD color screen with high enough resolution (180,000 pixels) to convince even an old "black and white is better" diehard that you can adjust manual focus effectively (horizontal resolution measured 400-lines in the viewfinder).

Tapes are loaded from inside a very well sealed-up compartment on the right. The same compartment holds the lithium ion battery. On the other side of the camcorder are manual override controls, and a small LCD status screen showing time code numbers, manual settings, and audio recording (16-bit or 12-bit).

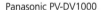

Panasonic PV-DV1000

One minor complaint is the way the camera turns on, which might tend to accidentally erase stuff. Panasonic has abandoned the common three position Camera-Off-VCR power switch. Instead, the switch that we've come to think of as the standby switch — the lever surrounding the run/pause button — is the power switch. The camcorder always powers up in the camera mode. To go into VCR mode you must press a button on top of the camcorder - tiny lights indicate whether Camera or VCR mode is selected.

The optical range of the zoom lens is 10x — the same as the Sony DCR-VX1000. Digital electronics extend the range to 20x, but resolution noticeably suffers when you're all the way zoomed in — especially when watching on a big-screen TV. Power zoom operates at just two speeds — taking about eleven seconds, or five seconds, to sweep from full wide angle to full telephoto (optical range only). There's also a Turbo-Zoom mode that takes about one and a half seconds to go to the most extreme zoom setting (in either direction), but you can only use this feature while the tape is paused (that's one less way to nauseate people with excessive zooming).

There's a very smooth, intuitive manual focus control ring around the lens. The 6 - 60mm lens has an f1.6 speed rating, and 60mm filter thread diameter. The lens comes with a detachable protective filter, attached to rubber anti-flare lens hood.

The manual iris override is adjusted by a knob located in the lower front left corner, below the lens. A button in its center selects between iris and high-speed shutter adjustments, both of which get displayed in the viewfinder. Instead of absolute f-stop numbers, in manual iris mode the display shows degree of adjustment, from f-6 to f+6 (calibrated in one-stop increments). However, you can see absolute f-stop readings through the use of the excellent auto-exposure lock button, accessed via a tiny pop-open panel along the left side. This button makes it easy to zoom in on someone's face, lock the exposure, and then zoom out for proper framing — thus semiautomatically compensating for backlight or spotlight exposure situations.

Three other buttons in this compartment activate manual focus, video gain boost (selectable up to +12dB), and white balance — an excellent manual setting performs both black balance and white balance adjustments.

The battery lasts about an hour and is recharged by hooking up the power adaptor cord, without removing the battery An LED meter on the adaptor indicates charge progress (charging takes about 80-minutes). An innovative power save switch, below the viewfinder, automatically turns off the viewfinder, zoom, and autofocus whenever the camcorder is pointing down.

The picture quality of recorded images is excellent. Horizontal resolution is a hair below Sony's three-chip model, around 480-lines. What's most striking about the image is not just the detail, but the stability. The picture appears rock solid. Vertical edges — such as poles and building edges — appear perfectly straight, with none of the jaggedness that shows up in other formats.

As far as raw picture quality is concerned, this camera performs fine. But start invoking some of the special effects, and quality suffers. A slide switch below the viewfinder selects normal or wide-screen recording. The wide-screen mode looks really impressive on a wide screen set — I hooked it up to Panasonic's 50" wide-screen projection TV, and at first glance it looked terrific. But technically, I noticed resolution suffered. A quick test with a standard resolution chart revealed that vertical resolution had dropped from about 330 to 250-lines.

The Electronic Image Stabilizer (EIS) also cuts down picture detail — I measured vertical resolution around 300-lines and horizontal resolution around 380-lines. The worst offenses occurred when combining the features — with both EIS and wide-screen recording active, I measured vertical resolution of just 200-lines, and horizontal resolution of 250-lines.

The culprits are the image sensors, whose combined resolution is just barely enough to satisfy the data-thirsty needs of the DV format. Each of the three image sensors has 270,000 pixels, and the resultant "pure camera" (without recording and playing back) horizontal resolution measured 500-lines — which is exactly what the DV format is capable of capturing on tape. For straight recording the image sensors are good enough, but start using just a subset of the picture — for letterbox (wide screen), image stabilizer, or digital zooming — and picture quality falls below what you'd expect from the DV format.

The PV-DV1000 has a 5-lux low-light rating; and in comparison seems slightly less sensitive than Sony's DCR-VX1000, which has a 4-lux rating. Most camcorders with three image sensors are less sensitive than one-chip models, because the light from the lens gets divided three ways by a prism. But in practice you'll be very impressive by any MiniDV model in low light, because the signal-to-noise ratio is so much higher than with other formats.

Still and slow-motion playback are rock-steady — totally free of jitter — but the picture appears to be just a field — not a frame — (vertical resolution is reduced). A Frame Record mode, in the setup menu, gets around this problem, but the picture appears jittery at normal playback speed. There's also Photo mode recording, in which a still frame occupies six seconds of playback time. Fast searching, as with other DV equipment, exhibits block-like digital motion artifacts. Fast forward and rewind times for a 60-minute tape are just over a minute.

The built-in audio recording and dubbing capabilities put the PV-DV1000 ahead of both Sony models, and should be of particular interest to anyone who might want to try making a music video using in-camera editing techniques.

The PV-DV1000 offers nearly the full range of audio flexibility that the DV format encompasses — including the ability to switch between CD-quality 16-bit stereo recording (with 44.1kHz sampling), or slightly lower quality 12-bit recording (with sampling at 32-kHz) that provides a total of four audio tracks. The 12-bit mode limits the high end of the frequency response to about 15-kHz, but for this slight sacrifice you get the ability to conveniently add music, narration, sound effects etc. Two of the 12-bit tracks are recorded along with original video, and two more can be added later using the audio dub feature. If you don't intend to add more audio later, you can get the best quality by selecting 16-bit stereo recording in the camera menu.

The playback menu lets you listen to either pair of 12-bit stereo tracks by themselves, or mixed together. You can also monitor just the left or right channel from each. When I tried audio dubbing over a 16-bit recording the original 16-bit track did not disappear — it ended up on the left side (or at least half of it), with the newly dubbed track on the right. But notably lacking, in the audio department, are a manual level control override, and headphone level control (though headphone level as supplied is ample).

The built-in audio recording and editing capabilities put this camcorder in a category by itself. Its ability to record the high quality 16-bit soundtrack makes it, in essence, a DAT-quality audio recorder in its own right (the microphone mini-jack and preamp circuitry are the weakest elements here). And the ability to perform glitch-free in-camera video-insert edits, while monitoring that 16-bit sound, makes the PV-DV1000 absolutely the camcorder to get for making music videos.

A standard set of line A/V and S-video output plug connections are available via a special adaptor cable — it has a flat razorblade sized connector that slips into a slot in the back. There are no digital audio connections.

There are also no A/V line input connections, and no digital video dubbing connections. This is perhaps the biggest weakness of the PV-DV1000 when compared with the Sony models. Because DV recordings are digital they can theoretically be copied over and over with no degradation — making the format perfect for editing. But without a digital dub connector, the PV-DV1000 won't let you make such copies.

If you can live with the PV-DV1000's analog output jacks, as part of an editing system, then you can hook the camcorder up to existing edit controller equipment (such as FutureVideo's V-Station and Videonics EditSuite) via a five-pin mini-DIN "System E" edit control interface on the back of the camcorder. With this hookup you get the benefits of time code and automated insert editing (from the microphone jack and camera).

Among the introductory consumer models for the DV format, this one may represent the best overall value if you're interested in doing a lot of in-camera editing. If you're thinking about buying the PV-DV1000 you're no doubt comparing it with the two Sony models. Compared to Sony's one-chip, this three-chip unit has better picture quality. Compared to Sony's more expensive three-chip, this camcorder has better audio and video insert capabilities, but lacks digital dubbing, and has inferior image stabilization. Considering the price differences, these are reasonable trade-offs.

For anyone with ambitious video production projects, a limited budget, and a desire to do in-camera editing, Panasonic's PV-DV1000 camcorder is the one to get. And even for those who just want absolutely top-notch raw quality, for more casual family and travel video, the PV-DV1000 is a compact and easy to use contender.

Panasonic PV-DV1000 and Sony DCR-VX1000 are the top contenders in the semipro category. The Panasonic model (right) is smaller and has better in-camera editing and audio capabilities; but the Sony (left) produces slightly better image quality and has digital dubbing - an important feature the PV-DV1000 lacks.

Tough choice! Gerry Roth, the author's son, ponders the possibilities.

3 Camcorder Basics: The Camera Section

The camcorder can be thought of as consisting of two distinct parts—a camera, and a recorder (VCR). Before there were camcorders, there were "two-piece" camera and VCR systems used for shooting video on location.

A camcorder combines a video camera and a video recorder together (thus the name "cam-corder"). Expensive professional video equipment keeps these two parts separate, or "docked" together to make a combination unit that appears to be a large single camcorder. But such two-piece dockable units cost upwards of five thousand dollars.

For most low budget video producers, the single-piece, self-contained camcorder is the basic tool of videomaking. By understanding how it works, you'll be in a better position to figure out

Courtesy of Canon USA

why it behaves the way it does, and you'll be able to gain control over the camcorder for your own artistic or professional purposes.

The camera section of a camcorder includes the optical and electronic systems that create a video image to be recorded on the tape. It consists of the lens, an electronic image sensor, and electronic circuitry that converts the image into video signals.

The Lens

When you first start using a camcorder, much of your attention is focused on learning how to properly manipulate the three lens adjustments: focus, zoom, and iris (aperture).

The lens focuses a picture onto the surface of the image sensor, where varying levels of light are converted into corresponding electrical levels. Most camcorders have a permanently installed zoom lens, though a few have interchangeable lenses. The zoom lets you adjust the framing of your shots without physically moving closer or farther from your subject. This is a great convenience, since you can get a variety of different framings—such as a close-up, medium shot, and wide angle shot—all from a single location. The zoom can also be used to create a form of "camera

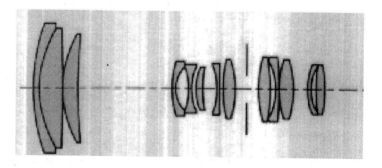

movement", by zooming in or zooming out on a subject as tape is rolling. The camera does not actually move, of course, but it appears to be doing so moving to the viewer. Excessive zooming is one of the most common problems that plague amateur video productions, however, so this effect should be used thoughtfully.

In the "power zoom" lens an electric motor smoothly glides from one focal length setting to another. Optical zoom ratios of 6:1, 8:1, 10:1, 12:1, and 14:1 are most common on camcorders. The zoom ratio describes the range of framings made available by the lens for a given subject shot from a given distance from the camcorder. A 10:1 zoom lens, for example, offers a wider range of framings, from the widest possible shot to the closest possible close-up than a 6:1 zoom ratio. (Digital zoom systems, discussed later, can extend these ranges to 100:1 or more, but the picture degrades. For this discussion, we're talking about optical zoom lens systems.)

Technically, the zoom ratio is a mathematical comparison of the focal length of the lens at the full wide angle setting to its focal length at the full telephoto setting.

What, exactly, is focal length then? This optical term has the same meaning for both photography and video. The focal length is a measure of the distance from the surface of the lens to the imaging device or film that the picture is being focused on (usually measured in millimieters). But with a zoom lens that incorporates numerous "lens elements" (lenses within the lens), the length of the lens does not really vary: rather, the distance between optical elements within the lens is varied to achieve the same effect. A typical camcorder might have a 10:1 zoom ratio, with adjustable focal length from 6mm to 60mm.

Objects appear bigger or smaller in the frame as the zoom is adjusted. The shortest focal length offers the widest view, while the longest focal length corresponds with the full telephoto setting, in which a subject appears bigger, filling up more of the frame.

There are other, more subtle effects that occur as you adjust a zoom lens. But before discussing these, remember one important point: The zoom setting does not determine the framing of your shots, that is, wide, medium, or close-up. The framing is determined by the combination of the zoom setting and your distance from the subject. That is, it is possible to frame a close-up shot of a person's face with the zoom at full wide angle, in the middle of its range, or at full telephoto simply by moving the camcorder closer to or farther away from the person you are shooting.

Wide Angle vs. Telephoto

As you change zoom lens settings, in addition to making objects appear near or far, other subtle optical effects occur. These effects are most pronounced when you go to either extreme of the zoom range.

In the full telephoto setting, distant objects seem to become compressed: There appears to be little space between them. If you've ever seen shots of city sidewalks filled with people, seemingly so crowded that everyone appears to be walking into each other, then you've seen this effect. (The film A Thousand Clowns has a good example.)

But beware of using extreme telephoto shots because there are serious risks to image quality. The biggest problem with telephoto settings occurs when you hold the camcorder in your hands, rather than mounting it on a tripod. Every little jitter and shake of your hands becomes grossly exaggerated, making it look like you are shooting through the middle of an earthquake.

The focus setting also becomes much more critical when the lens is zoomed all the way in (full telephoto setting). It can often be difficult to focus precisely using the small electronic viewfinder built into the camcorder. When the zoom is in the extreme tele-photo position, the "depth of field" (the range of what's in focus) becomes much more shallow. Thus, if a subject is in correct focus and leans a few inches forward or back, he or she may go out of focus. We'll discuss "depth of field" in more detail a bit later.

At the full wide-angle setting, the exact opposite happens: the distance between objects is exaggerated. If you're shooting a close-up of a person's face, you may notice the nose looming giganti-cally, while the little face recedes into the background. That's because when the lens is that close to the face, the distance from the lens to the nose is shorter than the distance from the lens to the top of the head. (That is, the lens does not create any distor-tion, but the perspective from such a position is inherently dis-torted.) When the camcorder is positioned further away from the subject, the distances of different parts of the face to the cam-corder become roughly the same, so the perspective seems more "normal".

For hand-held shooting (without a tripod) wide-angle settings are very forgiving. Minor shakes and vibrations are far less notice-able. The focus adjustment becomes much less critical, too. Prac-tically everything is in good focus at the wide angle setting because the "depth of field" becomes very deep, so that objects at many different distances from the camera are all in sharp focus. (We'll talk about this in more detail later.) Errors in manual or automatic focusing tend to be much less noticeable when the zoom is set to wide angle.

For hand-held shooting then, it is usually best to leave the zoom lens at or near the full wide-angle setting and physically move yourself closer to whatever you want to get closer shots of. But beware of the exaggerated perspective that can result from wide angle shooting.

Finally, note that somewhere in between the full wide angle and the full telephoto setting is what photographers sometimes re-fer to as a "normal" lens setting, because many people think the perspective offered at this setting is comparable to the perspective of the human eye. Of course, video and photographic images are quite different from human vision, so what constitutes a "normal" view for a camera only takes perspective into account. Humans can see, for instance, almost 180-degrees from side to side, where a camera sees a much narrower field. For those who are interested in how this "normal" setting is calculated, a more detailed explanation is provided later in this chapter.

Choosing a zoom lens setting for a particular situation depends on a lot of factors. Can you move the camcorder closer to or farther from the subject? Is the camcorder on a tripod, or hand held? Are you concerned about the degree to which background elements are in or out of focus? How much light is there? (As we shall see, light levels also effect the focusing.) What sense of perspective do you wish to convey?

There are no simple or formulaic answers to these questions; each situation is different. But the more you think about the factors involved, the more you practice shooting video, and the more you analyze the results to see how different zoom settings effect the image, the better you'll be prepared to face each videomaking challenge.

Zoom Speeds

Often the biggest thrill when you first get your hands on a new camcorder comes from playing with the power zoom lens. Suddenly you're looking through the electronic viewfinder, watching your very own personal TV show. But playing with the zoom is only fun when it is interactive, that is, when you are operating the control and watching simultaneously. Later on, when you passively view such shooting, it will often seem nauseating both for you and your audience.

The simplest camcorders have single-speed power zooms that smoothly glide from their full wide-angle to full telephoto positions in about five or six seconds. Most of the more advanced camcorders offer variable zoom speeds—a very handy feature. With the best variable speed zooms, you can creep along very slowly, taking over a minute to get from one end of the zoom range to the other. But most variable-speed models only take about ten to fifteen seconds, at their slowest speed, and instead of changing speeds gradually there's a noticeable shift as it jumps between two or three zoom speeds.

Most zooms in professional films and TV programs occur at slow speed. Usually, the zoom covers just a small part of the full range of the lens. At the end of a TV news report, for example, there will be a slight zoom in on the reporter's face as he or she concludes.

If your power zoom goes at only one speed, you may be able to operate it manually to achieve other speeds. But you'll find that it's very difficult to do this smoothly, especially at slow speeds. It's impossible to adjust zoom manually with newer inner-focus camcorder lens designs (the type that have no mechanical rings around the lens).

If you're shopping for a camcorder, you should consider this relatively obscure, but important difference between models. Variable speed zoom can really give your productions a professional touch.

If you already have a single-speed zoom lens on your camcorder, you might try practicing manual zooms to improve smoothness. Remember that in most professional film and television work, the zoom is very rarely utilized from one extreme to another; they're usually more subtle, so don't try to accomplish a zoom from full wide-angle to telephoto. Rather, practice shorter zooms that change the framing just a bit. Here's a tip for camcorders with manual zoom rings: Position the hand that will turn the zoom ring so that it feels comfortable in the spot where the zoom will end. Then, twist this hand back to the position where the zoom will begin. This way, your hand gets more and more comfortable as the zoom progresses, and you can "feel" the right point for the zoom's end, since the hand becomes untwisted.

Automatic Focus Systems

Automatic focus is a standard feature on practically all camcorders. Any lens (including the human eye) must be focused because when light reflects off of an object (to be recorded on film, video, or to be seen), it scatters in different directions. The lens bends this scattering light back into a focused image of the object. To do this properly, the lens must know, in essence, how far the light has been scattered.

The focus setting is thus based on the distance between the camcorder and the subject. Auto-focus is like an electronic tape measure that calculates this distance for you. But as we shall see, there will be plenty of times when you'll want to override it and switch to manual operation.

There are two common auto-focus systems, piezo electric and infrared. The infrared system emits an invisible beam of infrared light, and measures the time it takes for the reflection to reach the camcorder. The principle is very similar to radar, except rather than radio waves, infrared light is used. The piezo electric system electronically analyzes the image, and seeks out the sharpest possible edges, which occur when the picture is in proper focus.

Both systems work about equally well, perhaps with the slight difference that infrared systems are more likely to be confused by shooting through a pane of clear glass (they focus on the glass rather than what's behind it) because the infrared light gets reflected back by the window's surface. But piezo systems can also be confused, especially when shooting in low light, or when the subject is not in the center of the frame, is moving a lot, or has fuzzy edges.

There are many situations where you need to override the auto-focus and do the job yourself manually. In fact, there are so many occasions where the auto-focus system will fail that practically every single camcorder offers a manual override. In low light, many camcorders get confused and keep readjusting the focus, incessantly shifting back and forth. Also note that in low light the focus becomes more critical because the aperture is wide open (aperture is explained later in this chapter), making the range of focus quite narrow.

Some camcorders have trouble focusing on flat surfaces, like title cards or artwork. Instead of settling on a single focus setting, these camcorders will constantly readjust focus, with the image shimmering between focused and slightly blurred.

Manual Focus

In still photography, cameras often have a "split field" or "micro prism" focusing aid, built into the viewfinder. But the electronic viewfinders built into video cameras do not offer such focusing aids. Nevertheless, the zoom lens itself can provide a very accurate focusing aid because focus becomes more critical (that is, errors become more noticeable) as you zoom in.

To manually focus a professional zoom lens, zoom all the way in to see the subject with maximum detail. Focus the lens while fully zoomed in (the adjustment will be quite critical—a slight change will throw the subject totally out of focus). Then zoom out, and frame the shot the way you want it. A properly working zoom lens maintains the same focus throughout its zoom range.

However, on most low-cost camcorder lenses this internal adjustment, called "back focus," does not work the way it does on professional lenses. In this case, if you zoom in, set manual focus manuallly, and zoom out, the subject may go out of focus during the zoom out. (On professional lenses back focus is usually adjustable with a small screwdriver, but with consumer camcorder lenses, no adjustment is available.) If your camcorder's lens goes out of focus as you zoom out, you'll either need to switch to auto-matic focus, despite the flaws, or adjust both focus and zoom si-multaneously.

The best manual focus systems on consumer camcorders have a ring around the lens that provides very smooth adjustment. This ring, found on almost all semipro models (including the top MiniDV contenders) is actually an electronic control that operates the focus motor, but it feels as though it is mechanically linked to the optics.

One-shot Focus

Many camcorders with automatic focus also offer a focusing op-tion halfway between full automatic and full manual operation: one-shot focusing. To utilize the one-shot system, you press a but-ton when you have your subject centered in the frame. The auto-focus system is activate, but only as long as you hold the button down (on some models the viewfinder will display a sign indicat-ing when proper focus has been reached). Then, you can let go of this button, and the focus setting will stay where you left it.

If you don't want your subject framed in the center, you can use the one-shot system to automatically adjust the focus, then re-compose the frame as you like. If you know that your subject tends to sway from side to side, or if you're bothered by a jittery auto-fo-cus that shifts back and forth constantly, you can use the one-shot system to set a good "ballpark" focus, then just accept the fact that your subject may move in and out of focus slightly (this will often be less objectionable than the camcorder's more extreme shifts in auto- focus).

Pinpoint Focus

In the auto-focus mode, most camcorders primarily focus on what's in the center of the frame. This is called "center weight-ing," because the center weighs more heavily in the camcorder's auto-focus decision making. But how large is this center area? It varies from one model to another, but it is usually a rather large central portion of the screen.

You can experiment, using an edge between two different dis-tances, such as the frame of a doorway, to see at what point the auto-focus "kicks in." Start with the camcorder looking through a doorway, focused on what's beyond the door, with the door frame edge all the way to one side of the frame. Then gradually pan the camera so that this edge moves closer to the center. At some point, the auto-focus will begin to change the setting, to focus on the door frame.

Focus is based on distance between the subject and the camera. When depth of field is shallow, even nearby subjects at other distances will appear out of focus. Using a camcorder's autofocus system usually means focusing on what's in the middle of the frame, as in the center photo. Manual or pinpoint focus techniques let you focus on other objects in the frame, such as the stuffed animal in the rear (left photo) or the front (right photo).

Pinpoint focus is a feature found on some camcorder models that helps you get more precise control over auto-focus. When you press a button, the usual center weighting is abandoned and a more precise central area of the picture becomes all-important for the auto-focus system. A rectangular box usually appears superimposed in the viewfinder defining the precise focussing area. Press the button again and an even smaller box appears in the center of the viewfinder frame, indicating that the auto-focus is only concerned with this very precise "pinpoint" area.

Pinpoint focus can be especially useful when you're shooting distant objects that cannot fill up much of the frame, even when you're fully zoomed in.

Macro Range Operation

Older camcorders have a "minimum focus distance" for automatic operation, usually about three and a half or four feet. Subjects closer than this cannot be properly focused on using the auto-focus system. You must flip the lens into its macro range for such close-up operation. (Usually a button must be pressed on the lens to move the zoom ring into the macro range.) The macro range turns the zoom control into the focus adjustment, and the usual focus adjustment becomes largely irrelevant. In the macro range, you no longer have any zoom capability—the lens is at the wide angle setting all the time.

Newer camcorder models all offer auto-focus even in the macro range, but most still require that you first zoom all the way out to the full wide-angle setting before the auto-macro focus can work. The most automated lenses (including those found on Sharp's Viewcam line) automatically zoom out when the distance to the subject is too close for zoom operation. The latest camcorder lens innovation (found in JVC's GR-SZ9) allows full zoom operation even in the macro mode.

"Normal" Focal Lengths

When looking through a camera's lens the field of view is much narrower compared with human vision, but the perspective between objects seems about the same as when you look at them without a lens. That is, when you pick up a camera with a "normal" lens (or a zoom set at normal focal length, as explained in a moment) objects do not suddenly appear closer or further away—the view seems normal.

A mathematic rule of thumb used by photographers can be used to calculate the normal focal length for any camera or camcorder. Numerically, the normal focal length is about the same as the length of a diagonal line across the image area. Thus, for 35-mm still photography film, whose dimensions are 36-mm x 24-mm, the diagonal is about 43-mm (remember the old Pythagorean formula for calculating diagonals of a rectangle: A squared + B squared = C squared?) That's why most 35-mm cameras come equipped with lenses in the ballpark of 35 to 55 mm focal length. (A 50-mm lens for a 35-mm camera makes objects appear closer than a 40-mm lens.)

With video camcorders, of course, there is no film. An electronic image sensor, or imaging device, is the optical sensor on which the picture gets focused. The image sensor is quite small—usually just a fraction of an inch in size. Like all American TV screens, the image sensor has an aspect ratio of 4:3—that is, the screen is one third wider than it is high.

The specifications for camcorders often reveal the size of the imaging device, measured diagonally (just like a TV screen), which is typically 1/2" (on older models), 1/3" or 1/4". With a bit of metric conversion, that translates into 13mm, 8.5mm, or 6.5mm, respectively. Those numbers correspond with the normal setting for most video camcorders' zoom lenses since the normal lens calculation is based on the diagonal measurement of the image sensor frame. If a camcorder has a 6-mm to 48-mm zoom lens, and it has a 1/3" image sensor, then its lens is set at the normal position when it is at about 8.5mm.

You may not have previously paid much attention to the numbers on the zoom ring of your camcorder, but if you have an older model or a professional camera lens with these numbers, you should take a look at them. If you know the size of your camcorder's imaging device (often it's listed in the back of instruction manuals, or in catalog descriptions), then you know what a normal lens setting is for your particular model. (You might want to put a small piece of bright tape there, right on the side of the lens barrel, to remind you where the normal position is.)

Just about all new camcorders have inner-focus lens systems – they have no external zoom ring. Instead of calibrated focal length numbers, many models offer some form of viewfinder display of the zoom setting. Sometimes it's an uncalibrated bar graph; other times it's a series of multiplier numbers (x1, x2, x3, etc.). If your camcorder displays these numbers, you can calculate the focal length setting by multiplying the wide-angle focal length (the smaller of the two numbers in the zoom range) by this zoom factor, to find the normal setting. But it's a very rough approximation.

Note that this normal setting is usually rather close to the full wide-angle setting—it is nowhere near the middle of the zoom range. Of course, every shot requires careful consideration as to how the zoom should be set, and many photographers think that the normal focal length is the most boring of all. But even if you never shoot at this setting, knowing where it is can be useful as a point of reference, so that you'll know when you're shooting in the telephoto range, and when you're shooting wide angle.

Automatic And Manual Iris

Video camcorders incorporate an automatic iris or aperture system that sets the exposure level. The terminology here is identical to still photography.

The aperture, or iris (the two terms are photographically synonymous), of a lens controls how much light is allowed to pass through the lens to the image sensor. It works much like the iris of the eye: a hole through which light passes gets bigger or smaller, depending on the amount of light present. As the light level increases (such as when you go from indoors to bright sunlight), the aperture opening gets smaller. The image sensor is correctly "exposed," that is, it works best, creating a full range of possible brightness levels, when it receives a certain amount of light. The goal of the auto-iris system is to keep the light level that reaches the image sensor constant, at this ideal exposure level, even though the actual light levels the camcorder is "seeing" vary quite a bit.

Photographers usually measure the aperture in terms of "f-stops". The f-stop number represents a mathematical proportion of how much light is allowed to pass through the lens. Without getting into the nitty gritty arithmetic details, the numbering system represents the amount of light entering the aperture in inverse proportion. That is, an f-stop of 4 really represents the number 1/4, and an f-stop of 8 represents 1/8. Thus, the higher the f-number, the less light is allowed to pass through the lens to the image sensor. In the standard sequence of f-stop numbers, furthermore, each new step represents half as much light, or exposure level, as the step before it. The standard sequence is f1.8, f2.8, f4, f5.6, f11, f16, and f22, with f1.8 allowing the most light in, and f22 the least.

Only the fancier consumer camcorder models offer precise readouts of f-stop settings in the viewfinder. As explained a bit later in this chapter, knowing what f-stop your camcorder is shooting at can help give you an idea of the depth of field—the range of things that will be in good focus.

Manual Aperture Adjustment

Most of the better camcorders offer a manual iris control that lets you turn off the automatic system and take matters into your own hands. Although not absolutely necessary, this can be an invaluable feature when dealing with complex lighting situations.

What constitutes a complex situation? Any time the light reflecting off of your subject is substantially different from the average amount of light in the frame, the auto-iris system will respond to an inappropriate light reading. For example, suppose you are shooting a wide shot of someone standing in the shade in a park on a sunny day. Because the bright sunlight on the grass and in the sky reflect much more light than your subject in the shade, the auto-iris will lower the amount of light passing through to the image sensor. But this low amount of light may make your subject in the shade appear totally dark, while correctly exposing for the background.

With a manual iris control, you can compensate for this by opening up the aperture to the correct exposure. Without a manual iris control (or a "BLC" button—see below), you'll either have to accept a dark subject or recompose the image so that your subject occupies more of the frame. Remember that the auto-iris is based on the average amount of light in the frame, so if you move closer to your subject or zoom in so that the entire frame is filled with the area in the shade, then the average amount of light will be much lower, and the iris will open up, giving you the correct exposure for your subject.

Back Light Compensation and Exposure Lock

Many camcorders have a back light compensation (BLC) button, in addition to or instead of a manual iris control. Unlike high speed shutters, which let less light in, the BLC button increases the amount of light reaching the image sensor by opening up the aperture to a lower f-stop number. To use the BLC button, you cannot be in extremely low light, because the camcorder's lens will already be allowing in as much light as possible, so the aperture can't open any more. Use the BLC button when shooting subjects in front of a bright background, such as a person speaking in front of a white wall. Since the camcorder's auto-iris adjusts to an overall average of picture brightness, the white wall will cause it to let less light in, darkening the face you are really interested in seeing. Press the BLC button and your camcorder's lens will open up a little bit (usually a half or full f-stop), brightening the face of your subject.

Manual camcorder exposure controls can also be used as an "exposure lock." This technique is probably the best way to compensate for complex lighting situations. As mentioned earlier, zooming in on a subject will tend to yield the right exposure from the auto-iris, because the averaging system sees nothing besides the subject in a close-up shot. With exposure lock, you zoom in on the subject just so that the camcorder can learn the correct exposure. Next switch to manual exposure, and the camcorder will remain set (locked) at this iris setting. Then recompose the image the way you like and the camcorder's aperture remains at this setting.

Depth Of Field and Aperture Setting

"Depth of field" is a photographic term that describes the range of what's in focus. Suppose you focus the lens at an object exactly ten feet away. When the depth of field (or depth of focus) is shallow, only objects a few inches closer and farther—say from nine and a half to ten and a half feet away—will be in sharp focus. But when the depth of field is deep, then everything between five and twenty feet may be in focus.

Depth of field is related to the photographic f-stop settings that determine how much light a lens lets in. The lower the f-stop number, the more light is let in, and the narrower the depth of field becomes. Camcorders with only an automatic iris (which adjusts the f-stop for you) allow you little direct control over the depth of field. But as we shall see a bit later, you may be able to trick the auto-iris, using the high- speed shutter to control depth of field.

Still photographers and professional cinematographers usually have the luxury of working with lenses that have precisely calibrated depth-of-field guides marked on them. There are also books of charts, published by the American Cinematographers Society, that let you look up depth of field for any particular focal length lens and distance to subject. But most videographers don't make such detailed study of depth of field. In fact, as mentioned earlier, many camcorders don't even offer manual overrides, and only rarely are calibrated f-stops readouts available, which would be a prerequisite for any depth-of-field calculations. Most inexpensive camcorder lens apertures simply adjust from open to closed, and part of the skill you must develop in shooting video is being able to estimate what the depth of field is, with any particular camcorder, under different lighting and lens conditions.

You can't really trust the camcorder's viewfinder to judge what is in focus and what is not, because the small screen can make slightly out-of-focus objects look sharp. This problem gets even worse with color viewfinders, because they have much lower resolution than black and white viewfinders.

When depth of field is a critical factor, it can be advantageous to hook up the camcorder to a larger screen, such as a regular TV set, so that focus can be clearly checked.

When you shoot in low light, you often have no choice of iris—the camcorder must allow the maximum amount of light in to create a decent image. In outdoor light however, you have more control and flexibility. Most camcorders will automatically close the aperture to a higher f-stop, creating a wide depth of field. Usually, for casual shooting, a wider depth of field makes things easier because you don't need to worry about focus as much.

For creative dramatic effect, you might want a shallow depth of focus. Suppose you're shooting a dialog between two people, for example, and you want each one to glide in and out of focus as they speak. If one is slightly closer to the camcorder than the other, you can selectively control which speaker is in focus if you have a narrow depth of field. This technique is called "selective focus".

The high speed shutter allows you to accomplish this, even with camcorders that do not have manual iris controls. By selecting a higher shutter speed, you will force the camcorder's automatic iris control to let in more light, by switching to a lower f-stop. Of course, there must be enough light to work with for this technique to be useful. (A bit later we'll cover how the high speed shutter works. For now, just keep in mind that it can be helpful for setting the aperture—a higher shutter speed sets the lens to a wider aperture, resulting in less depth of field.)

F-stop Numbers and Lens "Speed"

The exact f-stop numbers are also a concern when shopping for a camcorder, because manufacturers often boast about the "speed" of their lenses. The term speed is borrowed from photography and refers generally to how sensitive to light something is. A "fast" film with a high A.S.A. sensitivity rating can work in lower light than a "slow" film, for example.

The speed of any lens, regardless of whether it's for film or video, is simply a statement of its widest possible aperture—that is, its lowest possible f-stop number. Since the f-stop number represents what proportion of the light in the frame that is allowed to pass through to the image sensor, it makes sense that a more efficient lens will allow more of the light to pass through. The closer the f-stop number gets to 1, the more light is passed through, so that the fastest lenses are rated around f1.2 or f1.4.

A faster lens contributes to better low-light performance, but it does not tell the whole story; the sensitivity of the image sensor must also be taken into account.

The Image Sensor

Video differs from film in many ways, but one distinction is crucial to understanding how camcorders work: at the heart of a video camera (or camcorder) is a light sensitive surface called the imaging device, or image sensor. This is a permanent piece of the hardware. The image sensor is something like a TV screen in reverse: instead of emitting light, it is sensitive to light; Instead of converting electrical energy into light energy, like a TV screen, the image sensor converts light energy into electrical signals.

With film, there's a new imaging surface with each frame, and with each new roll of film. You can change the sensitivity of a film camera simply by changing film to a "faster" film, one with a higher "ASA" or "ISO" rating, as it is called, indicating that the film is more sensitive to light.

With video camcorders, the sensitivity of the image device is permanent. You can not improve performance in low light by buying a fancy brand of videocassette because the magnetic tape does not affect sensitivity to light. A camcorder's ability to work well in low light depends primarily on the sensitivity of the image sensor, and the widest possible aperture setting that the lens is capable of (lens speed). A third factor in low-light sensitivity, the ability of the camcorder to electronically boost a weak (low light) video signal, will be discussed a bit later.

Note also that with film, you don't have to worry much about hurting the film surface by overexposing it, since, at worst, a frame or two of film will be ruined. With video, if you damage the image sensor, it will affect everything you subsequently shoot. You must therefore take more care to protect the camcorder's imaging device from the sun and severely bright lights, because a permanent "burn" in the imaging device will be seen in everything else you shoot.

Video Imaging Devices

This problem of burning used to be quite severe with older, "vidicon" vacuum tube imaging devices found on some of the earliest camcorder models. Practically all of today's camcorders have solid state "chip" imaging devices, called CCD or MOS image sensors. These chip-type imaging devices are less susceptible to burning, but it's still not advisable to point them directly at the sun for more than a few seconds (especially at high noon, when the sun is brightest), because a permanent spot can get burned in.

CCD stands for "charge coupled device," and is a more generic term than MOS. Within the image sensor, tiny electrical charges are passed from one picture element cell to the next until they reach the edge of the array. Hence, the charges are said to be electrically coupled. MOS stands for "metal oxide semiconductor" and represents one particular way of manufacturing CCD chips. There is practically no visible difference between MOS and CCD chips, but there are significant design differences among all image sensor chips. The main differences, resolution and light sensitivity, will be discussed later. First let's see how the chip images differ from film images, and learn why video does not look quite the same as film.

Video vs. Film Texture

The "chip" imaging devices, when overloaded by pointing at a bright light, create bright white streaks up and down the entire frame. These streaks occur because the overload translates into leakage of the electronic signal from one element of picture information to the next.

Such streaks are one of several texture differences between video and film images that subtly cue us to which medium we are watching. With film, bright light "overloads" create a softer halo around the light source due to the chemical nature of photographic imaging. Film images also have a fundamentally different texture than video images because the "grain" of the film—composed of particles that respond to light—is slightly different for each frame. There is a continual sense of subtle change everywhere in the image, simply because the "dots" of light that make up each frame are slightly different from one frame to the next. At twenty-four frames per second, the standard rate for cinema, this constantly changing texture gives film a grainy quality.

With video, since the image sensor is the same for all frames, the texture is smoother, less grainy (albeit coarser in terms of picture detail), with less random difference from one frame to the next. The most noticeable thing about video images, however, is that they are made up of hundreds of horizontal "scan lines." These scan lines, which you can see simply by taking a close look at any large TV screen, serve to limit how much detail can be conveyed in a video image. Just as the tiny dots which make up a newspaper photograph limit the image detail, video scan lines similarly do not show fine details. It is estimated that the standard 35-mm film used in cinema can show about six to twelve times more detail than even the best of today's video systems. (This is what "high definition TV" (HDTV) promises to change, as described in a later chapter. Later, we'll also examine the technicalities of the scanning process, and describe how images are recorded onto videotape.)

One, Two, or Three Chips

The video color imaging system utilizes three colors—red blue and green—with separate imaging elements for each color. Through combinations of these three primary colors in varying combinations, most—though not all—of the colors in the visible spectrum can be created. Shades of brown can be difficult for the color video system to do justice to.

One of the main distinctions between relatively inexpensive consumer camcorders and fancier broadcast camcorders is that most camcorders have a single image sensor for all three colors. A filter system lets only one of the three colors fall on individual picture elements, creating a dense matrix of red, green, and blue sensors. All professional broadcast cameras, and many industrial models, have three different image sensors—one for red, one for green, and one for blue. These are the "three-chip" cameras.

Three-chip cameras produce slightly better image quality than one-chip cameras but cost a lot more. An alternative is the two-chip camera, which has one image sensor for fine black-and-white detail and another for color. The improvement in picture quality over one-chip cameras is noticeable. In a two-chip camcorder, one chip is generally used for the black and white signal (which is equivalent to the green signal, since green is roughly in the center of the color spectrum), while the other chip is devoted to red and blue.

Although low budget video producers often bemoan the fact that they can't use fancier, professional tape formats, it is really the camera quality that makes the most noticeable difference. Look at an off-the-air VHS recording of a news show or soap opera or other program shot with 3-chip or 3-tube cameras. These will look better than your camcorder footage, even though you're looking at the same VHS tape quality. The difference is in the cameras that produce the images. TV stations and networks, with big budgets and big advertising accounts riding on them, can afford to use the best possible equipment. You can't. The difference is relatively minor, but be aware that it exists.

Pixel Numbers

The surface of a chip type image sensor consists of hundreds of thousands of individual picture elements, called "pixels." The pixels are organized in a vast matrix of rows and columns. The more pixels there are in an image sensor, the more finely it can resolve detail in an image. Pixels are analogous to the tiny dots that make up photographs in newspapers. The smaller the dots, and the more there are, the better the image quality.

Camcorder specifications often boast about the number of pixels in their image sensor, with top models offering over 500,000 (multiply that by three for three-chip models). Note, however, that a very high-resolution image sensor is only advantageous if you can record it with a high-resolution tape format, like S-VHS, Hi8, or MiniDV. Therefore, if you're concerned about recording fine detail, you should opt for one of these formats. (High resolution image sensors are now commonly used in standard resolution camcorders as a way to provide electronic image stabilization and/or digital zoom functions.)

There is a relationship between the number of pixels and the resolution of the camera section of the camcorder, but be forewarned that the arithmetic can sound somewhat complex. It works out that an image sensor with 400,000 pixels will yield a horizontal resolution of about 400 lines.

Horizontal resolution, described in more detail in the section on tape formats, is a measure of how much detail a video camcorder or camera picks up. The measurement is only taken horizontally because the vertical resolution is fixed by the video scanning system, which consists of 525 scan lines for each video frame. But the vertical resolution is not actually 525. If you put a test pattern with 525 points of detail from top to bottom on the screen, the scanning system will blur it. Tests have shown that the maximum number of points of detail is about 0.6 times the number of scan lines, so the effective vertical resolution is always about 330.

Now, if you want to follow the complex mathematical conversion of pixel numbers into horizontal resolution numbers, consider the following:

Not all the pixels are used to form the image—some are outside the boundaries of the image area. As just explained, the effective resolution, with a test pattern, is only about 0.6 times the number of pixels available across a column or row. Finally, horizontal resolution numbers are expressed as 0.75 times the actual number of test pattern points that can be seen across the width of the screen. Why? To make the numbers comparable with vertical resolution, since the screen is three-fourths as high as it is wide. Thus, a TV picture with a horizontal resolution of 330 has the same resolution number vertically and horizontally, but can actually resolve 440 points of detail horizontally and 330 vertically.

"Lux" And Light Sensitivity

The "lux" rating is a measure of light sensitivity; it is roughly equivalent to the idea of "film speed" in photography. But unlike a film camera, you cannot simply change the sensitivity by changing film. In a video camcorder, the sensitivity to light is a fixed feature regardless of which brand or type of tape you use.

Generally, the lower the lux number, the more sensitive to light the image device generally is, although the speed of the lens and the ability of the camcorder to boost the signal electronically are also factors. In theory, a rating of one lux is equal to illumination by a single candle of a three foot (one meter) square area. But there has been a lot of hype in lux ratings (in 1995 manufacturers agreed to a uniform standard for meausuring camcorder lux ratings—previously, each manufacturer used their own measurement system). What constitutes a good image is subjective. You'll be hard pressed to get good results with just a single candle illuminating your subject; but, in general, the lower the lux level the better a camcorder will be for indoor and nighttime shooting.

Practically speaking, most camcorders require about 150 to 250 lux to produce good, crisp looking images. Still, the judgment as to what constitutes an acceptable video image is highly subjective. A hobbyist recording a baby's first steps might be perfectly satisfied with an image quality that a corporate video client (hiring a videographer to tape a conference) would find totally unacceptable.

Camera Electronics: Automatic Gain Control

In addition to the automatic iris system, which determines how much light will reach the image sensor, most camcorders also have an electronic system to automatically amplify weak electronic signals coming from the image sensor in low light. This system is called automatic gain control (AGC).

With AGC (or manual gain boost—see below), it's important to note that electronically boosting the signal is not the same as opening the aperture to let more light in. When you amplify a video signal—as with an audio signal—you amplify everything, including both the desired signal and the undesired noise. Suppose, for example, that you have an audio cassette with a weakly recorded signal on it. To listen comfortably, you must crank the volume on your amplifier all the way up. The signal will be loud enough to hear, but all the background hiss and tape noise is much louder too.

The same thing happens with video signals. The video noise appears in the picture as static—speckles of white and color that are especially apparent in the black and dark areas of the picture. When you boost the video signal, it becomes more noisier, grainier. That's why some consumer camcorders, and most industrial models, give you the option to turn the AGC off. (Camcorders that do not have an on/off switch for the AGC are always in this automatic mode.) Suppose, for example, that you want to shoot a dark scene at night. With AGC, all the dark parts of the picture will be boosted to a muddy grey, and they will be filled with video noise. By turning the AGC off, you keep the picture dark. You may not see people's faces as clearly as if the AGC were on, but the entire image may be more striking, and better convey the sense of darkness.

Video AGC systems are usually based on the entire frame and generally respond more to "peak levels"—the brightest spots—than to the average brightness level. If there's a bright area anywhere in the picture, then the overall level will not be boosted. But some of the newest "fuzzy logic" AGC systems can actually create different settings for different parts of the frame (much like the photographic darkroom techniques of "dodging" and "burning in").

Video Gain Boost

The fancier consumer camcorders, and practically all industrial and professional video cameras, offer a manual "gain boost" switch to electronically amplify a weak video signal resulting from shooting in low light. Sometimes the switch is calibrated in units of "gain", or amplification, such as "+6dB" or "+9dB." (The "decibel," or dB, is a unit of electrical comparison that can be used to measure amplification. With every 6dB of boost representing a doubling in video signal level.) Most camcorders don't have such fancy calibrations, just a switch that says "Gain Up" or "High Sensitivity." Either way, the manual gain boost is slightly different from an AGC switch, in that when you flip it on, it will always boost the signal. AGC only kicks in when brightness is low.

The gain boost switch is generally used when shooting in low light, such as outdoors at night and in dimly lit interiors. It always adds visible picture noise in the form of flashing colored speckles all over the screen, especially in dark areas. It's the visual equivalent of what happens when you have a weak audio recording: you can boost the level, but you'll also hear a lot of noisy tape hiss.

Fader

Just as the electronic circuitry can boost a video signal, it can also reduce the signal, cutting it all the way down to zilch, if necessary. Consider your stereo system's amplifier, which has a volume control that goes all the way down to zero. That's exactly what happens when you use the fader feature.

Almost all but the simplest camcorders offer a fader control that lets you begin and end scenes by fading to and from black. Some camcorders fade to white, and some give you the choice of black or white. The fade is a very basic element in the grammar of moving image storytelling. It conveys a sense of time passing, or the end of one scene and the beginning of the next.

Usually, the fader control is activated by pressing a button before shooting begins. Nothing will happen in the viewfinder, except perhaps an indication that the fader is on. Next, when you start the tape rolling, the screen will go black (or white). Gradually, the picture and the sound will fade in.

To fade out, you must usually press the same button again, while tape is rolling. You can easily shake the camcorder doing this, so it's a good idea to practice touching the button without having to look for it. If your camcorder has a remote control with fade and pause buttons, you can mount the camcorder on a tripod and operate it by remote control to eliminate this camera shake. When you press the pause button, the camcorder won't stop instantly. Rather, tape will roll for several seconds, as both the image and the sound fade out.

Note that the time a fade in or out lasts is usually fixed at about two seconds. However, camcorders with manual iris control let you fade manually at other speeds by opening and closing the iris to fade in and out.

Fancier camcorders incorporate additional digital fade features, described in the next chapter.

White Balance Color Adjustments

The white balance control is a color adjustment to compensate for different lighting conditions. Remember from physics class that the color white is actually a mixture of all the colors in the visible spectrum. The three most common types of white light are sunlight, incandescent, and fluorescent. Each has a slightly different mix of colors, creating a slightly different shade of white. Outdoor light, created by the sun and the sky, tends to have much more blue in it than artificial indoor light. Incandescent electric lights tend to have much more red in them, while fluorescent lights tend to be quite green.

In human vision, our eye-brain system compensates for these differences, so all appear "white" to us. As we walk from indoor to outdoor light, visual cues about what color the sky should be, what color a white car should be, etc., alert us to the shift in lighting. We don't notice any change in color because human perception is linked with memory.

A video camcorder's automatic white balance attempts to provide similar compensation, by electronically adjusting the relative strengths of the red, blue, and green signals. That is, when you move the camcorder from indoor light, which has more red, to outdoor light, which has more blue, the automatic white balance automatically reduces the electronic sensitivity to blue, and increases the sensitivity to red. But there will be times when you need to override the automatic white balance, especially when different types of light are mixed.

Suppose you're shooting indoors, with incandescent lights, but there's also some sunlight coming in through a window. Every time you move the camera from an area illuminated by sunlight to an area illuminated by electric light, the colors will seem to shift. White walls will cycle through unsettling shades of pink and blue during the pan. Viewers will certainly notice these color changes.

In this situation, you can get more consistent colors by switching to manual white balance. Choose one setting or the other—for whichever type of light is dominant in the scene. The other light source will create a different color tint in part of the picture, but at least it won't change constantly. Shooting at the incandescent setting, for instance, will result in making the window (and everything outside) appear blue. Whereas setting the camcorder for outdoor light, will cause the areas around the incandescent lights to look red. Ideally, you should shoot in just one type of light for natural color rendition, though the real world is often far from ideal when it comes to shooting in available light. When shopping for a camcorder, note that the best manual white balance systems offer a "lock" or "hold" setting, rather than just two or three fixed settings for outdoor and indoor lighting.

To use a white balance lock, hold a white card in front of the camcorder, making sure that it reflects the actual light that will be illuminating your subject. Zoom the camcorder in to the card so that the white fills the screen, and "lock" onto this color balance. This is like saying to the camcorder, "Look, this is white. If you see this as red, re-balance your circuits so there's less red and more blue and green, because the lighting must have too much red in it." All professional video cameras utilize this white balance lock system.

Technically, the mixture of colors that makes white is called the color temperature of the light (see chart at the end of this chapter). The more on the blue side of the spectrum a light is, the higher the color temperature. Incandescent light is usually around 3,000-degrees Kelvin, on the color temperature scale. Specially balanced video lights are usually rated at 3,200-degrees. Fluorescent light is 4,500-degrees but is not recommended for shooting video — it makes faces look green. Outdoor light varies from about 5,600 to over 7,000-degrees.

For indoor shooting, 3,200 degrees has become the standard color temperature. It is not particularly superior to, say 3,400, or 4,000, but since it is a standard, it is easier to work with. The camcorder's incandescent setting is 3,200, and professional photoflood lights are 3,200, so it makes a nice match. At professional film and video supply stores you can buy orange-colored cellophane (the color is called C.T.O. – color temperature orange) to put in windows to convert higher-color temperature sunlight into 3,200 degree tungsten light (incandescent). You can also buy blue-colored cellophane (C.T.B.) to convert photoflood lights to the 5,600-degree color temperature of outdoor light (at mid-afternoon).

CAMCORDER SETTINGS	NATURAL LIGHT CONDITIONS	KELVIN COLOR TEMPERATURE	ARTIFICIAL LIGHT SOURCE	COLOR TINT MIXTURE
▲(Amber Filter Range)	• Fair weather, blue sky	10,000	• Color television	Bluish
	• Slightly cloudy sky	8,000		
	• Cloudy or rainy sky	7,000		
		6,500	• Fluorescent lamp (Daylight)	
"OUTDOOR"	• Sunlight in clear weather at midday	6,000	• Camera flash bulb	
		5,500		
	• Average sunlight in clear weather	5,000	• Blue lamp for photography	
"AUTO"	• Sunlight 2 hours after sunrise and before sunset	4,500	• Fluorescent lamp (White)	Whitish
		4,000	• Normal flash bulb	
		3,500	• Fluorescent lamp (Off-white) • Tungsten lamp for photography	
"INDOOR"	• Sunlight 40 min. after sunrise and before sunset	3,200	• Halogen lamp • Iodine lamp	
(Blue Filter Range)	• Sunlight 30 min. after sunrise and before sunset • Sunlight 20 min. after sunrise and before sunset	2,800	• Tungsten lamp • Acetylene lamp • Kerosene lamp	Yellowish
▼		2,000	• Candlelight	Reddish

Courtesy of Philips Consumer Electronics

4 VCR and Camcorder Tape Basics

All modern camcorders and VCRs work on a similar principle of tape recording called "helical recording." The tape is drawn out from the cassette and wrapped around a small polished cylinder a few inches in diameter called the "head drum" (see diagram below). The drum is split in half (see next diagram), and a set of tiny "video heads" spin around within the slit between the top and bottom halves. The video head is the device that can either magnetize the tape according to electrical signals it receives—to record—or sense the magnetism on a previously recorded tape and create corresponding electrical signals—to playback.

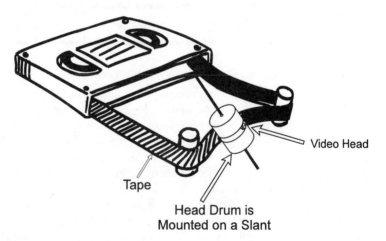

Video Head

Tape

Head Drum is
Mounted on a Slant

A helix

Helical Recording

The head drum is mounted on a slant relative to the tape, and the resulting tracks across the tape are long, slim, diagonal paths from the top of the tape to the bottom. If you connected the bottom of one such diagonal track to the top of the next, it would form a helix—a three dimensional spiral—hence the name helical recording.

The advantage of helical recording over the less sophisticated "stationary head" system used in standard audio cassette players is

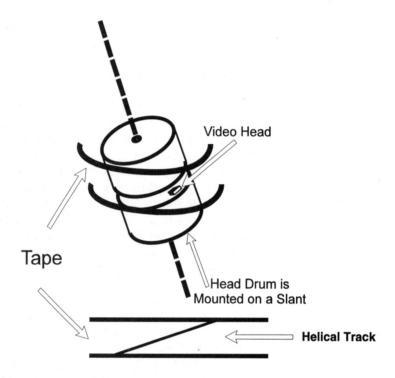

Video Head

Tape

Head Drum is
Mounted on a Slant

Helical Track

that more information can be recorded using less surface area of
tape. Video signals change very rapidly. The finest picture details
might last for less than a millionth of a second in the rapidly
changing electronic video signal. To record these signals requires
moving a lot of tape past the head very quickly. Instead of moving
the tape hundreds of times faster than audio tape, the helical recording system has the head move rapidly past the tape, accom-
plishing the same effect. If the circumference around half the
head drum is three inches and the head spins sixty times per second, then the effective tape-to-head speed is one hundred eighty

A video head drum

inches per second—quite a bit faster than the approximately two inches per second rate at which ordinary audio cassette tapes pass their heads.

Each of the helical tracks is the magnetic equivalent of a frame of movie film, with an important difference. A television image consists of a series of 525 horizontal scan lines, from the top of the screen to the bottom. At any given moment the video signal electronically describes the brightness and color at a particular point along a particular scan line.

There are 30 complete sets of scan lines—frames—created each second. But the basic unit of the television image is not the frame. A system called "interlace" makes the image look less jittery by first scanning all the odd scan lines, then the even scan lines, then the next set of odd lines, etc. The movement of the light from the top of the screen to the bottom thus occurs sixty times per second rather than thirty, and there is less perception of flicker. Each half-frame of the video signal—a set of odd or even scan lines—is called a "field."

Each of the diagonal helical tracks recorded by a VCR or camcorder thus represents one field of video information—two successive tracks constitute a frame. And the video head drum contains a minimum of two heads, placed 180-degrees away from each other. As soon as one head finishes recording the odd field, the other head begins recording the even field on the next diagonal track, and so forth.

Beyond this broad principle, the specific details of videotape formats vary. In addition to the main helical tracks, most video tape formats also incorporate several traditional stationary head tracks, sometimes referred to as "linear tracks." The details of recording these tracks may seem overly technical, but they play a major role during video editing. These differences also determine what you can and can't do with each format.

A complete frame consists
of 525 scan lines

A field consists of half the
lines in the frame

Resolution

Technically, there are three main areas in which the differences between broadcast and consumer video equipment can be seen. (On the audio side, the quality of some consumer equipment can be every bit as good—though not always as flexible—as professional quality equipment.) These three picture related criteria are resolution, signal-to-noise ratio, and timing stability.

Resolution is the amount of detail that can be seen in the video image. The resolution numbers are always stated as "horizontal resolution" because as far as vertical resolution is concerned, all American video equipment conforms to the same 525-scan line standard. As explained earlier, this yields an effective vertical resolution of 330, as measured using visual test patterns consisting of black and white lines that converge in increasing density (see diagram below) because the 525 scan lines function like a screen through which the test pattern is seen.

The broadcast-quality standard is to have the same level of detail in both the vertical and horizontal dimensions. The horizontal resolution standard for broadcast quality is therefore

A professional resolution test pattern. Courtesy of Accu-Chart.

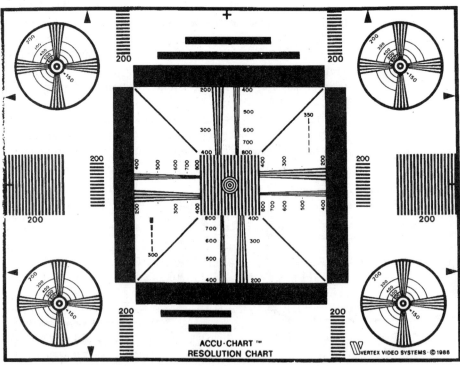

commonly stated as 330-lines. But remember that a TV screen is a third wider than it is high (see diagram below)—it has an "aspect ratio" of 3:4 (height to width). To compensate for this, the horizontal resolution numbers are stated as the number of individual points of detail one can discern along three-fourths of one horizontal scan line. In other words, a broadcast-quality video signal with a horizontal resolution rating of 330 lines can actually discern 440 points of detail along each individual scan line.

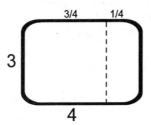

If you're familiar with computers, you'll no doubt relate this concept of resolution numbers to "pixels" in a computer display or image sensor. But note that the electronic video signal is an analog medium. Whereas each pixel represents a distinct piece of information in a computer, the video signal is a continuously changing voltage level where, in essence, one point of detail blurs into the next. Most importantly, as successive copies of the signal are made, the quality of the signal deteriorates. (If it were digital information, each copy would look identical to the original.) This degradation is called "generation loss."

S/N Ratio and Generation Loss

Just as audio cassette tapes have background hiss that you can readily hear during quiet moments on a tape, videocassette tapes have background video noise that is visible on the screen in a variety of ways: flashing speckles of white and colors that are particularly apparent when looking at dark backgrounds, very brief streaks across the screen, and variations in color and brightness in areas of the screen that should be uniform in color and brightness. All these picture defects are manifestations of mixing randomly occurring electronic "noise" with the desired video signal.

The technical name given to the degree to which a videotape system can suppress this noise is called the "signal-to-noise-ratio," or S/N ratio. It is measured in units called decibels (dBs). The bigger the S/N ration in dBs the less noise there is. Because of the complexity of the video signal, there are several different S/N ratios that are simultaneously at play, affecting different parts of the signal. VCR technical specifications commonly list three video S/N ratios: brightness level (luminance), color saturation (chroma amplitude), and color tint (chroma phase).

These noise levels build up with each successive copy of a video tape, just as background hiss gets louder when you copy from one audio cassette to another. Higher S/N ratios allow for less generation loss.

Some video producers working with modest (but not rock bottom) budgets choose to use the low-budget camcorders as an "acquisition format"—shooting their raw footage in either Hi8 or S-VHS, and then "bumping up" the tapes (copying them) to broadcast quality formats with better video noise suppression for editing. Since editing in professional formats can cost over a hundred dollars per hour, a low budget desktop editing system (also called an "off-line" editing system) can be used to make most of the editing decisions, thus minimizing the expense of renting the broadcast-quality facility for the final "on-line" edit.

Time Base Accuracy

Perhaps most important to TV broadcasters, is the accuracy of the timing of the video signal. In order for you to see a video image on the screen, there must be coordination between the device creating the signal—such as a camera or VCR during playback—and the TV or monitor receiving the signal. When a camera is sending information about the seventy-fourth scan line, for instance, the TV's cathode ray should be generating that seventy-fourth line.

The entire process requires precise coordination and synchronization. The TV, or video monitor, receives a signal which says something like, "Go to the top right corner of the frame, draw a line, go back to the left edge, draw the next line, go back to the left edge, draw the next, etc." If the timing with which the information is sent is inaccurate, the image can appear unstable or scrambled.

To demonstrate that the timing stability of consumer video equipment does not match the tight tolerances of broadcast-quality equipment, try shooting a straight vertical line, such as a pole extending from the top to the bottom of the frame, using a consumer camcorder mounted on a tripod or other stable surface. Copy the tape to another videocassette, and then make another copy from that one. Play the third generation tape back on a large screen TV or monitor, and look for imperfections in the vertical line. You'll probably find points where it is slightly jagged, deviating from a straight line. Consumer video equipment often cannot record and playback the sequence of scan lines with the perfect timing required to make the line look absolutely straight. When broadcasting a video signal to many TV sets, it is crucial that the signal be timed perfectly to prevent some sets from receiving scrambled or rolling images.

However, a slightly mis-timed signal usually falls within the window of tolerance when delivered to the TV set with a strong signal level. You can hook up your VCR to your TV with acceptable results because the TV compensates for slight timing inaccuracies. But the timing errors accumulate with each successive generation (copy) of the signal. A time base corrector, or TBC, can rectify errors in video signal timing, bringing consumer equipment up to broadcast standards. Most professional format VCRs have built-in TBCs.

S-Video Connections

S-Video connector, located above standard phono jack A/V output connections on camcorder.

A special type of "S-video" jack is found on all S-VHS, Hi8, and MiniDV camcorders. It keeps the black and white (luminance) signal separate (that's what the "S" stands for) from the color (chroma) signal. The S-video connection, when used with an S-video color monitor (a TV set with direct video input jacks) helps eliminate the interference that sometimes occurs between the luminance and chroma portions when they are combined, such as the "moire" (shifting grid) effect that occurs when very closely spaced lines are shown on TV. This can often be seen on TV news, when a speaker is wearing a black and white tweed jacket.

The S-video connection—contrary to what salespeople may tell you when you're shopping for a camcorder—is not required to see the improved resolution of S-VHS, Hi8, and MiniDV. In fact, the difference between using the S-video connection, and the standard composite (combining everything together) "line-video" jacks found on most VCRs and camcorders is quite minimal (assuming the equipment on both ends of the connection are high resolution devices—such as a Hi8 camcorder and a high-resolution color TV-monitor without an S-video input).

Finally, while we're on this subject, note that there is one basic distinction between professional analog videocassette formats like Betacam, and M-II and consumer video formats like VHS, S-VHS, 8mm, and Hi8: In pro video recording equipment, the luminance and chroma signals are recorded onto separate tracks of the tape; while in consumer equipment, they are combined onto a single track. This is true even for the S-VHS and Hi8 systems that feature S-video connections. The S-video connector provides separate wires for the luminance and chroma signals to travel through, but with the analog formats (S-VHS and Hi8) they are still recorded as one signal on the videotape. (In tech jargon, consumer formats are therefore called "composite" formats, while pro formats are called "component" formats. All digital systems, including MiniDV, are component systems.)

. . . .

Tape Loading And Operation

When you insert a videocassette into a camcorder, the tape is loaded by an electromechanical system that pulls the tape out of the cassette and wraps it around the tape heads. The heads are the interface between the worlds of electricity and magnetism: They convert the electrical signals which represent the picture and sound, into magnetic pulses that are recorded onto the tape. During playback, the heads do the opposite. They sense the magnetic patterns on the tape, and convert the magnetism back to electrical signals.

Camera / VCR Operation

Virtually all camcorders have the ability to play back the tapes they record. This becomes important not just when you finish your production and want to see it, but also as you go about shooting. In fact, that's one of the biggest advantages of videotape technology over film—you instantly get to see how things are coming out.

Camcorders are usually designed to operate in two modes: "camcorder," and "VCR." This setup helps promote ease of use and minimizes the possibility that you'll accidentally erase things. Sometimes the switch that toggles the camcorder between these two modes is built into some kind of cover, such as a plastic door that conceals the VCR controls. If you want to play a tape back, you must first slide open the compartment to reveal the "play" button. This automatically switches the camcorder into the VCR mode.

Since there are so many variations from model to model, it is hard to be specific, but you should learn which controls work in which mode on your particular camcorder. Some buttons will only work in the camera mode, while others will only work in the VCR mode. Understanding this distinction becomes particularly important with regard to the flying erase head (described below).

Some camcorders offer special effects, like slow-motion and high speed search. Usually, the quality of these effects will not look as good as on a home VCR, because extra tape heads are required, but again this varies from one model to the next. If you're particularly interested in special effects, you should seek out a camcorder model with digital effects (see below).

Quick Review

Most camcorders have a quick review button that will automatically show you the last three or four seconds of what you shot. The advantage of using the quick review feature, rather than just playing back the tape, is that you do not have to leave the camera mode and press a long sequence of buttons in the VCR mode just to see if the tape came out. As soon as the quick review ends, the camcorder is paused right at the spot where your last shot ended, ready to begin recording something new. It's a convenient way to check that the shot worked and to remind yourself of the content of the last shot.

Tape Speeds

Both the 8mm family and the VHS family of tape formats offer several speeds. MiniDV is designed to work at one speed only. Without getting overly technical, let's say for now that no matter what format you use, the best recordings will always be made at the fastest tape speed. Most 8mm family and many full-size VHS and S-VHS camcorders will only work at this fastest speed, called SP, for "standard play". Some newer 8mm models offer LP speed, which produces four hour of recording time from a standard two hour tape. In VHS, the slower speed is usually called EP, for "extended play," or SLP, for "super long play". The EP/SLP speed is one third as fast as SP. Thus a standard T-120 videocassette yields two hours at the SP speed or six hours at EP/SLP. (An intermediate four-hour "LP" long-playing speed is rarely found on VHS camcorders, but is occasionally found on VCRs and 8mm equipment.)

The slow EP/SLP speed shows up most often on VHS-C and S-VHS-C camcorders, since the smaller tapes can only record twenty minutes at the regular SP speed with standard thickness tape (which is recommended – thinner tapes, which tend to get chewed up more easily when editing, can extend that time to forty minutes). If you do have such a camcorder, you should bite the bullet, accept the time limitation, and use the SP speed. Note that industrial video editing equipment will only accept tapes recorded at SP speed, so if you shoot at EP, you won't be able to edit tapes at professional facilities.

If you're shopping for a camcorder, note that, in general, the tape heads that record and play back the video signal can only be optimized for a single speed. Most two-speed camcorders sacrifice quality a little bit at each speed to arrive at a compromise design. Some camcorders feature separate heads for each speed. Without separate heads, it is generally best to get a camcorder that only runs at the SP speed so that there is no compromise in quality.

Flying Erase Head

The flying erase head lets you insert new material in the middle of a previously recorded tape with smooth edits that are virtually unnoticeable on playback. All Hi8 and 8mm models have this feature, but only some VHS-family camcorders do. All MiniDV camcorders have the equivalent of a flying erase head, allowing for perfect insert edits.

The flying erase head is essential for editing video because, as we shall see when we look at tape editing, in video you can never physically splice the tape. All editing is accomplished through selective copying, or dubbing of tapes, so erasing and replacing tape material precisely becomes important. Only with a flying erase head can you perform insert edits, by rerecording new material over old.

Because of differences in the way audio is recorded, not all flying erase head camcorders offer the same capabilities: Most 8mm and Hi8 models can only insert picture and sound together, while most VHS-family models (VHS, S-VHS, VHS-C, and S-VHS-C) can only insert video (leaving the old sound). The MiniDV format is capable of all possible edits, but not all camcorders include this feature. To invoke the flying erase head, most VHS family camcorders must be switched to the VCR mode; while most 8mm and Hi8 models (as well as MiniDV models) perform A/V insert edits in the camera mode. (This is covered in more detail later.)

Audio Recording

All Hi8 and 8mm models have AFM sound, which stands for audio frequency modulation. In nontechnical jargon, AFM is high-fidelity—it has good reproduction quality. Newer and better camcorders usually have AFM stereo; older models have AFM mono.

All VHS and S-VHS models have "linear audio". It's not as good as the stereo VHS Hi-fi tracks found on a few camcorders and many VCRs in terms of audio fidelity, especially at the EP speed.

The MiniDV format offers a choice of superb quality stereo or very good quality 4-track configurations. Not all models offer both choices, however, so check specifications.

These tracks, their utilization, and more specific information about how the audio and flying erase heads work are covered in more detail in the chapters on low budget tape formats.

5 Other Camcorder Features and Frills

The rest of the features that you'll find on a camcorder offer extra convenience and production capabilities.

The Viewfinder

The electronic signal from the image sensor does not only go to the recorder section, to get converted into magnetism and recorded onto tape: It also usually gets fed to the viewfinder (except on the cheapest models).

Most camcorders have a black and white or color electronic viewfinder (EVF) that looks like a little TV set, built into the camcorder. The absolute least expensive toy camcorders have optical viewfinders that do not show you the electronic image, but rather, use a simple lens to give you an idea of what the image sensor is seeing. Electronic viewfinders are preferable, because they give you a much more accurate indication of how the image is actually being recorded.

The main functions of the viewfinder, of course, are to help in framing and focusing images.

The viewfinder also serves as a display of your camcorder's status. The simplest models may just have a light that goes on and off when the tape is running or in pause, respectively. More sophisticated viewfinders superimpose numbers and text over the image—indicating such things as whether tape is rolling, elapsed time, whether you're using manual or automatic white balance, manual or autofocus, manual or auto iris, tape speed, high shutter speed, zoom setting, fader mode, and whether you've engaged the title or date system (see below).

When shopping for a camcorder, always consider how easy it is to see the viewfinder. If you wear eyeglasses, you may appreciate the diopter found on most models. The diopter is an adjustable lens, in front of the viewfinder, that may help you to focus on the viewfinder screen without wearing glasses. This lets you take better advantage of the rubber eyecup to block ambient light from your view.

Color Viewfinders

Professional TV camera viewfinders are usually black and white. There are a number of reasons, all of which revolve around the limits of today's technology and TV picture tubes (there are "LCD" color viewfinders—see below). LCD screens are considered inadequate for professional focusing, where seeing every detail is crucial. It is very difficult to build color TV tubes that are less than an inch in diameter, due to limits in manufacturing technology. Color screens require much more power than black and white, which would drain the camcorder's battery faster. Color picture tubes also emit more unhealthy radiation than black and white tubes, so it's not a good idea to put your eye a few inches away from them. Finally, note that to get the benefit of a color viewfinder, you'd have to be absolutely certain that its color and tint levels were set accurately. Without some sort of built in self-calibration system for these color adjustments, you would never know if the camera's white balance was off, or if your viewfinder was out of adjustment.

But on the consumer side of the business, most of the mid to high priced camcorder models have "LCD" (liquid crystal display) color viewfinders. It's the trend of the future. LCD screens can be built small, consume less power, and don't have the radiation hazard of cathode ray tubes (CRT's). But, they can be difficult to view in outdoor light, have poor resolution (making it harder to focus), and the colors you see on the screen aren't always the same as what you're recording—because there's no way to calibrate them. Eventually these bugs may be worked out, and color LCD screens may catch on, even with professional equipment—this is certainly one area to keep an eye on as camcorder technology is continually updated and improved.

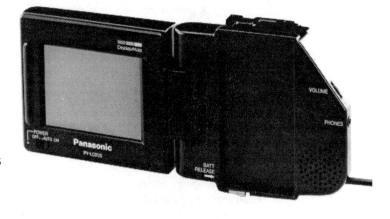

Panasonic's PV-LCD35 accessory can add a 3.2" viewscreen to some camcorder models.

Sharp's ViewCam replaces the traditional viewfinder with a large LCD screen.

The best color viewfinders now have about 180,000 pixels, which is almost enough to do good critical focusing. (The best image sensors have over 500,000 pixels.) Many camcorders have far fewer – in the range of 80,000 to 120,000 pixels, which effectively limits vertical and horizontal resolution to about 200-lines each. By contrast, even the cheapest black and white CRT models can usually show the full resolution of the tape format.

Although wearing the Virtual Vision Sport is a bit funny looking, it frees you from the need to look through the camcorder's viewfinder.

The Virtual Vision Sport is a viewfinder accessory you wear like sunglasses. You can also watch TV with it. Courtesy of Virtual Vision.

But color viewfinders are more fun to work with, giving you a better sense of what the recorded image will actually look like when you watch it in your living room. It also alerts you to problems with the camera's white balance, such as occur in mixed lighting situations.

The large viewscreen, pioneered by Sharp's ViewCam line of camcorders with built-in three to five inch LCD color screens, represents a completely different viewfinder approach. These camcorders are great for travel, and many other situations where you might want to see things played back, without the fuss of hooking up to a TV monitor. They're also great for more casual videotaping projects—you can prop the camera on a table at a night club, for instance, and enjoy the act while taping the show. And the best thing about most of these models is that you can flip the screen around for "self recording" – you can hold the camera at arm's length and see yourself as you tape.

But viewscreens tend to be hard to see in sunlight, appearing washed out. Sony's "Vision" camcorder line addresses this issue by offering both a large color viewscreen and a traditional black and white viewfinder. Panasonic offers an accessory for many of their camcorders that adds a 3.2" LCD screen, creating essentially the same setup.

Time and Date

Perhaps the most common special camcorder feature is the time and date "stamp" that lets you superimpose the date and time on one corner of the picture, as you record. Most camcorders give you the option to record this for just a few seconds, or continuously. Additionally, some camcorders are now offering an "age" feature that lets you enter your children's ages once, and automatically keeps track of how old they are as time goes by. Some models offer different time zone settings.

Title Systems

Many camcorders provide the capability to add titles, electronically. Two types of titling systems are commonly found—character generators, and page superimposers.

Character Generator Titlers

A character generator lets you superimpose titles (such as names, locations, etc.) over video as you shoot, by "typing in" the titles ahead of time. We say "type" in quotes because most models don't actually offer a full typewriter-style keyboard. Usually, one or two buttons are used to select the letters of the alphabet. Some models use rotating wheels to select characters, making it faster to "type" in names. Models vary in the number of lines of text, location of text, size of text, "pages" of memory (the number of different sets of titles you can store), and ease of selecting characters.

Digital Superimposers

A digital superimposer creates titles from printed cards and art-work by electronically "remembering" their outlines and then su-perimposing these shapes, in a variety of colors, over the image you're shooting. (In photographic terms, this works like an "orthochromatic" frame memory—because the stored image has super high contrast—essentially pure black and white.)

This system lets you get more creative with your titles, com-pared with the clunky looking block-type of character generator titles. But the CG titles can be much faster to set up, since no original artwork is required, and professional CG systems have much sharper edges on the titles, giving them a more profes-sional look (see the Titles chapter). Some camcorders with the digital superimposer let you store two or more pages of titles in electronic memory.

Note that this is not the same feature as the digital special ef-fects found on some camcorders (see below).

Electronic High Speed Shutters

Practically all new camcorders incorporate high speed shutters that function much like the adjustable shutter speeds on 35-mm still cameras—except that there is no mechanical shutter in a video camcorder. Because video images are created through scan-ning, the scanning simply takes place faster at the high shutter speeds.

To fully understand how the high speed shutter works will require a more technical description of video scanning. Earlier, I explained that a video frame consists of 525 scan lines. The scanning process is

A complete video frame consists of two fields

A video field consists of half the scan lines in a frame

actually a bit more complex than I described, because video systems actually scan out every other line (i.e., line 1, 3, 5, 7, 9, 11, etc.)

A single video frame consists of two video fields—two sets of scan lines representing the odd and even numbered lines, from one to 525. The merging of these two coarser images into a single fine image is called interlacing. At normal speed, video runs at thirty frames per second; which is the same as sixty fields per second. Video shutter speeds are stated as the amount of time required to scan out a single video field—half a frame. Thus, one sixtieth of a second is the "standard" shutter speed.

The high speed shutter systems speed up this scanning process, so that an image is taken in a few hundredths, or thousandths, or even ten-thousandths of a second. But note that the image sensor acts like a short-term memory system for such high shutter speed videography—that is, the image may be scanned in a thousandth of a second, but it still gets recorded in the usual sixtieth of a second. The image device takes the picture in super fast, and then holds it for a fraction of a second until it can be recorded on tape at normal speed.

So what use do these high speed shutters have, if they don't change the rate of recording?

The recording speed never changes, but the playback speed can. To see the effects of high speed shutters, you must watch the recorded tape either in slow motion, or frame by frame. Some camcorders allow such playback by themselves, while others will only record with a high speed shutter, and require that you play them back on a good VCR with slow motion playback.

Most VCRs, in slow motion and still-frame playback, show just a 'field" at a time—not a full frame. That's why the shutter speeds correspond to the half-frame field rate. (Remember that video consists of 30 frames per second, but the "standard" shutter speed for all video cameras is stated as one-sixtieth of a second.)

Sports is the main use for the high speed shutter. You can analyze all sorts of athletic movements—golf swings, swim strokes, tennis, baseball, etc.—utilizing the high speed shutter and slow motion playback to study or depict exactly how the body moves. Without the high speed shutter, a single frame (or more accurately, a field) of a golf stroke would appear blurry. This is also relevant if you intend to use a computer to do a "frame grab"—recording a single video frame onto a computer disc.

As I mentioned earlier, for serious videography, the high speed shutter can also help you control the depth of field of your video image. That's because when there is sufficient light to work with, by increasing the shutter speed, you force the automatic aperture to open up, thus reducing the depth of field.

Self Timer

Many camcorders offer a "self-timer" feature that operates much like still-camera self-timers. It's designed to let you put yourself into the picture, before the camcorder starts recording. Press the start button, and you have ten seconds, or so, to get yourself in place. Of course, proper use of this feature requires that you mount the camcorder on a tripod or on a table, and that you carefully frame the image and know where to go stand—or sit. Self-timers make it easier for you to star in your own productions.

Intervalometer (Time Lapse)

A less known feature that shows up on some camcorders is the intervalometer, which often goes by other names such as time lapse recording, or just time recording. When set up for intervalometer recording, the camcorder will automatically shoot a very short amount of tape—such as 1-second—at fixed intervals. Thus, for example, by shooting one second every minute, a complete day can be condensed into just twenty four minutes of recording. At a ratio of one-second every ten seconds, a complete sunset sequence can be condensed into just twelve seconds.

You've probably seen time-lapse sequences of flowers opening and closing in science TV shows about nature. If you're interested in time-lapse cinematography, you might want to watch the film *Koyanisqaatsi*, available at video rental stores. This film features music by Philip Glass, accompanying extensive and dramatic use of time-lapse shooting.

Normally, when you leave a camcorder in pause for more than five minutes, it shuts off automatically to prevent damage to the tape and heads. With time lapse recording, this feature no longer applies, since the camcorder actually records a short segment of tape every few minutes.

Animation

Video animation is another feature found on some camcorders. The idea is to let you shoot a single frame at a time, so you can create animated effects, such as moving clay figures ("claymation"). Unfortunately, video camcorders are not quite as precise as film cameras in this regard. Instead of shooting a single frame, most camcorders offering this feature shoot from four to ten frames at a time. So the resulting animation looks less smooth than those done with film. Video animations can, however look quite good, and you get to see the results instantly.

If you're shopping for a camcorder that can do animation, look for a model that can record the fewest number of frames at once. Remember that video runs at thirty frames per second, so a camcorder that can record five frames at a time will give you an animation rate of six images per second—with each image lasting for a sixth of a second.

. . . .

Digital Special Effects

Digital Special Effects, allow you to store full-color freeze-frame images in electronic memory, and then mix them with a "live" camera image. One of the best uses for this is to create a "pseudo-dissolve" between two scenes: One shot ends with a freeze-frame, and then this freeze-frame dissolves into the beginning of the next shot. It's not a true dissolve, because real dissolves cross fade between two moving images—one fades in as the other fades out.

Other possible digital effects include wipes, mosaic patterns, and split-screens. You can also create stroboscopic effects at varying rates - the freeze frame system repeatedly stores a frame and holds it for two or three frames, then freezes another frame and holds it, and so on.

Mosaic Fade

A "mosaic fade" digital effect allows you to begin and end each shot with a transition to or from a digitized box pattern, in which the box sizes get progressively larger (for fade-out) or smaller (fade-in). It's a nice, useful transitional effect.

Digital Zoom

Digital zoom is probably the most commonly available digital special effect. A center portion of the image sensor is blown up to fill the entire screen. As a result, resolution degrades as you digitally zoom in more. Digital zooms typically operate in two ranges—a "safe" range might go up to 20x, to prevent too much loss of picture detail. Then the second range (usually selectable from a viewfinder menu system) goes up to 64x or 100x, but at these extreme magnifications, images are practically unrecognizable, due to the loss in detail.

Dual Camera & Twin-Cam

Dual Camera or TwinCam is an exciting feature that lets you mix two camera images together into a single recorder section. Some models let you use chroma key to substitute the image from one camera wherever the other image is blue or green (like the weatherperson on TV!); or create split screen images that mix signals from the two cameras together. You can also dissolve from one camera to the other. With TwinCam models, both cameras point at the same subject; with Dual Camera models, the second accessory camera can be pointed in any direction.

Remote Controls

Most camcorders include a wireless remote that can start/stop the tape, operate the zoom, character generator, and other features.

Many camcorders also feature a remote jack that is useful for video editing. Usually, these jacks are the same size as miniature headphonejacks. Some offer only the basic run/pause capability. The best remote control jacks, are called "Control L" or LANC jacks. They can be recognized by the miniature 5-pin connector, or by the letter "L" next to a jack similar to a mini-headphone jack. In the Editing section, we'll see how these jacks let you hook up the camcorder to very sophisticated edit control systems.

Image Stabilization

Image Stabilization is a very useful feature found on some consumer camcorders. Image stabilization began in the 1980s with Cinema Products' Steadicam camera mount system for the Hollywood film industry (see "Tripods" chapter). When Panasonic introduced its Electronic Image Stabilization (EIS) feature to the consumer marketplace in the late 1980s, the relatively large, clunky system used mechanical manipulation of the image sensor to compensate for the slight shake and jitter of handheld camera operation. Then Panasonic switched to an all-electronic system that uses just a subset of the image sensor's full field of view—the exact borders of this subset keep shifting as the image jitters. But Panasonic's (and most other brands') digital EIS system reduces the overall resolution of the stabilized image, because a portion of the image sensor has less detail than the full sensor.

In 1992, Sony introduced its version of image stabilization in the CCD-TR101 Hi8 camcorder. Utilizing mechanical compensation based on a fluid filled variable angle prism. Sony's SteadyShot system (since renamed "Super Steady Shot" and improved) was jointly developed with Canon, and works very well, with none of the motion-lag artifacts that plagued earlier mechanical systems. Sony has since built the optical system into many of its Hi8 and MiniDV models, but note that many Sony 8mm

Variangle Prism

The "Shake-free" Effect

Flat glass

High-refraction
index liquid

Bellows

Prism

Lens Imag

Under Normal Conditions

Under Compensating Conditions

Optical image stabilization, based on a variable angle prism, literally bends the light to compensate for camera shake. It is usually preferable to electronic/digital systems.. Courtesy of Canon.

models use an electronic (digital) stabilizing system (not optical), so you must check specifications carefully. Canon incorporates optical stabilization in most of its top models, as well as in an accessory lens for its L2 and L1 camcorders.

The effectiveness of stabilization is most noticeable when the lens is fully zoomed in to the extreme telephoto range. Flip Steady Shot on, and it looks more like you are watching Television, not jittery amateur video. The system cleverly provides more compensation as the lens is zoomed in, so when you pan or tilt on

An accessory image stabilizing lens for Canon's L2 and L1 camcorders utilizes the same technology as found in Sony's Steady Shot optical stabilizing system.

a wide shot there's no feeling of resistance to the movement. It only eliminates minor and quick jitter, however, so you must still hold the camera as still as possible. It improves image quality significantly in almost all hand held shooting, as well as recording from the windows of moving automobiles, airplanes, trains, etc.

Best of all, there's no sacrifice in image quality when you use optical stabilization.An active prism mechanically moves the image that the high resolution image sensor sees, so all of this sensor's pixels are utilized all the time. The result is full 500-line horizontal resolution when used with the MiniDV format, and full 400-line horizontal resolution with Hi8.

In an interview on the Nickelodeon cable network, the amateur videomaker whose work is most well known to the American public, George Holiday, stated what was going through his mind as he shot the Rodney King beating. "All I kept thinking was that I've got to try to hold the camera steady," he said. Lawyers for the policemen on trial used the shakiness of the image in their defense (arguing that you can't really see what's happening because of the shake).

Eye Control

Perhaps the most technically innovative frill ever offered on a camcorder, eye control allows the user to start and stop tape, and select which part of the frame the autofocus system focuses on, just by looking at different areas of the viewfinder screen. The eye control system was introduced to the world of camcorders in 1995 on Canon's ES5000 Hi8 model (it was introduced in Canon's still photo cameras a bit earlier).

Eye control works by pointing a harmless invisible laser beam at the eye, and then detecting where the reflection lands on an image sensor. Similar technology has been used to give pilots control over instruments (so they don't have to divert their eyes to a control panel), and by advertising researchers who measure where on the screen viewers are looking during a TV commercial (eye tracking).

Before using eye control, you must customize the camera with a simple setup procedure. Operating the system requires a certain mental discipline. Wisely, the eye control system can be disabled if your eye gets weary or you get confused.

6 The Ultimate Camcorder

Ever since Sony introduced their first-ever Handycam in 1985, and JVC launched VHS-C camcorders a short time later, I have been writing reviews of new camcorder models for various magazines. Over these years I've seen lots of goofy features come and go, and I've seen lots of clever innovations catch on and spread from brand to brand. I've also had the chance to personally play with many different camcorders for extended lengths of time—taking them on vacation and shooting with them semi-professionally—so I've gotten to know the ergonomic side of camcorders quite well too. (One misplaced button, and you're accidentally turning the whole thing off instead operating the fader!)

Having found fault, here and there, with just about every camcorder ever made, I thought it might be interesting to let my imagination wander and conjure up what—in my mind, at least—could serve as the ideal. Perhaps the powers-that-be in Japan might even pay some attention, and produce the thing...

Well, I know I'm really dreaming on that last one, but for the sake of anyone who does care... here goes: My idea of the Ultimate Camcorder.

Everything, and Tiny

My ultimate camcorder uses a new video format—let's call it UltraDV. The UltraDV tapes are the same size as today's MiniDV cassettes, yet they are better in several ways. In addition to the video track, the UltraDV tapes offer eight synchronized audio tracks, any of which can be recorded independently. You can also record these audio tracks first, and then add new picture later, without affecting the sound. Thus, UltraDV is perfect for making music videos, and for creating serious video productions using in-camera editing techniques—including the addition of music, sound effects, narration, and ambience tracks after the initial shooting is over.

UltraDV has digital video recording, with quality that's the same as the component recording process use in the D-5 professional format (that's 4:2:2 recording, with 10-bit luminance,in video engineering jargon, for you tech heads). There's no data compression (such as MPEG), so the format offers superb high quality "raw" digital information.

If all that sounds rather complicated and elaborate, rest assured, the UltraDV format can also be easy to use. Like today's camcorders, my ultimate model—let's call it The UltraCam—would include a "full auto" switch that would disable all the manual adjustments, and operate everything automatically, with the same ease as today's point-and-shoot models.

Automatic focus would include macro operation right up to the lens' surface, of course, and the UltraCam macro wouldn't require you to zoom out for the close-up macro system to work (unlike today's models).

Luscious Lens

Speaking of the lens, a 20:1 optical zoom range seems about right, if it's truly to be an UltraCam. But I'm not talking about super-telephoto zoom settings here—we'll leave the UltraZoom function to digital electronics and an ultra high resolution image sensor (see below). I'm talking about wide-angle. Zoom back on the UltraCam, and you're practically at a fish-eye setting—super wide angle. Never again will your back be up against the living room wall, trying to get a shot of seven people sitting on the couch and love seat, and seeing only five at a time in the viewfinder. The UltraCam can zoom back.

The zoom would be variable speed, of course, and the slowest speed would take a full minute to go from one end of the 20:1 range to the other. Besides the usual rocker control for the zoom, a separate speed dial and trigger button would make it easy to operate the zoom slowly without having to worry about maintaining constant pressure.

The manual iris override would offer full-range, calibrated f-stop controls. A video gain boost would enhance low-light performance (with amplification up to 24-decibels.) Best of all, in infra-red illumination system would illuminate people's faces in dimly lit rooms, without annoying them with bright lights. (Special color compensating circuits, of course, would make the infra-red illumination look like ordinary color, or would shift things to black and white.)

Dual Viewfinders and Stabilizers

Why have to choose between a black and white CRT viewfinder, and a color LCD? My UltraCam, like Sony's Vision series camcorders, has both. To save battery power, you can switch either one on and off. The black and white viewfinder is better for focusing, while the color one is better for playback and for checking white balance.

The color viewfinder is a big 4" screen—similar to Sharp's best Viewcam models. But unlike those models, my LCD screen detaches—to minimize weight and bulk when necessary—and it has an easily replaceable light bulb. (I recently had to replace the lamp on a three-year old active-matrix color pocket TV, and it was a very difficult repair job.)

Image stabilization reaches a new plateau of perfection in the UltraCam. Taking the best of what's good and making something even better, the UltraCam's ultrastabilizing system uses both the optical and digital stabilizing techniques. First, the lens compensates by physically moving (optical stabilization). The second stage of image stabilizing uses digital techniques (similar to Panasonic models.) But there's a big difference: The image sensors (yes, plural) all have HDTV resolution—about 1-million pixels each. This means that only a fraction of all the available pixels are needed to produce a very good quality NTSC (today's TV) image. So the image stabilizing system has a lot more elbow room to move about in. The result is that UltraCam not only gets rid of the minor camera shakes, it gets rid of the major shakes as well.

These high resolution image sensors also facilitate another great UltraCam feature: Digital UltraZoom. Have you ever checked out one of today's camcorders with 64x or even 100x digital zoom? Zoom all the way in, and the picture devolves into an abstract pattern of huge colored rectangles. Not so with the UltraCam—the high resolution image sensors provide high quality images even when the digital zoom is at 100x.

The UltraCam has three image sensors—like Sony's CCD-VX3. All professional TV cameras have this feature—it produces sharper color detail, with less picture noise. But these image sensors work even better in low light than today's sensors, which results in an astoundingly low 0.01-lux rating for the camcorder's light sensitivity. Which means you can shoot in extremely dimly lit rooms, and outdoors at night.

Editing Galore

For editing, the UltraCam has time code, of course, and a wired remote control system (like Sony's LANC jacks) that allows full machine control and communication with a computerized editing controller system. But the UltraCam improves on Sony's RC time code system in a couple of ways. For one thing, the time code can be easily copied from one tape to another, so—for intensive editing—you can make "workprint" copies of the camcorder originals (assuming you've got two UltraCams).

The UltraCam's time code system also has a built-in "window dub" feature—so you can make copies of a tape on your VCR with the time codenumbers superimposed on the screen.

As mentioned earlier, UltraCam can do video dubs (leaving earlier audio recordings), as well as audio dubs on any (or all) of eight independent sound tracks. Because sixteen separate jacks (inputs and outputs for 8 tracks) would occupy too much room on the camcorder, a separate adaptor box is used (at home) for mixing and overdubs. A digital fiber optic cable connects the adaptor box to the camcorder.

In-camera digital editing features include dissolves, fades, wipes, and chroma-key. (A second accessory camera can plug into the UltraCam for the chroma-key feature.) Still frame and strobe are also provided, of course, along with a time-lapse recording system.

Animation gets a big boost in the UltraCam, compared with today's camcorders. Capable of recording just a single frame at a time, UltraCam finally lets low-budget video animation achieve the same smoothness as film animation. (Today's models record four to seven frames at a time when they do animation.)

But UltraCam goes beyond anything ever offered yet, by finally bringing another basic film feature to the low budget video world—variable frame rate. I'm not talking about high speed shutter (of course UltraCam has that, too)—I'm talking about truly recording the tape at rates other than the standard 30 frames per second. So you can record a couple embracing at the beach at 90 frames per second, and when you play it back, it will appear in slow motion (one third speed.) Or record a complete sunset (normally four minutes) at 3 frames per second, and then watch it playback in less than half a minute.

For titling, UltraCam offers an optional plug-in character generator, as well as a digital superimpose system. For maximum versatility, it also has a pair of video-through jacks—so you can process the video signal any way you want on the way from the camera to the recorder section of the camcorder.

For hooking up to advanced editing systems, as well as for improved playback, the UltraCam includes not just a built-in full-frame time base corrector (TBC), but an external sync input so you can mix images without any additional TBCs. In fact, the signal from the UltraCam is so good that even professional TV engineers will agree that it is truly broadcast quality.

Manual Everything

Neophytes will have no problem operating UltraCam in full automatic mode, but for those who understand the value of manual overrides, it's nice to know they're all there.

Beginning with manual audio recording level and headphone level controls. Continuing with manual iris, focus ring, and white balance adjustments.

But advanced semi-automated controls make it even easier for semi-pro users to set everything just right. A pinpoint focus/exposure system lets you locate a cross-hair target over a subject's face—the camcorder automatically focuses on this and adjusts exposure for it.

A viewfinder display indicates the current focus distance. The UltraCam thus doubles as a distance measuring device.

Back to Basics

Ever wonder who wrote the law that camcorder batteries should run out after about an hour of use? The UltraCam's battery lasts for eight hours—a full work day. And it weighs less than today's lithium ion batteries, of course, and recharges in less than fifteen minutes.

The buttons on the UltraCam are designed around the human hand. Each finger rests on a button—it's like a typewriter keyboard. For point-and-shoot operation, of course, all you need is one button (start/stop), and perhaps the zoom. But advanced users will appreciate the careful thought put into the location and shape of these controls. The top of each button is shaped differently, to make it even easier to find by feel. The power control is far away from everything else, and easy to find for novice users.

The microphone on the UltraCam goes far beyond today's crude zoom-microphone technology. It's adjustable from am omnidirectional to a hyperbolic (shotgun microphone) pickup pattern. In the shotgun mode, a cross-hair overlay appears in the viewfinder, and you can adjust the position of this target using buttons similar to the electrical remote controls for side-view mirrors in automobiles. Using these controls, you can aim the microphone with pin point accuracy at the mouth of someone speaking ten or twenty feet away. This results in vastly improved sound when recording from more than a few feet's distance from the subject.

For recording from even further distances, UltraCam includes a built-in wireless microphone receiver. So there's no fuss hooking up an external unit. Just switch on the wireless transmitter (supplied), and UltraCam automatically senses the wireless signal.

For compatibility, UltraCam comes with an adaptor that lets you play UltraDV tapes on ordinary VCRs. (OK, maybe this takes the biggest leap of faith, but we're imagining, right?)

And UltraCam's size is downright tiny—about the same as today's smallest camcorder models. But for semi-pro use, it features slide out, lightweight aluminum supports that let you shoulder-mount it, like a professional camcorder. A drop-down mini-tripod system is also built-in.

UltraCam weights about one pound, including tape, battery, and LCD screen. It comes with a foam padded carrying case—about the size of a tissue box—that protects it enough so that you can put it in the trunk of a car without worrying about damage. Speaking of cars, the UltraCam's power adaptor/recharger plugs into an AC outlet anywhere in the world, as well as into an automobile cigarette lighter socket.

UltraCam's price? Well, since we're dreaming, why not go all the way? Look at today's 35mm still cameras—for about $500, you can get a very professional unit. So why not with camcorders—if not now, sometime in the future? UltraCam carries a manufacturers suggested list price of $599.95, but if you shop carefully, you may be able to find it on the street for about $475. So check those ads!

7 Camcorder Production Tips

When you're shopping for a camcorder the advanced features, buttons, lens sizes, and other gizmos seem all important. But after you unwrap it, charge up the battery, and start taping, all those technical details seem to fade. More basic questions arise—when to shoot, how to use the zoom, and in general, how to make an interesting tape.

Here are tips that can help you shoot video with polish and style, and avoid some of the pitfalls that can make video productions boring and tedious to watch.

• Keep the Lens Wide

First-time camcorder users love to play with the power zoom lens, but there are several advantages to leaving the lens set all the way back at its widest angle setting. This advice is especially relevant for beginning videographers.

At the wide angle lens setting, the jitter that results from handheld camera movement is minimized. Try this test: Shake the camera at a constant rate while zooming the lens in or out. The shake will be very visible and annoying when you're zoomed in, but will be far more subtle at the wide angle setting.

Another advantage of wide angle shooting is focus. All camcorders have auto-focus circuitry, of course, but none of these systems are perfect. The more zoomed in the lens is, the more critical focus becomes. Try this experiment: zoom in on an object, and manually change the focus slightly. Notice how exact the focus setting must be—a small change makes the object fuzzy. Now, zoom out to the wide angle setting, and change the focus manually. Note that there's hardly any difference in the focus. When you leave the zoom set at wide angle, practically everything in the frame is in sharp focus.

Of course, when you keep the lens set at wide angle you take in a wider shot—you can see more of the people in a room, more of an outdoor panorama, etc.

• Be Brief

This can't be said enough. No matter how quick you think a shot should be, your audience will probably think it should be even shorter. Try to keep your tapes topical, and have some idea of how long they should be before you start shooting. For example, a birthday party is a fine topic for a tape, and ten minutes might be a good length. So, if there are twenty guests, each one should be on-camera for no more than thirty seconds.

Today's generation of camcorders can readily shoot very short segments—as short as one second long. Utilize this capability. Be very conscious of when tape is rolling. One of the most common mistakes beginners make is not knowing when the tape is paused and when it is recording. Unless you're recording someone speaking, or a specific action, you should keep the shots down to one or two seconds in length—just enough for the audience to recognize what is going on. Press the start button, count a beat to yourself, and press it again to pause. That's it. Whenever you're using the camcorder like a still camera—to show a house, a car, a statue, a park, etc.—use this technique. (This assumes you're editing in the camcorder—if you know for sure you'll be editing later on, then shoot longer segments ensure that you have enough.)

• Cut, Don't Zoom

A zoom lens is standard on every camcorder made, but most beginners misunderstand how zooms are used in professional video productions. Turn the sound down on your TV for a few minutes and watch for a zoom. You'll find that the use of the zoom is subtle and is not that common. Very rarely will you see an extended zoom from an extreme wide angle shot to a close-up.

Most of the time, in professional productions, a cut rather than a zoom is used to switch from one framing (wide, medium, close-up) to another. How do you "cut" with a camcorder? Pause the tape.

If someone is speaking, for example, start by recording the person in a wide shot. Then, at the end of a sentence, pause the tape, and quickly zoom in on the person's face. Wait until another sentence is about to begin, and start the tape rolling again. Upon playback, you'll see a much more effective cut from a wide shot to a close-up.

Think of the zoom as a tool that lets you get all different kinds of framing without having to physically move closer to or further from the subject. The main purpose of the zoom lens is to make a variety of shots available from a single location—but not to record the act of changing the framing using the zoom.

Before you hit the zoom controls, hit the pause button. Only show the zoom when you want to convey a sense of action, and when the intermediate shots that the zoom passes through are interesting to look at. Beginners might try disciplining themselves by setting the goal of shooting tapes with no visible zooms at all—the zoom lens is used extensively, of course, but not while tape is rolling. This is a standard film-school exercise.

• Hold the Camcorder Steady

If you compare your camcorder shots with professional TV productions, the camera shake will probably stand out as a bigger difference than anything else, including lighting, sound, etc. The problem of camera shake comes from holding the camcorder in your hands.

Ideally, a tripod or mounting system like the Steadicam JR should be used, although most people find these accessories too cumbersome to carry with the camcorder. The solution, whenever possible, is to improvise a tripod. Use a tabletop and salt shaker to prop the camcorder up (the salt shaker goes in front, to angle the camcorder up. Don't expect the camcorder to hold itself in position with such improvised supports—use one hand to hold it in position. This will vastly improve the stability of the shot over a purely handheld shot. Outdoors, use the roof of a car, the branch of a tree, the back of a park bench, a chair, or whatever else you can find at approximately the right height. A mini tripod (with 6" legs) and/or monopod can be a cheap and lightweight alternative. Though not as sturdy as larger tripods, they're certainly more convenient to carry.

When you must handhold the camcorder, be especially observant of tip number one—keep the lens set at wide angle, so that shake is less visible.

• Use the Language of the Moving Image

The camcorder is a relatively new invention, but the language of moving images has been around for one hundred years, since the birth of cinema. Study this language by watching TV and films, and use this language in your own productions.

Begin your scenes with a fade in. Start with an establishment shot (a wide shot) that shows where things will be taking place. Cut between wide shots, medium shots, and close-ups. Try not to cut to the same framing—that is, if the last shot was a wide shot do not make the next shot a wide shot—make it a close-up.

Use techniques like intercutting and foreshadowing to build tension and suspense into your production. You don't have to be shooting a murder mystery to utilize these techniques—intercutting shots of the burgers on the grill as they cook, between shots of the family in the backyard, can build dramatic tension for the moment of truth when the burgers are served.

End each scene with a fade-out.

• In-Camera Editing Saves Time

Most novice camcorder users think editing is something that takes place after the shooting is over, but only elaborate professional style productions are edited this way. Most people edit as they shoot. This is called "in-camera editing."

As you shoot, imagine that the tape you are making is the final production. There will be no after-the-fact editing. If you record someone speaking, and they ramble on endlessly, then go back to the last point in the tape that was interesting and re-record over the boring part. You must be ruthless about this if you're going to keep the tape moving and maintain viewer interest.

Don't be shy about shooting second and third takes when people speak directly to the camera. Most people enjoy the chance to try it again, just like the stars. Rewind the tape and erase over the "bad" take, and keep doing this until you get it right.

You do not have to shoot everything in sequence, especially with the 8mm format (and Hi8). You can leave the first two minutes of a tape blank, begin shooting, and then go back later to place a beginning in the opening two minutes. You can shoot two minutes of someone speaking, listen to the tape, pick out three short ten-second spots that you want to save, and use the insert editing feature to record over the minute and a half that you don't want to save. This creates an intercutting effect—you recorded the person speaking in one continuous take, but in the finished tape it will seem as if the person speaks, then something else happens, then the person speaks some more, than something else happens, and the person speaks again.

• Pay Attention to Lighting

You don't need fancy lighting equipment and crews to light your videos well—you need an astute eye. Analyze your shooting environment for lighting, and situate yourself to take best advantage of available light.

If you're shooting indoors during the day, for example, and there's a window with lots of light coming in from the outside, then you should place yourself right in front of the window, looking in towards the center of the room with the light from the window coming from behind.

If there is a fluorescent light straight above someone you are taping, the light will be blocked by the top of the person's head, and the face will be in shadow. Ask the person to step back a couple of feet, so that the light is diagonally in front of and above the person's face, illuminating it better.

Use the "backlight compensation" and iris adjust controls on your camcorder only as last resorts. Whenever possible, you're better off manipulating your camera and subject positions so that use of these controls is unnecessary..

• Use Lights Thoughtfully

The reason why a single light looks so harsh is because most professional TV studio lighting arrangements are based on the so-called "three-point" lighting system: A key light is the strongest, illuminating the face from one side. A fill light on the other side softens the shadow area, making the other side of the face visible but darker than the key light side. A backlight, located behind the subject pointing down, illuminates the hair, top of the head, and shoulders, preventing these areas from blending into the background and giving the image a more three dimensional look.

If you're working with just a single light, which would create harsh shadows by itself, try finding spots where other lights will serve as fill or backlights. Try bouncing the light off a ceiling, or better yet, use a white umbrella reflector (available at professional photo supply stores). Spreading the source of light over a wider area softens the shadows, creating gradations of darkness rather than just pure lit and pure unlit areas of the face.

• Listen

Try turning the sound down on your TV for half an hour, so that you can see but can't hear. Then try the reverse—turn the brightness down to black, but listen to the sound. Which version is more intelligible?

Sound is probably the most neglected aspect of beginners' videotapes. Unless you're going to do a lot of fancy editing after the shooting is over, you should be just as interested in recording good sound, while you shoot, as getting a good picture.

When you record people speaking, start and stop the camcorder at the beginning and ends of sentences. There is a rhythm to speech that will cue you as to when a thought is about to end. Be ready.

Try to include music or narration when you shoot scenic shots, especially if the shot lasts more than a second or two. A car radio, a Walkman cassette player, or a street musician can be called into service to add improvised musical accompaniment.

Wear headphones when you shoot outdoors. There is a lot of wind noise even in mild weather. The only way you can hear it is if you monitor the sound while you shoot. There are a few full-size camcorder models that have built-in speakers on their sides, but for most camcorder users, headphones are needed to monitor the sound while shooting. You can usually use headphones from a portable cassette player.

Getting good sound pickup boils down to a few basic rules: Get the microphone as close as possible to the sound source without causing overload distortion. Use an external microphone (wired or wireless) whenever the person speaking is more than a few feet from the camcorder's built-in microphone. Set manual recording level, when available, so the loudest signals hit the 0-VU point on the meter. Watch out for hum pickup problems whenever making wired connections, and eliminate them before recording. And always wear headphones to monitor the sound — you wouldn't shoot without looking at the viewfinder, would you?

• Impose Structure and Tension

Life may be unstructured and random, a series of coincidences and happenstance, drama, in contrast, is more ordered. Your tapes will be more engaging, and more accessible to viewers, if they follow this well tested dramatic formula: introduce your characters, establish a conflict, and resolve it.

This technique need not be heavy-handed. Two dogs in the backyard fighting over a dropped bun, for example, is conflict enough for a family video.

Husband and wife travelling in a car, fighting over who got them lost in the first place, is conflict.

Which brings us to your instigative role as a videomaker. In a fun, friendly way, you can spice up your tapes by getting people to argue about things—even if they are stupid things. Don't forget to wrap things up at the end. One dog eats the bun and wanders off triumphantly into the sunset. The couple kisses as they arrive at their destination. Two guys arguing over sports shake hands. The party's over and the cleanup begins. Fade out.

• Keep Shots Short

OK, it's true that this was said earlier, but it is so important I can't emphasize it enough. (Go back to the second tip and you'll see this repetition was foreshadowed.)

Watch TV and count aloud each time the shot changes—from a wide shot to a close-up, from one person's face to another, from whatever to whatever. You'll rarely count above ten seconds before there's another shot. Things move at a brisk pace in TV-land.

Try to think like a TV news producer—in "sound bytes." You don't want to record everything someone says—just the pithy, catchy phrases that express the essence of it without going in to too much detail.

Don't be afraid to ask people to repeat things they just said, if the tape wasn't rolling. Sometimes, when doing casual interviews, it is best to keep the tape paused while someone first explains what they want to say, and then ask the person to repeat selected ideas and phrases with the tape rolling. This is not the same as putting words into someone's mouth (though that's perfectly valid too)—it is a form of editing and refining as you go along.

By keeping shots short, you can also help compensate for some of the flaws that are associated with not following the other tips listed above. A poorly lit shot that lasts five seconds is less bothersome than one which lasts for five minutes.

Suppose you're shooting Mount Rushmore with no good sound—just wind noise. A fast paced seven second travelogue sequence—a three second wide shot, and one second close-up shots of each of the four presidents—would be much more interesting to watch than a two-minute long shot filled with zooms and wild panning.

Drive all the way to Mt. Rushmore just to shoot seven seconds of video? Admittedly, it takes discipline. But that's what it's all about.

• Get To Know Your Camcorder

The relationship you forge with your camcorder over the years can be as emotional as what occurs between man and car. Each camcorder model has a personality. Learning to locate key buttons by feel takes time, and taking full advantage of all the features may take even longer.

Camcorder proficiency occurs in stages. The first stage is getting control over the most basic stuff — starting and stopping the tape, using (and not abusing) the power zoom, manual override controls, holding the camera steady, and knowing when to turn the camera off because lighting is poor, sound pickup won't work out, etc.

Once you feel confident that you can competently capture picture and sound onto tape, the real fun begins. Now it's time to not just capture moments, but express a vision. Instead of worrying whether each individual shot will come out, you can start focusing your attention on the big picture — the overall production.

• Tell A Story

Perhaps the most important single ingredient most beginners need to add to their productions is the sense of storytelling — what filmmakers call the narrative element — a story with a beginning, middle, and end. Within the world of alternative cinema, there are non-narrative experimental videos that are widely respected works of art. But most beginning camcorder enthusiasts are striving to create more traditional work — except perhaps for music videos, where normal rules go out the window and experimental cinematic styles are mainstream.

Before embarking on a shoot, the crucial questions to ask yourself are: Who is the intended audience — family, friends, a public access channel, clients? How long do you envision the finished work being? How will it begin and end? And what will be your production strategy — in-camera editing, film-style (single cameras shoot-to-edit), or multi-camera?

• Select An Appropriate Format

The tape format you work in and type of camera you shoot with should correspond with your distribution plans. Usually most people wish to achieve the highest picture and sound quality possible. For anyone just starting out now, buying a camcorder for professional or semi-pro use, the three-chip DV camcorders (Sony's DCR-VX1000, Panasonic's PV-DV1000) are clearly the way to go. But of course, most people are still working with older equipment.

Super-VHS and Hi8 are considered standard for wedding videos, low-budget documentaries, student films, etc. The base-level 8mm and VHS formats are acceptable for home-video quality level, but should be avoided for anything beyond that (except, that is, when your goal is to appear as a home video clip on broadcast TV).

• Consider A Studio

So far, the assumption has been that you're shooting with one camera. Certain types of programs, such as talk shows, sports events, and concerts necessitate multi-camera production. This is also how most TV sitcoms, game shows, and news programs are shot — in a studio where several cameras feed into a switcher that selects which camera will be recorded, at any given moment, onto tape.

You can accomplish this multi-camera setup on a low budget with just about any two or three camcorders (different formats don't matter), an A/V mixer such as Videonics' MX-1 or the Panasonic WJ-AVE7, and a VCR to record the selected signal. You could also record separate camcorder signals on separate tapes, but this "iso-cam" approach can turn into an editing marathon.

• Scout The Location

Whether you scout a location weeks in advance, or arrive on the scene with the event you're there to tape already in progress, you'll need to assess the lighting, sound (look for quiet spots with a minimum of background noise), and electrical power (where you can plug in battery chargers and lights?). The only difference between advance scouting and by-the-seat-of-your-pants shooting is the amount of time you'll have to figure things out.

Try to avoid using a camcorder light — it annoys people and usually creates harsh shadows and very dark backgrounds behind illuminated subjects. Look for windows (during daylight hours) or well-lit areas that you can use to base your shooting. Take the time and effort to move subjects into better lighting — most people are cooperative.

• Compose The Picture

When framing, think in terms of wide, medium, and close-up shots. Such thinking is absolutely essential to in-camera editing, because each time you pause the tape you should substantially change the framing (such as from a medium shot — waist up — to a close-up). Otherwise you'll end up with a "jump cut", in which the subject seems to suddenly jump into a different position.

Pay close attention to people's eyes. Eyes should generally appear at a height of about two thirds to three-quarters of the way up the screen. If someone is looking slightly up or down at another person, carrying this angle between wide, medium, and close-up shoots will contribute to the realism of the scene. This is called the eyeline.

As you frame shots, try to maintain screen continuity. If someone is on the left side of the screen in a wide shot, keep them on the left in close-ups. Cinematographers obey the "180-degree rule" religiously — draw an imaginary line between two subjects' heads, and stay on one side of that line to keep left-right screen relations consistent.

• Optimize Manual Settings

Perhaps the most important thing to understand about manual overrides is that they can *not* take any bad situation and make it good. If someone is standing five feet away and a statue is located one hundred feet away, and it's nighttime and dimly lit, no manual exposure or focus setting is going to get them both in sharp focus.

Hollywood producers spend small fortunes avoiding just these situations — thousands of watts of artificial lighting are used to bring things in balance. That's why scoping the location and identifying spots that are good for you is so important. The manual controls don't necessarily solve problems, but they do give you more control over the tough choices. When someone stands in front of a window, for example, you can choose to have the face appear properly exposed and the window all white, or you can expose (and focus) for what's outside the window, having the person appear in silhouette.

When shooting indoors during daylight, try to turn off all artificial lights and illuminate the room with daylight. Sunlight and incandescent lamps have different color temperatures, making things appear too blue or red, respectively, when they get mixed together. Setting the manual white balance will not make everything look fine in mixed lighting, but it will keep the colors from shifting wildly every time you pan to or away from the windows.

• Take Advantage of Lens Accessories
Consumer video cameras usually have permanently mounted lenses, thus limiting a major area of control that's available in professional videography. But with lens filters and adapters, you can greatly influence the picture you get. Perhaps the most useful accessory for an event videographer is the wide angle adapter. This extends the wide angle range of your camcorder's lens — instead of seeing four people with your back against the wall, you can see seven.

Filters can provide a variety of useful effects, from warming up skin tones (giving your subjects a healthy glow), to creating mysterious looking fog, to shooting rays of light out from bright objects (star filter). They're sold by the combination of what they do and what size threads they have — the front of your camcorder's lens should indicate the thread diameter (the Greek letter phi usually appears next to this number, which ranges from about 35 to 65mm.).

• Avoid Sloppy Camera Movement
Shooting moving objects is arguably the most difficult aspect of camera work, and it comes up all the time when recording school athletics, Little League, etc. This is an area where inexpensive tripods give themselves away, too: Even an inexpensive tripod can provide good support when locked down for a static shot. But start panning or tilting the camera, to follow the action, and cheap tripods will look jerky. Better tripods all have fluid heads, which help smooth the camera movement.

One of the best ways to shoot action without degenerating into sloppy camera moves is to keep the camera still, and let the action move across the screen. Let the players or characters appear in frame on one side and disappear on the other — then cut to another shot. A character disappearing out of frame also lets you switch screen direction, too, so someone who was running towards the right in one shot can be running left in the next.

The problem with this approach is it limits you to wide shots. If you want to see the sweat on someone's face while they're running, you'll probably need to pan the camera sideways to keep the face in frame for several seconds. In this type of shot, leave "nose room" in front of the person's face. If someone is running towards the right side of the screen, place them not dead center but somewhat to the left. This creates the appearance of space that they are running into. For in-camera editing, start the pan before you start the tape rolling — this will give you a chance to get "in sync" with the action, so that when the shot begins the subject is already framed properly.

Remember that there are two ways to get close-up shots — by zooming the lens in, and by physically moving closer to the subject. You'll find that moving yourself closer makes it easier to keep a subject in sharp focus and to follow the action smoothly, rather than using extreme telephoto zoom.

• Prepare Scripts and Storyboards

Perhaps no other aspect of videomaking is as emotionally evocative as the script. I know people who have staked their dreams and aspirations on script writing; and I know filmmakers who curse the very concept of the script, and swear they'll never use one.

In professional television, of course, scripts are considered absolutely essential not just for dramatic productions, but for news reports, documentaries, and even music videos.

The storyboard offers a visual form of scripting that helps you think out each shot in a production. It's a series of comic book style panels, each containing a simple stick figure sketch showing the key elements — the framing of your subject(s) and background.

Visualizing the flow of shots before the production begins is crucial if you intend to use in-camera special effects, such as dissolve to/from a still frame, fade, or strobe. Ditto for in-camera titles — these should be prepared in advance and stored in the camcorder's memory.

• Choose Your Strategy

Broadly speaking, there are two overall strategies available to most camcorder users: In-camera editing, and post-production editing.

With in-camera editing, where you create the finished tape as you shoot (with no plans for further editing later), you must be absolutely ruthless during recording. Every time you shoot for more than a few seconds, you must go back and carefully evaluate what you want to keep, and re-record over every section that needs to be eliminated. The advantage of this strategy is that it's fast and dirty

— you walk out of the event with the finished tape. In-camera editing is highly recommended for all but the most serious projects, because it eliminates the biggest problem that plagues most camcorder enthusiasts: shelves and shelves loaded with tapes, waiting to be edited.

If you've never really tried in-camera editing, here's a good way to begin: The next time you're about to zoom in on someone's face, pause the tape, then zoom in while the tape isn't rolling, get the camera in good focus again, and start tape rolling.

The post-production editing strategy lets you shoot much more loosely, with multiple takes and out-of-sequence shooting, but there will be a big price to pay for this down the road: wading through hours and hours of rambling footage is tedious. If you've never tried in-camera editing, it's a good idea to practice in-camera a few times before shooting-to-edit. When shooting to edit, you should have a list of specific shots — picture compositions — you hope to get, and keep in mind the technical needs of your editing system (see box).

The main advantage of editing after the fact is that you get to defer decisions. Instead of deciding on the spot whether something you just shot is good or bad, whether you want to use the wide shot or the close-up, you can make these decisions later, when things are calmer and you can evaluate the options more objectively.

• Shoot to Edit for Flexibility

Shooting to edit affords you a more luxurious style than in-camera editing. You can record the beginning and end of a production at the same time, shooting out-of-sequence and with multiple takes. You can shoot the same thing several different ways, from different angles, and determine which one looks the best later.

But that doesn't mean you can shoot freely without any concern for how things will cut together. Raw footage that maintains screen continuity (left right relations), has reaction shots and cutaway shots that can be used while people speak, and includes opening and closing segments does not just happen. You have to make it happen. Before shooting, imagine yourself sitting down in the future to edit the project — what kind of shots will you need? Make a list and shoot it — be sure to include opening and closing shots, and establishing shots showing where the action is taking place (a home, a building, church, banquet hall, etc.).

• Allow For Pre-Roll

Depending on the particular editing system you'll be using, you'll probably need to allow for pre-roll time: Begin recording with the camcorder at least five seconds before the start of anything you plan to use in the final edit. This will give the editing system time to get the VCRs up to full speed prior to the edit point, without any glitches. This rule should apply to every shot — don't yell "action!" until you count to five.

The very first minute of a tape should be recorded with the lens cap on. This portion of the tape tends to have more dropouts than the rest, and recording a minute of black will also provide your editing system with plenty of pre-roll time. Never shoot something really important right at the very beginning of a tape — in the first few seconds (as can happen when you arrive late to an event, pop a fresh tape in, and start recording the main ceremony). Many editing systems will refuse to copy these first few seconds, due to the lack of pre-roll time.

• Avoid Blank Spots

Blank areas in the middle of a tape are another problem to avoid if you'll be using an automated editing system. Such blank areas stop the flow of counter (or time code) numbers to the editing system, wreaking havoc. Many editing systems will cancel out of the operation when they hit such a spot. Blank areas are generally created when you take a tape out of the camcorder in the middle, then put it back in and continue recording. In such instances, you should carefully locate the end of the last recorded spot on the tape, and begin from there. Err on the side of erasing the last few frames of what was previously recorded, rather than leaving a spot blank.

• Take Notes

Having accurate notes — called logs — of what's on each tape at each moment (with an hour:minute:second entry whenever there's something new) can help minimize the time you spend editing, especially with big projects that consume hours and hours of tape. A production assistant can perform this task during shooting — essentially beginning the editing process right there.

• Have A Plan

The more you shoot and edit, the more they seem like two sides of the same coin. Though editing takes place after shooting is over, successful shooting usually begins with an editing plan in mind. It's the yin-yang of video production.

Perhaps the worst attitude to have — though it's quite common —is, "I'll shoot everything I see now, and then figure out how to edit it later." Just as even a master chef cannot take a bunch of rotten ingredients and create a gourmet meal, no amount of editing skill can save the day when the camera work is shaky, out of focus, and poorly framed.

If I had a dollar for every student I've seen spending hours and hours tediously and precisely editing a project that was originally shot in the most half-assed sloppy manner, I'd have enough money to buy a new Mini-DV camcorder. A little time and effort invested on the front end of a video project — planning the shots, framing carefully, shooting re-takes to correct errors, etc. — will pay off handsomely in the finished production.

8 Tripods

Pedestal camera mounts used in professional TV studios cost quite a bit more than most camcorders. Fulmar Pedestal 3702, courtesy of Vinten.

Of all the accessories and gadgets you can buy for your camcorder, none will consistently improve everything you shoot as much as a tripod. For all the talk about subtle technicalities like resolution numbers and S/N ratios, the most obvious difference between professionally shot video and home efforts has nothing to do with formats and specifications—it's in the framing of each and every shot. And the starting point for any serious discussion about framing is the ability to keep the picture steady.

Fortunately, tripods are also the most universally compatible camcorder accessories. Regardless of whether your camcorder is a super deluxe semi-pro dreamboat, or a humble point-and-shoot loss leader, it's guaranteed to have a tripod socket (screw threads) on its bottom.

Sure, you've no doubt seen TV news crews shooting public events without using tripods, but note two points: A professional TV news cinematographer has years of experience learning how to keep a shoulder-mounted (not handheld) camera as stable as possible; and even with all that skill, the picture still looks shaky. Just watch a local TV newscast and observe. The shaky field-report images are literally "anchored" by the far more stable shots of the news anchors in the studio (where handheld camerawork is strictly taboo). And not even all the field shots are shaky—even TV news crews try to use a tripod whenever time and space permit.

Outside of news (where production values tend to be sloppier) tripods are considered an absolute must—for drama, comedy, action-adventure, suspense, etc. (The only exception is for shooting the occasional point-of-view shot, such as in hor-

Mohawk MTR-2150 compact tripod. Courtesy of Coast Manufacturing.

ror films, where you want viewers to experience each footstep. But 99% of the film will still be shot with tripod.)

If you just want to start the camcorder running and capture one single static shot at a time, almost any tripod can do an adequate job holding the camera still. But if you want to be able to do camera moves on a tripod—pans and tilts—then you'll find there's a big difference between shoddy inexpensive tripods and fancier models.

In fact, the heaviest, sturdiest pneumatic pedestal mounts used in network TV studios (which smoothly glide up and down at the touch of a button) cost tens of thousands of dollars. Even the simple-looking wood legged tripods commonly used in 16-mm student film productions (such as the Sachtler 7+7, or the metal-leg O'Connor 50) cost thousands of dollars. Tripods used by TV news crews carry similar price tags.

Good Head

What makes these professional tripods so expensive? Once you go beyond building an extremely sturdy base, the main difference is in the head.

The tripod's head is mounted on top of the three legs, and it is to this head that you attach the camcorder (or camera). The cheapest heads, found on tripods costing under about $100, are simply a collection of nuts and bolts that facilitate camera mounting. A half notch up from this level of quality are "spring loaded" heads that use a metal spring to provide resistance when you tilt the camera up or down.

The best tripod heads are always "fluid heads". A viscous liquid that is permanently sealed inside the head provides smooth resistance to both up/down (tilting) and left/right (panning) motion.

The advantage of a fluid head is simple: Smooth camera motions. But the disparity between the smoothness of cheap and expensive fluid heads is enormous. Beware of fluid-head-hype—ever since camcorders became popular, a lot of cheap tripods hit the market claiming to have fluid heads, but with performance not much better than spring-loaded heads. (Visit a professional video or film supply store to see how smooth the heads on over-$500 tri-

Vision 30 professional tripod head. Courtesy of Vinten.

pods are, so you can learn how to gauge the smoothness of less expensive models.)

All fluid head tripods are rated for the maximum weight they can handle. If you exceed this limit, the tripod won't necessarily break, but the head's performance will be severely compromised—in other words, your pans and tilts will look jerky.

All good tripods have lock down knobs or levers to limit the camera's motions—so that when doing a pan the camera won't accidentally tilt, or vice-versa. Better heads also have drag or resistance adjustments to control how hard you must push to make the camera move.

Although zooming the lens is the one camera movement that doesn't really require a high quality head, you'll still need a solid, stable tripod if you intend to touch the camcorder controls. Otherwise, every time you press the zoom buttons the camera will shake. A wireless remote control with zoom buttons can be very useful in this situation. A shaky tripod will also shake the image whenever you start and pause the tape, unless you use a remote.

The fanciest camera movements require physically moving the camcorder forward/back (dollying) or sideways (trucking). A set of dolly wheels under a tripod can facilitate such motion in studio environments where the floor is very smooth. (Note that professional filmmakers almost always prefer to use a set of railroad-style tracks, and a matching cart, to achieve smoother and more controlled motion.)

Practically all tripods use a series of telescoping tubes or leg extensions to vary the height. Many video tripods also have an elevator column to raise the camera a foot or more above the top of the point where the three legs meet (a crank usually facilitates this up/down motion.) On cheap tripods, this tube tends to be the first down motion.) On cheap tripods, this tube tends to be the first part to get rickety. In general, you should avoid using the elevator column, and adjust height by extending the legs (always extend the thicker legs first). This produces maximum steadiness.

The heavier a tripod is the more stable it is. This is basic physics. A four pound camera atop a one-pound tripod is top heavy; but on top of a ten pound tripod the center of gravity is much lower. Unfortunately, heavy tripods are inherently heavy—that's why most casual (not professional) videographers don't want to lug them around, and why there are so many lightweight models on the market.

Two Tripods In Every Pot

In my view, the best solution to this dilemma is to own two tripods—a heavy duty true fluid-head model for the most serious projects, and an extremely compact, lightweight no-frills-head model for more casual taping (vacations, friends, family, etc.). For the serious work, consider Bogen's 3046 video tripod, equipped with the 3063 "mini" fluid head (the combination is sold as Bogen's 3140, for about $325). A valuable accessory for this system is the bubble head level (Bogen #3115), which helps ensure that the top and bottom of your frame are parallel to the horizon (about $40). All top-notch professional tripods have built-in bubble levels. Other heavy duty models include Bilora Pro930S ($399.95 list), the Miller System 10A (about $575), and the pricy but top-notch Peter-Lisand Ultra-250 (about $1,000).

Bogen 3140

For ultimate portability, Cullman's Magic One tripod folds to fit in a 15" ξ 5½" ξ 1½" case, and offers reasonable sturdiness but the head is of the most basic design (no fluid, no spring, about $140). Bilora's 6144 tripod is a couple of notches larger (it collapses to 20" long), but has a much better "fluid effect" head (about $185). Coast's Mohawk MTR-2150 is similar.

For the serious hobbyist who wants to get the fluidity of handheld camera movements but wants the steadiness of professional cinematography, there's the Steadicam JR (about $500), which I'll describe in more detail in a moment. It's a unique handheld counter-weight camera mounting system that can help you create very smooth looking walking shots without a dolly or track system.

If you're purchasing your first tripod, choose a model that will satisfy the majority of your needs. If you live near a big city, you can probably find a local media or public access center that rents heavy-duty tripods and other grip equipment (such as the Steadicam JR) for occasions where your needs go beyond the basics.

If you're setting up shop as a semi-pro or professional video producer, by all means splurge and get the best tripod you can possibly afford. Not only will it impress your clients, it will also impress you by improving your camera movements. And one great thing about spending money on a good tripod is that, unlike fancy video equipment, it won't become obsolete in five years. I've had my two tripods for ten years, (I've even trekked one around the world in a backpack,) and both still work like they're brand new.

The Steadicam JR

The Steadicam JR offers a different type of image stabilization. It is a unique camcorder accessory designed for the serious video enthusiast. It can help add a professional touch to low budget productions. Like its much more expensive big brother, the professional Steadicam (which sells for $40,000!) the JR stabilizes camera movements during hand held shooting—allowing you to walk through rooms, up and down staircases, and ride in vehicles with very steady shots.

Steadicam JR camcorder stablizing system from Cinema Products Corp.

Note that this is *not* the same function that electronic and optical image stabilization provides. EIS basically steadies the shake that occurs when you try to hold a shot still. The Steadicam JR does stabilize still shots, but its real thrill comes from stabilizing motion shots—pans, walking "tracking" shots, and "booming" shots (moving the camera up or down vertically). EIS doesn't stabilize these moving shots.

To make the comparison more blunt, EIS is basically a "fix up" technology that corrects one of the biggest problems plaguing amateur video (camera shake). The Steadicam JR is a more creative tool designed to give the serious video hobbyist and semiprofessional producer the opportunity to get elaborate Hollywood-style shots without paying Hollywood prices. Its list price is $600.

The Steadicam JR must be customized for your particular camcorder. The process is confusing, tedious, intimidating, and

The professional Steadicam SK mounting system consists of operator's vest, camera mount, and stabilizer arm (camera not included).

time consuming—but fortunately, after about two hours, you'll be in Steadicam heaven.

Steadicam JR is a weight counterbalance system that moves the center of gravity of the mounted camcorder down below the point where you hold the camcorder. The setup procedure is literally a balancing act—you must select and install weights, and adjust trim controls, to get the unit perfectly balanced.

Garrett Brown, the inventor of the Steadicam (who won an Academy Award for the professional model) hosts a one hour long instructional VHS videocassette that accompanies the Steadicam Jr. It is an excellent production, and is the saving grace of the setup procedure. The tape provides a wealth of information, and does not insult your intelligence wasting lots of time with basics.

The Steadicam JR will work with any camcorder that weighs less than five pounds—including most MiniDV, 8mm, Hi8, VHS-C, and Super-VHS-C camcorders, but not all full size VHS and Super-VHS camcorders. You may have to use the lightest available

Steadycam JR

battery with some models. A supplemental guide lists initial weight settings for many camcorder models.

The Steadicam JR is more than just a mounting system—it incorporates a high brightness/low glare 3.5-inch black and white LCD viewfinder that is an integral part of the Steadicam system. The screen is different from that found on pocket TV's—it is optimized for use in any lighting condition, including bright outdoor light. The viewing angle of the screen can be difficult booming operations (moving the unit up and down), but otherwise it performs quite well.

A low power "Obie" light completes the Steadicam's electronics system. The "Obie" is apparently named after actress Merle Oberon. If you like this type of Hollywood insider jargon, you'll love the presentation of the Steadicam JR instructions. The Obie provides an increment of extra light for faces of people who are a few feet from the camera. It's a soft fill light that creates a warm glow.

Both the screen and the light are powered by four alkaline "C" batteries (battery life is 9 hours without the light, or 2 hours with it). They're automatically triggered by a video signal from the camcorder, so you don't need to turn the Steadicam on and off separately. A remote pause switch near the Steadicam JR's grip lets you conveniently stop and start the camcorder, if it has an appropriate jack.

One hand supports the weight of the system using the pistol grip, while the other hand gently points the camera. Separated by a gimbal that provides mechanical isolation, the supporting hand can move all over the place without affecting the camera angle. Operating the Steadicam JR is a skill that requires some practice—professional Steadicam cameramen make a living out of this skill alone. But even without much experience, you'll find the Steadicam Jr. impressive. A simple tour of an apartment becomes breathtakingly smooth. It's easy to walk backwards and keep the camera steady, and to bring it down low to a child or pet's level.

The Steadicam JR may be a bit serious for the most casual camcorder users, but it is a fantastic production tool.

PART II

Tape and Editing

9 Low Budget Tape Formats

Choosing a format depends on a trade-off between picture quality, budget, portability, and compatibility (see chart for a full comparison). MiniDV is clearly the best. Super-VHS and Hi8 are more reasonably priced, and still offer superior performance compared with the 8mm and VHS-C formats.

One thing to consider in selecting a format is what kind of editing facilities are available to you. Many videographers own their own camcorders, but when it comes time to edit they rent the use of professional editing equipment for an hourly fee. Such editing facilities are available in most big cities (if there is none in you community, it might be a business worth starting up). You must, of course, find editing equipment for the same format tape you are shooting in. (Desktop Video Systems, the publisher of this book, provides a convenient and accurate service – send in the coupon at the back of the book for more details, and a starter kit.)

Utilizing high-end consumer/low-end industrial video equipment to best advantage requires some understanding of the technical details, and limitations, of each format. But before diving into detailed descriptions of the competing camps, it may be instructive first to take a quick look at how these formats evolved, and to see how they compare.

Format	Record Time*	Horiz. Res.	Size	Camcorder Price	Tape Cost
VHS	120-min.	240	full	$500-1,500	$2
VHS-C	20-min.	240	mini	$500-1,500	$3
Super-VHS	120-min.	400	full	$1,000-10,000	$8
S-VHS-C	20-min.	400	mini	$1,000-7,000	$7
8mm	120-min.	250	mini	$500-1,500	$4
Hi8	120-min.	400	mini	$900-10,000	$8-15**
MiniDV	60-min.	500	mini	$2500-15,000	$15-25

*Recording time for a standard length videocassette, at fastest (highest quality) tape speed. Longer length videocassettes may be available, but use of thinner tape and slower (EP) speed is not recommended.
**MP (metal particle) type Hi8 tape is less expensive, but EP (evaporated particle) is recommended for serious production -- it has fewer dropouts.

Video Format War

The 3/4" format, still in use today, was introduced back in 1971 by Sony, and was the first industrial format to use a cassette, instead of open reel tape. A few years later Sony introduced Betamax, the first successful consumer VCR format. But when the dust settled, VHS was victorious in the first consumer video format war. Betamax is now almost extinct in the United States, though today's camcorder purchasers now have seven other tape formats to choose from: VHS, S-VHS, VHS-C, S-VHS-C, 8mm, Hi8, and MiniDV.

Before agreeing on the MiniDV format, a fierce format war lasting over twenty years was fought between Sony and JVC—Japanese rivals who have competed to receive lucrative licensing fees for videocassette formats.

It started in the mid 1970s, when Sony fought an expensive lawsuit because the American movie industry claimed that VCRs violate copyrights. Sony battled Hollywood all the way to the Supreme Court, and won, but meanwhile JVC was stomping Sony in the marketplace, and winning. Sony introduced an improved "SuperBeta" format featuring better picture detail, but the popularity of JVC's VHS with video rental stores reached landslide proportions.

By the mid 1980s, Sony concentrated their energies on a new camcorder videocassette format: 8mm. The name evokes memories of 8mm and Super-8 home movies.

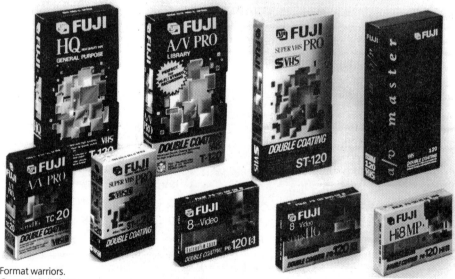

Format warriors.
Courtesy Fuji Photo
Film USA

The advantage of 8mm is size: 8mm videocassettes are about a sixth as big as VHS videocassettes, yet can hold the same two hours of video with equal picture quality. Sony's Handycams made camcorders truly portable, and suitable for casual use.

JVC's defense: a "compact" 20-minute "VHS-C" videocassette that could be played on a home VCR, using an adaptor. (8mm videocassettes cannot be played on regular VCRs—the camcorder must be connected to the television for playback.)

JVC also offered improved picture quality with "Super-VHS" and mini-sized "S-VHS-C" equipment that increases horizontal picture detail—from 240-lines to 400-lines. (Remember, vertical resolution is identical for all formats.) S-VHS became the premium camcorder format; and S-VHS VCRs offer the best quality for off-the-air taping.

Sony then countered with Hi8—an improved version of 8mm that is equal to Super-VHS in picture quality. (Sony also managed to resuscitate Betamax with a technically superb, albeit expensive "ED-Beta" format. There are some videophiles who swear by ED-Beta, but it is so obscure that it's hard to find camcorder and editing equipment.)

Finally, in 1995 Sony, Panasonic, and JVC introduced camcorders in the MiniDV format, apparently settling the format wars for the foreseeable future – at least as far as the serious semipro producer is concerned. But MiniDV costs considerably more than the other formats.

Beyond the technicalities of each format, note that the availability of a remote control jack play a large part in determining what editing capabilities can be achieved with a particular piece of equipment. The next several chapters describe these points in detail. But first, here's an overview of the pro's and cons of each of the available low budget camcorder videocassette formats.

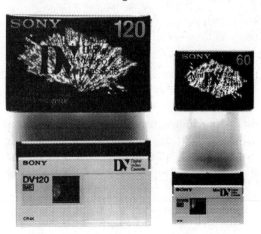

The full size DV cassette, on left, holds up to 270 minutes. MiniDV camcorder format, on right, is smaller than 8mm cassette and holds 60 minutes of digital video. Courtesy of Sony.

Quick Comparison of Videocassette Formats

Here's a quick rundown of the pros and cons of each of the low-budget camcorder videocassette formats:

VHS

• **Advantages:** Uses same tape as most VCRs. 2-hour recording time on inexpensive $3 tapes. Camcorder can play rented movies, too. Fancier models have flying erase heads, and allow separate audio and video editing. Less expensive.

• **Disadvantages:** Bigger size, horizontal resolution of about 240-lines. Remote edit "mini-jack" not as good as LANC/ Control-L.

8mm

• **Advantages:** Very compact size. 2-hour recording time on $4 tapes. Hi-Fi "AFM" mono sound is standard; stereo on some models. Flying erase head assures smooth editing on all models; some also have LANC remote edit jack. Less expensive.

• **Disadvantages:** Tapes must be copied to play on home VCRs (but can be played directly from the camcorder). Horizontal resolution about 240. Cannot edit audio and video separately (except with "PCM" sound, as explained later).

Super-VHS

• **Advantages:** High-resolution, more finely detailed pictures with horiz. res about 400- lines. 2-hour recording time on tapes costing $8 to $15. Some models allow separate audio and video editing. Doubles as VHS camcorder.

• **Disadvantages:** Large size (same as VHS). Tapes must be copied to play on most home VCRs (but can play on camcorder or S-VHS VCRs). Remote "mini-jack" not as good as "5-pin" type. More expensive.

Hi8

• **Advantages:** High-resolution pictures with horiz. res. about 400-lines. Compact size (same as 8mm). 2-hour recording on $6 to $20 tapes. Flying erase head is standard. LANC/Control-L edit control jack on some models. Hi-Fi "AFM" mono sound is standard; stereo on most newer models. Doubles as 8mm camcorder.

• **Disadvantages:** Tapes must be copied for home VCRs. Cannot edit audio and video separately. More expensive.

MiniDV

• **Advantages:** Best picture quality with highest resolution (500-lines), highest signal-to-noise ratio, and extremely compact cassette size. Digital dubbing on some models permits editing with no generation loss. Flexible, excellent sound tracks. Audio/video dubbing on some models.

• **Disadvantages:** Tapes cost about $15 to $25 each; must usually be copied for playback on home VCRs. Most expensive.

VHS-C

• **Advantages:** Compact size. Tapes can be played directly on home VCRs using an adaptor. Some models have audio/video dubbing. Inexpensive.

• **Disadvantages:** 20-minute recording time (1-hour at inferior quality "EP" speed) on tapes costing about $4 each. 240-line resolution.

S-VHS-C

• **Advantages:** High resolution picture (400-lines), compact size (same as VHS-C) Audio/video dubbing and hi-fi sound on some models.

• **Disadvantages:** 20-minute recording time. Tapes cost about $6 each; must usually be copied for home VCRs. More expensive.

ED-Beta

• **Advantages:** 500-line horizontal resolution. Professional features. Hi-fi sound.
• **Disadvantages:** Very expensive. Tapes must be copied for home VCRs. Questionable future of Betamax format – ED-Beta is all but extinct.

. . . .

Tape Brands

Is there a difference in blank tapes? The short answer is yes, but differences are subtle among major brands, and off-brands should be avoided always. Stick with Japanese and American manufacturers for the best quality—Scotch, TDK, Maxell, and Fuji.

But within brands and tape types, differences between standard grade and high grade variations can be dubious. Walk into any well-stocked store to buy blank videocassettes, and you'll be confronted with a dizzying selection of brands, grades, and prices.

In some respects, a VCR is like an automobile: You have to feed it fuel—blank tape—of which there are dozens of nearly identical choices, all suitable for your VCR, whether it's a Rolls or a Neon.

Unlike premium gasoline, which costs 10% to 30% more than regular, premium grades of blank videocassettes can sell for three or four times what standard grade tapes cost. Are blank tapes any more different from each other than gasoline formulations? Can you really perceive any improvement by switching from a standard grade to premium?

"The makers of good tape are finding it harder and harder to differentiate between the tapes," says Dick Skare, Technical Services Engineer for 3M Magnetic Media Division, makers of Scotch brand tapes, who I once contacted for a magazine article I was writing about blank tapes. "If you've been hearing stories or rumors about one tape, within a brand, not being necessarily better than another one, there's a grain of truth to it."

Over a decade ago, when Consumer Reports magazine published one of their first detailed studies of blank videocassettes in November 1986, they found only minor differences between practically all the brand name tapes they tested. Most startling of all, they found that in some cases, lower grade tapes actually outperformed higher grades!

Three premium grades of TDK tapes—"E-HG Super Avilyn", "Extra High Grade Hi-Fi Super Avilyn", and "HD Pro Super Avilyn"—were all rated within a hair of each other, and the cheapest (E-HG) rated the best. Scotch's lowest-priced "EG" tape, which sells for $3 to $5 on the street, outperformed the higher-priced "EG+" tape, and was equal to Scotch's "EXG Camera" tape ($8 to $10). "Sometimes, the only thing higher about a higher-grade tape is its price," said the magazine.

"We took issue with the Consumer Reports tests," said Skare. "They're not specialists in the subtleties of tape testing." Scotch's different grades are created by the company's own testing of production lots, sorting the tapes into grades after they're made. "Sometimes when we've made "EG+", we have more tape than we have orders for, so we'll put it in an "EG" box," Skare said, explaining what may have happened in the magazine's test samples.

Hype is rampant in the marketing of blank tapes. Which grade is best: "Super", "Pro", "High-Grade", "Premium", or "Extra Quality"? The superlative names are meaningless. Special tape labels make appeals to various upscale consumers—such as camcorder owners and hi-fi buffs—but these tapes don't necessarily perform any better than their cheaper cousins.

In some cases, the only claimed advantage is the packaging. Scotch's "EXG Camera" tape—list price, $12.69—is marketed for use in video camcorders, and has the same tape formulation as the $9.99 list priced "EXG" tape. The differences, according to Scotch: "EXG Camera" has anti-static treatment to keep dust and debris from sticking to the tape, it comes in a plastic box to keep dirt out ("EXG" is packaged in a plastic sleeve), and the hubs inside the cassette are colored bright red to help prevent accidental erasures.

What to Look for in a Blank Tape

"Dropouts" are the most visible difference between blank tapes. During playback, they appear as short horizontal streaks of missing picture information, occurring for just a fraction of a second. They're caused by microscopic magnetic particles dropping off of the tape surface.

A study once published by the now defunct Video Review magazine found Scotch's lowest-priced "EG" tape had more dropouts than any of Scotch's higher grades; but a similar test commissioned by Video magazine, published around the same time, found just the opposite: "EG" had *fewer* dropouts than five of Scotch's higher priced tapes. And Consumer Reports gave all Scotch tapes the same excellent rating for dropouts. Thus, sample to sample differences, or test procedures, may be more significant than any real differences between grades.

Numerous tapes are designated as "Hi-Fi", but in fact, most experts agree that if you own a Hi-Fi VCR (they cost $400 and up) *any* blank tape you use will give you truly superb audio quality (better, in fact, than any cassette deck), and "Hi-Fi" grades are indistinguishable from standard grade tapes.

Only with less expensive (non Hi-Fi) VCRs, costing $200 - $500, can very slight differences between blank tapes be heard. Even then, there is no certain correlation between tapes designated as "Hi-Fi" and their audio performance. One study found BASF's "Chrome SHG Hi-Fi" tape to actually have lower fidelity than BASF's two cheaper grades!

"Super-VHS" recording system offers noticeably better picture detail, but at a steep $700 - $1200 price for the VCRs. It also requires a higher-priced tape ($8 - $15) with extremely fine magnetic particles. In this case there's no hype: it's impossible to make a decent Super-VHS recording using regular VHS tape. But the word "Super" on a tape package does *not* mean that it's Super-VHS. Some manufacturers use "Super" to label their *lowest* grade of tape! Only the official S-VHS logo (a frilly S on the left of a standard VHS logo) identifies true Super-VHS tapes.

The same is true for Hi8: You must purchase specially designated Hi8 tapes. If you put a regular 8mm tape in your Hi8 camcorder you'll get a regular 8mm recording—the camcorder automatically switches according to the tape type. With Hi8, however, there are two different formulations available: MP and ME. Metal Particle costs about a third to half less than Metal Evaporated, but there is a slight difference in quality. ME has fewer dropouts and tends to stand up better in editing.

Recommendations

For use in regular (not Super) VCRs, the lowest priced name brand tape is probably your best bet. Consumer Reports once found Scotch's "EG" performed a bit better than other standard grade tapes. Runners-up included Fuji "Beridox", TDK "HS", Maxell "EX", and the paradoxically named Panasonic "Premium Standard".

If you care enough about picture quality to spend extra for blank tape, buy a Super-VHS camcorder or VCR. Any advantage of using fancy tape with a regular VCR is minimal. For good audio, buy a Hi-Fi VCR, and ignore all blank tape claims.

Absolutely avoid so-called "unlicensed" tapes of unfamiliar brands. Some can actually damage your VCR. Since they usually cost just a few cents less than the cheapest name brand videocassettes, it's silly to risk using them.

Want to experiment? Try this: Buy two tapes—the least and most expensive made by Scotch, TDK, Fuji, or Maxell. Record the exact same program on both, and play back a short portion of each twenty times to see how it endures repeated viewings. Then try copying each to another tape, and look at the copies. If the two recordings don't appear different to you, save your money. Dressing a VCR in an emperor's clothes can be costly.

But for camcorder originals, it pays to splurge. If you're shooting in Hi8 and it's a serious project (however you define that), spring for the higher priced ME (Metal Evaporated) tapes, rather than the cheaper MP (Metal Particle) tapes that have more drop-

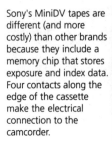

Sony's MiniDV tapes are different (and more costly) than other brands because they include a memory chip that stores exposure and index data. Four contacts along the edge of the cassette make the electrical connection to the camcorder.

outs. With Super-VHS and S-VHS-C, there's only one grade of tape available, making life surprisingly simple.

With MiniDV, there are currently two types of cassettes available: The ones from Sony cost more, and incorporate a built-in chip that keeps track of index information. Other brands, including Panasonic, lack this chip and cost less. The chip makes no difference in picture or sound quality – it's simply a convenience for locating segments during playback.

The Nitty Gritty of the Formats

In this book, we're concerned primarily with ten tape formats, divided into four families – VHS, 8mm, MiniDV, and 3/4". These are today's low budget formats. The next several chapters examine these families, and the variations within each, in detail.

25 years of videocassette evolution. From left to right: 3/4", Super-VHS, Hi8, VHS-C, and MiniDV. The smallest cassette, on the right, records for the same amount of time as the one on the left (60 minutes) and has vastly superior picture and sound quality.

10 The VHS Family: VHS, Super-VHS, VHS-C, S-VHS-C

There are four variations of the VHS format, offering compact size mini-cassettes for camcorder use and 400-line resolution for top notch picture quality. Of the four variations, full size Super-VHS offers the best overall quality, but any of these formats can be used in low budget video.

All of the VHS variations record onto the tape similarly, so we will treat them all as one family of equipment in this discussion. But note that the higher quality S-VHS format requires a higher quality tape formulation, and records the helical tracks using higher speed (frequency) signals. (Most older VHS format VCRs cannot play these S-VHS recordings at all, but some newer VHS models offer "quasi-S-VHS"playback—providing a clear picture, but at reduced resolution.)

Control Track
Helical Video (and Hi-Fi Audio)
Linear Audio (stereo shown)

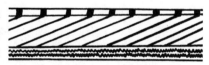

Video Track

The helical video track on VHS-family tapes takes up the lion's share of the tape surface (see diagram). A minimum of two rotary heads are required to record and playback these tracks, because the tape is only wrapped half way around the head drum—the heads take turns, alternating which one is recording or playing back each successive track.

In addition to the helical video tracks, several other tracks also exist on VHS-family tapes:

Audio

The VHS format family offers three different sets of audio tracks—linear, Hi-fi, and a long ago announced but still unmarketed digital. But most VCRs and camcorders only offer linear and hi-fi, or just linear.

Linear Track(s)

The linear audio track is the most universal—it is found on every VHS format piece of equipment. It is usually monaural (one channel), although some older consumer VCRs and many industrial VCRs offer stereo (two channel) linear audio. Each of these stereo tracks is simply half the width of the mono track, so compatibility is maintained.

The linear track is recorded as a straight line along one edge of the tape (see diagram) Most VCRs can erase and record over this track without changing the video track—a process that is called "audio dubbing."

Technically, the quality of the linear track(s) ranges from mediocre to poor. At the SP speed, frequency response, at best is from about 100 to 12,000 Hz within a plus or minus 3-dB range. This is comparable to an inexpensive audio cassette deck using standard tape. The audio S/N ratio is around 40 to 45-dB, again similar to an inexpensive cassette deck. But at the slower EP speed, the frequency response drops down dramatically—the range is limited to 100 to 5,000 Hz—barely better than a telephone line. (EP speed should not be used for serious tape production and editing anyway, because video quality is also reduced.)

Hi-fi Tracks

Many consumer VCRs, and a few camcorder models offer VHS Hi-fi tracks in addition to the linear tracks. The Hi-fi tracks are always in stereo (two channel), and have excellent audio quality. Frequency response is typically from 20–20,000 Hz plus or minus 3-dB. The S/N ratio is typically around 80-dB. These numbers are better than the best audio cassette decks, and approach compact discs in quality.

The VHS Hi-fi tracks are recorded helically, just like the video signal, in the exact same area of the tape where the video gets recorded. In order to see them properly in our diagram, you'd really need a three dimensional view—because the Hi-fi audio gets recorded at a different depth in the tape. The technique is called depth modulation, and in practice it can be a bit finicky—VCRs sometimes require that a tape play for several seconds before sensing the Hi-fi tracks. A pair of separate heads spinning within the head drum are used to record and playback the Hi-fi tracks.

If the Hi-fi audio signal is recorded at too high a level, it can interfere with the video signal, creating video disturbances. Because Hi-fi and video tracks are recorded in the same area of the tape, the hi-fi tracks also reduce the video S/N ratio slightly. For these reasons, the fancier industrial VCRs often have a switch to turn off the Hi-fi recording process.

Practically all prerecorded movies in the VHS format (for rental or sale) have Hi-fi audio tracks, which is why Hi-fi is a popular feature on VCRs. The Hi-fi tracks can be useful for editing, but it takes a bit of planning and ingenuity to utilize them fully, as explained in the section on editing. The problem is that with most VCRs, you must record the video signal and both of the Hi-fi tracks at the same time. You can't go back and change one without the other. Thus, it is not possible to do audio dubbing, as with linear track recording.

PCM Audio

The VHS format may offer additional audio tracks that take the form of "PCM" digital audio (pulse code modulation). Like VHS Hi-fi, these tracks are also recorded through depth modulation, but the recorded signal more resembles the 8mm format's PCM audio tracks (see below). The full technical specifications were not yet released at the time this book went to press.

Control Track

The VHS format, as well as all other videotape format *except* for 8mm and Hi8, also has a "control track" that runs along one edge of the tape (like the linear audio track). On the control track a control head records a series of rapid pulses that tell the spinning video heads where to find the beginning of each helical track. The control track is like an electronic version of the sprocket holes found along the edges of movie film—it tells the equipment where to find the beginning of each new field.

As we'll see in a moment, the newer 8mm videocassette format requires no control track, because auto-tracking electronic circuitry can automatically advance or retard the tape so that the video heads spin accurately across the center of each helical track.

. . . .

VHS Index/Address Track

Newer equipment in the VHS format incorporates an "index/address track". Actually, this is a way of encoding digital information into the control track. The system, called VIASS (VHS Index/Address Search System) encompasses two different levels of capability —the simpler address system lets users "mark" up to twenty different points on a tape. The more sophisticated index system allows users to record a unique code number at up to one thousand different points along a tape.

Many VHS and Super-VHS camcorders automatically record an address track signal each time the camcorder begins recording, to make it easy to find the beginning of each new recorded segment during playback. Many high-end VCRs also have this feature, making it easier to find the beginnings of programs that have been recorded.

Although the index number system at first sounds like a great method to locate points on a tape for editing, it has some severe drawbacks: First, there is no way for external edit control equipment to receive the index/address information, so the utility of VIASS is basically limited to whatever capability is built into the VCR or camcorder that can read the electronic code. Additionally, there are limitations to how closely you can space two consecutive index points, making it difficult to index during short duration (tight) editing.

11 The 8mm Family: Hi8 and 8mm

The 8mm format is technically different from all video formats that have preceded it in that it is the first tape to utilize all-helical recording (see diagram). Earlier formats, including VHS, divide the width of the tape into numerous sections, with helical video in the center, and linear audio and control tracks occupying space along the edges. Part of 8mm's ability to pack the same amount of electronic information into a much smaller space (two hours of recording in less space than the VHS-C format's thirty-minute cassette) comes from eliminating all the linear tracks. (There is space reserved for a single linear track, but it hasn't been used in current models of equipment). 8mm also benefits from newer metal particle tape formulation technology. Also, a digital auto-tracking system finds the center of each helical track, so that the spinning heads don't read between the tracks.

Each swipe of the rotary heads can record and playback a variety of information—and (perhaps the most marvelous capability of all)—in fancier 8mm equipment the heads can actually switch from play to record as they swipe across the tape—to add time code or PCM audio while leaving the original video and AFM audio intact.

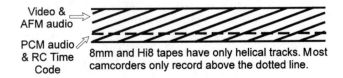

Video & AFM audio

PCM audio & RC Time Code

8mm and Hi8 tapes have only helical tracks. Most camcorders only record above the dotted line.

Video Track

As with the VHS format, 8mm's video track takes up most of the tape. But the video signal occupies a discrete portion of the helical tracks—not the whole thing (see diagram) The recording process is similar to VHS—each helical track holds just one field, or half a frame, of video information; the two heads are alternately recording or playing back these tracks, so that the tape need only be wrapped halfway (180-degrees) around the head drum. With

8mm, the size of these tracks is smaller than VHS, thanks to more dense metal particle tape formulations and smaller heads. The Hi8 format, like Super- VHS, requires an even finer tape formulation than the standard- quality 8mm format.

. . . .

Audio

8mm and Hi8 equipment offer two different audio recording and playback systems—AFM and PCM. Each offers very high quality audio fidelity, but the editing flexibility with 8mm's standard AFM track is more limited than with VHS's standard audio track.

AFM Track(s)

The system for recording audio frequency modulation (AFM) is technically similar to FM radio. The audio signal modulates, or changes, the frequency of a much higher radio frequency. Instead of broadcasting this radio frequency, the camcorder mixes it in along with the video signal and records it on the exact same helical tracks as the video signal.

Technically, the advantage of AFM is that it has excellent frequency response and low noise, thanks to the superior helical recording process. On the down side, the AFM audio is inextricably married to the video signal—you can never change one without also changing the other. You must edit material onto another tape to change the picture or sound —it is therefore impossible to perform an "audio dub" with an AFM track.

Most older 8mm and Hi8 camcorders have monaural AFM audio; while newer models have AFM stereo. Although the quality of AFM stereo is quite good, unfortunately the separation between the left and right channels is not nearly as good as with the VHS Hi- fi stereo tracks (or 8mm PCM, discussed next). This is ordinarily not a problem for normal stereo recording, but makes it impossible to use the tracks for entirely different purposes—such as normal audio on the left and time code on the right, or English on the left and Spanish on the right.

The bleed-through between the left and right channels stems from the way AFM stereo gets recorded. To maintain compatibility between stereo and mono equipment, AFM stereo camcorders record a monaural AFM track, and a second "stereo difference track" that contains the mathematical subtraction of the left and right signals (L minus R). On playback, if this stereo difference signal is sensed, the camcorder (or 8mm format VCR) introduces special circuitry to derive the left and right channels from the two signals (L+R and L-R). This is the same system used for stereo FM radio.

PCM Tracks

Most 8mm/Hi8 VCRs, and a few of the top camcorder models offer additional audio capability in the form of digitally encoded PCM audio tracks. PCM stands for pulse code modulation—technically, this acronym stands for one of several methods by which digital information can be encoded into another medium as pure numbers—that is, it is a way to record numbers onto magnetic tape. The PCM tracks employ only a very simple method of data compression, and have only a limited amount of tape surface area to record data, resulting in quality that is not quite as good as that from Compact Discs.

(Technically speaking, 8mm's PCM recording system records 8-bit samples at a rate of 32,000 samples per second. This results in frequency response limited to about 15-kHz—not quite as high as the 20-kHz top end of ideal human hearing—but nevertheless quite good, and certainly superior to the VHS linear track.)

The most remarkable thing about the PCM audio tracks is that you can record them after the video and AFM tracks have already been recorded—you can use them to do an "audio dub." As the spinning rotary heads swipe along the surface of the tape, they switch from play to record as they pass from the video to the PCM area of the tape.

When you perform this audio dub function using most consumer equipment, the bottom of the picture temporarily disappears, hiding the switch over point. However, upon subsequent playback the bottom of the picture reappears. Repeated PCM recordings on the same tape can damage the bottom of the picture, according to reports from some users, due to the delicate nature of this play/record switchover process.

Sony's CCD-VX3 3-chip Hi8 camcorder. Prior to MiniDV it was the reigning champ of low budget production.

PCM audio is always in stereo, and the two channels are recorded as completely different sets of numbers, resulting in excellent stereo separation between the tracks.

Unfortunately, however, most consumer VCRs and camcorders that offer PCM audio make it very difficult to get full control over the combined power of the PCM and AFM tracks, because they are not available from separate output jacks, you must use one or the other.

8mm Time Code Track (RC and Industrial)

The 8mm/Hi8 format also includes space along each helical track for time code information, to identify each frame of the tape for precise editing. There are two different, incompatible time code systems—an industrial format and a consumer format. Time code recorded with one system cannot be read by the other system, according to Sony, although they make an industrial deck that can read both (the 9850).

The consumer time code system is called RC time code—for rewriteable consumer (also referred to as RCTC - pronounced "arctic.") Like PCM audio tracks, the RC time code is recorded along a short section of each helical track, and the heads can switch from play to record during each swipe. Thus, the time code can be added to a tape after it has already been recorded—a major benefit for people who wish to edit tapes they've already shot.

The information from the RC time code track is available to sophisticated edit controllers, including all FutureVideo models, through the LANC remote control jack. This means that even the non-SMPTE time code versions of certain models of FutureVideo's editing equipment can benefit from having an RC time code camcorder as part of the editing system. But the RC time code information cannot be copied on to another tape—a problem if you want to use "workprints" for editing (see below).

12   The DV and MiniDV Format

The introduction of the Digital Video Cassette (DVC) and MiniDV tape format in 1995 was the most exciting thing to happen to the world of low budget video production in years. This new camcorder format truly brings, once and for all, the quality and editing capabilities of professional video equipment to the consumer. It has better resolution and less noise than several pro formats. Because it's digital you can make perfect copies, and edit without worrying about generation loss.

While adding yet another choice to the crowded existing field of six popular camcorder tape formats (8mm, VHS-C, full-size VHS, Hi8, S-VHS-C, and Super-VHS), the DV cassette also promises to finally put an end to the camcorder format war of the past decade. In fact, the first two of some 55 manufacturers to introduce products using this new format — Sony and Panasonic — have been arch-rivals of the format wars, with Sony pushing 8mm and Panasonic pushing VHS-C (though Panasonic's parent, Matsushita, has quietly made 8mm as well as VHS-C units for other brand names.)

The First Models

Make no mistake about it: At least initially, the DV cassette format will not be slugging it out for dominance in the $500 camcorder category. The DV cassette is a high-end product, competing with the Hi8 and Super-VHS formats for the pro-sumer market — for the serious enthusiast, wedding videographer, film student, public access producer, etc.

Sony DCR-VX1000

The first wave of MiniDV camcorders included two semi-pro models from Sony and Panasonic, a James Bond inspired ultraminiature model from JVC, and a Viewcam model from Sharp. Prices range upwards from about two thousand to over four thousand dollars. Several models, including the Sony DCR-VX1000, the Panasonic PV-DV1000, and Sharp's VL-D5000U — have three image sensor chips, similar to

Panasonic PV-DV1000

Sony's old CCD-VX3 model. Three-chips are considered de rigueur for all professional video cameras, because they provide better picture detail and less picture noise. But most consumer models have just one image sensor chip. Sony's lower priced DCR-VX700 is a one-chip offering, as is GR-DV1 spycam model from JVC (also marketed under RCA's brand name).

The hour-long MiniDV camcorder tapes cost about fifteen to twenty-five dollars each. Sony's version of the tapes include a memory chip that provides indexing features to locate segments on a tape; while other brands don't have this chip and cost less (the chip only gets activated in Sony camcorders). A larger size DV cassette for VCR use holds up to 270-minutes.

Technically, these camcorders offer images that are much better than anything to date — with horizontal resolution of 500-lines, and video signal-to-noise ratio of 56-dB, which is on par with and even superior to some of today's professional formats (including Beta SP, MII, and the old 1" Type C formats), and much better than the 45-dB S/N ratio and 400-line resolution of Hi8 and Super-VHS equipment.

Editing Nirvana

Like all digital media, the DV format has the ability to make copies with virtually no signal degradation. Which means that for video editing, a kind of blissful nirvana has finally been reached.

For years, the problem known as generation loss has plagued video editing. Recall that unlike film, videotape can't be spliced, so all videotape editing takes place through selective copying. But with analog formats, each copy of a tape has a noticeably degraded image. The reason why you need to go down several generations is because as your editing plan evolves you begin to see additional changes and refinements — this is what professional editors call going from a rough cut to a fine cut.

With analog tape formats, going beyond about four or five generations of copies meant making the picture unviewable, so all forms of elaborate editing equipment has been devised to create edit decision lists and off-line/on-line systems that ultimately have one goal: After all the creative decision-making is over, you go back to the original tapes and edit from them, so that the edited master consists of second-generation copies.

With DV's digital dubbing capability, those machinations are now unnecessary. If you edit a sequence together, and then see a few seconds you'd like to trim away, you can just make a copy of the entire tape, minus those few seconds. And you can do this again and again. With professional digital video formats, somewhere between about fifty and one hundred generations are generally considered acceptable — very minor problems from tape dropouts do accumulate, so you can't copy infinitely.

Solid and Stable

Another big technical improvement comes in the timing stability of the video signal. A video image consists of a series of scan lines stacked one on top of another. (As discussed previously, in the standard American NTSC video system there are 525 scan lines in each frame, of which 490 are actually used to form the picture.) But minor timing errors creep into most recordings with consumer camcorders, resulting in scan lines that don't stack up absolutely perfectly when the tape is played back. Just record a picture of a straight vertical line, such as a lamppost or flagpole, and look closely at it on playback (preferably on a big-screen TV) to see the problem. Professional analog video recorders always incorporate a digital memory system called a time base corrector, or TBC, to correct this problem.

But since DV cassette recordings are digital in the first place, there's no need for a TBC, and the recordings appear rock solid, with absolutely no wavering in the picture.

This also means you can use DV cassettes to play directly into digital video computer devices — such as the Video Toaster, or non-linear video editing systems — without the need for a TBC. (Though with a Toaster you'll still need a TBC to feed two DV tapes in simultaneously for image mixing.)

Audio Flexibility

The audio tracks on the DV cassette are digital too. The format actually provides for two systems of audio recording: For highest recording quality, the audio tracks are configured as a two-channel stereo system with CD-quality recording — 44,100 samples per second, with 16-bit quantizing. But for more flexibility and greater editing capability, you can also configure the audio as two sets of stereo tracks (four channels, total) with slightly inferior, though still very good quality — 32,000 samples per second, with 12-bit quantizing. (The "raw" signal-to-noise ratio of 12-bit audio is 72-

dB, but the format uses a non-linear quantizing scheme, similar to the PCM tracks in 8mm, to boost S/N ratio to 96-dB.)

The advantage of the four-track configuration is that you can record original sound with the video, and then dub in additional music, narration, or sound effects on the other two tracks, and then mix it all together. (Note that the four tracks must be recorded two at a time — in stereo pairs, and that only the first pair can be recorded at the same time as the picture.)

Taking advantage of this audio dubbing capability may require an editing VCR (exception: Panasonic's PV-DV1000, which has built-in audio dubbing). The DV format also facilitates insert video editing — letting you leave the original sound, while recording new pictures. Although VHS and Super-VHS have had this capability for years, it only works with the lower quality linear track — not the Hi-Fi tracks. So the DV format is the perfect medium for garage bands to produce their own low budget music videos (and in particular, Panasonic's PV-DV1000, which, through insert video editing, lets you do it all using in-camera editing techniques.)

Firewire connector, located in lower right corner on the back of Sony DCR-VX1000 camcorder, is labelled, "DV IN/OUT."

Firewire Connection

To do digital dubbing, for post-production editing, you need a digital input/output connector. Among the early MiniDV camcorder entries, only Sony's models include this crucial connection. A tiny jack labelled "DV In/Out" on the back of Sony's camcorder models represents what is arguably the most powerful connector ever put on a camcorder. This single jack, which has been nicknamed the "firewire" connection, is a super high speed two-way serial port. It carries video, audio, time code, and control information in either direction. Just connect the jack on one camcorder to another, and you can dub in either direction (the camcorders automatically know which way the information should go, depending on whether you press the play or record buttons.)

In effect, the Sony camcorders (and VCR) offer two different systems of machine control: the firewire connector, which also carries video and audio, and the LANC connector, which can be hooked up to many existing edit controllers.

At least initially other MiniDV camcorder manufacturers have omitted the firewire connection – perhaps because the firewire chips, which transfer data at an astounding 25 megabits per second, are too new; or perhaps because of the same copyright issues that delayed introduction of the DV format VCRs. (The movie industry fears there will be rampant piracy – illegal copying of movies – when digital dubbing becomes widely available. A similar conflict between the music industry and electronics manufacturers delayed the introduction of digital audio tape by some three years, back in the 1980s.)

The DV Cassettes

The Digital Video cassette comes in two sizes – the MiniDV cassette, intended for camcorder use, is less than half the size of an 8mm cassette (measuring 66 x 48 x 12mm – that's 2-5/8" x 1-7/8" x 1/2" and holds up to 60 minutes. The standard size DV cassette, for VCR use, is about three times bigger (measuring 125 x 78 x 15mm), or approximately one fourth the size of VHS. It holds up to four and a half hours – thinner tapes may produce even longer recording times in the future.

Besides recording 60-minutes of moving video, DV camcorders also have a special still frame mode. Up to 580 images, individually indexed, can fit on a standard length tape. During slide-show style playback, each still frame lasts for about 6 seconds.

	Dimensions (w/d/h: mm)	Recording time (SP mode: min.)	Volume(cm³) (Mini. DV=1)
Mini. DV	66 × 48 × 12.2	60	39 (1.0)
8mm	95 × 62.5 × 15	NTSC: 180 PAL: 120	89 (2.3)
VHS-C	92 × 59 × 23	NTSC: 40 PAL: 45	125 (3.2)
DV	125 × 78 × 14.6	270	142 (3.6)
VHS	188 × 104 × 25	NTSC: 180 PAL: 240	489 (12.5)

The tape is 6.35mm wide. Veteran audio recording buffs may get a kick out of the conversion to English measurements: that's quarter-inch, just like the old open reel and 8-track formats. Though the width may be old-fashioned, the tape technology is certainly the most advanced ever. The tape's magnetic surface is made from double layers of evaporated metal particles, with an over coat of hard carbon to minimize tape wear. This extra protection is needed because of the speed of the head drum, which rotates at 9000 RPM (8mm and VHS heads spin at 1800 RPM).

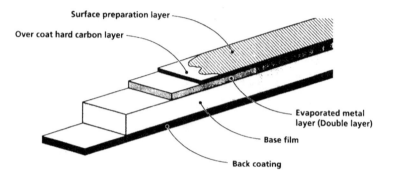

The head itself is smaller too -- just 21.7mm diameter (8mm has 40mm head drums; VHS has 62mm full size). The width of each helical track is just 10-micrometers (VHS track width at SP speed is 58-micrometers, and 8mm is 20.5-micrometers).

		DV	8mm	VHS
Diameter		ø 21.7	ø 40.0	ø 62.0
Relative speed	**NTSC**	Approx. 9.9 m/s	Approx. 3.8 m/s	Approx. 5.8 m/s
	PAL		Approx. 3.1 m/s	Approx. 4.9 m/s
Rotating speed	**NTSC**	9000 rpm	1800 rpm	1800 rpm
	PAL		1500 rpm	1500 rpm
Track pitch		10 µm	20.5 µm (SP)	58.0 µm (SP)

The DV Tracks

Unlike traditional analog videotape, which uses a single helical track to record each field of video (recall that two interlaced fields equals one complete frame), DV uses 10 helical tracks to record each frame. The helical heads are thus spinning at a rate that can record 300 tracks per second (30 frames/sec. x 10 tracks/frame) – it's a two-head system, similar to 8mm (plus a flying erase head), with each track representing 180-degrees of rotation around the head drum. The heads thus spin at 150-revolutions per second, or 9000 revolutions per minute.

Besides recording video information, each helical track includes three other sections – one for audio information (immediately following the video), and two sub-code sections at the very top and bottom of each track, which provide tracking signal, time code data, Index ID, and still-picture ID codes. (That's for American NTSC video which runs at 30 frame/second; with European PAL video, which runs at 25 frames/second there are 12 helical tracks per frame.) Each helical track thus contains some 2.5 million bits of data – in a track that's roughly one tenth the width of a human hair!

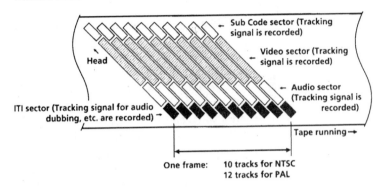

Sub Code sector (Tracking signal is recorded)

Video sector (Tracking signal is recorded)

Head

Audio sector (Tracking signal is recorded)

ITI sector (Tracking signal for audio dubbing, etc. are recorded)

Tape running →

One frame: 10 tracks for NTSC
            12 tracks for PAL

The total amount of data that can be recorded on this tape is astonishing – the digital bitstream rate is 25 million bits per second. Nevertheless, that's not nearly enough to record a "raw" digital video signal, which requires about 160 million bits per second for a broadcast-quality TV signal.

DV's Data Compression

Digital video data compression makes this new format possible. DV compresses the video data by a 5:1 ratio, after lopping off the very top and bottom of the picture (the unseen scan lines). The compression system is based on the same DCT (Discrete Cosine Transform) still-frame image conversion process that's used in JPEG still photography compression. All data compression is based on eliminating repeated information. But DCT is fundamentally different from MPEG (as used in DSS satellite TV) in that each frame contains complete information for that frame. With MPEG, about 15 frames of tape prior to a selected frame need to be played, because the compression is based on change from frame to frame. This has greater efficiency (the MPEG data stream is just 1 to 4 megabits per second), but makes video editing cumbersome.

From the lens to the image sensor, everything in a MiniDV camcorder is essentially the same as with traditional analog camcorders. But after the image sensor, the digital processing and recording kicks in. The RGB information from the image sensor(s) is first converted into YUV information, which can be more efficient than RGB, because of well-established research showing that the human eye is far less perceptive of color detail than black and white. All digital VCR systems, including DV, provide a more detailed black and white image, accompanied by a more coarse color signal – that's what the ratios of 4:2:2 (found in pro digital formats) and 4:1:1 (as in DV) are all about.

Those numbers represent sampling rates, but in a roundabout way. They're roughly multiples of the color subcarrier frequency, which is 3.58 MHz. The three component signals – Y (luminance), Y-R and Y-B (R is red, B is blue – these are called the color difference signals, also known as U and V), are thus sampled at different rates. In the sampling process, each analog signal – basically a voltage representing relative brightness or color value at that point – is converted into an 8-bit digital signal by an A/D (analog to digital) converter, similar to the way digital audio gets recorded (8-bits of binary information produces 256 different value levels – with the three 8-bit factors, there are 16.7 million different color possibilities). The digitized picture information next moves onto the DCT compression chip, which takes in a frame's worth of information (consisting of some 450,000 samples of data, or roughly 5.4-megabits of information) and compresses it by a 5:1 ratio. This compressed data next gets error correction bits added (to catch tape dropouts and other errors that may occur), and gets recorded onto the DV tape.

Signal		Sampling frequency	Remarks
Y signal		13.5MHz	H : Over 500 lines
R-Y and B-Y	NTSC	R-Y : 3.375MHz B-Y : 3.375MHz	Color band width is three times wider than analog VCR's.
	PAL	R-Y or B-Y : 6.75MHz	Color band width is six times wider than analog VCR's.

Comparison With Broadcast Digital Video

Although the picture from DV cassettes appears fantastic, in technical engineering terms there is one noteworthy difference, compared to professional digital video formats. There are currently four main digital video formats used in broadcasting, called D-1, D-2, Digital Betacam, and D-5, the newest format. (Several other formats have come and gone, too — these seem to be the survivors.) The formats vary in physical characteristics — D-1 is the biggest, Digital Betacam the most compact — and they also vary in digital recording technicalities.

The big technical difference between the pro digital formats and DV is all pro formats utilize a 4:2:2 sampling scheme; while DV cassettes utilize 4:1:1 sampling.

As explained earlier, the three numbers refer to multiples of the color subcarrier frequency, which in American NTSC TV is at 3.58-MegaHertz (MHz). Thus, the 4 in 4:1:1 means that the sampling rate is approximately 14.32-million samples per second (4 x 3.58) — that's about three hundred times faster than the standard audio CD sampling rate of 44,100 samples/second. Actually, DV's sampling rate is slightly less than 4x the chroma subcarrier — it s about 13.5-million samples/second, but the ratio gets rounded off.

The difference between pro and consumer digital video is in the second and third numbers, which refer to the three-part YUV method for encoding color signal information. If you're familiar with computers, you're probably already comfortable with the idea of RGB encoded video — that is, breaking the video signal into separate red, green, and blue images. But RGB encoded via requires more data per frame, compared with YUV encoding, because it treats color and black and white equally (in RGB, white and gray are represented as equal levels of all three colors).

YUV Encoding

Broadcast engineers have known for years that human perception of color and black and white information are not equal — our NTSC color-TV broadcast system is based on the idea that you can have a finely detailed black and white image, combined with less detailed color, and it looks very acceptable.

The Y in YUV refers to luminance, which is the technical name for the black and white portion of the video signal. U and V are mathematically derived color components, using a two-dimensional graph to represent most of the colors in the spectrum. (The two color signals are derived by subtracting the luminance, which represents the sum of all three colors, from individual color signals. They re thus referred to as the R minus Y and B minus Y chroma signals.)

The fact that the sampling rates for these chroma signals are half what professional digital video formats use means that, theoretically, DV cassette recordings will have slightly less color detail. In all other respects, the color signal is comparable with professional formats.

For most viewers, this difference is negligible. Even at the sampling rate of 3.58-MHz, the color detail is still better than analog broadcast TV. And for recording black and white video, there's no difference whatsoever (in this case, you get technically rewarded for being arty.)

Data Compression

But in another key respect — data compression — the new DV cassette format pushes the envelope of what broadcasters are already doing. The D-1 and D-2 formats use no compression whatsoever — the tape records the raw digital data stream. Digital Betacam compresses it by a modest 2:1. As mentioned earlier, DV cassettes utilize 5:1 data compression — twice as much as any pro format.

Anyone who has spent anytime viewing the DSS satellite signal, which employs MPEG data compression, knows that the system occasionally exhibits compression artifacts or motion artifacts — in other words, errors in the compression/decompression process. The image may freeze for an instant, or appear in mosaic. This form of picture degradation is very different from traditional video gremlins, like static, wavy lines, ghosts, etc. And it only occurs rarely.

MPEG was deemed an inappropriate compression system for the DV cassette, because it requires the accumulation of information over the course of several frames to decode the signal. Instead, DV cassettes utilize a compression algorithm based on DCT — for Discrete Cosine Transfer. Without getting too into the math of it, the main difference is that each frame stands on its own, with all the information needed to decode that particular frame. This makes it much more suitable for video editing, where you might only want to record a frame or two a time, such as for animation or claymation. (Recall that video in the U.S. runs at 30-frames per second; in most foreign systems it's 25-frames per second).

Determining whether the DCT system is perfect, or slips up occasionally, will require the test of time. As of this edition of the book, I have personally logged several dozen hours of editing with

MiniDV (going between two camcorders), and haven't yet seen an error (except for some obvious camcorder foul-ups where the tape would play fine on another camcorder, indicating that the recording itself was OK.) Certainly there's every reason to believe it should work perfectly — with a bitstream rate of 25-megabits per second, there's a lot more room for data than in the 1 to 4 megabits per second MPEG bitstreams (as used in DSS satellite-TV). DCT is already widely used in professional photography, as part of the JPEG still-picture compression system.

No Generation Loss

Generation loss — deterioration of picture quality with each successive copy — has been the Achilles heel of video editing ever since videotape was introduced back in the 1960s. Professional video began going digital a few years ago, thus solving the problem for big-budget productions. Now, the new Digital Video cassette format — DV — promises to eliminate generation loss problems for video enthusiasts and low budget producers, allowing a practically unlimited number of copies with no deterioration in the image.

In tests conducted for Video magazine shortly after the DV format was introduced in 1995, I (along with Technical Editor Lance Braithwaite) found that twentieth generation copies of DV tapes looked virtually identical to the camera originals. (We copied back and forth between two Sony MiniDV camcorders using Sony's VMC-2DV Firewire dubbing cable.)

As far as home video editing is concerned, this isn't just another improvement — like Hi8 was to 8mm — this is a genuine revolution. Experience with professional digital video formats, which have been around for several years, indicates that you can go one hundred generations with no appreciable loss, and DV appears to perform the same.

I've done some fairly extensive editing between two DV camcorders, and have not yet seen problems arise from "chewing up" a DV tape by repeatedly pausing and rewinding and stopping over the same section of tape, as might happen in a gruelling series of editing sessions. The tape, which is just one-quarter inch wide, does seem fragile however. To be prudent, if you're editing with DV you might first want to run off a copy of the tape as a backup just in case problems arise — this backup will be virtually identical to the original.

DV incorporates its own error correction scheme to compensate for dropouts that inevitably occur in the extemely fine helical tracks. Although ten tracks are required for each frame of video, the compensation system can render a clear image from any eight of these ten tracks.

DV represents a fantastic price breakthrough in video editing. Previously, professional digital video recording equipment has cost upwards of $25,000. DV brings prices down to the consumer ballpark. Two DV camcorders will set you back from $6,000 to $8,000, depending on models selected.

If your idea of editing video is eliminating the worst errors — like the times you left the camcorder running when you thought it was off — then the DV difference may not seem that significant. But for anyone with more ambitious video editing aspirations — such as for making music videos, travelogues, wedding videos, documentaries, public access programs, student films, etc. — DV's digital dub capability is absolutely astounding.

As explained earlier, because of the helical recording process employed in all modern video tape formats — including VHS, S-VHS, 8mm, Hi8, as well as DV — all video tape editing is accomplished through selective copying (dubbing). Edit controllers add sophisticated and precise control over the process, to locate particular points for copying, and select the type of copying to be done (video and audio combined, or separate video insert or audio insert). With all formats that have preceded DV, each successive generation of copies looks noticeably worse than the previous generation. Working in S-VHS or Hi8, a limit of about four or five generations has generally been considered the practical edge of the envelope of what's allowable — using top notch VCRs, blank tape, and time base corrector (TBC) can squeeze perhaps another generation.

Four generations may sound like a lot, but for serious editing it's not. Imagine producing a documentary this way. The "raw footage" is the first generation. You choose your favorite segments from this raw footage — this represents "selected takes" — the second generation. You roughly arrange these takes in the order you want to use them in — this represents your "rough cut", the third generation. Next you trim the beginning and end points of each segment, tightening things up. This represents the "fine cut" — the fourth generation. Finally, you edit in synchronized music, sound effects, narration, and any other audio elements you want, and perform the "final mix". This brings you to the fifth generation, representing your edit master. From this master, you make distribution copies to give out to people — these are sixth generation.

And this scenario hasn't even included the need for revisions — what if, after performing the fine cut editing, you see something that bugs you and want to change it? Add another generation. Professional film editors typically go through a scene dozens if not hundreds of times, constantly evolving from rough to fine cut with each pass.

Prior to DV, elaborate video editing solutions have been devised to get around this generation loss problem. With edit decision list technology (EDL), the edit controller stores the frame numbers for the beginning and end points of each segment in a production. To make revisions without going down another generation, you change the frame numbers in the EDL, and then the edit controller automatically re-performs all the edits for you using first generation tape. With EDL edit controllers, you can keep changing things and changing things, without having to redo all the edits manually. But this process is still very time consuming.

Nonlinear editing systems make editing quicker and more intuitive. You first transfer all the raw video and audio footage into computer data, using a video capture board, and store it on the computer's hard drive. Then software such as Adobe Premiere is used to edit the data. You can rearrange things over and over, with no deterioration in quality, because the images are stored as binary data. The generation loss problem is licked, but with today's computer technology the quality of the digitized image is inferior to tape — with noticeable jerkiness (slow frame rate) and loss of detail — unless you spend upwards of about $15 to $20,000.

With DV, just like with non-linear editing, the video and audio signals are converted to digital data that can be copied over and over with practically no loss. But unlike non-linear systems, DV's compression ratio is so low that the quality of the digitized image is excellent (today's hard disks can't record that much data so quickly). For the cost of two camcorders, or a camcorder and a VCR, you can edit back and forth and back and forth, thus trimming and rearranging things at will, with no concern about losing quality with each generation.

DVC and DVCPro

The DV camcorders all use MiniDV tapes, which hold up to one hour. The larger full-size DV (also called DVC) tapes hold up to 270 minutes, and are intended for use in DV format VCRs.

These two consumer tape cassettes are industry-wide standards that have been agreed to by virtually all camcorder manufacturers. Additionally, Panasonic's industrial video division has gone off on its own and introduced DVCPro. This semi-compatible format uses the same tape, but is much more expensive – the introductory camcorder and VCR models each list for more than $15,000.

Panasonic AG-EZ1. Essentially the same as the consumer PV-DV1000, this model is sold through the industrial division.

In terms of pure picture and sound quality, the specifications for DVCPro are identical to consumer DV.

The technical difference is in the speed of the tape and the width of the tracks. DVCPro runs the tape twice as fast as MiniDV, resulting in more surface area for each bit of information. According to Panasonic, this results in a more reliable recording, less prone to have signal dropouts, especially if you chew the tapes up during editing. It's a good point, but in my view ridiculously overpriced for the difference. (If you're worried about chewing tapes up, just run off absolutely-perfect digital dubs of the camera originals, and edit from the dubs. Save the originals as a backup in the event of catastrophe.)

According to Panasonic, another benefit that will make the DVCPro format superior to consumer DV will be the ability to play and copy tapes at 4x normal speed, thus facilitating fast digital downloads for use with nonlinear editing systems.

Panasonic's first DVCPro format industrial/broadcast camcorder, the AJ-D700, features three higher resolution (410,000 pixels) image sensors (compared with Panasonic's industrial MiniDV model, which is identical to the PV-DV1000), and weighs about 11-pounds, including lens (like all pro camcorders, lenses can be interchanged).

The DVCPro format is semi-compatible with MiniDV in that all DVCPro equipment can playback regular DV / MiniDV tapes, but not the reverse. At first glance the existence of DVCPro may

Panasonic AJ-D750
DVCPro VCR

seem a bit odd, but viewed from the perspective of the format wars between Sony and Matsushita, it makes perfect sense. Sony's broadcast and industrial divisions have enjoyed great success with Digital Betacam, while Panasonic's fledgling D-5 format has not. Panasonic needs a pro digital format, and it's a tribute to how narrow the difference has become between consumer and pro gear that they've turned to DV for inspiration.

HDTV-Ready

DVCPro's double-speed operation, in which a "60-minute" tape lasts just 30-minutes, is actually part of the industry-wide standard for the DV format. It's specified as the speed DV equipment will run at when the tape format is upgraded to handle HDTV (high definition television), with twice the number of scan lines.

With HDTV DV equipment, which is not yet available, everything gets doubled: There will be 20 helical tracks for each frame, recorded at a bitstream rate of 50-megabits/second.

A True Breakthrough

Meanwhile, the DV cassette is unquestionably a fantastic advance in camcorder technology, and video empowerment. Anyone thinking about buying a semi-pro type camcorder should take a serious look at this format. Even with two camcorders you can do a lot of advanced editing, and Sony's first editing VCR affords maximum utilization of all the available features in this format (including insert video and audio dub editing).

This format can put you in a whole new league — you'll be literally rubbing elbows with the pros, at least as far as technical quality is concerned. Yes, the MiniDV format promises to finally eliminate any concerns about camcorder footage not being broadcast quality — consumers will now have equipment that's just about on par with the pro gear. Which means that in the future, content and technique will matter more than format.

If you are a filmmaker, student, wedding videographer, or serious video enthusiast, the new MiniDV cassette format is definitely for you. It may be pricey, at first, but it's well worth it.

13   The ³/₄" U-matic Format

The first edition of this book didn't have any information about the 3/4" format. I foolishly assumed that this quarter century old format would be gone by the time the book got published. But though it's a bit of a dinosaur, ³/₄" is still alive and kicking—especially at college film/video departments, public access facilities, and media centers that got up and running in the 1980s. If you're producing low budget video, you're likely to encounter it.

Historically, the ³/₄" format has done a lot to change the face of television. Introduced by Sony (which holds the patents) back in 1971, the ³/₄" U-matic format was the first successful video cassette format. Prior to ³/₄", videotape always came on open reels, and had to be threaded around complicated tape paths.

Although incredibly clunky by today's standards, ³/₄" was the first portable video format that was deemed good enough for broadcast television (with the aid of a time base corrector, a device that cost upwards of five thousand dollars when it was first introduced). Consequently, by the mid-1970s, most of the TV news business had switched from shooting field news footage in 16mm film, to shooting in ³/₄".

But the low cost of ³/₄" also made it accessible to industrial video users, such as in-house corporate video, libraries, and schools, and to public access centers. The format thus transcended several different budget categories; but because of its inferior technical quality when compared with the costlier 1", and the older 2" professional tape formats (as well as the Betacam and MII formats that followed later), ³/₄" never gained acceptance for use in prime-time network television.

Technically, the original ³/₄" format has horizontal resolution only slightly better than regular VHS and 8mm—about 260-lines (considerably less than the 400-line horizontal resolution of Hi8 and S-VHS). But the format has slightly better signal-to-noise ratio

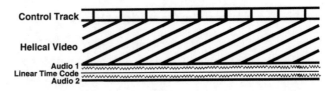

than even the best S-VHS and Hi8 gear, and, as explained below, may offer better audio, too.

In the mid-1980s, an improved "SP" version of ³/4" was introduced, boosting horizontal resolution to about 350-lines. Although ³/4 SP has become common in professional environments that continue to use U-matic, at most media access centers it costs significantly more to work in ³/4 SP, compared with plain old ³/4". (At one college where I've taught, freshmen students got access to regular ³/4", while sophomores got access to ³/4 SP.)

One very noteworthy difference between the higher and lower quality versions of ³/4", compared with the Hi8 / 8mm and Super-VHS / VHS dichotomies, is that tapes recorded with the higher quality ³/4 SP system can be played back on a regular (non SP) ³/4" deck. This total compatibility does not exist with Hi8 and S-VHS.

The tape itself is ³/4" wide, and it runs quite a bit faster than VHS family or 8mm tapes. So there's a lot more tape surface area passing the heads each second. Theoretically, this could produce far superior picture and sound, but the format was practically abandoned by the broadcast world long ago, and doesn't take advantage of the latest tape technology. The closest thing, physically, in the professional arena is the D-2 digital format, which comes in cassettes similar in size and tape width to ³/4". But D-2 is light years ahead in quality, and costs more than just about any other video format, except HDTV.

Theoretically, the comparatively big ³/4" format should also be more durable and hardier than other low budget formats—standing up to excessive wear and tear when locating edit points, for example, without stretching and creating glitches. But that will only be true if the editing equipment is relatively new and well maintained. The format has been around a long time, and there's a lot of funky old equipment out there.

There are two sizes of ³/4" cassettes—this format was the forerunner of the VHS / VHS-C dichotomy. The big ³/4" cassettes fit in the full size (not portable) tape decks, and hold up to one-hour (there's only one speed available). The smaller ³/4" cassettes are required for use in the portable decks. They hold up to 20-minutes, and they also fit in the larger editing-system decks, without the need for any adaptor. Tapes cost from about $12 to $20, depending on size and length.

When To Consider Using ³/4"

There's no such thing as a ³/4" camcorder—the tapes are simply too big to make a one-piece camcorder feasible. All "portable" ³/4" systems are two piece, consisting of a camera, connected by cable to a shoulder-strap dangling battery-operated tape deck. (These systems, and their ½" open-reel predecessors, were commonly referred to as "porta-packs" in the late 60's and early 70's.)

You can buy used ¾" portable systems for about $500 to $2,000 these days, but they're hardly worth it. The cameras almost always use tubes, and these are likely to have burns (permanent spots) in them (check carefully if you're shopping); and the portability just isn't there.

Buying a used ¾" editing system may occasionally represent a good deal, but note that the equipment can require a lot of maintenance (have a technician check the system out, and keep the technician's number handy for service.)

But as I said at the beginning of this chapter, in general you don't want to consider buying ¾" equipment. The reason most low-budget producers end up working in ¾" is because they are renting access to ¾" editing equipment.

There are probably more low-cost ¾" editing systems available for hourly rental, at about $10 to $25 an hour, than any other format. And many schools offer extensive ¾" editing facility access in association with courses in video production. So you may find yourself thinking about editing in ¾" simply because it's available locally.

You should avoid going down a generation just to get access to editing equipment. So if you shot your original footage in Hi8, for example, and you're interested in working in ¾" (sometimes it's the only format a public access channel will accept, and it can have audio advantages), you should look for interformat editing that goes directly from Hi8 to ¾ SP (if you edit onto regular ¾", you'll lose picture resolution).

But then again, if you can get free or very cheap access to ¾" editing, you may find yourself transferring your camera original materials to ¾", trading off picture quality for saving money. (One advantage, if you do this, is that you'll be preserving your camera original tapes—protecting them from getting chewed up in the editing process.)

. . . .

The Audio Advantage

In my view, the main advantage that ¾" now holds over both Hi8 and Super-VHS is in the audio department. Although both Hi8 and Super-VHS both offer audio tracks with superior raw quality (Hi-fi stereo in the case of VHS, and AFM stereo with Hi8), neither of these hi-fi systems has the flexibility to edit picture and sound separately.

For making music videos, the ¾" format can be your best choice. The raw quality of the standard pair of audio tracks on ¾" is not as good as VHS Hi-fi or 8mm AFM, but they're far more flexible to use.

When you edit a music video, you want to first lay down the audio track—with the best quality possible—and then edit in pictures to match (video insert editing). MiniDV is clearly the best format for this, but it's expensive. Hi8 and 8mm don't let you do video insert edits except with the most expensive industrial VCRs (even if you have PCM audio)—they're the worst formats to edit music videos onto. Super-VHS and VHS let you record the linear audio track(s) first, and then insert picture. But even the otherwise stellar Panasonic AG-1980 has just a humble monaural linear audio track—you need fancier industrial models, costing upwards of $3,000 to get stereo audio. And even in stereo, the linear track does not technically match the audio fidelity of the two linear tracks available in $^3/_4$" (the faster tape speed and wider tracks make $^3/_4$" inherently better.)

The difference is not gigantic—the high frequency audio roll off of the linear track on a good Super-VHS deck might be around 12,000 Hz, while on $^3/_4$" it might go up to 15,000 Hz. And the audio signal/noise ratio on $^3/_4$" might be better than VHS linear by just a few decibels too. But hey, for a low budget music video, why not try to get the best audio quality possible? Squeezing the specs is what it's all about.

Some of the newer $^3/_4$" decks include a separate audio track for use with longitudinal SMPTE time code. Depending on your raw material, and the precision your specific project calls for, this feature can be a distinct advantage over Super-VHS. (Most $^3/_4$ SP decks include built in VITC time code.)

. . . .

An Inexpensive, Intermediate Format

A student in a class I taught recently had already shot a music video using a Super-8 film (not video) camera, and wanted to precisely sync it up to the song. She wanted to know which video format to work in. Much as I wished to have a newer, zippier answer for her, when all was said and done I had to recommend $^3/_4$". Since the original footage was film, she could have it transferred to any video format she wanted. And as long as the original format wasn't an issue, the stereo audio advantage and low-priced editing access of $^3/_4$" made sense for this project (DV VCRs were not yet available then).

She could start with a "blackened" video tape (one which has already been formatted, much the way floppy disks are formatted—see "blackburst"), then do an insert-audio edit of the complete song (transferring it from a CD, DAT, or high-quality audio cassette recording), and then insert the short video segments (transferred to ³/₄" from film) to match the song.

When the editing was completed, she could take the ³/₄" edit master to a tape dubbing facility, and run off copies on VHS (with Hi-fi sound). The ³/₄" format thus serves as an intermediate format—as a bridge between the original footage, and the final release copies.

The same approach could also be used if the original footage was shot in Hi8 or Super-VHS, but you'd have to look harder to find interformat editing facilities that go directly from Hi8 (or S-VHS) to ³/₄", at a reasonable hourly rate. Remember: You don't want to go down a generation just to gain access to a particular editing facility.

The slight advantages of ³/₄" only make sense if you'll be renting editing time (but not shooting time), and want to keep the budget as low as possible. For better quality with rental-oriented production, shoot in Betacam, or Betacam SP (daily camera/recorder rental rates can be almost as cheap as ³/₄", and the quality is noticeably better.) For lower production-package (shooting) rental prices, with as-good or better picture quality (depending on whose opinion you want to believe), you should shoot in Hi8 or S-VHS.

Nowadays the ³/₄" format only makes sense when viewed in its historical context. If it were introduced today, it would fall flat on its face. It is clearly on its way out. But there are literally hundreds of thousands—if not millions—of schools, libraries, corporate video departments, cable systems, and even broadcast TV libraries, just filled with aisles and aisles of recorded programs on ³/₄". A vast collective investment has been made in this quarter-century old format, and this explains its longevity. It also explains why you can rent editing time so cheap.

A Few Words About the Fancier Stuff

As I mentioned in the introduction, this book is not about the professional equipment used by major television networks. But if you've read this far, you may still be wondering just what it is they're paying so much for—why do the professional VCRs, for example, cost upwards of $10,000?

Among the analog formats discussed so far—Hi8, 8mm, Super-VHS, S-VHS-C, VHS, VHS-C, and even ³/₄" and ³/₄ SP—all share one technical difference with the fancier Betacam, Betacam SP, M-II, and 1" formats: They utilize a "color under" recording system that simultaneously records the luminance (black and white) and chrominance (color) portions of the video signal onto the same helical track on the tape.

The professional analog video tape formats—Betacam SP, MII, etc.—uses what the industry calls a "component" color recording system, in which luminance and chrominance are each recorded on separate helical tracks.

This component recording system produces better signal/noise ratios, and results in better multi-generation editing. Specifically, besides less picture noise, component video technology produces less horizontal color shift when editing down several generations (in lower budget formats, as you go down generations, you'll see colors move to the left or right of the edges of the objects they're supposed to be contained within.)

All digital video recording systems—D-1, D-2, D-3, Digital Betacam, D-5, and MiniDV—are inherently component systems, and all offer the best multi-generation capability of all. As explained in the chapter on the DV and MiniDV format, there are differences between this low-budget consumer format and the professional gear. But whether that difference is worth the cost, which can run upwards of $30,000 for a professional digital VCR, is debatable.

Besides improved quality, all professional formats (both analog and digital) also offer slow-motion and still-frame playback that's good enough to broadcast on TV and to copy onto edited tapes (MiniDV has this quality too); they've got more audio tracks (usually four) that are more flexible to work with; and they've always got built-in VITC SMPTE time code record/playback systems.

Yes, technically speaking, professional videocassette formats do offer much more than the humble Hi8 or S-VHS videocassette.

But are they worth ten times the money? They're certainly not ten times as good. They're not even twice as good. And compared to MiniDV, the professional digital formats are just slightly better. For anything other than mass media applications, spending money on pro formats is probably a waste. But when you're trying to mass communicate in a really big way—like network TV—you want to look as good as everyone else who is using the medium.

If a potential client calls you and wants you to videotape some event, and they want the best quality, don't hesitate to offer Betacam at a ridiculously high price (somewhere between $800 and $1500 a day). Then hit the yellow pages and see where you can rent a Betacam package for $300 to $500 a day (usually with a camera operator). OK, it's not the creative work you dreamed of when you started your video business, but you've got to admit it's a nice spread, for making a few phone calls. That's the world of pro video.

14 Erase Heads and Editing

Each format has its own quirky advantages and disadvantages when it comes to editing. Much of this discussion revolves not only around how the tape gets recorded, but how it gets erased.

All VHS-family equipment has a stationary erase head—a head in a fixed position that is located early on in the tape path—before the tape reaches the other heads. That way, a tape gets erased before it gets re-recorded (see diagram). The linear audio track can also be selectively erased, making audio dubbing possible on many VCRs and camcorders.

But the stationary erase head does a very crude job with the video signal, because it begins and ends at different parts of different helical tracks. That is, when the erase head switches on or off, the action does not define a single precise moment in time, because there are many different diagonal helical tracks that are all stretched across the erase head. (See diagram—the vertical line of the erase head cuts across dozens of helical tracks.)

In addition, there is a space between the erase head and the video head drum, resulting in a "glitch" whenever you try to insert new material in the middle of previously recorded material: At the end of the inserted material, when the erase head and video recording heads switch off, there will be a short portion of tape left

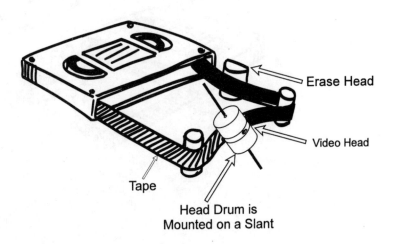

Erase Head

Video Head

Tape

Head Drum is
Mounted on a Slant

"Glitch" area left at end of insert

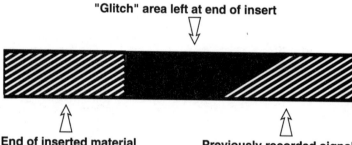

End of inserted material   **Previously recorded signal**

between the erase head and the video head drum. This portion of tape has been erased but not recorded on—resulting in a screen filled with static for a short time.

The Flying Erase Head

The flying erase head solves this dilemma of locating the erase head and the videoheads in different places, by putting an erase head right inside the same spinning drum where the helical video heads are located. "Flying" means the same thing as "helical" or "rotary"—the heads are spinning around in the head drum. This is an absolute necessity for smoothly inserting new material in the middle of previously recorded material, without a glitch.

In the VHS format, the flying erase head allows you to erase and rerecord the picture (and Hi-fi audio) track, while leaving the

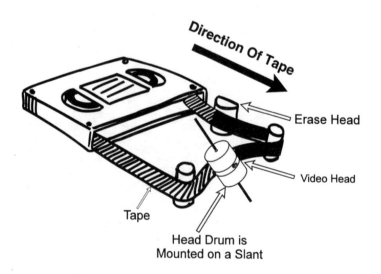

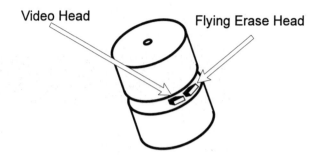

Video Head — Flying Erase Head

original linear audio track intact. This is called "video dubbing" or "insert video editing."

In the 8mm/Hi8 format, the flying erase head is the only erase head—there is no stationary erase head, and there are no linear tracks. When you record new video, you must always record new AFM audio along with it. (The consumer 8mm models also re-write the PCM audio track at the same time and do not allow for video only inserts.)

The same is true for the MiniDV format, except that, since the signal is digital (it lacks subtlety, being either a 1 or 0), there's no need for a separate erase head. But the system works the same as flying erase head systems, and permits selectable video and audio insert editing.

Other Limitations

The MiniDV format is clearly superior for editing purposes. But with any of the formats, your use of the available audio tracks will require a tradeoff between the number of tracks, the ability to dub audio after video has been recorded, and the quality of the tracks. Many low-budget producers shoot in Hi8 and edit on to Super-VHS, but many others shoot in Super-VHS and edit onto Super-VHS, while still others shoot in Hi8 and edit onto Hi8. Each of these variations has certain advantages and disadvantages; all are a big notch below the quality you'll get shooting and editing in MiniDV.

Additionally, manufacturers of consumer video equipment have cleverly tried to keep excellent consumer equipment from stealing business from the more expensive industrial video equipment by limiting the flexibility of the audio systems in consumer and low-end industrial equipment. Most notably, you usually cannot get all the different audio tracks out of separate jacks, for individual processing and mixing. Instead, a crude "mix" switch on the equipment forces you to listen to one set of tracks, or a 50-50 mix. This is particularly cumbersome when you wish to add SMPTE time code signals to a tape, as explained later (exception: Panasonic's AG-1980 S-VHS deck).

There is a cottage industry of VCR repair shops that can custom modify VCRs and camcorders to enhance the audio capabilities — by bringing each output to a separate jack, and by letting you listen to the audio at faster search speeds (most VCRs mute the signal). You can locate businesses that offer such technical services by checking classified ads in video specialty magazines, or asking at stores that specialize in industrial and desktop video equipment. These modifications are by no means necessary for video editing, but can enhance your ability to add time code after tapes have been recorded, or to add synchronized sound effects and music.

15 The Language of the Moving Image

Low budget video producers wear many hats—camera operator, director, sound technician, editor, etc. It may sound backwards, but in order to really understand how to shoot properly, you must first understand what editing will involve. Then you, in your role as camera operator can supply you, in your role as the editor with the raw materials needed to get the job done professionally.

In conventional film and video production, there is general recognition of a language of moving images that has evolved over the ninety-odd year history of cinema and TV. This same language is spoken by domestic, foreign, Hollywood, and independent film and television editors alike. Everyday Americans are just now learning how to "write" in this language that they have been reading for over half a century. There is something empowering about cutting from a wide shot to a close-up, and having it "work". The feeling, for adults, might be akin to what a child must feel when he or she makes his or her first sentence.

Conventional editing (as opposed to avant-garde and experimental techniques) attempts to "hide the seams" of the edits by making them as unnoticeable as possible. The goal is never to jar the viewer or call attention to the edit; but rather, make each transition from one shot to another appear smooth and 'natural'.

Here is a quick guide to some of the most basic editing conventions, followed by a more detailed discussion of both the aesthetics and technicalities of video editing.

Quick Guide to Editing:

- **Avoid "Jump Cuts"**. When you cut from one shot of a person to the exact same shot of the person at a different point in time, it appears that he or she suddenly "jumped" from one position to another. The solution is to cut between different framings of the person—such as from a wide shot to a close-up; or to "cutaway" to a neutral shot of something else—like the "reaction shots" you always see in TV news of a reporter nodding his/her head, or taking notes.

- **Maintain Screen Continuity**. If a chase is moving from the left of the screen to the right of the screen in a wide shot, maintain this screen direction in subsequent close-ups. Similarly, if two people are talking, framed so that one person is on the left side of the screen and the other on the right, maintain these left-right relationships in all shots. Edit in a neutral shot (from head on, or behind) before switching screen direction.
- **Cut on Action.** As soon as some action occurs, cut a fraction of a second later, and continue the action in the subsequent shot. For example, if someone picks up a pen in a wide-angle shot, cut to a close-up just after the pen rises from the table, and continue the action in a close-up of the pen approaching a sheet of paper. (The same action must be repeated in two scenes for this effect.) By cutting just at the moment of action, viewers are distracted from the edit, and hence less aware of it. (It's like a magician distracting you with one hand while performing the trick with the other.)
- **Fade-out and fade-in** to convey the passing of time. Accessory products like Panasonic's MX-series and AVE- mixers, Videonics' MX-1, JVC's JX-SV55, or simpler "black boxes" costing under a hundred dollars can accomplish this after shooting is over; or you can use the camcorder's built-in fader as you shoot.
- **Be brief.** In editing, less is often more. Remember that your audience must watch the completed production at a fixed rate, and video "skimming" (searching or fast forwarding by the viewer) is cumbersome and insulting to the producer (you!).
- **Intercut** between two or more shots to show simultaneous action and create dramatic tension. Anticipating the arrival of party guests, for example, you can show the host's nervous face, then the doorbell, then the face, the door, the face, a clock, the face, etc.

The Art of Editing

Editing is the art of visual storytelling, and can be the most creative aspect of video production. But many people don't appreciate the importance of editing, and video camera owners often leave their "raw footage" unedited. The procedure is a bit tedious, but the results can be thrilling. You don't necessarily need any extra equipment to start editing your own videos, although there's no limit when it comes to buying fancy editing equipment.

If you've been making home movies with a camcorder for the past year or two, you may approach editing out of necessity. Even the stars will squirm when they sit for hours on end watching, in their entirety, tapes of your vacations, family events, etc. Selecting the best shots from the mountains of footage you've accumulated may at first seem a bit like the biblical story about Abraham sacrificing his own son (in this case, your precious footage), but the sacrifice is justified.

On a more sophisticated level of production, editing becomes an integral part of videomaking—not just a cleanup process to get rid of the mistakes. Practically all serious video and film directors "shoot to edit"—that is, they gather together in the camera a series of planned shots which may seem boring when viewed as raw footage, but ultimately spring to life when they're later edited together into an interesting, fast paced sequence.

Video editing has two distinct aspects—editing aesthetics (the art of editing), and the more technical mechanics of editing. The artistic side of it is more fun, and you don't need any fancy equipment to try out techniques—in-camcorder editing will do fine. So we'll look at the aesthetics first, and then return to the technical.

Editing Aesthetics

How many famous film directors can you name? How many writers? How many actors? Now, how many editors can you name? If your answer is zero, you're not alone. Although editing is certainly among the most creative aspects of movie production, there can be no doubt that editors get short shrift in the glamour and fame of Hollywood filmmaking.

An excellent treatise on this very subject is Ralph Rosenblum's *When The Shooting Stops, The Cutting Begins.* The author, who has edited films for Woody Allen, Sidney Lumet, and other famous directors, offers a fascinating, behind-the-scenes glimpse at how the final cut of a film comes together.

The creative role of editors, working in dark, windowless rooms far from the glamour of Hollywood's sets, is generally underappreciated, Rosenblum laments.

Any attention or credit given to the editor can detract from the apparent skills of other key personnel. If it becomes known that an editor decided to re-arrange scenes, create montages, or otherwise change the film from the original script, the director loses credit as the film's auteur. Similarly, when an editor pieces together segments from five different performances of an actor's monologue because no single take was perfect in all respects, the editor is essentially covering up the actor's flubbed lines and the cameraperson's faulty focus.

The editor is like a seamstress whose goal is to connect different pieces of material together in such a way that no one notices the seams. Except for the occasional montage sequences, in which a series of overlaid images are set to music to create a mood or condense a lot of narrative action into a very short amount of time, the editor's intent is usually to be unnoticed by the viewer.

Some experimental/avant-garde film and video makers have rebelled against this philosophy, complaining that it is manipulative. Rather than using slick editing to tell a story in such a way that the audience forgets all about changes in camera angle, these filmmakers make their edits very noticeable so that viewers remain constantly aware of the acts of filmmaking and film viewing.

What follows is a quick rundown of the basic rules of grammar for the language of moving images:

Overall Structure and Pacing

Practically every film and television program begins with an "establishment shot", to tell the viewer where the story is taking place. The establishment shot can be very simple —for a wedding, it can be a single outdoors shot of the church or synagogue. In the case of a feature film or TV show, it can be a complex series of shots beginning with wide aerial views of a city, and ultimately leading to a particular window in an office building where the action is about to take place. The establishment shot(s) doesn't necessarily have to be the first thing you record with the camera, because through editing you can rearrange the sequence at will. The important thing to remember is to get such a shot sometime during the production.

It may sound overly simple, but every story has a beginning, middle, and end. Editing imposes this structure even where it may not exist in real life. You should introduce your characters at the beginning of your story, allow them to develop in the middle, and bring them to some kind of conclusion at the end.

Even the most humble home videos can follow this structure. For example, if you're shooting a family vacation, you can begin with the packing—the anticipation of what's to come. Will there be bears? Will our plane crash? Will the toilet paper be soft?

The introduction can be very short, but should not be ignored. The longest section of the story should be it's middle. When editing, you must keep a sense of proportion and discipline as you weave the story's elements together. Just because you shot twenty minutes of fireworks on the 4th of July doesn't mean you have to use it all! Generally speaking, the shorter each segment is, the better.

In editing a video program for a professional or academic presentation, you should also consider the appropriateness of the material to the medium. Video tends to do a good job communicating broad ideas and outlines, but often the details of what you're talking about can be explained best through a printed handout with graphs and other statistical data. Be particularly careful about presenting information which only a small subset of your audience will understand, for example, technical jargon, or new developments which require a lot of background to grasp. Be sure to include relevant background material in your finished pro-duction—even if you have to shoot additional footage and edit it in.

Finally, remember to include an ending to your story. Don't worry that there really isn't an end (i.e., continuing research, etc.)—your purpose in ending is to wrap up the story told on video, not the real events on which it's based. If you're taping a wedding, end with a shot of the bride and groom sailing off into the sunset. At your backyard barbecue, the cleanup squad stuffing paper plates into garbage bags bring the drama to a close.

Often, when a story has no natural ending, you must create one. Think of how many times you've heard a TV news report which ended with the line, "only time will tell," or, "Now it's up to the legislature (or courts or jury) to decide." If more research is needed, say that at the end. If more time must pass before side ef-fects can be assessed, say that. The conclusion of your video pro-duction is merely a convenient way of saying goodbye to the audience—don't worry about drawing overall conclusions to the story.

Visually, you can create a feeling of closure by going back to a very wide shot, such as the establishment shot. We're now leaving this place where the story occurred.

Since editing allows you to shoot out of sequence, it's often most convenient to get the opening and ending shots at the same time. If you're concluding a report, you can use an audio-only voice-over, in conjunction with the ending image, to announce that the future is in the hands of God, science, politicians, the people, or whatever.

Camera Angles

The idea of using a wide angle shot to establish the site of the ac-tion becomes relevant each time your story moves from one loca-tion to another. In general, edit each new scene to start with wide shots, giving the audience a broad perspective on where the char-acters are in that location, and in relation to one another. Con-tinue the scene by moving into medium shots and close-ups of the characters in action.

For example, in shooting a back yard barbecue, you might first show a broad view of the yard from a neighbor's porch or your roof. Next, a series of medium shots, showing people from the waist up, can convey a sense of the family busy with preparations—your spouse preparing the meat, Joey lighting the fire, the kids fighting over the hula-hoop—etc. The close-ups, which should be intercut, during editing, with the medium shots, can show texture and detail: the molding of the meat into patties, the match touching the charcoals, etc.

The Zoom Blues

Beware of the zoom lens! Without doubt, the single most common violation of the basic rules of moving image grammar by amateur videomakers is the overuse of zoom lenses, as described earlier. The zoom lens offers an extraordinary convenience in that, from a single vantage point, you can gather wide, medium, and close-up shots. Think of the zoom lens as not one, but as five or six different lenses which just happen to be combined together. (Many professional cinematographers still prefer to use "prime" lenses [single focal length lenses,] because they consider the optical quality superior to that of a zoom.)

In general, it is almost always better to cut (edit) from a wide shot to a medium shot or close-up than to zoom between the same shots. Try this experiment to prove it: First, shoot a wide shot of several people sitting in your living room, zooming and panning to close-ups of each face.

Second, start with the same wide shot of the people, but then pause the camera without zooming in. Zoom in on one person's face, and start the camera rolling again. Stop it after a second or two, frame the next person's face, and then start rolling again. Do the same for each person in the room. Now compare the results between the first and second trials. You will no doubt agree that the second version, in which you suddenly cut from a stable wide shot to a series of stable close-ups, looks a lot better than the first in which you zoom in from the wide shot to the close-ups.

It can be nauseating to watch incessant zoom-ins and zoom-outs. Unless you are trying to convey a sense of action, zoom shoots are usually irrelevant and should be edited out. Use the zoom to frame a shot, *then* start the camera rolling, without touching the zoom again until you're ready to frame the next shot.

To discipline yourself in this regard, try leaving your camera's zoom lens at one particular setting—wide angle, or "medium" (halfway to telephoto)—for several hours, using only that particular focal length. If you need a close-up, walk closer to the subject. The choice of an optimal zoom setting—or focal length—for each shot depends on many things, including how much of the picture should be in focus, and how prominently the main subject should appear in front of the background.

If you're editing material which has already been shot with incessant zooming, try to cut out the zooms as much as possible. If the camera was stable for a few seconds on a wide shot, zoomed in, and then was stable on the close-up, you can either edit directly from the wide shot to the close-up; or, if there is important audio material during the zoom (someone talking, for example), then you can edit in a "cutaway" shot to cover the zoom.

Jump Cuts and Cutaway Shots

Suppose you've videotaped a lecture, so the material you have to edit is all "talking head"—a medium close-up shot of the person speaking. Through editing, you want to condense the ninety-minute speech to a more tolerable twenty minutes. (Distributors of educational films and videos say that twenty minutes is the maximum time for in-classroom screenings before the squirm problem becomes unbearable.)

Whenever you edit from one point in the lecture to another, you will see a "jump cut". The speaker's face will suddenly be in a slightly different position, the hands will seem to suddenly jump from one place to another, and visually, the edit will be extremely noticeable, even if the audio edit sounds smooth, with one sentence ending and a new one beginning.

For many years, jump cuts were universally avoided in professional film and TV work, but in the 1950s French "new wave" filmmakers began deliberately using this edit to jolt the audience and make them more conscious of the act of editing. These days, jump cuts convey a sense of "reality", and are used frequently by "hidden camera" style commercials to make viewers think they are watching a documentary rather than a commercial. To give edited video productions a polished look, avoid jump cuts whenever possible.

The "cutaway shot" is the simplest method of eliminating jump cuts. It is usually a picture-only edit. First the end of one of the lecturer's sentences is edited to the beginning of a new sentence taken from a different point in the lecture. The jump-cut is "covered" by cutting away to an illustrative image, or other shot, for a few seconds, then returning to the speaker.

The "reaction shot" is the most common form of cutaway shot. In the case of the lecture, it would be a shot of the audience—either in aggregate, or just a few people nodding their heads, rapt with attention. Note that reaction shots are almost always recorded out of sequence—either before, during a break, or after the lecture—and edited in later. Note also that technically, you will need an editing VCR or camcorder capable of insert video edits to accomplish this effect (see the next section).

TV news reporters use reaction shots all the time to cutaway from their interviews. After a reporter asks the basic question (i.e. "Are you a corrupt politician?") they might pose follow-up questions to ferret out a coherent answer. Later, when the interview is edited, pieces of answers to the follow-up questions are put together, so that the response sounds like an answer to the original question. The resulting jump-cuts are eliminated by editing in reaction shots of the reporter nodding, taking notes on a pad, etc.

Since news crews usually work with just one camera (except for big-money productions like *60 Minutes*), these reaction shots are almost always recorded *after* the interview is over: The cameraperson changes positions, turning away from the interviewee, and focuses on the reporter. Often, at this point, the reporter will repeat the main questions, which can then be edited in place of the original questions, giving the effect that a camera was trained on the reporter during the interview.

You can also use cutaway shots of the speaker's lecture material. For a lecture on "Homeless Americans" you can cutaway to shots of actual homeless people on the streets. If the lecture is about a new artificial heart pump, you can cutaway to a drawing of the device, or a shot of the working prototype.

Cutaway shots should usually be edited in for just two or three seconds, unless they are particularly complex or compelling. Avoid repeating the same cutaway shot. For audience reaction shots get several different close-ups of people watching, as well as several medium and wide shots of the whole audience. If you're using diagrams or other subject-related cutaways, try to insert each at the most relevant point of the lecture.

Screen Continuity

Screen continuity is an important editing consideration which must really be thought through beforehand, during shooting. Screen continuity amounts to this: If someone starts out on the left side of the screen, keep'em on the left. If someone else is on the right, keep them on the right.

In a two-person interview, for example, you'll often shoot "over-the-shoulder" of the person asking the questions, to see the face of the interviewee. If the back of the head of the questioner is on the left, and the face of the interviewee is on the right, then when you edit in the reaction shots, you should maintain the

The 180-degree rule: Draw an imaginary line between the two characters. To maintain the left-right relationship, keep the camera on one side of this imaginary line (around the semicircle).

When you cut to a close-up of A, the left-right relationship will be maintained.

And when you cut to B's close-up, A will still be on the left, and B on the right.

same relationship: The back of the interviewee's head should now be on the right, and the face of the questioner on the left.

An easy way to remember this while shooting is the "180-degree rule". When you first setup the camera, imagine drawing a line through the heads of the two people. Imagine a semicircle around that line, representing 180 degrees of arc. As long as you keep the camera positioned anywhere in the semicircle, you'll maintain screen continuity. If you cross over the imaginary line, you'll reverse the left-right relationship.

In editing, you can cover over breaks in screen continuity by using neutral cutaway shots. These can be shots of whatever the people are talking about, which do not show either of the people. Editing chase scenes offers a classic exercise in maintaining screen continuity. If the good guys start on the left, chasing after the bad guys on the right, then all subsequent shots should show both the good guys and the bad guys running toward the right of the screen.

When editing, maintain this direction in wide shots, medium shots, and close- ups.

You can change the screen direction, in editing, in either of three ways: First, you can show the actual characters changing direction: by turning around a corner, for example. Second, you can show a switch in perspective by physically moving the camera from the first position to the second while the tape is rolling. (This is difficult to do smoothly with low budget tripods and dollies, however.)

Finally, (and usually most easily), you can switch, in editing, from a series of rightward-moving shots to a series of leftward moving shots by cutting to a neutral, head-on shot in between. That is, if a man is first shown running to the right, and you want to edit to a shot of him running to the left, you should first cut to a shot of him running directly towards the camera (neither left nor right) and then cut to the changed direction. Or cut to another shot which doesn't show him at all, such as his point of view.

Just watch an old *Hawaii Five-0* rerun, or any other action/adventure TV show or film, for a demonstration of these techniques. Try watching a chase scene in slow motion to see what's going on in the editing.

Simultaneous Action

When editing many home videos, you can increase the sense of tension and excitement by intercutting between two or more different events to create simultaneous action. For example, suppose you're editing twenty minutes of tape you shot when your family had a barbecue. The first ten minutes show the kids tossing a ball around. Then there's five minutes of your spouse cooking the burgers, followed by five minutes of table chatter as everyone eats.

After editing together an appropriate introduction, you can spice up the production by intercutting between your spouse and the kids. Start with your spouse's handling of the raw meat, explaining the special recipe. Then cut to the kids picking up a ball and throwing the first few tosses. Then cut back to your spouse placing the patties on the grill. Then back to the kids falling all over each other as they try to catch a wild throw. Back to your spouse flipping the ground beef over. Then to one of the kids imitating a major league star. Back to your spouse preparing buns. And so on.

At the end of the sequence, you can bring the two events together when your spouse calls the kids to the table to eat, and then cut to the table chatter segment. Even if the kids actually played ball two hours before your spouse started cooking, the intercut editing will create the feeling that these two events occurred simultaneously.

Recurring Themes

Similarly, you can edit a recurring visual theme into your production to set a mood or add a comedic element. For example, suppose you got drunk one night on vacation and shot twenty minutes of ocean waves lapping up against the shore. Most people would be pretty bored to watch those waves, but rather than just throwing them out, you could intercut short five or ten second segments of them between each day's events. The waves would thus serve as visual punctuation to separate scenes, giving a sense that another night had passed, as well as conjure a seaside ambiance.

Along the same lines, suppose your family hit the road for a few weeks to take a vacation, and every time you wanted to stop to eat the kids began arguing over whether to eat at Hojo's or Pizza Hut. By recording five or six such fights, or taking just a single fight and dividing it into five smaller parts which you intersperse throughout the final edited production, you can add a comedic thematic element.

Cutting on Action

To "hide the seams" of your editing, make your cuts immediately after an action begins.

Let's say you're editing a lecture, and have a variety of wide, medium, and close-up shots of the speaker. Instead of using cutaways, you can avoid jump cuts by editing between different views of the same person. The size of the person's face must change dramatically from one shot to the next—such as from a wide shot to a close-up.

Suppose the speaker drinks from a glass of water throughout the lecture, and you want to cut between a wide shot and a close-up as he pauses to take a sip. You'll really be cutting between two *different* occasions where he sipped the water, but if he used the same hand and stayed in pretty much the same position, the edit will look fine.

Start with the wide shot, and then, just a moment *after* he begins picking up the glass, cut to the close-up of him bringing the glass to his lips. Cutting on action not only helps "cement" the two pieces together, but also helps you compress time: You needn't show the raising of the glass through the air—just the beginning of the action (in the wide shot) and the end of the action (in the close-up). If you study the editing of TV commercials in slow motion, you'll find this technique is used repeatedly.

Montages

The word "montage" simply means "editing" in French, but in America the term has come to mean a quick visual sequence incorporating lots of different images which all relate to a single theme, usually set to music or to non-synchronized sound.

Montages are a great way to edit together sections of your travel videos, since you often come home to find that you've got good images but poor audio. Suppose you travelled through France for a few weeks and shot famous spots in Paris such as the Eiffel Tower, the Louvre, the Champs Elysee, etc. These are purely visual, and you can easily edit them together with music. Be sure to include shots of the family pointing, laughing it up, etc.

You can connect a staged shot of someone pointing a finger (as if saying, "look at that!") to another shot of the Eiffel Tower. The cut will look great—even if you actually recorded the finger pointing several days later on a street which was nowhere near the Eiffel Tower.

Rather than putting scenes together by following the order in which they were shot, the edits will look much smoother if you carefully note where the main subject of each shot is on screen as the shot ends, and connect it with a new shot whose subject is at roughly the same place on screen.

As you edit, put your own finger right on the TV screen on the point where the main action has just occurred (i.e., someone pointing to the sky). The audience's eyes will be drawn to this spot. Next find a shot of the Eiffel Tower framed so that it first appears at the same point on screen. If you've got a child waving at the end of one shot, try to have the main focus of the next shot be framed right where the waving hand was. Using this visual technique, you can edit together many completely different images into a smooth, cohesive sequence.

Fades and Dissolves

Up until now, all of the edits discussed so far have been "straight cut" edits, in which the first frame of the new shot occurs immediately after the last frame of the old shot. This is the most common, basic edit. The straight cut edit usually implies a sense of "real time": each new shot shows the next thing that has happened.

Fades create the feeling that a considerable amount of time has passed between the end of one shot and the beginning of the next. The fade to black at the end of one shot, and fade up from black at the beginning of the next is a basic video editing technique. The longer you keep the screen black, the more time will seem to have elapsed, but don't go beyond a few seconds or your audience may mistakenly think the program is over.

Film editors often use the dissolve, instead of the fade to black, to create a similar sense of time passing. However this effect is very expensive to achieve with videotape, requiring at least five to ten thousand dollars of additional equipment (discussed later). Recently, it has become possible to create a slightly different type of dissolve using the digital effects found on some of the newest, top-of-the-line camcorders. These effects allow you to freeze a frame at the end of one shot, hold the frame in memory indefinitely, then dissolve to live action in the next shot. The effect's meaning is similar—a stylized sense of time passing. But you are limited to performing these edits in the camera—you can't add them later on, unless you have a fairly sophisticated editing system with digital effects (such as a Panasonic WJ-AVE or MX-series mixer, or a Video Toaster and time base corrector).

Editing can be a highly creative, highly rewarding process—but it can also turn into a nightmare of tedium and frustration. The key to making video editing work for you lies in proper planning of both your shooting strategy and editing strategy, as well as a good understanding of the technical abilities and limitations of the equipment you'll be working with.

Shooting to Edit vs. 'In-camera' Editing

Before you start shooting, you should already know what your editing strategy is. There are two general approaches commonly used—'in-camera' editing, and post-production editing. Many advanced camcorder models incorporate numerous advanced in-camera editing features that let you create smooth transitions, sometimes with special effects, every time you stop and start the camcorder.

In-camera Editing Saves Time

It's time-consuming to sit down with your raw footage and edit it together long after it was originally shot. Many of the editing techniques described here can actually be performed "in-camera"—that is, as you are shooting. You'll save time later on, because much of the editing will have already been done. The disadvantage of in-camera editing is a degree of sloppiness: you can't belabor your edit decisions, carefully picking exactly which frames to cut on, or re-perform the edit if you're unhappy with the results.

As a rule of thumb, industrial video editors often estimate a sixty to one ratio of time spent editing to completed tape. To create a reasonably slick ten minute video, expect to spend roughly ten hours editing it. Obviously, the more in-camera editing you do, the smaller this ratio will become.

In-camera editing works great for recording family events like barbecues, parties, etc. At a back yard barbecue, you can cut from a wide shot of the tofu-burgers being flipped over to a close-up of one tofu-burger as it is crumbles apart on the grill, just by using the stop/start button on the camcorder. The more practice you get editing after-the-fact, the easier in-camera editing becomes.

However, in-camera editing has some severe limitations that makes it appropriate only for the most casual videotaping applications. First and foremost is the lack of flexibility. Once you record something at a particular spot on a tape, you are stuck with it in that position. Suppose, for example, that you produce a ten-minute long edited tape, but at a point five minutes into it there is a twenty-second long segment that you'd like to eliminate. With in-camera editing, you have no choice but to try to fill in this twenty seconds of tape with something else—by shooting something new that will get inserted there. You can't just shorten the tape.

One place where in-camera editing should usually NOT be used is when recording a lecture, or interview, or documenting a live, unplanned event. In these situations you can't know what a speaker might say next, or what turn of events might demand the camera's attention.

Shooting to Edit Yields More Polish

A post-production editing strategy lets you concentrate more on shooting when you are shooting, putting off editing decisions until later, when things are calmer. It is, therefore, the method that all professional video and film producers use. If you're shooting a dramatic piece and go through several "takes" of an actor's performance, for example, you'll have the luxury of looking at the various takes later to decide which is best.

Editing after the shooting is over also provides the major benefit of allowing you to shoot out of sequence. This vastly speeds up the shooting process. Suppose you are shooting a dramatic scene that calls for a wide shot and two close-ups of people speaking. If you edit as you go along, you'll have to constantly move the camera back and forth to switch from a wide shot to one close-up to the other. By shooting out of sequence, you can first shoot the complete scene as a wide shot, then one close-up, and then the other. With just three camera positions you'll create the raw material that, when edited, may result in dozens of shot changes.

You can shoot a whole story out of sequence, scheduling shooting according to the convenience of your crew, talent, locations, etc. If a story begins and ends at an airport, for example, there's no need to visit it twice—you can shoot the beginning and end on the same visit.

When you shoot with the intention of gathering raw materials for future editing, you are "shooting to edit." In an organized production, each days's shooting will be carefully planned out using scripts, storyboards, shot lists, or a combination of these preparations.

Pre-production, Production, and Post-production

Professional video and film producers divide their projects into three distinct phases: pre-production, production, and post- production. This division of the work involved in creating a finished videotape or film helps clarify the deadlines for the various elements that feed into a production, and streamline the overall efficiency of time and labor.

The pre-production phase is the planning stage. This can involve the writing of scripts, storyboards, budgets, location scouting, selecting props, wardrobe, etc. Equipment rentals, finding a crew, planning meals, parking, etc. should also be taken care of in advance. Technically, the overall editing strategy should be planned in advance too—paying particular attention to how time code may be used.

The production phase is the actual shooting and sound recording—gathering the raw materials for editing. In big budget productions, the construction of sets and lighting plans may take up weeks of time before any shooting actually begins. During production, careful notes are taken about what scenes, shots, and takes are on each videocassette. These notes will be a big help later on, when the editing project gets going.

Post-production is everything that takes place after the shooting is over—editing, mixing in music and sound effects, adding credits, graphics, etc.

One-camera vs. Multi-camera Shooting

In professional video production, there are two different overall approaches commonly used to create a program. The one-camera approach is generally used for news, action/adventure, and dramatic programs. One-camera shooting is sometimes called "film style" shooting by video producers, because it is the same method that most feature film producers use. A single camera is used to shoot things out of sequence, with the assumption that it will be woven together later through editing. As mentioned earlier, in one-camera news production, an interviewer usually asks the questions again, after the interview is over, so that the camera can swing around into a different position to show the reporter's face.

In studio television production, also called multi-camera shooting, there are two, three, or more television cameras all operating simultaneously. During the production of a situation comedy, for example, one camera will keep a wide shot showing two or three characters, while other cameras get close-ups of the individual actors. The director of a multi-camera production functions very much like the editor of one-camera productions—picking and choosing which shot to show when. Unlike editors, though, studio TV directors must make quick decisions with no time to ponder the advantages and disadvantages of each shot.

Typical News-Style Production using Special Effects Generator

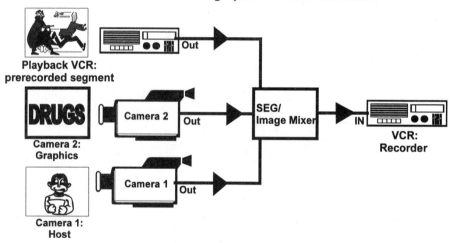

1-Host appears with graphics in box in corner of screen
2-Graphics replaced by beginning of prerecorded segment on playback VCR
3-Prerecorded segment fills entire screen
4-Host appears with next graphic

For this reason, multi-camera television is generally considered sloppier and less precise than one-camera production. But it has the advantage of speed—when the shooting is over, a completely finished tape, including sound effects and credits, can be finished. The tradeoff for this speed, though is spending much more time planning and rehearsing which camera will get which shot when, and accepting the inherent sloppiness when somebody goofs. Multicamera setups cost a lot more money, of course too. For some "live" events, like sports, multi-camera production is the only way to properly capture the action, since you could hardly expect two competing teams to reenact their plays for wide shots and close-ups.

Using time code, you can shoot simultaneously with multiple cameras that are each recording onto a separate tape, for editing later. Wireless microphone equipment (explained later, in the Audio section) transmits time code from a single time code generator to several different camcorders, so that each has the same moment in time identified with the same frame number. This setup, or a variation of it, can get expensive, but it greatly facilitates the editing process later on.

Storyboards, Scripts, and Shot Lists

There are numerous types of scripts that are commonly used in professional video production. A shooting script—the most detailed type of script—includes not only the exact lines of dialog that each actor will say, but also information about how the actors should move through a scene, and how the camera will be set up for various shots.

Storyboard of a backyard barbecue

Most low budget video productions do not require such a high level of detail—after all, a wedding video is more of a documentary than a fictional drama—but can benefit from simpler forms of scripts.

A storyboard is a sort of visual script, consisting of a series of cartoon like panels. Each box is framed like a TV screen, and you sketch a very rough cartoon drawing of how you'd like to see things framed. A simple dialog scene, for example, might have a storyboard with three basic shots—a wide shot showing both people speaking, and close-ups of each person.

A shot list is an even more streamlined variation—instead of drawing cartoons, you simply make a list of all the shots you need to get. This generally requires the least amount of work, and can be a very handy reminder of what you need to get for a given shoot. As you get each shot, you can cross it off the list. A wedding video shoot, for example, might have the following items on a shot list:

> exterior view of chapel
> bridal preparations
> family arrivals
> parents of bride and groom - interviews
> walking down the aisle
> the service
> wedding vows
> aunts and uncles at reception
> friends at reception
> bride and groom drive off or say good-bye

"Takes" and the Clapboard

When shooting drama, or news reports in which the reporter wishes to retry the same lines over and over again, you'll end up recording numerous "takes" of the same thing. Later, in editing, you'll decide which takes to use in the completed tape. Professional video and film directors commonly use a simple chalk slate, or "clapboard", to identify each take on the tape. The clear identification of each take makes it much easier, when editing, to remember which take is which in figuring out which to use. This is also a particularly useful technique when you're editing without the benefit of time code, since the counter numbers that will be used to identify the different takes are less reliable than time code numbers.

Recording Time Code As You Shoot

Depending on what format you're shooting in, what equipment you have, and what your other audio needs are, it may be impossible for you to add SMPTE time code to camera original footage after the shooting is over. This will be the case whenever you need to record time code on 8mm AFM or VHS Hi-fi audio tracks. To record time code on these tracks, it must be recorded at the same time as the picture—necessitating the use of a portable time code generator. Ideally, the time code numbers should start and stop as the tape rolls, so that there are no gaps in the time code when the camera original tape is played. (Whenever the time code numbers change, it takes the time code reader several seconds to lock onto the new numbers, so a good amount of tape should be recorded when there is a lapse in code numbers—such as if you accidentally leave the time code generator running while the camcorder is paused). Portable battery-powered time code generators, such as FutureVideo's TCG series and several models by Horita, are automatically triggered to stop and start generating time code whenever the camcorder is paused.

Note that with MiniDV camcorders and Hi8 models equipped with RC time code, all this is unnecessary – time code is automatically recorded whenever you start the tape rolling, and stops whenever you pause the tape, creating a smooth, continuous set of numbers.

Maximizing Audio Tracks

The biggest frustration for low budget video producers often stems from the audio side of video. The consumer camcorder formats make it cumbersome, at best, to record both synchronized (live) audio and SMPTE time code onto the same tape. In some situations, such as with most 8mm camcorders, you'll have to choose between recording live sound, recording time code, or going down a generation (to VHS or Super-VHS) to get both original audio and time code onto the same tape.

If you intend to work with time code, you should have this figured out before you start shooting. You may need to carry a portable time code generator with you, as you shoot, to get the time code onto the first generation camera original tape.

A Super-VHS camcorder that offers Hi-fi audio is probably the best bet for recording SMPTE time code along with original audio.

Besides time code, you should also try to figure out how music and sound effects can be added to your tapes, as you edit them.

185

Again, the specifics will vary depending on which format(s) you're working with and which audio features each has. In your planning, distinguish between items that need to be in perfect synchronization, and those sounds (such as background ambience) that can run synchronously (and use an audio cassette recorder for non-sync sound).

In the VHS format, the linear track can offer the ability to add one or two synchronized tracks after a recording is made, using the audio dub feature. 8mm equipment that has PCM audio can also add two additional audio tracks.

On a higher budget, the standard SMPTE time code can be used to synchronize an 8-track or 16-track audio tape recorder to the videotape, offering professional quality audio-for-video production and mixing capabilities. Similarly, SMPTE to MIDI (musical instrument digital interface) converters can synchronize musical instrument synthesizer equipment to a videotape, with frame accuracy.

Logging Your Tapes In Preparation For Editing

One of the more tedious, but important parts of organizing an editing project is to create accurate logs of what is on each tape. Such logs become especially important when you're editing footage that doesn't necessarily go together in any particular sequence—such as two hours of footage of a street fair.

Although it is time consuming to make these logs in the first place, it generally pays off in the end: Think how long it would take to search through two hours of tape to find a particular shot that you remember seeing somewhere on the tape but don't know where it is.

Edit decision list software can aid in the logging of tapes by automatically keeping track of time code or index counter numbers as you play a tape. By using the "mark in" command on the edit controller, you can repeatedly have the computer store the time code or counter number on successive lines of the edit list, jotting down a brief description of each new shot or event.

Then, to edit your first rough cut of selected items from this list, you can copy only those events you wish to use onto a new list. This new list will gradually get modified and trimmed, resulting in your final edit decision list.

16 Shopping for an Editing VCR

Just about any VCR can be used for the most basic video editing, but as your projects get more ambitious, and you gain more experience, you'll begin to appreciate the advanced features offered by VCRs designed especially for editing. These features can provide better accuracy, more editing flexibility, cleaner looking edits (free of "glitches"), better search controls, and remote control capability for hookup to edit controllers and computers.

Just as with camcorders, you have a choice of formats when choosing an editing VCR. Because the higher resolution capability only adds a few hundred dollars to the price of a VCR, and most people who are serious about editing usually want the best picture quality possible, all of the better editing VCRs are either Super-VHS or Hi8 format. Each has advantages and disadvantages for editing. The current top low-budget (compared to professional gear) contenders in each category—Panasonic's AG-1980 (Super-VHS) and Sony's EV-S7000 (Hi8)—cost about $1500 to $1800 each, yet offer features that just a few years ago would have cost many times that price—such as built-in time base correction, time code, and computer control interfaces.

But at a somewhat higher price, and not yet in stores as this edition of *The Low Budget Video Bible* was going to press, Sony's introductory DV format VCR, the DHR-1000, is truly an editing dream machine. In conjunction with one of Sony's MiniDV format camcorders, you can copy segments back and forth endlessly, without ever worrying about generation loss.

Regardless of which format you choose, the basic tape editing process will be essentially the same: Your camcorder (or another VCR) will be used as the "source" deck, to play the tapes back on. The editing VCR will be used for recording selected segments from the source. There's no need for the source and editing VCR to be of the same format—you can, for example, edit from a Hi8 camcorder to a VHS VCR.

For the simplest editing operation, just hook up the video and audio outputs of the camcorder to the video and audio inputs of the VCR, and use the pause control on the VCR to eliminate portions of the camcorder tape you don't like. But as you get more involved re-arranging material (copying it out of sequence), and trying to edit at very specific points, you'll find the manual pause button coordination too tedious and inaccurate. That's where automated edit controllers come in, along with the need for remote control jacks to hook them up to (see below).

A "flying erase head" is essential for an editing VCR. It's the technical component that ensures video edits will look clean — without any error in the timing of the video signal (a "glitch") at the point where one picture changes to another (the "edit point"). Practically all VCRs selling for over $500 have it, and many selling for less also have this feature.

All 8mm and Hi8 VCRs have flying erase heads, too. But there can be a distinct advantage to editing onto the Super-VHS or VHS format, because you can insert new video images while leaving the original camcorder audio (this is called video insert editing, or video dub). You can also leave the original picture while replacing the sound (audio dub) with VHS and S-VHS.

With 8mm and Hi8 equipment you can't generally do video-only inserts (except using the fanciest industrial equipment, as explained later). Most 8mm and Hi8 VCRs can add a new stereo soundtrack — called PCM sound — to the original (AFM) sound (you generally can't do this with VHS and Super-VHS, unless you have a hi-fi camcorder). But if you want to edit together a music video, for example, you need to be able to first record the soundtrack and then cut in shots to match (video inserts). For this reason, many low-budget video producers prefer to edit onto Super-VHS.

The MiniDV format allows for all possible video and audio insert editing, but most camcorders don't support all these features. That's where a MiniDV editing VCR becomes very useful.

Jog/Shuttle Controls

Perhaps the one thing that cosmetically distinguishes practically every editing VCR is a big (about 2" diameter) jog/shuttle dial, usually located on the right side of the deck. Although some manufacturers — including Sony — have tinkered with the design

and developed cheaper knockoffs, a true jog/shuttle control consists of two parts:

The shuttle is a ring around the outside of the control that normally rests in a center position, and can be turned to the left or right. In either direction (backward or forward), the tape can be moved in slow motion at several speeds (such as $1/2$, $1/5$, $1/10$), at regular speed, and at several levels of fast search speeds (such as 2x, 5x). The farther you turn the dial, the faster the tape goes.

The jog dial is for precise location of individual frames. It has a detent, like an old telephone dial, for you to put your index finger in. You rotate this dial around and around—in either direction—and each circle advances or reverses the VCR by one frame. You can thus count the number of frames by counting the number of times your finger has gone around.

Many manufacturers have incorporated the shuttle part of the control into their mid-priced VCR designs, but have omitted the frame-by-frame jog dial. So when shopping for an editing VCR, check these controls carefully.

The ability to precisely locate frames tends to be just as important—if not more so—on the source side of the edit system as on the record side. This is one reason why professionals scoff at the idea of using a camcorder as the source—a "true" editing system, in their view, consists of two editing VCRs, so that you have the benefit of true jog/shuttle controls on both sides of the system, to conveniently locate edit points on both source and recorder.

The Panasonic AG-1980

Panasonic's AG-1980 Super-VHS format VCR is a true workhorse of low budget video editing. It is the successor to the AG-1970 and AG-1960, which basically defined in the late 1980's and early 90s what top value in a low-budget editing VCR could be. Technically it's not a consumer model—the AG designation indicates it's part of Panasonic's industrial video line (their consumer VCR models are designated with the PV prefix). But priced around $1500, it's not out of line with top consumer models, and no comparable of-

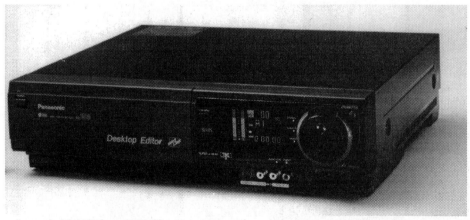

Panasonic AG-1980 Super-VHS VCR

ferings in either Panasonic's or JVC's consumer lines come close (JVC, which is half-owned by Panasonic's parent company, Matsushita, is the creator of the VHS and Super-VHS formats.)

The biggest advance, compared with its predecessor (the AG-1970), is the inclusion of separate input and output jacks for the linear audio track. This is a true rarity – and addresses something that I have been complaining about for the better part of a decade. This feature alone puts the AG-1980 way ahead of all other S-VHS decks in this price range.

Like its predecessor, the AG-1980 has a true jog shuttle control, a framing servo system that ensures even more perfect edits than a flying erase head alone (it synchronizes the VCR to the incoming video signal just before the edit occurs), and full flexibility to edit video only (video insert), audio only (audio dub), or both (A/V insert).

The AG-1980 also has a built-in time base corrector, for rock-solid playback stability. Which means you can use the AG-1980 with products like the Video Toaster, and other computer video devices, without having to purchase a separate TBC (which costs upwards of $700. Note that to combine two VCR signals together in the Toaster you'll still need separate TBCs—the built-in TBC is only good for using the VCR signal by itself, or mixed with graphics.) A color saturation level control lets you adjust the picture from black and white to cartoon overkill.

An excellent remote control jack on the AG-1980 provides two-way communication for computerized edit control systems. (In one direction go commands telling the VCR what to do, in the other direction the VCR reports back its precise tape location.) It is a 5-pin jack that resembles an S-video connector (but the pins are laid out differently). The remote control system is Panasonic's own—it's similar to Sony's LANC connectors (see below), but incompatible. Therefore, you can't use a Sony editing controller on a Panasonic editing VCR, and vice versa.

Panasonic makes an excellent manual (one edit at a time) editing controller, the AG-A96. Two AG-1980s and one AG-96 and presto!—you've got a complete Super-VHS editing system. Hooking the AG-1980's remote control jack up to a computer, using an interface such as FutureVideo's EditLink system, opens up even more possibilities: The system serves as a bridge between Sony's LANC remote jack and Panasonic's 5-pin jack, so it can edit from Hi8 to Super-VHS or vice versa. And the editing system can automatically execute a long series of edits (up to 1000 events), in the form of an edit decision list (EDL).

In the audio department, the AG-1980 has excellent VHS Hi-Fi sound, with separate left and right level controls, as well as a headphone jack with its own level control. But the linear track—

which is the only one the audio dub editing works with—is limited to monaural sound. As mentioned earlier, this track is available via separate jacks from the Hi-Fi sound, which can be very useful for recording separate narration or music tracks, or even SMPTE time code. (There's no built-in time code.) You can also hear this sound track during rapid searching and slow motion – a useful feature for cuing up edit points.

The Sony DHR-1000

Though we make every effort to keep this book impeccably up-to-date, because of the obvious time it takes to make revisions and print runs, some of the products mentioned may have become discontinued by the time you read this. But only one product – the VCR I'm about to describe – may not have even been introduced yet.

Sony's DHR-1000 is the first DV format VCR intended for the consumer market. Panasonic has already introduced a DVCPro model, the AJ-D750, but with a list price of over $15,000 it's out of the range of low budget video. My guess is that, when introduced, the DHR-1000 will sell for around $3,500. Sony had not yet announced a price as we were going to press, but had demonstrated the DHR-1000 at numerous trade events. I've had the

Sony DHR-1000 DV format VCR

chance to personally play with it and verify that it works. (if it's not yet available by the time you read this, what's holding it up is the copyright issue – the movie industry fears rampant pirating, and is negotiating with the consumer electronics industry over copy protection.)

The DHR-1000 accepts both the 60-minute MiniDV cassettes, and the full size 270-minute DV cassettes, which are slightly bigger than 8mm tapes. The machine is designed from the ground up for editing. Instead of front panel controls, a removable edit control panel has everything you need to control not just the VCR, but another DV format VCR or a compatible Sony MiniDV camcorder as well.

A single large jog/shuttle control operates both source deck and recorder in the editing system. Edit in and out points are entered in the traditional way. Edit buttons let you select between video-only inserts, A/V inserts, or audio dubs. During recording you have full control over the DV format's audio options, choosing betwen 2 track 16-bit mode or 4 track 12-bit recording. Manual recording level control is available

The rear panel has a full complement of traditional analog audio/video input and output jacks. This lets you transfer your existing footage to DV, and copy your edit masters back to regular VHS for distribution. There's also Sony's standard LANC edit control jack, for compatibility with edit controllers such as from FutureVideo and Videonics.

But what really makes the DHR-1000 shine is its front-panel "firewire" jack. This is the digital dubbing link that, when connected to another DHR-1000 VCR or to one of Sony's MiniDV camcorders, allows you to make absolutely perfect copies back and forth. You can go down dozens of generations, with practically no loss in picture or audio quality. This makes the DHR-1000 a true editing delight, because you can evolve from a rough cut to a fine cut by simply recopying over and over.

The Sony EVS-7000

Sony's EVS-7000 Hi8 VCR is quite a tempting dish, though there's one major drawback. It has a built-in RC Time Code system, which means that, when hooked up to appropriate edit control equipment, it can provide the most automated and repeatable editing of just about any consumer VCR.

The RC time code gets recorded automatically on fresh tape as it's recorded, or it can be added to previously recorded camcorder tapes (professionals call that "post striping" time code). The time code is communicated, electronically, through the

VCR's LANC remote control jack—which is actually a sophisticated computer serial port interface. A computerized edit controller, such as Sony's own RME-1000, or less expensive products such as Video Director from Gold Disk or Thumbs Up from Videonics, automatically receives this time code information and tells the VCR to go forward or reverse, fast or slow, to get to a specific selected point on the tape.

Depending on your needs, you might choose to use the EV-S7000 as the source VCR, or as the recorder. Time code tends to be most useful on the source side, to locate specific points in the raw footage. (A "dream" Hi8 to S-VHS system might pair the EV-S7000 as the source, with Panasonic's AG-1980 as the recorder.)

In the audio department, the EVS-7000 has both AFM stereo hi-fi recording (common on many better camcorders), as well as a set of additional PCM stereo audio tracks. (PCM is almost never found in camcorders, except for Sony's old semi-pro model, the CCD-V5000.) The PCM tracks can be dubbed in, without affecting previously recorded video or audio, and are very useful for adding narration and/or music on tapes that are already edited for picture (such as tapes that have been in-camera edited).

But, as mentioned earlier, this deck (along with most others in the Hi8 format) has one inherent editing disadvantage compared to VHS: No video insert editing ability.

Other Consumer VCRs

Most major Japanese VCR manufacturers offer a top-of-the-line editing VCR, but unfortunately, they're generally not as versatile as the two above mentioned models because they don't have the high level two-way remote control interfaces (Sony's LANC, or Panasonic's 5-pin jack).

Some Sony VCRs have a simpler one-way remote control jack, called Control-S, that works basically like the old wired remote controls. These jacks areno better than using infrared remote signals to control the VCR, such as the way Videonics' Thumbs Up edit controller works.

Many editing VCRs have a "synchro-edit" jack. They're designed to be used with a camcorder of the same brand, for semi-automated editing. Press just one pause button, and both the camcorder and VCR start running simultaneously.

Some VCRs and camcorders offer automated assemble editing of up to 8 scenes, using the synchro-edit system. Usually the scenes must be recorded in the same order as they appear on the original tape. Perhaps the most sophisticated system in this category is JVC's Random Assemble Edit feature, found on some of their high-end camcorders (including the GR-SZ9). It lets you automatically re-arrange several scenes, and works with many brands of VCRs via infrared remote. The word "random" refers to the fact that edited sequences can put the selected scenes into a different order than they occur in on the original recording.

Runner up awards for a Super-VHS VCR go to Sony's SVO-2000 industrial S-VHS model and the SLV-R1000 consumer deck. The consumer deck features Sony's LANC remote control interface, for use with Sony and third-party edit controllers. Editing capabilities are very similar to the old AG-1970—you can do audio dubs on the mono linear track, video inserts, or A/V inserts. In fact, this is currently the only consumer VCR with a full-fledged two-way remote control jack. But there's no time base corrector, and Sony's "Dual Mode Shuttle" control is not as good as a true jog/shuttle, because it lacks the frame-by-frame jog dial. And there's no independent linear audio jack.

(Note that some older Sony VHS format VCRs, and most Betamax models also have the LANC jack, which is also called Control-L. Some older Panasonic VCRs, especially portable models, also have the 5-pin remote control jack. But the trend has been towards eliminating these jacks from mid-priced VCRs, and only putting them on top models.)

Panasonic's PV-S4690 also gets an S-VHS runner up award. Though not as versatile as the industrial AG-1980, this consumer model does include a Matsushita 5-pin edit control jack, as well as audio and video insert edit capabilities.

In the Hi8 department, where not many VCR models have ever been introduced, runner up award goes to Sony's discontinued CVD-1000—the CVD stands for computer video deck, but it is commonly called the "Vdeck". This unique model came neither from Sony's consumer video division nor its industrial division, but rather from Sony's computer products division. Fortunately, at under-$1500, it's priced lower than Sony's top consumer VCR. What distinguishes this editing VCR from the rest of the pack is that it's designed specifically to be operated from a computer—there's no jog/shuttle control, and the front panel buttons are minimal. There's no display either. The remote control interface is a new Sony protocol called VISCA, that hooks right up to the standard RS-232 serial port found on almost any computer. There's already quite a bit of software available to control it, including Gold Disk's Video Director, Homrich's EZV2, and FutureVideo's Edit List Manager.

The Vdeck looks simpler than an ordinary VCR—there's no front panel display, no shuttle control, no flashing clock, no index number counters, no audio level controls or VU meters. These functions are provided by computer software the Vdeck is used with.

The overall editing capabilities of the CVD-1000 are very good —with one glaring exception: It can't do video inserts. But it does automatically record and read RC time code, it can add time code to previously recorded tapes, and can add new soundtracks to camcorder tapes using its PCM audio dub mode. You can thus edit accurately, and add synchronized music and narration to camcorder tapes that have already been shot.

The VISCA remote control jack is actually a serial communi-cations connection that hooks up to any IBM-compatible, Macintosh, or Amiga computer's serial port. Unlike other remote control jacks (like LANC), VISCA allows multiple VCRs to be daisy-chained to a single computer serial port. A tiny front panel light indicates when VISCA communication is established. Sony's companion Vbox converts VISCA to work with LANC (Control-L) remote jacks found on many Sony Hi8/8mm camcorders and VCRs.

The Vdeck can record new audio on the PCM tracks, while leaving a previously recorded picture and AFM audio, but, as mentioned earlier, it's biggest problem is that it can't add new pic-tures to old audio (video inserts).

Two sets of video and audio output jacks are provided on the rear panel. Ironically, there are four audio tracks (AFM stereo and PCM stereo) and four audio output jacks, but it's impossible to get each track out of a separate jack.

There's a front-panel mini-sized stereo microphone jack, but no headphone jack. Combined with the lack of audio VU meters, setting PCM level accurately is almost impossible. When using a microphone, you can't monitor sound with a speaker (since there'll be feedback), so you must make a test recording and play it back—a tedious ritual.

Compared to using a camcorder as a source deck, CVD-1000 offers the editing advantages of RC time code, and two additional synchronized audio tracks (left and right PCM).

Special Features On Industrial Models

Many fancy consumer VCRs offer a variety of special effects, such as PIP (picture in picture), slow motion, and freeze frame. But if you intend to use such effects in your edited project, note that these effects must usually be invoked on the source (playback) side of the editing system. Also, for slow motion and still frame effects, it is imperative that the playback VCR have digital special effects—otherwise, after editing the effects will look too jittery. All MiniDV, and almost all professional format VCRs can do slow motion and freeze frame, but only the best industrial S-VHS and Hi8 models can do it.

Higher priced industrial VCR models costing between $2000 and $6000 not only offer better performance—in terms of less signal degradation with each copy, better frame accuracy, and standard computer serial port remote control interfaces—but unique editing abilities not found on consumer models. If you want to do video insert edits with Hi8, for example, so that you can leave previously recorded audio (on the PCM tracks) while replacing the video (the standard way music videos are edited), you'll need to shell out over five grand for the top-of-the-line Sony EVO-9850 industrial Hi8 VCR, or the slightly less expensive EVO-9650 (see below).

In Super-VHS if you want to do insert video edits while leaving the Hi-fi audio intact, there's only one VCR currently available that can do it: JVC's BR-S378U. This is actually an entry-level industrial model, comparable to the Panasonic AG-1980. But it lacks the all-important remote control jack that makes the AG-1980 so versatile. Strangely, even JVC's costlier Super-VHS decks lack the unique VOS (video on sound) feature, which is great for making music videos.

None of the aforementioned VCRs can record single frames of video, as needed to do high quality animation work. For that job, Sony's EVO-9650, about $5,000, is the ticket. It can also do Hi8 video inserts.

Without one of these special animation VCRs, the shortest intervals you'll be able to record will be around four to seven frames at a time. Since video runs at thirty frames per second, that translates to about an eighth to a third of a second, which is fast enough for crude animation, but not as smooth looking as recording each frame separately.

For single-frame recording, you might also want to look into the Personal Animation Recorder, from Digital Processing (the same company that makes the Personal TBC). It uses hard disk storage, instead of tape.

Getting Started

Don't let all this talk about fancy editing VCRs scare you off. There's no limit to how much you can spend for this type of equipment—some broadcast VCRs sell for over $50,000! Ultimately, it's your editing creativity that counts most. If you've never edited video, start by playing around with a basic home VCR, until you at least get enough experience to appreciate the advantages of the fancier models. Many projects don't really require fancy equipment—it all depends on how many cuts you need to make, how accurate they need to be, and how much fooling around with audio mixing and insert editing you want to do.

Rank novices might begin by simply assembling together the best moments of tapes they've shot. For a fun exercise that doesn't involve sacrificing your own material (it's often hard to part with stuff you've shot yourself), try editing a network TV program recorded off-the-air. Take an hour-long drama, for instance, and try cutting it in half. (I'm using the term "cutting" figuratively here—remember: videotape should never be physically spliced! All editing is done through selective copying.) As you gain experience, you'll see what frustrates you the most working with more basic home equipment, and you'll develop a better idea of which features you'll want when you're ready to spring for a full-fledged editing VCR.

17 Tape Editing Technology

Editing is the next frontier in home video. Home videos usually lack the sparkle and pizazz of professional film and video productions, not so much because the equipment is inferior (indeed, some of today's most sophisticated camcorders actually rival broadcast equipment in technical specifications), but because it's usually used in a casual, arbitrary fashion.

Which is not to say that top notch movie stars, lavish sets, props, lighting, special effects, make-up, and lush multi-track audio don't make a difference—they do. But even without these big budget extravagances, the camcorder is an extremely powerful communication tool. Just like a pen or typewriter, however, the tool alone does not create a work of art.

The Basic Home Editing Setup

Videocassettes resemble audio cassettes in appearance, but technically, the method by which signals get recorded—helical recording—is quite a bit more complex. The helical recording process (explained in Chapter 4) is used for all video formats—VHS, S-VHS, 8mm, Hi8, VHS-C, S-VHS-C, MiniDv, Betamax (Super Beta, ED Beta) and all professional video formats.

Videotape *cannot* be physically spliced, like regular audio tape or film, to accomplish editing. For one thing, helical recording makes it impossible to separate one frame from another. Worse still, severe damage to the VCR can result from splicing videotapes, because the spinning video heads move so rapidly (sixty revolutions per second) that any slight aberration in the tape's surface can chip them. (Some stores actually sell videocassette splicing blocks, but at best, you can use these to repair a precious, but damaged tape. Never play a splice past the video heads. Stop the tape before reaching the splice, and fast forward beyond it to resume play.)

In video, all post-production editing is accomplished by selectively transferring, or "dubbing" material from one tape to another. The system used to make these transfers can be very simple, using equipment you may already own; or it can be quite complex—network television editing suites can cost over a million dollars to build, and rent for hundreds of dollars per hour to use.

Regardless of how sophisticated or primitive the editing equipment is, an analog copy of a videotape never looks quite as good as the original. This is the whole advantage of digital video formats, such as MiniDV and DV – the ability to make perfect copies. But when you edit by selectively copying from one analog tape to another, you "go down a generation" in quality. With most home video equipment (except DV), you are limited to about four or five generations of deterioration before the picture becomes unstable and difficult to view.

The solution to this dilemma is digital video, as exemplified by the MiniDV and DV format. But the price of building a MiniDV editing system is still relatively high, compared with Hi8 and Super-VHS equipment. Fortunately, some of the same edit controller devices, described a bit later, can work with all three formats (Hi8, S-VHS, and MiniDV). This makes it easier to start off working in one of the cheaper formats, and then move up to MiniDV when you can afford it.

The most basic home video editing setup requires no additional equipment beyond a camcorder and VCR. You hook up the video and audio outputs, from the camcorder, into the video and audio inputs of the VCR—just as if you were going to make copies of the camcorder tapes. The only difference is that now you'll be making very selective dubs: Instead of copying an entire tape at a time, you'll copy just short segments, and rearrange the sequence for better dramatic effect. Leave the recording VCR in the record mode, the playback camcorder (or VCR) in the play mode, and press the pause buttons on each to simultaneously start dubbing.

Incidentally, you don't necessarily need a camcorder to edit: Using this hookup between two VCRs, you can edit "found footage" instead of material you shoot yourself. Nor do you need a VCR to edit. You can just as easily edit between two cameras. This basic editing setup will have you jockeying frantically between the two pause buttons on the camcorder and VCR, trying to compensate for the slight differences in time that each takes to release from pause. For casual editing—say, transferring scenes that last for several minutes each—the precision will be adequate.

But for tighter, faster paced editing, you'll find that using the "pause" buttons limits accuracy to about half a second or a second. Inevitably, the beginnings of some scenes get cut, or the end of a scene runs on past the point where it should end.

To minimize the hassle of coordinating the "pause" buttons, many camcorder and VCR manufacturers—including Hitachi, RCA, Sony, JVC, Toshiba, and others—incorporate an "edit" or "synchro-edit" mini-jack that lets you control *both* the camcorder and VCR's "pause" functions from a single button.

It's a useful feature, but note that in many cases the camcorder and VCR must be made by the same manufacturer for it to work properly. Also, the accuracy is only slightly improved, because the VCR and camcorder may still take slightly different amounts of time to release from pause.

Technical Quality and the Flying Erase Head

The technical quality of the edits depends on your equipment. Examine the seams—the edit points—by watching in slow motion as the edit passes through. With some VCRs, there will be a "glitch" or timing error at each edit point. The picture may roll, or become unstable, for as little as a frame or two, or as much as several seconds. A more subtle, but common error is the appearance of a "rainbow effect" for a few seconds after the edit occurs. Colors appear to shimmer before settling down to their correct values.

The flying erase head, described in detail in Chapter 4, can eliminate these problems, and is thus a highly desirable feature for any VCR or camcorder to do video editing. Without a flying erase head, the videotape gets erased by a stationary erase head located several inches in advance of the video recording heads (in the same way that an audio cassette deck has the erase head placed about an inch before the record head). This creates short sections of tape that have been erased but not recorded on, or recorded on twice without being erased—the underlying reasons behind many editing glitches. Installing a "flying" erase head within the video head drum, just a slight fraction of an inch in advance of the video recording head, solves these problems.

Specifics vary with regard to the flying erase head, depending on format and model. Some VHS equipment will only utilize the flying erase head when you insert new video material while retaining the old audio. With 8mm camcorders, however, the flying erase head is always operational, and you must always record new sound along with the picture (it's technically impossible to add new pictures to previously recorded sound, without going down a generation).

The Pro Gear

Beyond the world of home editing is industrial and semi-professional video gear that can improve edit quality in four significant
ways: stability, accuracy, synchronized multi-track audio, and
multi-image effects.

Fancier editing VCRs, such as industrial Super-VHS and Hi8
models costing about five thousand dollars, offer glitch-free edit
quality with rock solid timing stability, so that edits never tear or
break up.

Using an electronic labelling system called "SMPTE Time
Code" (Society of Motion Picture and Television Engineers), each
frame of a videotape is identified with a unique code number so
that edit points are precisely stored and executed, with accuracy
within one thirtieth of a second.

Time code also facilitates synchronizing an unlimited number
of audio tracks, so that music, dialog, sound effects, and background ambience can be separately recorded, edited, and mixed
in.

Beyond the "straight cut" from one image to another is "A/B
roll" editing—letting you mix together two different recorded images at the same time (an "A" roll and a "B" roll of videotape).
This allows you to dissolve rather than cut from one shot to another, or to create split screens, wipes, and other multi-image special effects.

Technically, A/B roll editing requires precise electronic synchronization of the video scanning process for two different recorded images. Currently, Panasonic's WJ-AVE7, MX-10, MX-12,
MX-30, and MX-50 "image mixers" are among the least expensive
accessories that can achieve this; as this book was going to press
two similar video mixing devices—from Sony and Videonics—
were being introduced. Prices run from about a thousand to five
thousand dollars, excluding the VCRs. The "Video Toaster" offers
a pricier image mixing system—starting at about five thousand
dollars, including two "time base correctors" to synchronize the A
and B video signals (the Toaster is covered in more detail later).

But before buying such exotic equipment, you might want to
check out a local cable-TV public access center, or a video editing
rental facility, to see how fancy editing equipment gets used. Such
facilities are available in most big cities at rates of ten to fifty dollars per hour, and can be found in the Yellow Pages under "Video
Production Services".

JVC RM-G870U
industrial A/B roll edit
controller for S-VHS
decks.

Low Budget Desktop Video Editing

Videotape cannot be physically spliced, as previously explained, because the spinning video heads and helical tracks make it dangerous and imprecise. All editing of videotape therefore takes the form of electronic editing—transferring electronic signals around within a tape, or from one tape to another.

Many high-end camcorders and VCRs offer a substantial amount of "in-camera" editing capability—letting you edit tapes as you go along, and go back to insert things and dub in audio.

But practically all professional video producers, and many serious video hobbyists find in-camera editing too limited, because of the fixed time constraints that it poses. What if you shoot an hour of footage and want to condense it down to fifteen minutes? Since you can't splice the tape, there is no way to shorten the original tape.

As explained earlier, electronic video editing is the process of selectively copying portions of one tape onto another tape. The original videotape—also called the "raw footage," "master," or "camera original" tape—remains unchanged during the editing process. Sections of the tape are cued up and played, while another VCR records them.

Edit controllers automatically coordinate the action of two or more pieces of video equipment, such as a camcorder and a VCR, or two VCRs. Since editing is essentially a copying process, these two VCRs (or camcorder and VCR) are generally referred to as the "player" or "source" machine and the "recorder" or "editing" machine.

In addition to providing a centralized, convenient remote control for both pieces of equipment, the edit controller improves the precision of editing by electronically identifying specific points on both tapes and using those points to coordinate the editing action. More sophisticated edit controllers can store a lengthy list of edit points—called an EDL or edit decision list—that can be repeated again and again. For the most precise editing, the EDL lets you see a "rough cut" of your editing project, then fine tune the edit points until you have a "fine cut", without having to relocate all the editing points yourself.

Types of Edit Controllers

There are a number of different types of edit controllers on the market, selling from hundreds of dollars to tens of thousands of dollars. They vary in terms of the precision of the editing, the type of equipment they can work with, and their ability to store and modify edit decision lists.

An edit controller by itself does not create a great editing system. The quality of the edits is primarily determined by the VCRs that are used for editing. The edit controller simply facilitates convenient access to the inherent editing capabilities of the VCRs. For maximum editing power, the edit controller should be able to take advantage of all of a VCR's editing features—the best editing setup for any given budget will have components that are well suited for each other.

Specific items to look at in evaluating editing systems are its cuing capabilities (how it locates specific points on a tape, and how accurately it gets there); the availability of different editing modes (picture only, sound only, insert and assemble); and the method of interconnection between the VCRs (or camcorder) and the edit controller, how accurately it edits, and how "clean" (glitch-free) are the edits it makes.

Consumer Infrared (IR), Industrial, Hi-end Professional (CMX)

The simplest edit controllers are designed for use with consumer equipment, utilizing infrared remote control signals to mimic the commands from a VCR's wireless remote control. The problem with the wireless system is that it is a one-way street—the edit controller can send command signals to the VCRs, but the controller does not receive information to find out the location of the tape on the VCRs, nor its current mode of operation. To get around this limitation, various schemes have been devised—all with some drawbacks. By rewinding the tape to the beginning and counting time from that point while the tape is playing, a fairly accurate edit can be performed. That's the logic behind Videonics' DirectED products. But to find numerous out-of-sequence edit points with this precision may require many playings from the beginning of a tape. Some IR editing controller systems, like DirectED, make a copy of the original tapes, and add their own time code numbers to the copy. These numbers become part of the video signal. The drawback to this system is that you must go down a generation just to add the time code, and there is no comparable code on the recorder side of the editing system—just the player side.

The next category up in edit controllers is variously called "semiprofessional", "prosumer", or "low end industrial". This is the category that FutureVideo's edit controllers fall into. These desktop edit controllers generally use remote control cables to link the edit controller to the source and recorder equipment. The advantage of cables, over infrared, is that a two-way link is established: Not only can the edit controller command the VCRs (or camcorder and VCR), but the VCRs tell the edit controller where they are in the tape, and what it's doing at the moment. This leads to far more accurate and reliable editing than can be accomplished with infrared, and it generally takes less time, too.

Both consumer and industrial edit controllers are designed to work with VHS-family and 8mm/Hi8 equipment. The most advanced professional edit controllers, and high-end industrial models, generally work with a higher grade of tape equipment—utilizing the 1", Betacam, MII, D-2, or 3/4" tape formats. Some models work with the fanciest (industrial) versions of Super-VHS or Hi8 VCRs, and can combine them with equipment in the professional formats. The professional formats' control cables can carry more information than with the consumer and low-end industrial equipment, leading to more precise editing with a minimum of glitches. However, for the vast majority of non- broadcast applications the Hi8 and Super-VHS desktop video equipment provides more than adequate precision and edit quality.

On-line and Off-line Editing

A company called CMX pioneered the development of computerized edit decision list systems for professional videotape editing, and established a set of standards for computerized lists of video edit points. Consequently, many other brands of edit controller equipment provide CMX-compatibility, or CMX-conversion capability. Although for most low-budget producers this CMX compatibility is meaningless, at a somewhat higher budget level it offers powerful capabilities.

Editing time using professional format equipment can cost hundreds of dollars per hour. It is prohibitively expensive to pay such high rates to sit and ponder how an edited sequence should look.

Many professional editing jobs are therefor first thought out using less expensive desktop or industrial editing equipment. This is called the "off-line" edit. Then, after the edit points are all figured out, the original professional format tapes are edited "on-line" (at hundreds of dollars per hour) using the edit decision list created with off-line equipment. If the off-line editing system can create a CMX-compatible computer file (like FutureVideo systems can), the edit point numbers can be readily transferred from the low budget system to the big budget system.

Alternatively, even some video producers who shoot in Hi8 or Super-VHS choose to transfer all the footage to a professional format for editing. This is called "bumping up" the tape to a fancier format. The advantage is that in the professional formats there is less generational loss as each copy is made, and there is wider editing flexibility with regard to adding audio tracks, special digital and slow motion effects, and combining multiple video signals together. Most producers who bump-up their Hi8 and S-VHS format tapes will also develop their edit decision lists using inexpensive desktop video equipment, and then transfer the CMX file to a big budget professional editing suite as the final act of the editing process.

How Edit Controllers Work

All videotape edit controllers perform a somewhat similar process, though details vary. The process begins when the user selects a set of "edit points"—specific moments in time on the original tape that represent the beginning and end of a segment to be transferred. The user also selects a beginning point on the recorder VCR, where this material is to be transferred to. The edit controller can then be told to go ahead and perform the edit—to actually locate the points, playing the source VCR while recording on the recorder VCR. To do this properly, the edit controller will "preroll" both the source and record tapes—that is, the tapes will be up and running at full speed before the editing begins, so that there is no problem with acceleration time.

When an edit controller has decision list capability, the edits do not have to be performed one at a time. Instead, the editor can specify a lengthy list of editing points, and then have the editing system automatically locate each set of points and perform all the edits—assuming that all the source material has been recorded onto a single tape. (More on this below.)

Remote Connections

The method by which an edit controller connects to the player and recorder in an edit system makes a big difference in what capabilities, and accuracy, the edit system has. Here is a summary of the major types of remote control connector systems. These obscure jacks (or the lack of them) play a central role when editing.

LANC and 5-pin Connectors

The LANC (also called Control-L) and Matsushita (Panasonic) 5-pin connectors offer the best communication between the edit controller and the VCR (or camcorder). These remote control jacks, along with Sony's abandoned VISCA protocol (see below), are the only ones found on low budget equipment that offer full two-way communication between the edit controller and the VCR (or camcorder).

Sony's LANC jack, also known as a "Control-L" connector, is located to the right of the headphone jack on this camcorder. It looks similar to the headphone jack, but takes a smaller submini size plug.

The LANC and Matsushita 5-pin remote control connections are two-way serial communications ports. The edit controller can send commands to the camcorder or VCR for complete motion control (pause, search, slow motion, play, stop, etc.), as well as edit mode control (assemble, insert, dub). The VCR, or camcorder, sends back information to the edit controller about its current location in the tape (index number or hours:minutes:seconds).

There are two different systems in use because of the ongoing format war between Sony and Matsushita (parent company of JVC, which also owns Panasonic, Quasar, Technics, and numerous others). They are essentially similar, except that the Matsushita 5-pin system communicates at a faster rate of data exchange, resulting in more frequent and rapid updating of the tape location information to the edit controller.

Matsushita 5-pin remote control connector, labelled "System E" on this Panasonic PV-DV1000 MiniDV camcorder.

Over the years, the Matsushita 5-pin connector jack has remained essentially the same. It appears on numerous pieces of Panasonic industrial video equipment, as well as some consumer video equipment, including Panasonic's current top Super-VHS model, the AG-1980, and Panasonic's PV-DV1000 MiniDV camcorder. It is usually labelled "Remote", (or "System E") and is recognizable as a small round jack with five little holes arranged in a grid (similar to, but smaller than an S-video jack).

Sony's competing system has undergone some evolution over the years. Originally named Control-L, or Ctl-L, this jack initially took a very similar form to the Matsushita 5- pin jack—a small circular jack with five little holes (but the layout was different than Matsushita's). However, since this is really a serial communications port in which dozens of different commands can be communicated through digital codes sent over the same communications wires, the jack was subsequently made smaller by converting it to a subminiature mini phone jack—reducing it to a tiny single hole, smaller than the microphone jack found on most camcorders. This newer Control-L jack is a stereo sub-mini jack (three connections), but it offers all the same capabilities that the larger 5-pin jacks offered. Sony also changed the name from Control-L to LANC—for Local Application Network Control—with onlys slight changes in what the jack can do.

Sony's LANC jack now spans three different tape format families: Hi8 (and 8mm), Super-VHS (and VHS), and MiniDV (and DV). With Hi8 models equippend with RC time code, as well as all MiniDV and DV models, the LANC jack communicates time code information to the edit controller.

The Matsushita 5-pin jack spans two formats: Super-VHS (and VHS) and MiniDV. Time code only gets communicated through the jack with MiniDV equipment.

Finally, one difference that has been observed in certain pieces of consumer equipment—but may not reflect an inherent problem with the communications link—is that some of Sony's Super-VHS format VCRs that have LANC are not as reliable in maintaining a consistent pre-roll time as are Panasonic's industrial VCRs with the Matsushita 5-pin connection. A VCR's built-in pre-roll time is only relevant when using the VCR for the recorder side of the editing system. With some Sony models, the pre-roll time varies from 20 to 30 frames, resulting in 10-frame errors (one third of a second).

One advantage of third party editing equipment—–such as from FutureVideo and Videonics—is that they are compatible with both of these systems. By contrast, edit controllers made by Sony (or designed specifically for use with 8mm camcorders, like

Videonics' Thumbs Up) usually work only with LANC, and equipment made by Panasonic usually works only with the Matsushita 5-pin remote jack.

Firewire

The Firewire connection is the newest interface for low budget video, and is found only on MiniDV and DV format equipment. Unlike all the other connectors mentioned in this section, Firewire, which is formally known as IEEE 1394, carries much more than remote control information—it also carries the video and audio signals. This connector was introduced on Sony's MiniDV camcorders. Fortunately, since there were no Firewire based edit controllers available when these camcorders first appeared, Sony's MiniDV camcorders also have Control-L remote jacks, making them compatible with existing edit controllers. (See the chapter on the MiniDV and DV format for more information about Firewire.)

Remote Pause and Synchro-Edit

Many camcorders and VCRs have a simple remote control jack that can be used for starting and pausing the tape. The simplest variations are called "remote pause" jacks, while a more sophisticated variation is called "synchro-edit". Both are designed to allow one piece of equipment—such as an edit controller or a compatible VCR—to control the pause/stop function on the other. Unfortunately, most synchro-edit jacks require purchasing a camcorder and VCR from the same manufacturer. The more sophisticated systems can store six or eight editing events in memory, and automatically perform the edits. But compared to using a separate edit controller, the synchro-edit system is crude.

With some edit controllers (including FutureVideo's), the remote pause connection can be used on the recorder side of the edit system, to selectively record and pause the tape (assemble editing—see below). The connection is made using the GPI jack (see below).

The synchro-edit or remote pause terminal can also be used on the player side of an editing system to start a second player (the "B-roll" in an A/B-roll editing system) to begin playback.

Infrared Remote Control

Most VCRs and many camcorders have wireless remote controls that use coded infrared light to provide one-way command. Some consumer edit controllers, like the Videonics Thumbs Up and Gold Disk's Video Director, mimic these infrared light codes, thereby duplicating the motion controls. However, since the infrared system is strictly one-way, the edit controller cannot know where it is in the tape. Infrared controllers therefor cannot usually do insert edits—they can only assemble edit.

Control-S

The Control-S jack is a one-way remote control jack that functions much like the infrared remote control receptor—through this jack, all motion control information can be communicated. Unlike the more sophisticated Control-L jacks, however, Control-S does not communicate the location of the tape, and is consequently not as useful for editing. The Control-S connector is only found on older equipment—conceptually, it dates back to the era before IR wireless remote controls became standard equipment on VCRs.

VISCA Control

VISCA promises to offer a new breed of full-fledged computer controlled VCRs that utilize a standard RS-232C serial port connector to communicate motion control and position. This remote control system is called "VISCA"—for Video System Control Architecture. VISCA is a Sony protocol.

VISCA provides all of the remote control capabilities of the LANC and Matsushita 5-pin interfaces, and represents the current state-of-the-art in desktop video editing interfacing. In particular, VISCA models are generally superior in their ability to record single-frame animation. However, at the time this was written, the only VISCA equipped VCR were Sony's CVD-1000 Hi8 format "Vdeck" (about $1,500), and a slightly lower priced 8mm deck. No VHS-family VISCA equipment exists.

General Purpose Interface (GPI)

As its name implies, the general purpose interface (GPI) is a versatile connection to additional equipment that can be put to a number of different uses. The jack is usually a simple two-wire mini-phone jack, but the signal that appears on the jack is often programmable from the equipment it appears on .

The GPI uses standard digital "on" and "off" signals to communicate with other pieces of video equipment that have appropriate remote control jacks. On FutureVideo edit controllers, for example, the GPI can be programmed selectively to go on for the duration of an edit, or to go on for just a brief moment at the beginning and end of an edit, or to do the opposite—going off at the specified times.

The most basic use of the GPI jack is to coordinate editing when using consumer video equipment that has only a "remote pause" or "synchro-edit" jack. For example, in hooking up an editing system to edit from an 8mm camcorder with an LANC jack to a VHS format VCR with a remote pause jack, the GPI would be used to stop and start the VCR. (That is, the GPI is used instead of the LANC/Matsushita 5-pin jack to remote control the recorder).

In more advanced time code editing systems, where both the player and the recorder have LANC or Matsushita 5-pin jacks, the GPI can be used to help put continuous time code onto a Hi-fi track (in VHS) of the edited tape. As the edit controller performs a series of edits, the GPI can selectively run and pause a time code generator, so that a smooth, continuous time code track gets recorded onto the tape. (These time code numbers can become important for subsequent insert editing).

The GPI jack can also be used for triggering special effects during the transition, in editing, from one shot to another. In this way, for example, the GPI can command an image mixer to record a freeze-frame at the end of an edit, and then gradually dissolve from this freeze-frame at the beginning of the next edit, creating a "pseudo-dissolve." Many Video Toaster users take advantage of the Toaster's GPI for this purpose.

The GPI is also useful for advanced A/B roll editing, in which full motion dissolves between two scenes, as well as numerous other special effects, are created through the use of a separate image mixing device capable of synchronizing the two non-synchronized source tapes (the "A roll" on one VCR and the "B roll" on another). The GPI can be used to trigger a second source VCR or camcorder (the "B" roll) that has been manually cued to a selected location on the tape. It can work with "synchro-edit" camcorder and VCR jacks for this purpose. (Other technical considerations in A/B roll editing are discussed in more detail a bit later).

Other effects, like fades, digital wipes, solarization, etc, can also be triggered on image mixers like Panasonic's MX-12 and the Toaster. Titles from an electronic character generator can be triggered to automatically superimpose and drop out. And the GPI can also trigger practically any other video equipment offering basic (run/pause) remote control operation.

The RS-232C Interface for Computers

Some industrial VCRs offer RS-232C remote control jacks. This allows a computer to remote control them directly. Practically all IBM, Mac, and Amiga computers have an RS-232C port already built-in.

IBM, Macintosh and Amiga computers can also be used as edit controllers, in conjunction with other specialized equipment, such as the FutureVideo edit controller hardware that communicates through the RS-232C port to a separate box. The box then communicates with the camcorder and/or VCR using LANC or Matsushita 5-pin protocols.

Some special effects generators, such as Panasonic's WJ-MX30, incorporate an RS-232C port which can be used for computer controlled, automated special effects—a useful feature for advanced A/B roll decision-list editing.

The RS-422 Interface

RS-422 is found on more expensive industrial and broadcast VCRs. It provides a similar remote control function. However, most computers do not have a built-in RS-422 interface, making it more difficult to connect. For Macintosh computers, the Sundance edit controller (a software & hardware combo product) lets you interface to RS422 cables via the mac's printer or modem port.

. . . .

Editing Accuracy

The accuracy of a video editing system is dependent on several factors:

- The ability of the system to figure out exactly where it is on each tape (player and recorder tape locations).
- The ability to repeatedly locate a tape position when prerolling during editing (minimizing tape slippage).
- Consistent and predictable preroll time of the record deck, so the editing controller can reliably compensate for any delays from the time it tells a VCR to do something to the time it does it.
- Quick and stable communication of the tape status signals from the VCRs (or camcorder) to the edit controller, to maintain synchronization.
- The ability of the edit controller to compensate for errors that can occur when bad data is sent to the controller due to noise on the tape or stretching of the tape.

Most modern editing systems—even the least expensive consumer edit controllers—can compensate for time lags in the control process, simply by knowing which model VCR they are hooked up to and what its time delays are. The focus of editing accuracy—at least as far as choosing an edit controller is concerned—thus revolves largely around the method by which the edit controller finds out where it is on the tape.

As mentioned earlier, some of the crudest infrared editing systems get no such location information from the VCRs—they simply count how many minutes and seconds have elapsed since the tape was rewound and started playing. Accuracy is generally limited to about a second or two, at best, and can drift as more time goes by.

For desktop video and industrial applications, editing accuracy of less than a second is generally needed. There are several different systems which camcorders, VCRs, and edit controllers use to keep track of where they are on a tape, varying in accuracy from less than a second to within one frame of the selected edit points:

Hours:Minutes:Seconds Tape Counter Displays

Most 8mm/Hi8 camcorders, and the better VHS/Super-VHS equipment offer a "real time" or "linear time" counter display. The readout is in the form of hours:minutes:seconds, such as 1:23:40. If the VCR or camcorder has a Control-L (LANC) remote control jack, then this counter information can feed into the edit controller to provide reasonably accurate information about where the tape is located. However, if an edit decision list is going to store a series of edit points, it is crucial that the tape be periodically rewound to the beginning and the counter reset to 0:00:00 to maintain accuracy.

The more you move around through a tape, searching through edit points, the more often the VCR or camcorder is likely to lose track of a frame or two, thus throwing off the editing accuracy. Also, note that every time you eject one tape and insert another, the counter automatically resets to 0:00:00. This means that you may have to keep rewinding tapes back to the beginning just to set the counter properly, even though the material you need for editing may be located an hour into the tape and take quite a long time to find. (FutureVideo's EDL software can help you get around this problem by specifying alternate reference points in the middle of a tape.)

Index Number (4 Digit) Editing

Older VHS-family equipment tends to use a simpler 4-digit index counter system, rather than the hr:min:sec display. The numbers from the 4-digit counter are also electronically communicated to the edit controller system through the Matsushita (Panasonic) 5-pin jack, but these numbers do not correlate with any specific lengths of time. Rather, they are arbitrary counts of how many times one of the rollers that the tape glides over has spun around. These numbers tend to be less accurate than the hr:min:sec display, especially in terms of accumulating error as the edit system executes a lengthy decision list. (And since the counters vary from machine to machine, an edit list created with one VCR cannot be later used with another VCR.)

Control Track Editing

Since video signals consist of thirty frames per second, neither the hr:min:sec display nor the index counter system provide accuracy to a specific frame. Industrial video editing systems that do not use time code are called "control track" editors. Dating back to 1970s, the control track system uses electronic counters to keep track of pulses that the VCR sends out each time the frame changes. These pulses originate from the control track of the tape, where each new frame is marked off, and are communicated through cables that tethered the VCR to the edit controller.

The control track system can provide editing accuracy within a few frames, when performing each edit one at a time—the way many industrial video edit controllers work. However, for editing a long decision list, a large amount of error can accumulate as the VCRs accidentally slip here and there and miss a frame.

Within camcorders and VCRs that have hr:min:sec displays, something very similar to a control track system is used to count frames. Every thirty frames constitutes one second, and increases the count by one. Even in the 8mm/Hi8 format, where there is no control track per se, it is a simple matter to electronically count the frames. VCRs and camcorders that use this principle will stop counting when there is no recorded signal on the tape—when it is blank—since there are no frames to count.

With desktop video equipment, the advance of each frame is electronically communicated through the Control-L/LANC or Matsushita 5-pin cable, but the communications protocols are different for the two systems. The serial communications system on both allows the edit controller to request the VCR or camcorder to report back its exact location (in HR:MIN:SEC:FRAMES), but most of the Control-L/LANC equipment only reports back its location to the nearest second. The most sophisticated desktop video edit controllers, such as FutureVideo's products, can calculate precise frame numbers by first waiting for a change in the number of seconds, and then counting frames from that point.

. . . .

Time Code: SMPTE, VITC, RC, and MiniDV

The best way to locate edit points, and achieve accuracy to a specific frame of a videotape, is to use time code. Time code is a sytem that labels each frame of a video tape with its own unique frame number. With time code, when you select specific frames for edit points, there's no question which frame you've selected. You can remove a tape from the camcorder or VCR, and put it back in, and the number identifying that frame will remain the same (unlike counters, which will automatically reset to zero whenever you insert a tape.)

There are four different systems for recording time code on tape that you're likely to encounter: SMPTE, VITC, RC, and the MiniDV format's own built-in system. With MiniDV and RC-equipped Hi8 equipment, the time code is part of the format itself (see chapters on 8mm and MiniDV for more info.) SMPTE and VITC, by contrast, are more universal signals that can be recorded onto any tape format.

SMPTE stands for the Society of Motion Picture and Television Engineers, a trade organization that established this standard in the late 1970s, to facilitate the development of edit decision list capabilities in professional video editing equipment.

Time code numbers generally appear in the format of HOURS:MINUTES:SECONDS:FRAMES, with the count advancing the seconds by one whenever the frames count goes from 29 to 00. (That is, the next frame after 0:59:59:29 is 1:00:00:00.) Additionally, the SMPTE time code system also sets aside a small amount of electronic space to record any information the user wants—such as a title, date, reel number, etc. These are called "user bits" of information.

SMPTE time code comes in two general forms—as an audio signal, or as part of the video signal. The audio signal SMPTE code can be readily recorded on any available audio track on a video tape, and is consequently more accessible for desktop applications. (See the Tape Formats chapter for a discussion of the audio tracks.) The SMPTE audio signal sounds somewhat like a computer modem, and uses a similar principle to encode a series of numbers into a warbling computer tone. The audio SMPTE system is sometimes called "longitudinal time code", because it used to be recorded along the edge tracks of a video tape (the linear track). However, today this is something of a misnomer, since the audio signal can be recorded on any audio track—including any of the helically recorded audio in VHS (the Hi-fi tracks) or 8mm (the AFM or PCM tracks).

Professional video equipment uses another form of SMPTE time code called VITC—vertical interval time code. The numbers get recorded in the picture part of the videotape signal, utilizing unseen scan lines at the very top of the video frame. (Closed captioning for the hearing impaired utilizes a similar process.) Most professional video recording equipment automatically inserts this time code into the picture information as it is recorded. But consumer camcorders cannot record VITC, and it is impossible to add this particular form of time code without going down a generation (making a copy of it). VITC is therefor problematic for use in desktop editing systems.

When not otherwise specified, the term "SMPTE time code" most commonly refers to the audio form, while "VITC" refers to the video form.

Both versions of SMPTE time code offer a "drop frame" variation which compensates for the fact that color video signals actually have a precise frame rate of 29.97 frames per second—not exactly 30 fps. With drop frame time code numbering, the frames are numbered as if the rate were 30 fps, but then a couple of frame numbers are skipped (dropped) every few minutes, to compensate for the slight time difference. With drop frame numbering, when the time code reads exactly one-hour past the beginning of a program, the number reflects the exact length of the program—not one hour and tens seconds.

Most time code generators give you the choice to record in either format. I generally recommend you choose the non-drop-frame mode, because it will prove less confusing when you edit later on, and need to subtract numbers in HR:MIN:SEC:FRAMES to figure out how long various audio and video segments last for. Also, if you want to maintain timing compatibility with 8mm RC time code (below), the non-drop-frame format is preferable.

Edit Decision Lists

Much of the power of today's sophisticated desktop video editing systems comes from their ability to automatically edit tapes, using an edit decision list (EDL) as their guide. Prior to the development of EDL capability, video editors had a very difficult time try-

File	Edit	Zoom	Effects	Ripple/Sort	UTR	Options	Help	Quit

Total Listed Time = 0:00:00.00   Elapsed Time =
SOURCE ■ 0:06:17.—   RECORDER ■ 0:01:32.—

		Source					Recorder		
STOP	<<RW	PLAY		FF>>	STOP	<<RW	PLAY		FF>>
<JOG	<!!	STILL	!!>	JOG>	<JOG	<!!	STILL	!!>	JOG>

REF	EVENT	EDIT	TRANS	SRC IN	SRC OUT	REC IN	REC OUT
001		VIDEO INS	CUT	0:00:00.00	0:00:00.00	0:00:00.00	0:00:00.00
002		VIDEO INS	CUT	0:00:00.00	0:00:00.00	0:00:00.00	0:00:00.00
003		VIDEO INS	CUT	0:00:00.00	0:00:00.00	0:00:00.00	0:00:00.00
004		VIDEO INS	CUT	0:00:00.00	0:00:00.00	0:00:00.00	0:00:00.00
005		VIDEO INS	CUT	0:00:00.00	0:00:00.00	0:00:00.00	0:00:00.00
006		VIDEO INS	CUT	0:00:00.00	0:00:00.00	0:00:00.00	0:00:00.00
007		VIDEO INS	CUT	0:00:00.00	0:00:00.00	0:00:00.00	0:00:00.00
008		VIDEO INS	CUT	0:00:00.00	0:00:00.00	0:00:00.00	0:00:00.00
009		VIDEO INS	CUT	0:00:00.00	0:00:00.00	0:00:00.00	0:00:00.00
010		VIDEO INS	CUT	0:00:00.00	0:00:00.00	0:00:00.00	0:00:00.00
011		VIDEO INS	CUT	0:00:00.00	0:00:00.00	0:00:00.00	0:00:00.00
012		VIDEO INS	CUT	0:00:00.00	0:00:00.00	0:00:00.00	0:00:00.00
013		VIDEO INS	CUT	0:00:00.00	0:00:00.00	0:00:00.00	0:00:00.00
014		VIDEO INS	CUT	0:00:00.00	0:00:00.00	0:00:00.00	0:00:00.00
015		VIDEO INS	CUT	0:00:00.00	0:00:00.00	0:00:00.00	0:00:00.00

A blank EDL. Courtesy of Future Video Products.

ing to revise edited work. Each edit had to be performed in sequence along the tape. If a ten-second mistake was later discov-
ered, say, fifteen minutes into a half hour edited tape, then the
editor would have to re-perform each of the subsequent edits from
that point on—essentially re-editing half the tape just to fix one
minor problem. Under these circumstances, it was no wonder why
so many video editors developed an attitude that allowed minor
mistakes to slip through.

Evolution from Rough Cut to Fine Cut

The EDL allows video editors to put the same kind of care and
precision into their editing that film editors put into movies, because it provides a convenient way to revise and change an edited
work.

Think for a moment about how professional film editors do
their job: First they look at all the raw footage for a given scene,
and select the "takes" (repeated performances) that they think are
the best, or that seem to go together the best to maintain a consistent feeling from shot to shot. All the other footage gets put aside.
Then, from this reel of "selected takes", they extract lines of dialog, reaction shots, cutaway shots, establishing shots, etc. as
needed to form a "rough cut" of the scene. The rough cut might
show two different versions of the same thing, or have elements

missing that will be added later (such as music, special effects, etc). The editor then proceeds to pare down the rough cut—making final selections of which shots to use when, pacing moments between lines of dialog, etc. Ultimately, what emerges from this process is called a "fine cut"—a precisely edited version of the scene that is ready for the subsequent stages of the post-production process (scoring music, mixing, etc).

The fact that you cannot physically splice videotape, to trim down edit points and rearrange shots, makes this revision process very cumbersome when compared with film. The EDL alleviates much of the problem, by automating the process of editing. With EDL capability, you can first create a rough cut by entering all the edit points for takes that you want to use. Then the computer can take over—spending several hours editing together the sequence of selected takes that you specified. The process may take hours, but if all the source material is on the same tape, it can be completely automatic. (If tape changes are required, you'll have to "babysit" the system, popping in new tapes as needed.)

When the editing system finishes this task, you can look at the tape and decide where you'd like to change things. If you're working with time code, you may be able to enter new edit points directly from the edited tape, making it very convenient to trim down the footage. (Otherwise, you may have to go back to the original footage to locate the revised edit points, or to guess the number of frames or seconds by which you wish to trim the edit point.)

After making a series of such changes, you can let the editing system utilize the revised EDL to create a new version of the edited videotape. Again, you may have to wait a while for the editing system to do this automatically, but when it's done you'll have a new "cut" of the project that you can analyze for further editing.

If you want to work on revising just one short sequence at a time, you can eliminate much of the waiting by having the edit system perform just a small portion of the EDL at a time—a sequence of just a handful of edits. Using this technique, you can rapidly move forward through the evolution of an editing project by checking the last few edits along with the latest one, to see how it "works".

Workprints

The idea of using workprints for editing, rather than original footage, began with film. Editing scratches and dirties film—so editors use copies of the original footage, that have corresponding edge numbers identifying each frame. After the editing is completed, a "negative cutter" conforms the original footage to match the edited workprint—a very tedious and time consuming process.

Thanks to time code, video editors can have a much easier time editing with workprints. The advantage is the same for video as with film—the act of editing inevitably causes some damage to the material being edited. The power of the edit decision list is its ability to be revised and trimmed. If your EDL goes through twenty generations of development, you may end up having the equipment reedit the same footage dozens of times. All that searching, playing, and pausing of the tape will lead to minor dropouts, stretches, and other slight glitches.

By using a workprint of the camera original footage, you can get the precision you want while maintaining the technical quality of the original footage. Only after you are absolutely sure that your EDL is finalized do you put the original tapes in and edit them.

The key to doing this precisely, of course, is having identical time code numbers on the original tapes and the workprints. Since audio SMPTE time code can simply be copied from the audio track on one tape to an audio track on another tape—even in a different format—it is the most flexible time code system for utilizing workprints.

A major limitation of the 8mm RC time code system is the fact that you can't easily copy the time code from one tape to another. However, it is possible to record slightly different SMPTE time code numbers on a workprint copy of a tape with RC time code, and then figure out the offset between the two sets of numbers.

With the MiniDV and DV format, thanks to digital dubbing the picture and sound quality on a workprint can be identical to that on the original. Therefor, you can actually perform all the edits in the final prodution from the workprint, and save the original as a safety backup in case the copy gets accidentally chewed up.

The Edit Decision List and Workprints

The edit decision list (EDL) forms the basis of workprint editing. You use the workprints to create an EDL, and then go back and edit the original camera footage using the same EDL. If you have time code on the original tapes, the match between the workprint edits and the final edits should be perfect. With control track editing, the match will be less precise. You can utilize the reference feature of the EDL software to help enhance the editing precision, by periodically providing index number reference points at noticeable events in the camera original tape.

Note that with the MiniDV and DV formats, if you're copying the signal digitally, you can edit by going down numerous generations without ever having to go back to the originals. This gives you a lot more flexibility with your decision lists, since there's no need to ever match the final decision list with the original tape. Each decision list represents the selected edits for that particular version, such as one decision list in which you selected takes, another list in which you put together a rough cut, another in which you trimmed the rough cut, another representing final trims.

Going Down Two Generations to Maintain Interformat Editing Consistency

A workprint, by definition, is a copy of an original tape. If you're editing between two different formats, such as from Hi8 camcorder tapes to Super-VHS, then the question will arise as to what format to copy the workprints to. Ideally, you should edit workprints that are in the same format as the originals, so that the equipment setup doesn't change from editing the workprints to editing the originals. That way, subtle timing factors that may be unique to your equipment will not change when you do your final edit with the original tapes.

If you don't have two pieces of 8mm equipment, but you shoot in 8mm, then it may prove advantageous to go down two generations to make the workprints—that is, first copying the Hi8 originals to Super-VHS, then copying the Super-VHS copies back to blank Hi8 tapes, which become the workprints for editing.

Assemble vs. Insert Editing

In the VHS-family and 3/4", as well as most professional analog video formats, there are two different technical variations of the editing process—assemble and insert editing. Note that these distinctions do not apply to the 8mm/Hi8 and MiniDV/DV formats (but if you edit from 8mm or MiniDV to VHS, then the distinction between assemble and insert editing is applicable, since the VHS format is on the recorder side of the editing system).

The difference between assemble and insert editing stems from the different types of erase heads available on VHS, Super-VHS, and most professional video formats. Since the 8mm format only has one type of erase head, the distinction does not apply.

In the VHS-family, assemble editing is what most people would think of as normal recording. Look at the path the tape takes through a typical VHS format VCR (see diagram). The tape first passes a stationery erase head, which erases the full width of the tape. Next, this erased (blank) tape has helical video tracks, linear audio tracks, and a control track recorded on it. As long as the tape keeps moving forward through this system, a continuous series of video, audio, and control track signals are created. Even if the tape is paused, the tracks can continue from where they left off, as long as the VCR or camcorder can get up to speed fast enough. (Many VCRs and camcorders have a "backspace" editing feature that brings the tape back slightly every time it is paused, giving it a short amount of time to get up to speed before it starts recording again).

But what happens if you wish to go back into the middle of a previously recorded tape and insert something new? Two problems will result: First, at the very beginning of the inserted material, there will be a short section of tape—representing the distance between the erase head and the video head—where the second image is recorded over tape that hasn't been erased. Usually the second image overpowers the first image, but the highly sensitive color signal becomes undecipherable to the VCR, resulting in a shimmering rainbow of colors during the first second or two after the insert edit begins. At the end of the insert, though, a far worse problem occurs. There will be a blank section of tape, again representing the distance between the erase head and the video head. This small section of tape has been erased and not recorded on. There is no way to eliminate this "glitch" in the tape.

That's how assemble editing gets its name—as long as you move forward on the tape, assembling a sequence of one shot after the next, the edits look smooth.

The main advantage of assemble editing is time—assemble editing requires no special advance preparation. In TV news, for example, experienced news editors may first perform a series of assemble edits to produce a smooth soundtrack of an interview that fits the specified time, and then go back and add several video inserts to cover visual problems such as jump cuts, poor focus, random zooming, etc.

Insert editing, on the other hand, is designed to deal with the specific problem of putting new material in the middle of a previously recorded tape. A flying erase head inside the video head drum makes this possible. The flying erase head erases the helical video track just before it is rerecorded onto by the video head—consequently, there are no glitches at the beginning or end of the insert.

In the VHS family, only the video and Hi-Fi audio tracks are recorded by the helical heads—so when you perform an insert edit, the linear audio tracks and the control track remain unchanged. This gives you the opportunity to add a new picture to previously recorded sound.

In the 8mm/Hi8 format, all information is recorded helically, and the flying erase head is the only erase head. Consequently, all edits can be thought of as insert edits. But since the AFM audio tracks are recorded helically, there is no opportunity to change the picture while leaving the sound intact.

Similarly, with MiniDV and DV tapes all the information, including digital video, audio, and time code gets recorded helically. There's no control track, except on Panasonic's much more expensive DVCPro format, which adds a control track to the tape. (See below for more info about insert edits.)

Using Inserts on Control Track Tapes (VHS)

Three types of insert edits are generally available with VHS-family equipment: video only, audio only, and audio/video (A/V). The video only insert is accomplished using the flying erase head, and the audio only insert is really the same thing as what is commonly called "audio dub"—selectively erasing and rerecording the linear audio track(s), while leaving the picture intact. With an A/V insert edit, you erase both the helical video track and the linear audio track, replacing them with new material.

If you're erasing both audio and video, how is this different from assemble editing? There are two distinct differences: First, the control track remains unchanged—you don't see this track, and you don't hear it, but it provides important internal timing information for the VCR. Secondly, since the video track is erased using the flying erase head and not the full-track erase head, you can insert material in the middle of previously recorded material without a glitch.

In essence, the A/V insert edit on VHS-family equipment is the same as the standard edit on 8mm equipment—allowing you to insert new picture and sound in the middle of something. If you need to insert both picture and sound in the VHS format, then you must use A/V insert editing.

A/V Inserts Can Add Stability

But many experienced video editors choose to use the A/V insert even when assemble editing would work—that is, they perform a series of A/V inserts as they move forward through the editing of a tape, utilizing A/V inserts even though they're not editing in the middle.

The reason for this approach is to maintain the smoothest possible control track. Since the control track determines the timing of the video frames, a sudden aberration in the control track signal shows up on a TV screen as a slight vertical roll in the picture—that is, the' first few frames of a "bad" edit occur a fraction of a second too early or late relative to the previous frames (before the edit), and so the TV's picture rolls until it manages to adjust and synchronize itself to the new signal. This defect in the timing of the tape is a video "glitch".

With assemble editing, the control track—along with all the other tracks—is recorded in short bursts that last for as long as each edit lasts. If the editing is tight—with shots that last only a second or two each—this provides ample opportunity for the control track to mess up. After hours of use, VCRs tend to get a bit sloppy, stretching tape slightly and not quite accelerating perfectly—the new control track may not pick up just where the old one left off.

To get around this problem, some video editors prefer to first lay down a single continuous control track, and then do all the editing as insert editing. The A/V insert is used instead of the assemble edit, and video and audio inserts can also be readily performed. Whether or not this approach improves upon the quality of assemble edits depends on the VCR you are using as the recorder. Many newer VCR models now edit in assemble mode as cleanly as in the insert mode, providing glitch-free editing.

Preparing VHS Tapes for Insert Editing with "Blackburst"

VCRs do not record the control track separately—it is recorded as part of the normal (assemble) editing process. In fact, the control track is created from the incoming video signal—internally, the VCR creates a pulse for each new video field (half a frame) and records it on this special track.

You cannot perform A/V insert edits on blank tape—A/V inserts require the existence of a previously recorded control track. To prepare a tape for A/V insert editing therefor requires the preparation of tape to be edited onto.

In theory, you could use any tape that has already been continuously recorded on. The recording must be at least as long as
the anticipated length of your editing project, with some pad for
running longer than expected (i.e., if you think you're editing a fifteen minute tape, prepare twenty five minutes of control track).

Since the control track that gets recorded on this tape will
form the basis of the video signal timing of the edited tape, it
should ideally come from a very stable and accurate source—such
as over-the-air broadcast television. The timing tolerances of a
broadcast TV signal tend to provide more accuracy than a typical
camcorder.

But there is another consideration that may make using a camcorder better for preparing control track tapes. The flying erase
head is generally considered weaker than the stationary head, and
may not fully erase all of the previously recorded video signal.
Therefore, the ideal signal to record for the purpose of creating a
control track is black. That way, there is no possible conflict between the old signal and the new signal.

In professional video jargon, such a signal is given a special
name—it is called "blackburst". Basically it is a signal that has all
the video timing information for the construction of each field
and frame, but no actual picture information. It appears as a
screen full of black (which looks quite different from a blank tape,
which is filled with static video noise speckles). The "burst" in
blackburst refers to the fact that the sensitive color reference signal—called the chroma subcarrier burst—is also included.

More sophisticated video editing facilities often include a
piece of equipment, called a "sync generator", whose main purpose is to create a highly stable source of this blackburst signal.

On a lower budget, you can create your own blackburst in two
ways: First, if your VCR has a manual video level control, or if
you have a "processing amplifier" with a video level control, then
you can try turning this level all the way down, so that the screen
becomes completely black, while recording over-the-air network
television (be sure to turn the audio level all the way down too).

Alternatively, working without any special equipment or controls, you can place a black lens cap over your camcorder, and
simply record black (using the camcorder as a camera, and the editing VCR to make the recording).

Note that whenever you are preparing blackened tapes for editing onto, it's preferable to record the tapes on the exact same VCR
that they will be edited on. Otherwise, sync problems can occur
during editing due to the very slight tolerance variations from one
VCR to another.

In addition to the black + control track preparation, most professional editors also put sixty seconds of color bars at the beginning of edited tapes. The color bars aid in adjusting the system the tape is played back on , and the sixty seconds of leader keeps the important program material away from the very beginning of the tape, where stretching and dropouts tend to create problems. A ten second countdown usually precedes the precise beginning of the program, with audio beeps from 10 to 3, silence and black on two, and fade up to program at 0.

A/V Dubs

As mentioned earlier, not all edit modes (assemble, video insert, audio dub, and A/V insert) are available within each variation on the VHS and 8mm formats. Here is a summary of what you can and can't do with each type of equipment:

Overview of 8mm and VHS Insert Editing

All 8mm editing is insert editing, and both the video and AFM audio tracks get erased and recorded together. Only the PCM tracks offer the opportunity to add new sound to old 8mm pictures, without going down a generation (editing). You can also dub new RC time code onto previously recorded 8mm and Hi8 tapes. But you can't add new video to previously recorded PCM sound.

With VHS equipment, the linear audio track(s) are recorded on a separate area of the tape from the video and VHS Hi-fi audio tracks, allowing maximum flexibility to change either audio, video, or both.

When you perform an A/V insert on VHS, all the audio tracks (linear and Hi-fi) as well as the video track get replaced. Any time code information also gets erased.

The "Audio Dub" (VHS and 8mm PCM)

Audio dubbing, also sometimes called insert audio editing, is a standard feature on most VHS equipment. But with 8mm/Hi8 equipment, it can only be found on a few top camcorder and VCR models that have additional "PCM" digital audio tracks. The standard AFM audio track(s) that all 8mm camcorders record are inextricably married to the video signal—when you erase one, you erase the other.

Note that with VHS, audio dubbing is only possible for the linear audio track. The VHS Hi-fi audio tracks are recorded along with the video signal, and get erased and rerecorded whenever you perform an insert video edit.

The "Video Dub" (VHS)

The insert video edit, or video dub, is generally available on low-budget equipment only in the VHS family (see below). The flying erase head, in VHS, lets you record new video and Hi-fi audio tracks, while leaving the linear audio track intact. Due to the existence of Hi-fi tracks, the term "video dub" or "insert video" can be a bit confusing. Think of it as "video plus Hi-fi audio dub."

When working with SMPTE time code, you may get into a situation where the time code is recorded on the Hi-fi audio, yet you want to do insert video editing that will destroy the time code signal with each insert edit. Depending on your specific equipment setup, it may be possible to replace the erased time code with new time code that gets recorded as the insert video edit is performed.

No "Video Dub" (8mm)

In the 8mm format there is no low budget equipment available that can do video-only inserts. The erase head erases both the AFM and PCM audio tracks when insert editing is done. Exceptions: Sony's two top of the line industrial Hi8 decks—the EVO-9650 and EVO-9850. Both cost over $5000, and can record new video and AFM while leaving the PCM audio tracks intact.

VHS Hi-fi and 8mm AFM Audio Follow Video

Once again, just for emphasis: In the VHS-family the Hi-fi audio tracks get erased and rerecorded whenever the video track is changed; likewise, in the 8mm format, the AFM and PCM audio gets erased and re-recorded whenever the video signal is changed. These limitations should be thought out in advance of shooting, whenever possible, so that the audio tracks can be best utilized for time code, music, sound effects, etc.

MiniDV and DV Insert Editing

With MiniDV and DV tapes, separate areas of the helical track are dedicated to video and audio, so by very rapidly switching the heads between playback and recording, it's possible to do both audio-only and video-only insert edits. Normal edits, in which both video and audio get recorded, are similar to A/V insert edits with VHS and 3/4".

Note that with MiniDV and DV's audio tracks, you'll only have the ability to dub in additional audio if the original recording was made with the 12-bit audio mode. With 16-bit recording, which is higher quality, all the available space in the audio area is taken up by the original sound. You may be able to completely replace this 16-bit stereo soundtrack, but you can't add to it. (See the MiniDV and DV chapter for more info.)

Time Code Editing vs. Control Track Editing

There are two big advantages to time code editing over non-time code editing, commonly called control track editing (even though 8mm has no control track the term is still used): accuracy, and repeatability. The accuracy comes from identifying each video frame with its own unique code number, allowing precision of plus or minus one frame with Super-VHS and Hi8 desktop video editing equipment. The repeatability means that the same edit can be performed again and again with the same precision—thanks to time code, the edit controller never gets confused about which frame was the one you really wanted. The repeatability of an edit decision list using time code makes it possible to evolve an editing plan from a rough cut to a fine cut using a workprint copy of the camera original footage.

Preparation for SMPTE Editing

If your equipment doesn't already have time code built-in (such as Hi8 equipment with RC, or MiniDV equipment) then you may want to consider adding SMPTE or VITC time code. To minimize generation loss, it is usually best to have the time code right on the camera original tapes. The edited tape will thus be second generation.

However, your ability to put time code on the tape may be limited by the equipment you have—consumer and low-end industrial video equipment is notorious for making it difficult to use time code on the audio tracks.

For this reason, it may sometimes be necessary to go down a generation just to add time code. The edited tape ends up being third generation. As a video producer, only you can decide whether this sacrifice in picture quality (third vs. second generation for the edited master) is worth the benefits gained from precise and repeatable time code editing. One great feature of Videonics' Thumbs Up edit controller is its ability to add VITC to copies of camera originals.

Audio Tracks for SMPTE Time Code

In the 8mm/Hi8 format, it is difficult to record SMPTE time code along with the picture, unless you are willing to sacrifice the regular audio (that is, unless you are shooting picture only, with no sound). The AFM stereo audio tracks found on many camcorders can theoretically record two different signals, but there is significant leakage between them. If you try recording time code on one channel and regular audio on the other, you'll hear a high pitched fluttering sound on the regular audio side. The PCM channel separation is superior in this regard, and 8mm PCM is suitable for use with SMPTE on one channel and audio on the other, but most camcorders don't have it.

The VHS format offers more opportunity to use time code on the audio tracks—especially if the camcorder or VCR offers Hi-fi sound. If the camcorder has Hi-fi, you can safely put time code on one channel (left) and regular audio on the other (right), with no leakage problem. This scheme has the advantage of leaving the linear audio track for synchronizing additional sounds (though you'll need a VCR that can play all three tracks simultaneously).

Note that you can also "post-stripe" VHS tapes (and 8mm with PCM audio) with SMPTE time code—keeping the original audio on the Hi-fi tracks and adding time code later, using the audio dub function, onto the linear track. But you'll need a VCR that plays these different tracks through separate output jacks at the same time—a crude "audio mix" switch won't do the trick. (Of course, with 8mm, the RC time code is far preferable to SMPTE time code, when available, because it doesn't tie up an audio track. With VHS, you have no choice—you must use an audio track if you want time code.)

Time Code on Source Side

For most editing applications, time code is most important on the source side of the editing system. The time code numbers refer to actual points on the original tapes. These time code numbers feed into the edit controller, but there is no need to copy them to the recorder side. The edited tapes can have their own time code numbers, if your edit system has the advanced feature of time code on the recorder side.

Time Code on Recorder Side

Time code can serve several useful functions on the recorder side of an editing system, even though these numbers don't refer to the raw material.

Suppose you edit a tape using assemble edits, and want to insert video-only edits over the already edited tape. Time code on the recorder side would give the edit controller precise information about where the insert video edits should go.

There are two ways the time code can get onto the recorder side tape—just as with the original footage. If the linear audio track (assuming you're working in VHS) is free, you can add the time code continuously as an audio dub, after all the assemble editing is completed.

Alternatively, you can record the time code as the edit controller performs each assemble edit, utilizing a time code generator that can be commanded to start and stop by the edit controller's general purpose interface (GPI). This setup has the advantage of letting you record the time code onto a Hi-fi audio track, but remember that the Hi-fi tracks will get erased when you perform an insert video edit.

One advanced, though workable technique to get around these limitations takes advantage of the fact that some Hi-Fi VCRs let you monitor the Hi-Fi tracks while dubbing onto the linear track. Taking advantage of this feature, you can first perform the assemble edits, putting the edited audio on one Hi-fi channel and time code on the other (using a GPI triggered time code generator). After all the assemble edits are complete, you transfer the entire Hi-fi audio track with edited sound onto the linear track, using the audio dub feature (you can also mix in music and sound effects as you do this).

Finally, you perform the video insert edits, always taking care to move forward through the tape. If the insert video edits are not spaced too closely together, there will be enough time code left after each edit for the edit controller to lock onto the time code and locate the point for the next edit. Of course, as each insert video edit is performed the time code gets destroyed, making it difficult to go back and change something if there's a mistake.

Making Hi8 and MiniDV Window Dub Tapes with RC Time Code

I recently resumed work on a film for which I had shot more than a dozen two-hour Hi8 videocassettes about five years ago. My goal was to add RC time code to the tapes, and run off workprint copies that I would use to make the editing decisions. Then I shot another ten hours of MiniDV footage (using Sony's camcorder), and had the same need. The problem with time code on both Hi8 and MiniDV is that you can't directly copy it to another tape.

But by cleverly using an accurate edit controller, you can get around that problem. Here's the procedure I followed, which is essentially the same for both formats:

1. (For Hi8 and MiniDV.) Fast forward and rewind the tape all the way through, to loosen it up and prevent layers from sticking together during subsequent operations. This procedure should be followed for all tapes stored six months or longer without playing. I use a portable two-way (forward and reverse) 8mm rewinder, the Sakar RE-88, which costs about $25, for this purpose.

2. (For Hi8 only.) Make a pristine backup copy of the Hi8 tape. All my original footage is shot on the more expensive ME Hi8 tape; I copy onto the cheaper MP Hi8 tapes for backup. By pristine I mean that no display appears on the screen—the purpose of the backup is to be insurance, in case a section of a tape (or an entire tape) gets ruined.

3. (For Hi8 only.) Add RC time code to the original tape, using the time code dub function found on every Hi8 camcorder or VCR that has RC time code capability. The time code should begin at the absolute very beginning of the tape, within the first five or ten seconds.

4. (Hi8 and MiniDV.) Make a copy of the tape, with matching RC time code numbers. To do this, you must first record a minute of time code onto a blank tape, then set up the edit controller (I use the FutureVideo V-Station for Windows) to do an edit that begins at 0:00:20:00 (that's twenty seconds into the tape) and ends at 2:10:00:00 (a little more than two hours, to allow for excess tape length – use 1:05:00:00 for MiniDV). For a window dub (with time code visible in the frame), you don't need a fancy window dub device—just get the playback VCR or camcorder to display the time code numbers in the video output signal (many camcorders will do this by pressing a display button.)

If you don't have the necessary equipment to create these MiniDV or Hi8 RC time-coded workprints yourself, mail in the coupon in the back of this book for information about a low-cost workprint dubbing service.

18   Building an Editing System

Since all video editing involves selective copying from one video-cassette to another, the question of which tape format(s) you'll be using gets more complicated. If all your equipment is in the exact same format—such as if you have a Super-VHS camcorder and two Super-VHS VCRs, then you don't even have to think much about interformat editing. But if you have an 8mm camcorder and a VHS format VCR, then you'll be doing interformat editing by necessity.

You Can Transfer Anything to Anything!

First, despite what some uninformed sales people may say—and what many novice video enthusiasts mistakenly believe—you can indeed transfer from any videocassette format to any other video-cassette format. There is no problem, whatsoever, going say from Hi8 to VHS, or from VHS-C to 8mm, or from Super-VHS to ³/₄", or from whatever format you choose to any other format. Of course, if you go from a superior quality format to a lower quality format—such as from Hi8 to VHS—there will be some subtle loss in detail (and perhaps sound quality). But there is total technical compatibility between all of these formats—as long as you have two VCRs (or a camcorder and one VCR) in the formats you wish to transfer between, you can do it.

The only exception to this is foreign television—that is, tapes that were recorded in other countries that do not conform to the

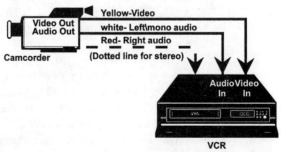

The basic hookup for making dubs and simple editing

American National Television Standards Committee (NTSC) 525-line 30 frames-per-second TV standard. Such foreign tapes utilize the European PAL or Soviet SECAM standards, and must be specially converted for playback on American NTSC equipment.

Generation Loss

The good news is that you can copy from any format to any other format, but the bad news is that – unless you're working in the digital MiniDV format – each time you make a copy, the quality of the picture degrades (as well as the sound, to a lesser extent). This degradation is common to all analog copying processes — photocopy machines, audio tapes, etc.—and is called "generation loss". Each subsequent copy of a copy, or generation of copy, looks and sounds worse than its predecessor.

With analog video recordings, about five generations is generally considered the absolute maximum amount of generation loss that is allowable. A fifth generation copy, compared against the camera original first generation footage, looks quite noticeably worse. Detail is lost, colors seem to smear across the edges that are supposed to contain them, and the timing of the video signal becomes much less stable.

If you can limit the generation loss to two or three generations, the technical quality of your video production will be much better than if you go down five or six generations. For example, if you are a wedding videographer, and you can edit the camera original tapes to create a second generation edited master, and then copy that master to make third generation distribution copies for the family, you'll have quite effectively limited your generation loss.

Contrary to popular video mythology, there is no real difference in generation loss between interformat and same-format editing. That is, if you shoot in Hi8 for example, the generation loss won't be much different between editing from Hi8 to Hi8 or from Hi8 to Super-VHS. On the other hand, though, if you edit from Hi8 to regular VHS, the second generation will of course be inferior because the VHS format is inherently inferior to both Hi8 and Super-VHS.

Alternately, some professional video producers choose to transfer their original footage to a format that is much better than the original format—such as from Hi8 to Betacam (that's professional broadcast quality Betacam, not to be confused with the lower quality Betamax). This process is called "bumping up" the tape, and is designed to minimize subsequent generation loss. The Betacam or 1" professional format copy does not look any better than the Hi8 or Super-VHS original, but the generation loss is much less. (Five generations of Betacam copies may look better than three generations of Super-VHS copies.) In the jargon of the broadcast industry, when professionals use Hi8 or Super-VHS with the intention of "bumping it up" in this manner, they say that they are using the consumer/industrial gear strictly as an "acquisition format."

As mentioned earlier, you can eliminate generation loss problems entirely by shooting and editing in the MiniDV format. Since each copy is identical to the original (when using the digital dub feature), you can start editing by selecting segments, then rearrange them in the next copy, then fine trim the edit points, then make final adjustments – going down ten or more generations along the way. With MiniDV, you can edit already edited tapes as much as you want; but with analog formats, editing edited tapes is a generation loss taboo.

Editing Edited Tapes

In designing an interformat editing system, such as one that will edit from Hi8 camcorder originals to Super-VHS, one consideration that should be thought through in advance is what will happen when you need to edit edited tapes?

Suppose for example that you are editing wedding footage from a Hi8 camcorder onto a Super-VHS master tape, and then want to copy the S-VHS master to VHS distribution copies. You'll need an additional VHS format VCR for this purpose, since the S-VHS unit can't copy to itself. You could save money on equipment by copying the master tape to Hi8, and then copying that Hi8 tape to VHS on the Super-VHS deck, but then the distribution copies are down to fourth generation—you'd be wasting a generation just to deal with the interformat problem on the cheap.

At a more sophisticated level, suppose you are working with several other people on the production of a cable television show, and there are numerous sub-producers contributing edited segments, or scenes to the program. You will need to edit their edited segments into a third generation master tape. Suppose the footage is all shot in Hi8 and then edited onto Super-VHS. What do you do with the edited segments on S-VHS if you're system is configured to edit from Hi8 to S-VHS?

In this situation, you'd have three choices: If the cable company would accept the edited master in the Hi8 format, then you could re-configure the same editing system to put the Super- VHS deck on the player side and the Hi8 camcorder on the recorder side. This would be the best solution, since it will entail no loss of quality and no additional expense. Alternatively, you could spend extra money and purchase (or rent) a second Super-VHS deck, so that you can edit from S-VHS to S-VHS. Or—the least desirable solution—you could go down an extra generation, just as with the wedding tape example, and give the cable company a fourth generation edited master.

The advantage of staying in the same format is that you don't have to worry about these questions of how to edit edited tapes—that is, until you must deal with an outside world using a different format.

What Do You Have Already?

Most people setting up a desktop editing system are not starting from scratch—typically they already own a camcorder, VCR, or both. So decisions about how to configure a same-format or interformat editing system usually begin with an assessment of what equipment you already own.

In addition to considering the formats of your equipment, you should also pay very close attention to what kind of remote control jack—if any—is available on each piece of equipment. The LANC (Control-L) and the Matsushita 5-pin remote control jacks are the best. Control-S, remote pause, and infrared control are not as good.

If you already have one piece of equipment with the Control-L jack, such as all of Sony's MiniDV equpment and most of the Hi8 and top 8mm camcorder models, then consider yourself ahead of the game. Most VHS format VCRs have only infrared remote control—resulting in less precise and less flexible editing. Notable exceptions to this are Sony's line of consumer VHS and S-VHS format VCRs, and Panasonic's low-end industrial and consumer equipment with 5-pin jacks. Purchasing such a VCR for the purpose of editing can substantially improve the overall performance of the editing system. A VCR with a "remote pause" or "synchro-edit" jack offers more limited capabilities, but will work with editing controllers using the GPI jack.

When configuring an editing system with equipment you already own, you should also consider what editing features your equipment has or doesn't have. For example, you may have an 8mm camcorder with a flying erase head, but have a VHS format VCR that has no flying erase head. In this case, you'd probably get cleaner looking edits by editing from VHS to 8mm (that is, from the VCR to the camcorder) rather than the other (more obvious) way.

With that said, here is a point by point rundown of the advantages and disadvantages of using each format on each side of an editing system. For this discussion, VHS refers to the entire family, as does 8mm. This discussion assumes you will be utilizing an edit controller device like the FutureVideo products, which can quickly reverse the roles of player and recorder simply by switching cables. Some edit controllers are not as versatile—requiring, for instance, that an infra-red remote control be available on the recorder side. In such cases, you may not have the choice of deciding which format to put on which side of the editing system.

VHS vs. 8mm on Player Side

Lower budget editing systems tend to use an 8mm camcorder as the source (player) machine, thus sparing the budget from the expense of buying two VCRs for editing. Since there are currently no VHS format camcorders that have Control-L or 5-pin remote jacks built in, but there are plenty of 8mm models with this feature, the 8mm format offers a clear advantage if you want a camcorder to serve double duty as half an editing system.

But if you're interested in using SMPTE time code, the VHS format can have a distinct advantage, if you can record on the Hi-fi tracks as you shoot. With VHS Hi-fi, you can record regular audio on one track and time code on the other; if you try doing this with 8mm's AFM stereo, the time code will leak through to the other channel.

Most consumer VHS-family camcorders do not offer hi-fi sound, but there are several industrial models that have it. A few high-end 8mm camcorders have PCM sound, which can also facilitate time code. And an 8mm camcorder with RC time code may serve your purposes just as well as SMPTE time code.

VHS vs. 8mm on Recorder Side

On the recorder side, you must draw a distinction between whether you intend to use an 8mm camcorder or an 8mm VCR as the recorder. That's because most camcorders do not offer the PCM digital audio tracks, resulting in very limited flexibility to separate the video and audio tracks. Most 8mm camcorders cannot perform audio or video dubs—both signals must be changed at the same time. Most 8mm and Hi8 VCRs (not camcorders) offer PCM audio, but you can usually only add sound to previously recorded pictures—not the reverse (you can't add new pictures to old sound).

VHS format VCRs that are designed for editing usually offer more flexibility, by allowing you to selectively change just the video or the linear audio track on a previously recorded tape.

. . . .
A/B Roll Editing

Until now, we have assumed that all the edits to be performed are "straight cut" edits, in which one image simply follows another. This is the simplest and most straightforward type of editing, and for many years was the only form of video editing available.

If you examine professionally produced videos and films, you'll find that the vast majority of edits are of the straight cut variety. But other transitions are used occasionally, requiring more complex, but affordable, video editing equipment.

The dissolve is probably the second most frequent transition, after the straight cut. Instead of having the first frame of the new segment simply appear after the last frame of the previous segment, a dissolve overlaps the two images, so that one gradually fades out while the other gradually fades in.

In video tech jargon, the ability to mix together two different images like this at the same time is called "A/B roll editing." The letters A and B refer to the two different tapes that will be combined.

A/B roll editing requires, at a minimum, three VCRs—two as source machines (to play the A and B tapes), and one as a recorder. Additionally, a device for mixing the two images together, and for synchronizing them, is also required.

(As explained below, such equipment has come down drastically in price in recent years—Panasonic's WJ-AVE 3 mixer is perhaps the cheapest way to accomplish these transitions.)

. . . .
The Time Base Corrector, Image Mixer, and Frame Synchronizer

If you just start playing two VCRs simultaneously, they will not be synchronized with each other—that is, one VCR may be telling a TV to scan out the very top of the frame, while the other VCR is scanning out the middle of the frame. In order to combine the two signals, they must be perfectly in sync—each scanning out the same exact point on the screen at the same moment in time. Devices called "time base correctors", or TBC's, perform this function. In a sophisticated editing system, there is a central "sync generator" that provides the master timing information. Each VCR is hooked up to its own TBC, and each TBC delays the signal from its VCR ever so slightly (by a fraction of a frame) to bring the signal into sync with the master signal. The resulting signals are then fed into an image mixing console, called a "special effects generator", or SEG, where they can be dissolved, or combined as split screens and wipes (one image seems to push another off the screen). This setup is used in all professional on-line editing facilities.

The Video Toaster (see below) is essentially an image mixing device.

On a lower budget, a device called a "frame synchronizer" can delay one signal by just enough time to bring it in sync with the other. Although frame synchronizers are not considered broadcast quality in terms of their timing stability, they are adequate for most industrial and low budget applications. The frame synchronizer also contains built in special effects functions—like dissolves and split screens. These can be controlled manually, or sometimes triggered from an external source, like an edit controller.

One Channel Digital Effects

Digital video effects can offer an even lower budget alternative to true A/B roll editing. Instead of dissolving between one moving image and the next, a "pseudo-dissolve" can be created in which one image ends in a freeze-frame, and then this freeze frame dissolves into the next image.

The advantage of the pseudo-dissolve over the true A/B roll dissolve is that the freeze frame is stored in digital memory. Only one source VCR is needed—the digital memory simply stores the last frame from the end of the last edited event, and mixes this frame in along with the moving image when the next edit event begins.

Utilizing the GPI as a Trigger

For one channel effects, a general purpose interface (GPI) can help automate the editing. Unlike the LANC and Matsushita 5-pin remote control systems, the GPI provides a simpler start/stop type signal. An edit controller can thus command an image mixer to dissolve.

The GPI on FutureVideo's edit controllers, for example, can be programmed to produce a pulse every time an edit begins. This pulse can then trigger a frame synchronizer, or digital video effects unit like the Video Toaster, to begin performing a selected effect as an edit begins. The effects unit will typically have a preprogrammed length of time for the effect, such as two seconds. Therefore, only the beginning of the edit needs to be transmitted to the effects unit.

At an even more advanced level, the decision list can include more information about what type of transition is to take place—

such as a cut, dissolve, or wipe. This information can then be automatically sent to the effects unit, so that it automatically switches from straight cut to dissolve as needed in the edit decision list. This type of transition mode information is not available from the GPI, but can be made accessible using a computer's expansion slots and internal data bus, along with appropriate EDL software (such as FutureVideo's EDL-2000/FX or Matrox's Personal Producer system) that can communicate with the special effects add-on computer circuit board.

The following sections discuss several popular low budget video editing devices—beginning with image mixers, and then edit controllers.

Image Mixers: The Video Toaster

Probably the most well known image-mixing device, in low budget video, is the ubiquitous Video Toaster. Everyone, it seems, has heard of the Toaster and wants to get their hands on it.

Made by a small, relatively obscure company called NewTek, the Video Toaster is a combination hardware/software product that turns an Amiga 2000, 2500, 3000, or 4000 computer into a sophisticated video production switcher—an image mixing console (also called a "special effects generator"). The Video Toaster also includes, as separate software functions, the ability to colorize, solarize, posterize, filter, and tint moving video images; a powerful character generator system; a "paint" system that lets you manipulate still images; and a 3-D animation system. Best of all, the Video Toaster meets all "broadcast quality" technical specifications—in resolution, timing stability, and noise suppression (signal to noise ratio).

Equipped with a Video Toaster, a low budget producer can now create many of the same fancy digital effects—like page flips and "squeeze zoom"—that we're used to seeing in big-budget network productions.

Commodore, the company that originally made the Amiga computers, went out of business in 1995, and then a German manufacturer took over the Amiga design, promising to produce clones of the A4000. Meanwhile, NewTek has introduced a PC based version of the Toaster, allowing it to work with a much wider universe of computers.

Image Mixing

The opening control screen on the Toaster reflects its primary use as a special effects generator, to visually combine two or more video signals together. For example, you could use the Toaster to

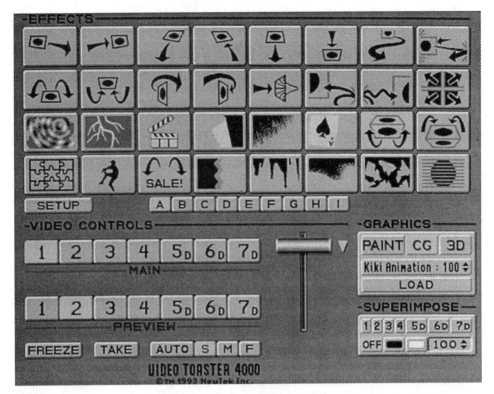

Video Toaster image mixing screen. Top four rows represent available special effects (there are six sets of these). Courtesy of NewTek.

overlay graphics on top of an image, or to dissolve (rather than cut) from one image to another, or to create a split screen with two different images, or it can create fancy digital effects in which images seem to zoom onto and off the screen, or turn like pages. These features make the Toaster a unique breakthrough bargain among low budget video switchers.

At first glance, the Toaster seems like the perfect companion product for video editing. But there's a big catch: As with professional broadcast switchers, all four of the Video Toaster's input signals must be perfectly synchronized with each other.

You can't just run two different VCRs into the Video Toaster, and expect to dissolve from the end of one scene to the beginning of the next. The two VCRs scan each part of their frames at slightly different moments in time. To combine them, the Video Toaster requires that you have available two TBCs to synchronize the signals from the two VCRs.

In fact, you need at least one TBC just to run any prerecorded video signal into the Toaster at all. Otherwise, tape signals from consumer VHS, Super-VHS, 8mm or Hi8 VCRs or camcorders are too unstable for the Video Toaster to deal with, and recordings appear as a series of jumbled scan lines.

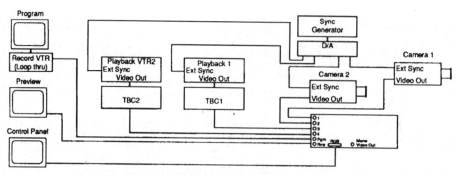

A full-blown Video Toaster system, including two VCRs, two TBCs, and two live video cameras. Courtesy of NewTek.

The cheapest TBCs currently cost about $800 to $1000, making the Toaster about a five thousand dollar proposition for editing applications (including the Toaster, the Amiga computer, and two TBC's.)

But there are lower budget possibilities—some camcorders and industrial VCRs incorporate full-frame time base correctors (partial frame TBC's won't do). You generally can't mix these signals together, but you can perform effects on a single video signal. Ditto for all DV and MiniDV equipment – the signal coming out is rock solid for single channel effects (so called A/X editing), though you'll still need TBCs to mix two together.

On an even lower budget—with no TBC's—you can use the Toaster with signals from a "live" video camera (or camcorder), or from a TV tuner. (On my cable system, the public access channels require time base correction, but all other channels can be "toasted" without TBC). One or more low cost (under $1000) TV cameras (not camcorders) with "genlock" capability (synchronizing to another signal) can be added to build a multi-camera TV studio.

Note that there is no problem recording the output of the Toaster using a regular VCR. The TBC's are only needed for use on the input side.

The Toaster can store two still frames of video in its two digital frame buffers and combine them with the four other "live" signals. Each time you "grab" a new frame however, all of the digital frame buffer's memory gets erased and reused. Still frames can be permanently saved on floppy disks—just one frame to a disk—or several dozen can fit on the computer's hard drive.

Low budget studios considering using the Toaster as an "on-air" switcher should note that the "Preview" monitor does not really let you see what an effect will look like before you put it through to the main "Program" output. It would therefor be difficult to use the Toaster in a live-TV context.

The Video Toaster.

Fanatics of the "S-video" connectors found on Hi8 and Super-VHS equipment may be dismayed to find the Toaster has no "S-video" jacks. But technical tests show that the Toaster does pass the full 400-line resolution of these tape formats.

Beyond frame grabbing and image mixing, the Toaster has numerous other capabilities. Here's a brief rundown:

Chroma-FX

"Chroma-FX" is a separate program that lets you change the colors in a moving or still image, or assign colors from a black and white image based on luminance (brightness) and location on the screen.

This feature is light years ahead of the tint control found on video processing gadgets, because you have far more control over what part of the picture the effect will be active in. It is also great for making psychedelic music video effects, and for creating interesting color backgrounds for character generator text, or product displays.

Character Generator

The ToasterCG character generator title system offers a good variety of fonts and type sizes, and can also utilize standard Amiga fonts. The text is very sharply defined, like professional broadcast equipment, and can be scrolled up the screen, as with credits. Pages of text can be composed with the CG program, stored on disk, and then can be readily called up for use in the image mixer.

Paint Box

The ToasterPaint system is extremely powerful because you can grab frames from live or recorded video signals (using a TBC for recordings) and modify them to your heart's content. You can readily clip and combine portions of images, and blur the edges between image segments.

Many ToasterPaint functions (such as adding character generator text) require you to work in the "2X" magnification mode in which you can only see one fourth of the screen at a time—a minor inconvenience.

Lightwave 3-D

This program does a great job calculating and rendering animations—multiframe sequences in which objects move around the screen. But unlike other popular Amiga animation programs like Deluxe Paint III, the Video Toaster's Lightwave 3-D cannot play the animation for recording on a regular VCR (at the standard thirty frames per second video rate). To utilize Lightwave 3-D you previously needed a VCR capable of recording just one frame of video at a time. Such VCRs are rare, and cost thousands of dollars. The Toaster 4000 can record several seconds of animation on the hard disk, and play it back in real time, thus making it appropriate for low budget animation production.

To Toast or not to Toast

When you run other programs on the Amiga (like Deluxe Paint) the Toaster will continue to superimpose the graphics over an incoming video image. (This is the same function that Amiga "genlock" boards provide.)

The Video Toaster is an extremely powerful image processing tool that lets you combine and create transitions between various video sources in dozens of interesting ways. Its fancy digital effects were previously unavailable on low budget video production gear.

In combination with an edit controller, two TBC's, and three VCRs, a package of $10,000 worth of equipment can now do things that previously required a million dollar's worth of professional broadcast equipment.

The Video Toaster is most suitable for a small production studio that wants to create a big-budget look, on a moderate (but not minuscule) budget. It is perfect for wedding videographers, institutional video production studios (corporate, libraries, schools, etc.) and places like cable-TV public access centers.

But working on a lower budget, digital A/V mixers such as Panasonic's WJ-MX30, Sony's XV-D1000, and Panasonic's WJ-AVE5 may be able to provide similar, though lower quality special effects.

Low-Cost A/V Image Mixers

The video mixer performs a feat that just a decade ago would have cost tens of thousands of dollars to accomplish: It can create special effects transitions—such as dissolves or wipes—between two totally non-synchronized video sources. The sources could be two VCRs playing tapes back, a camcorder and a VCR, two camcorders, or even two or more "live" camcorders being used as cameras to create a low-budget TV studio.

Panasonic pioneered this product category, with the WJ-MX10 (industrial) and WJ-AVE5 (consumer) models, and has periodically updated and extended the line. Panasonic's latest consumer model, the WJ-AVE7, packs a lot of production punch for the buck. But the newest entry in this field, the Videonics MX-1 Video Mixer, offers what is unquestionably the biggest bang you can get for $1,199 list. Videonics, best known until now for its editing products such as the Thumbs Up, DirectED, and TitleMaker (recently revised—see the chapter on Graphics), has achieved a breakthrough in price/performance.

Why an A/V Mixer?

So why do you need an A/V mixer? For the simplest video editing, they're unnecessary—just copy the footage you want from the camcorder to the VCR. In video editing jargon, that's called straight-cut editing. But what if you want to dissolve from one shot to another, or insert a box (such as an over-the-anchor's-shoulder news-style image)? In video lingo, such special effects are called

A/B roll editing, because the effects take place as transitions between two different rolls of tape (or film)—called the A-roll and the B-roll.

The A/V (audio/video) mixer appears to be very similar, at first glance, to another device that is a staple of studio TV production, called the special effects generator. But there's a big difference between these two products: The SEG requires that all incoming video sources already be synchronized. Such synchronization is common in a professional TV studio environment, because each of the cameras in the studio is fed a common sync signal. But in low budget video editing, when you're playing back two VCRs simultaneously, they're not synchronized.

A video signal consists of a series of 525 horizontal scan lines, swept across the screen 30 times per second. In order for two video signals to be in sync, they must be scanning the exact same spot on the exact same horizontal line on the screen simultaneously. Without synchronization, it would be impossible to dissolve between two video sources—things would become scrambled, with the bottom of one image appearing superimposed over the top of the other.

Professional video engineers use devices called time base correctors, or TBCs, to get videotapes in sync with each other. TBCs used to cost thousands of dollars, but nowadays the lowest priced units can be purchased for about seven or eight hundred dollars. You need two TBCs to do A/B-roll editing with an SEG, such as the Video Toaster.

But A/V mixers manage to synchronize the video signals without the need for external TBCs—thus significantly reducing the cost of A/B-roll editing for the low-budget producer. The A/V mixer accomplishes this by delaying one of the video signals by just enough time to match up with the other—this process is called "frame synchronization", as opposed to the costlier (requiring more memory) TBC technology.

The delay system is digital, and in converting the analog video picture to digital, it inevitably degrades very slightly. The amount of degradation is largely what distinguishes low-cost A/V mixers from higher cost models, and from professional SEGs. As you go up in price, picture quality is better maintained, with higher resolution and less introduction of noise.

The Videonics MX-1

Featuring a menu of 210 special effects, a deceptively simple-looking control panel, and what Videonics says is true TBC performance, the MX-1 is at the cutting edge of A/V mixer technology. Like the more sophisticated Video Toaster system (made by NewTek) the MX-1 is designed to work with one monitor serving as a control panel screen, with status indicators, and another monitor showing the "program output". But rather than requiring an expensive computer monitor (as the Toaster does), the MX-1 can use any video monitor for this display, which is called "Preview". (It's not really a true preview, in the sense that a broadcast SEG lets you see what an effect will look like before using it on the program output—but the Toaster lacks a true preview feature as well).

The MX-1 accepts four video inputs, all of which can be either S-video or line video (RCA phono plug). Three of these four sources can also have stereo audio signals mixed in the MX-1.

The MX-1's preview monitor shows you what's on all four sources, so you don't need to set up separate monitors for each. (Note however that the displays are rather crude, and they're shown at reduced frame rates, so it would be hard to edit precisely by looking at these screens. They're perfect for a low-budget multi-camera live studio environment, however.)

All effects take place between two of these sources—called the current source, and the next source. You can select a video-only transition, an audio-only transition (cross-fade), or—most useful— an audio and video transition.

Videonics MX-1

A "T-bar" (a big slide control) located on the left of the control panel lets you do the transition manually, and a big "Play" button does it automatically, at a choice of ten speeds.

The dissolve is the most basic video transition. As one source fades out, the other one fades in. Simple wipes across, or up and down are also possible. And then there are about 200 more effects, such as venetian blind patterns, reducing one image into a box and flipping it into the next, squeezing one image down to a line in the middle and then expanding it out again to reveal the next image, etc. It's a very impressive collection of transitions—but nine times out of ten, the basic dissolve is all you'll need. (Warning: Don't go crazy using these effects— overuse is the A/V mixer equivalent of incessant camcorder zooming! Effects should generally be used sparingly.)

The fancier the effect, the better it looks if executed automatically, rather than using the manual control, because the "T-bar" control tends to feel a bit spotty (like there's a sweet spot representing just a small part of its range where all the action takes place.) For use in conjunction with automated edit controllers (including Videonics' Thumbs Up), a sequence of up to 25 effects can be stored in memory, and then executed automatically via a GPI (general purpose interface) trigger jack.

Each of the video sources can be processed in a number of ways, including black and white, solarization, posterization, mosaic, strobe, two forms of negative images, and horizontal and/or vertical flip. These effects can be combined with the transition effects.

A freeze frame button is also provided, and the frozen frame can be mixed with an incoming source signal—this is perfect for creating so-called "A/X effects" from a single videotape source, such as ending one shot with a freeze frame and then dissolving into the next shot. (Unfortunately, freeze frames can't be stored after you've switched to one of the sources. Technically, they're really freeze field images, with half the resolution of a video frame.) A unique "Compose" button lets you create a screen consisting of smaller freeze frame images (as many as you want) as well as boxes or lines made from fully selectable background colors.

Chroma key is perhaps the most sophisticated special effect feature. It lets you superimpose one image over another, based on the background color—just like a TV weatherperson stands in front of a blue wall, but viewers see maps and radar patterns behind the announcer. The background color that will be replaced by the second image is fully adjustable—a cross-hair pointer gets placed over the color(s) you wish to select (in the first image). It works quite well, but it doesn't look nearly as "clean" as professional units—there are a lot of flashing speckles at the edges between the two images.

Overall, the Videonics MX-1 offers fantastic video production value. It has a really wide variety of effects, as well as very good raw picture quality (minimal degradation—in tech talk, the S/N ratio is rated at 56 dB, and bandwidth is 5.0 MHz—roughly 400 lines horizontal resolution). It sets a new standard of performance for low-budget video gear offering professional features.

Panasonic WJ-AVE7

Panasonic's newest consumer A/V mixer, the WJ-AVE7, offers both impressive performance and an impressive look for the $2,000 list price. The most powerful new feature is a dual-PIP mode that lets you insert two boxes of live or recorded video over a background—the same way debates are shown on interview programs such as Nightline.

Ergonomically, it's more enjoyable to operate than the MX-1, because instead of having to go into menus to select various parameter, the WJ-AVE7 offers more clearly labelled control panel buttons, knobs, and slide controls for the various functions. This panel also makes the WJ-AVE7 physically larger, and more impressive looking to clients.

A total of 96 special effects are available, organized in six wipe categories plus mix (dissolve). A slider control in the middle of the console can execute the effects manually, or an auto-take system can do it automatically, over a time interval that is fully adjustable (via rotary knob) between half a second and eight seconds.

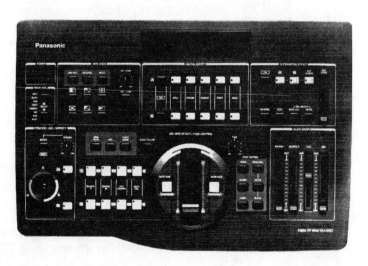

Panasonic WJ-AVE7

The audio signals from the selected sources can automatically follow the video signals, or they can be mixed separately. A simple four channel audio mixer is provided in the lower right corner of the console—the inputs are for source 1, source 2, a microphone (mini-jack input), and auxiliary input. Stereo VU meters are provided at the top of the console for checking audio levels.

There are two sets of A/V inputs, plus a third video input labelled "external camera". Any of the video inputs can be processed with strobe, mosaic, paint, or negative effects, or it can be frozen (and maintained indefinitely in memory) as a still. You can thus dissolve between two freeze-frame images (something the MX-1 can't do), as well as between a live image and a freeze frame (A/X editing). Technically, the frozen images have only field resolution, with half the vertical detail as a full video frame.

The tint and color saturation of the video signal can be adjusted via a very ergonomically friendly joystick control, which doubles as a positioner for locating boxes or other wipe patterns on the screen. You can quickly select between fading to white or black, or one of eight background colors.

A luminance keyer system is provided, to superimpose images over one another using brightness values (a weather person would have to stand in front of a black background to get maps to appear where the background is.) Unfortunately, there's no chroma-key.

However, there is a very useful second "downstream" luminance keyer, which is perfect for superimposing titles on top of whatever other effect has already been created. It offers fully variable key level (via a slide control), as well as the ability to add white or color borders around the superimposed graphics. Besides titles from a character generator (such as Panasonic's own WJ-TTL5, or the Videonics TitleMaker), you can also use a camcorder or video camera as a graphics camera, and superimpose hand drawn diagrams or hand lettered titles and logos. You can also use a freeze frame as a source for this "superimpose effect".

The only real drawback to this unit is that it is a frame synchronizer, and not a true time base corrector. That is, it adjusts the timing of one video signal to match up with the timing of the other, but the overall signal quality (in terms of timing stability) is only as good as the reference signal that it's syncing to. (A true TBC references itself to a solid sync source, not a comparatively less stable tape playback signal.)

But overall, the WJ-AVE7 Digital A/V Mixer offers a very good, easy-to learn special effects system for about a third the cost of a full Video Toaster setup. It represents the top of the consumer line (Panasonic's industrial A/V mixers, designated as WJ-MX units, cost upwards of a thousand dollars more.) Its design mimics

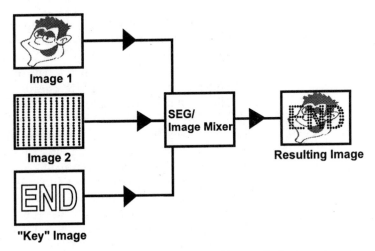

Image 1

SEG/ Image Mixer

Image 2

Resulting Image

"Key" Image

Keying is a process of superimpossing images. In this setup, the key image is never actually seen—but its shape serves as the decision-maker for choosing between the two images.

traditional broadcast TV SEGs, rather than the newer computer-based switcher (a la the Video Toaster). Rather than having to look at a preview screen to figure out what's going on, this WJ-AVE7 puts it all there, right on the console, complete with blinking lights and audio VU meters.

Panasonic WJ-AVE5 Digital AV Mixer

Panasonic's WJ-AVE5 is a real low-budget alternative to the Video Toaster. Introduced around 1991, it is a true breakthrough product that does something previously unheard of in consumer video equipment, and that used to cost tons of money even with professional broadcast TV equipment: It can combine two non-synchronized video signals, such as from two different VCRs, into a single video signal that can be recorded onto another (third) VCR. It is a special effects generator (SEG) combined with a frame synchronizer.

For low budget video editors and producers, this opens up a world of new possibilities: Instead of cutting from one shot to another, an edit can now incorporate a dissolve. It is also possible to superimpose one shot over another shot, or create split-screen effects showing two shots at once—all from previously recorded tapes.

Yes, it does "A/B roll editing"— as little as five years ago the starting price for such capability was upwards of ten thousand dollars. The "A" and "B" refer to the two different videotape signals. As explained earlier, in professional video systems two separate devices called time base correctors, or TBC's, are used to delay the video scanning information from each tape signal until they are in sync (this is the approach that the broadcast quality Video Toaster uses, albeit at much greater cost).

The WJ-AVE5 is not a full-blown time base corrector— rather, it is a "frame synchronizer" that has just enough digital memory to delay one signal so the other can catch up with it. This distinction may be of importance to those producing tapes for distribution over cable or broadcast TV, but for the vast majority of low budget video applications—weddings, family get togethers, parties, industrial documentaries, etc.—the WJ-AVE5 can be used, opening up a wide array of special effects heretofore unavailable on such a low budget.

In addition to synchronizing VCR signals, the WJ-AVE5 can also synchronize live video signals—from a camcorder being used as a TV camera (without recording on the camcorder's tape). Using two or three camcorders and the WJ-AVE5, you can create a multi-camera TV studio in your living room, basement, or anywhere else that you can dig up AC power (the WJ-AVE5 and WJ-AVE7 require 120-volts AC—they cannot be operated from batteries).

Previously, setting up a multi-camera studio required the purchase of special industrial video cameras with "gen-lock" or external synch capability (to get all the cameras to scan out their pictures in sync with each other). But the WJ-AVE5 lets you use any combination of video cameras, camcorders, or tape sources —making it much easier to scrounge up borrowed equipment as needed. The WJ-AVE5 accepts either composite video (standard) or S-video cables, and has output jacks for both composite and S-video.

Digital Effects

Additionally, the WJ-AVE5 can perform a host of digital special effects on a single video source—even if you are not looking to do A/B-roll editing or multicamera studio production, you may find these effects useful. Music video producers, take note: The digital special effects include strobe (variable speed), still-frame, mosaic, and "paint".

These digital effects are commonly found on some top-of-the line camcorder models, but the WJ-AVE5 gives you the luxury of deciding when and how you want to use these effects after the shooting is over—just as the pro's do it—in post-production. Additionally, you use the still-frame effect to create a "pseudo-dissolve" during editing—you can end one scene with a freeze frame, and dissolve to the moving image of the next scene.

These digital effects can also be combined with the image mixing functions—you can, for example, create a split screen between a strobed image from a tape and a mosaic image from a live camera.

A "multi" button multiplies the split screen effects so that, for example, instead of dividing the screen into two parts it can be split into four or eight. In combination with the five basic wipe patterns (two vertical splits, two horizontal splits, and circle), a total of 98 different complex wipe patterns can be created—among them, familiar cliches like the box which appears over a newscaster's shoulder (a position joystick lets you precisely locate it).

Titles, Audio

The WJ-AVE5 incorporates what video engineers call a "downstream keyer"—you can add another layer of graphics over the image already created in the mixer. This is commonly used for adding titles using artwork that is shot by an external video camera. Best of all, the WJ-AVE5's external camera input for this purpose can also be any consumer camcorder—it does not require any special sync signal (as professional models always do). You'll never actually see the true image from this external camera—only its outlines. The actual titles can take on the color of eight different background colors. These background colors can also be used in any other effect, as well.

An optional character generator, model WJ-TTL5, can be plugged into the front of the WJ-AVE5 mixer instead of an external camera, so that titles can simply be typed in. This character generator has considerably more power than what's usually built into camcorders—it can store ten pages of text (one with date, time, and stop watch capability), offers four different sizes of text, and scroll nine pages of titles up the screen (like standard TV credits).

The WJ-AVE5 can selectively add borders or shadows to the titles.

Finally, the WJ-AVE5 not only combines video signals, but audio as well. A separate audio mixer section can combine up to four different audio signals, including a narration microphone that can be plugged into its front panel. This mixing capability is relatively simple (compared with the sophisticated video effects) but adequate for adding recorded music or narration to an edited tape.

Overall, the WJ-AVE5 is very impressive. Similar, more expensive products have been on the industrial market for several years—like the MX-12—but this is the first consumer version. The main feature that it lacks (and which the industrial models have) is an external trigger jack so that it can be cued to automatically dissolve by a computerized editing system. To use it with an automated editor, you'll have to do the fades and other special effects manually.

The WJ-AVE5 is a very capable, versatile video production tool that can be a put to a number of different uses as situations arise. For A/B-roll editing, in particular, it brings to camcorder enthusiasts a capability that was previously reserved for the big boys—at a price (around $1400) within the reach of many small studios and home video setups. But it does degrade picture quality significantly, by limiting resolution and adding noise. Better, more expensive image mixers, like Panasonic's WJ-MX30 and Sony's XV-D1000 offer superior picture quality, for about twice the dough.

Sony XV-D1000

The Sony XV-D1000 has an extremely compact control panel, because the main electronic guts are contained within a separate rack mountable cabinet. A three foot cord connects the panel to the box, which contains three sets of A/V/S-video input jacks, two sets of outputs, and remote control trigger inputs.

The XV-D1000 switches between two rows of buttons—the A and B buses—via a T-shaped fader control. The feel of this control is not nearly as smooth as on the MX30 (a more complete description of which follows in a moment), but it's smooth enough, and there is absolutely no visible noise in the picture as you slide it. At the very beginning of some digital effects, like mosaic, the second image appears rather abruptly—but on the all-important fade (dissolve) effect, there's no such problem—onset is perfectly gradual.

The XV-D1000 is an all digital system—there isn't a single knob on the control panel. In addition to the basic dissolve, fade to black, and fade to white, about 30 wipe effects are available, as well as two unique mix modes: One converts a picture to black and white as it fades into the other, then converts it back. The other converts the picture to a scrambled mosaic, then descrambles to show the new image.

Beyond the basic corner, box, and circle wipes, several unique shape patterns are also provided—a star, a diamond, and (perfect for wedding videography) a heart. Unfortunately, there is no ability to create a soft edge at the border between one image and the other, when using the wipes. Venetian blind, random box, and an unusual rotating box pattern are also available.

Positioning a box or circle in a spot that's not in the center is a bit cumbersome, requiring the use of four directional cursor buttons instead of a joystick.

My favorite digital effect, called "after-image", provides psychedelic trails of moving images. Strobe and freeze frame effects are also available.

The freeze frame offers a choice of full-frame, or field (half-frame) display The advantage of the field display, though it loses resolution, is that it eliminates jittery motion artifacts that result from two successive fields being replayed (like a loop) thirty times a second.

If any of the three inputs are left unconnected, or if one suddenly goes bank, the XV-D1000 automatically turns them into a freeze-frame. Two frames can be stored—one on each bus—so you can perform effects between two still images.

Several, though not all of the effects can be combined together. Any effect can be triggered to occur automatically, at a rate you select, by pressing a big start button.

The XV-D1000 excels in its still frame and strobe memory—which holds two full frames, compared to the Panasonic MX-30's (see below) single field (half frame) still effect.

Effects can be programmed into ten user-defined memory button, which can be used in conjunction with more sophisticated edit control systems. A GPI—general purpose interface—jack allows any effect to be triggered by an external editing controller—such as Sony's own RME-700, or models made by third parties like Videonics and FutureVideo.

The audio capabilities are simple but useful. As you perform a transition from one signal to the other, the audio can automatically cross-fade, or it can stay fixed on one or the other. Besides the two selected input sources, a third auxiliary audio signal can also be mixed in. There's no microphone jack, and no headphone jack.

Overall, the XV-D1000 is a great unit, with very good technical performance (much better resolution than Panasonic's WJ-AVE5), but for about the same amount of money ($2500 to $3000) you could also get Panasonic's WJ-MX30.

Panasonic WJ-MX30

Panasonic's WJ-MX30 looks and performs much like a traditional special effects generator. Its control panel is big and impressive looking—an important consideration for wedding/low-budget industrial video facilities where impressing clients is a legitimate factor in the purchase decision.

A big, professional-looking T-bar controls the wipes and fades. (But unlike professional gear, it doesn't split apart into separate controls for the A and B busses.)

There are only eight pattern buttons, and four pattern modification buttons, but by pressing them multiple times, and combining them, a total of 107 patterns can be created. The wipes can have colored borders at the edges, in a choice of three thicknesses, and—unlike the Sony—soft wipe edges are also available.

Six digital video special effects are available—strobe, mosaic, paint, negative, monochrome (black and white), and still frame. Convenient knobs adjust mosaic size and strobe rate. Unfortunately, the mosaic effect cannot easily be used as a transitional device between the A and B busses, as the Sony allows.

My favorite feature is an "A/V synchro" audio trigger control for the digital effects. This triggers the effects to kick in only when the audio level exceeds an adjustable threshold—perfect for wedding video dance sequences. By feeding music through it and hooking up a feedback loop, more than an evening's worth of psychedelic video light show style entertainment is readily available.

Chroma saturation and hue adjustment are available, with separate adjustments for the A and B busses. The position joystick doubles as an R-G-B tint control.

In addition to black and white screens for fades and backgrounds (which Sony's XV-D1000 has), the MX30's Matte generator also creates basic color backgrounds, standard color bars, and gradient color backgrounds which get lighter near the top.

A separate, downstream luminance keyer lets you superimpose titles or other high-contrast effects over all the other effects. And a final set of program output switches lets you preview special effects before switching to them. (None of these features exist on Sony's XV-D1000.)

The audio mixer is basic, but offers a bit more than on the Sony. There are four separate slide controls, for input 1, input 2, an auxiliary device, and the front panel microphone input jack. A stereo VU meter at the top of the console displays the stereo output level, and as with the Sony, it will automatically cross-fade audio to follow video mixing and wipes.

The front of the unit also sports a headphone jack next to the microphone jack, a headphone level control, and an interface jack for an optional character generator (WJ-KB50).

There are several more advanced jacks beyond the three sets of A/V/S-video inputs (signal one, signal two, and an external key camera/auxiliary audio input). Most important, perhaps, is a preview output that works in conjunction with a separate set of A/B/effects program output switches. You can switch the output to what's on A, for example, while previewing an effect. This is a capability that even the highly-touted Video Toaster doesn't provide.

There are also "advance sync" output jacks for industrial VCRs that can lock onto this signal, thus improving A/B-roll editing performance. A GPI remote control jack works in conjunction with an eight-transition memory, similar to the way the Sony works. But an RS-232 serial interface jack is also provided, for remote control by computers.

My only real complaint about the MX30 is that each bus really has four inputs (signal 1, signal 2, external camera, and matte) but to select the external camera, you must press two buttons simultaneously.

The MX30 offers two luminance keyers, but unfortunately, as with the Sony XV-D1000, there's no chroma-key effect.

A standard RS-232C serial port remote control jack can interface with practically any computer—including IBM, Macintosh, and Amiga—with the appropriate software. (By contrast, Sony's interface system—the "I/F" jack—may be compatible with VISCA, but there are no available controllers to support it, yet. Sony seems to have a penchant for creating new standards and then failing to deliver a wide array of products to support them.)

Overall, the WJ-MX30 offers an attractive alternative to the Video Toaster, for several thousand dollars less.

Edit Controllers: Videonics Thumbs Up

Videonics' Thumbs Up edit controller is a lot more sophisticated than its humble appearance suggests. Advanced features include both VITC and RC time code, a video fader/enhancer processing system, the ability to create window dub workprint copies showing time code or index numbers, and a 124-event edit decision list digital memory. With the interconnection of Videonics' companion Titlemaker, Thumbs Up can automatically add dozens of different titles at specified points in the editing sequence. At $229 list, Thumbs Up is quite a bargain.

The only catch is that for best results, you need an 8-mm or Hi-8 camcorder with an LANC (or Control-L) remote control

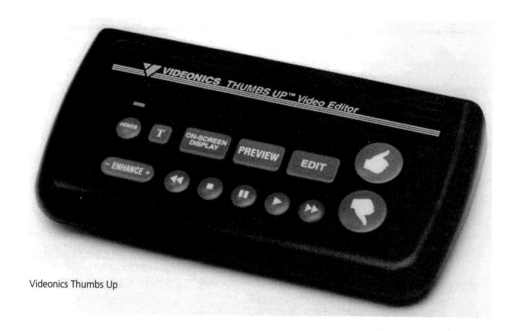

Videonics Thumbs Up

jack, or a Panasonic VCR with a 5-pin remote jack. Without such a jack (most VHS, VHS-C, and less expensive 8-mm and Hi-8 models lack one), you have two choices—either use Thumbs Up's non-automatic "instant edit" technique (a glorified pause control), or make a VITC time-code copy of the tape and edit from that (thus reducing overall quality by a generation).

Entering edit points is as simple as pressing the big thumbs up and down buttons while the tape plays, or in pause. When viewing the tape, a big thumb appears in the lower left corner, pointing up or down to indicate what is or isn't included. Making changes is easy—just press the opposing button to eliminate previous decisions.

The initial accuracy of the edits is approximately +/- 15 frames (half a second). To improve accuracy, trim adjustments are available for the start and stop points. . But after about five edits without time code, it starts drifting, and the +/- 15 frame accuracy becomes the rule.

With time code, +/- 3 frames accuracy is achievable, after running a test and adjusting the trims accordingly.

Thumbs Up offers another way to get time code onto recordings, even if your camcorder does not have RC time code (or a Sony MiniDV camcorder, whose time code Thumbs Up will also read): by making a copy with SMPTE vertical interval time code (VITC).

Adding VITC is quite easy: Press two buttons, and run off a dub of the camera original. The time code is hidden in the video signal, and—unlike some of Videonics' previous time code systems—no extra picture deterioration is visible, except for the usual degradation when making a copy. This generation loss is the big drawback of using Thumbs Up to add time code.

With VITC, editing accuracy is excellent—usually within one or two frames, and never more than three frames from the marked points (after carefully calibrating the trim adjustments).

If you can sacrifice portability, VITC can be added without going down a generation, by using a camcorder as a video camera, inserting the battery-powered Thumbs Up in the signal path as a VITC generator, and recording on another camcorder (with line input) or VCR. But it's cumbersome.

A jack on the back of Thumbs Up connects to Videonics' Titlemaker, triggering it to automatically change pages on cue. The title cues do not have to coincide with the edit points—for example, you can first have a woman's face appear, then fade in her name for a few seconds, and then fade out. This is a very powerful capability.

Videonics Edit Suite model AB-1 can simultaneously control up to four LANC or Matsushita 5-pin devices (camcorders or VCRs).

With both the Thumbs Up and the Titlemaker in the video signal chain, a slight increase in visible picture noise is noticeable, compared with the Thumbs Up by itself, which looks very clean. When the Titlemaker superimposes over the Thumbs Up's black generator, the signal gets very jittery, unless you simultaneously play a camcorder tape to serve as a video timing source.

Thumbs Up has some other limitations: It can't automatically edit tapes out-of-sequence. (It holds up to 124 editing/titling events in its memory, but you can't put something from the end of the original tape at the beginning of the edited tape, without re-sorting to manual editing techniques.) Also, you can't select individual scenes to fade up or down at—once you turn the fader on, every segment fades in and out. (Again, using manual techniques, you can overcome this.) And Thumbs Up can't automatically do insert editing, even if your VCR is capable of it (you can cue up an insert or audio dub manually, and use Thumbs Up to stop/start from pause).

Other minor complaints: Too many unlabelled "hidden functions" (such as pressing the Preview and Thumbs Up button simultaneously to record black); the on-screen display is a tad cryptic (filled with obscure, unlabelled number codes); and the two-instruction books are confusing—the "reference" manual frequently refers you back to the more basic "instructions".

But overall, Thumbs Up is an excellent value—packed with sophisticated editing power, yet unintimidating.

FutureVideo Edit Controllers

As mentioned earlier, FutureVideo Products makes an excellent line of computer-based desktop video edit controllers that work with both the LANC and Matsushita 5-pin remote control jacks.

These controllers generally take the form of a computer expansion card that gets installed deep within the bowels of an IBM-compatible computer. Other models are available as "black boxes" that hook up to Macintosh and Amiga computers. Prices run from about $800 to $2,000 depending on time code and A/B roll (3 VCR) features. Besides the VCRs, you'll also need a computer, and compatible software.

But for simpler applications, FutureVideo also makes stand-alone edit controllers that sell for around $600 to $1,000, depending on time code capability.

These stand-alone controllers can only store a handful of edit points—they're designed primarily for people who prefer doing "one at a time" editing. But some models also include computer

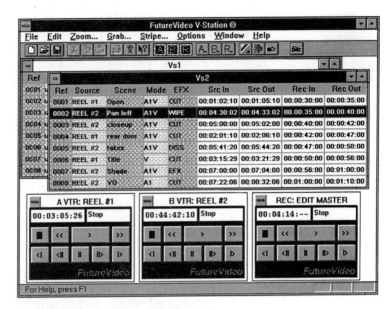

FutureVideo V-Station
for Windows

interface jacks, so you can upgrade the system later to have full EDL capability (with hundreds of editing events).

The main advantage of FutureVideo's edit controllers, over most competing products, is that they work with both Sony LANC and Panasonic Matsushita 5-pin remote control jacks. This capability is essential if you want to do interformat editing—shooting in Hi8 to take advantage of the portability and time code, for instance, and then editing onto Super-VHS to take advantage of the insert-editing capabilities. And unlike many simpler assemble-edit only products, FutureVideo's edit controllers always provide access to whatever insert-editing features the recorder VCR has.

The V-Station products are probably the best overall values in computer-based edit control. For about a thousand dollars (including EditLink hardware and V-Station software) you can transform your computer (IBM, Macintosh, or Amiga) into a very accurate time-code editing system—if you hook it up to a Hi8 or MiniDV camcorder with built-in time code. For a few hundred dollars more, the the system can read SMPTE time code, so you can get the same accuracy using Super-VHS equipment. It works with both LANC (Sony - Hi8) and Matsushita 5-pin (Panasonic - Super-VHS) remote interfaces. It's thus one of the most versatile low-budget edit controller you can find. Higher priced models in the FutureVideo line facilitate A/B roll editing, including automated Video Toaster mixer control.

In addition to FutureVideo's own software, several other edit control programs can command their controller hardware (available as either a PC card or as an external box, connected by serial port)—including Gold Disk's Video Director (which is itself a great video editing bargain—for about $125, your computer becomes a simple assemble-edit controller that works between any LANC camcorder and any VCR).

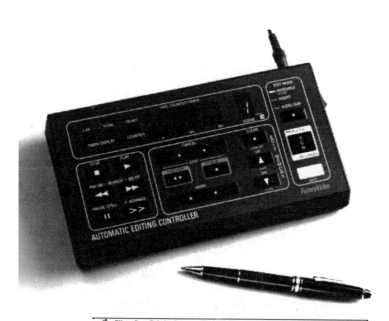

FutureVideo Edit Controllers. FV-3300, below, works with IBM, Amiga, and Macintosh computers (V-Station for Macintosh screen on right).

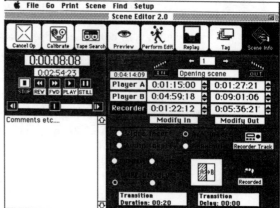

19 Nonlinear Digital Video Editing Technology

Nonlinear editing is the hot new trend in video post-production, and for good reason. It offers a far more intuitive, easy-to-use, and flexible user interface. It makes video editing much more like film editing, in that you can conveniently keep trimming away at edit points, evolving from a rough cut to a fine cut. It can also offer more synchronized audio tracks.

Nonlinear editing revolves around the idea of converting video and audio information into computer data, and editing this data with the same kind of flexibility that writers and publishers enjoy using word processing software. The term nonlinear comes from the random access to the raw footage—you can jump instantly from any point in the recording to any other point, without waiting for tape to rewind or fast forward.

The most well-known nonlinear editing systems are made by Avid and Media Logic, and were originally designed to run with Apple Macintosh computers, though Windows-compatible versions have been appearing lately. Price tags generally run from about $20,000 for a starter system, to upwards of $40,000 for broadcast-quality systems capable of storing several hours of raw material.

With professional nonlinear editing, once you get passed the basic picture quality issues, storage capacity becomes a paramount concern. It takes many gigabytes of hard disk drives to hold even a couple of hours of video. The exact formula for converting gigabytes to minutes of video recording depends on the nonlinear editing system used, and the selected data compression ratio. For organizing a big project like a feature length documentary involving dozens of hours of raw footage, deciding which footage is loaded into the editing system at any given time can become a real juggling act.

Unfortunately, for under-$10,000, right now there is no nonlinear editing system that offers picture quality as good as Hi8 or Super-VHS tape. Although these systems are very appealing in that they're more fun to use than traditional tape-based editing, for someone who wants to get the best possible output quality at the lowest possible price, they should generally be avoided, at least for now.

There's no question that nonlinear editing represents the future of video editing, and even by the time you read this book things may have changed. The new DVC digital video cassette format represents a very important step forward, that may ultimately lead to hybrid linear/nonlinear systems that offer the best of both worlds to low budget producers.

Because this is the hot new area of video editing, you can expect a half dozen or more new products to hit the market just in the time between when this book is written and when it's published. But the following sections attempt to at least provide a snapshot, in the mid-1990s, of where things are.

Digital Tape and Nonlinear Video

The technical problem of generation loss plagues practically all home video editing efforts. Every time you make a copy of a tape, it looks and sounds worse; yet, since videotape should never be physically spliced, the only way to trim edit points and evolve from a rough cut to a fine cut is through selective copying. Either the edited tape must be copied again to reflect the changes, creating generational loss, or all the edits after the point to be changed must be re-performed, a very tedious and cumbersome process, without the aid of such professional conveniences as electronic time code and computerized edit decision list technology.

Digital video recording can eliminate all the hassles of home video editing, potentially making video editing as easy as word processing currently is using computers.

"True digital," as exemplified by the DV and MiniDV consumer formats (as well as pro formats like D-2 and Digital Betacam) means the video signal actually gets recorded on the tape as a sequence of 1's and 0's—just as CDs record music, and computer floppy discs record text and data. Once any information—be it video images, audio, or computer programs—gets recorded in digital form, it can be copied and recopied almost endlessly, with no generational deterioration.

Some of today's fancier consumer VHS format VCRs offer "digital effects" like picture-in-picture, and freeze-frame, but these are not "true digital" VCRs. The picture and sound get recorded using the exact same analog techniques that are used in all VHS and S-VHS equipment.

Computer science has found ways to compress the enormous amounts of data to fit into less bandwidth, and this is largely where research in High Definition Television is focused. HDTV itself requires more bandwidth, even in analog form; and digital HDTV requires tons of bandwidth—a double whammy. This problem of bandwidth – data rates – is crucial to understanding why, with today's technology, editing with digital tape (MiniDV) provides better quality at lower cost that most nonlinear editing systems.

The MPEG-1 and MPEG-2 systems are the most widely known video compression technologies, though there are many others. These "high ratio" video compression schemes involve some compromise in picture quality, and suffer from visible compression artifacts, which generally become most noticeable during fast movements in the picture. By high ratio, I mean that the raw data is compressed by about a factor of about 50:1 to 150:1. The higher quality DCT compression scheme used in MiniDV and DV, by contrast, has a ratio of just 5:1, and there are virtually no visible artifacts.

Video data compression input boards make it possible to transfer raw videotape directly to a computer's hard disk, and edit it as digital information. Editing with this nonlinear system is several orders of magnitude faster than editing from tape, since access to any item of information on disk is extremely rapid. Such systems are clearly the future of low budget editing, but for the time being, tape editing systems still have a significant cost advantage.

The problem with low-cost nonlinear is the quality of the conversion, a process which usually takes place in the video input board. The speed of the computer's hard disk drive may further limit the quality of the video, and require you to use higher compression ratios with more visible artifacts. If you're willing to spend upwards of ten thousand dollars, you can put together a decent nonlinear system (though it probably still won't match the raw quality of MiniDV tapes).

But with less expensive nonlinear equipment, you generally won't have the resolution or frame rate quality that's needed to match Hi8 picture quality. Getting a computer video system to record video with VGA resolution of 640 x 480, at 30 frames per second, without glitches, is a challenge—and this basic standard is actually a bit worse than Hi8/S-VHS.

DVS (the publisher of this book) offers a unique low-cost computer-based nonlinear editing service for those who already have a computer, but don't want to purchase thousands of dollars worth of editing equipment. For those ready to take the plunge, DVS also publishes a newsletter with tips on the latest products, and offers a systems integration service to put together the best package of equipment. Send in the coupon in the back of this book for more information.

Quicktime and Computer Video

Imagine editing video on a computer, manipulating moving pictures and sounds with the cut-and-paste ease of word processing. Camcorder enthusiasts who have only dreamed of editing their footage on fancy "A/B roll" editing systems, with special effects at scene transitions, and precise frame accuracy, now have the opportunity to at least learn the principles of video editing, albeit with mediocre picture quality, thanks to the new world of digital video computer files.

Advanced techniques for compressing digitized video data have led to new computerized video file formats—QuickTime movies (Apple's format), and Video for Windows (from Microsoft).

For most computer users, these new file formats will not be used for video editing, but rather, for playback of prerecorded multimedia software. Already, computer CD-ROM discs commonly contain video files that playback historical film clips, or other video materials. Future software products (like spreadsheets and word processors) will include video clips to train new users, or provide help as needed.

But for camcorder fans, these new computer video capabilities provide fantastic new opportunities to dabble with some very fancy editing capabilities, at very low cost. Not only do you have access to a wide variety of special effects, but you also break free from the tedium of waiting for tapes to search to a particular edit point. As mentioned earlier, in video editing jargon, this non-sequential access is called "nonlinear editing".

Be forewarned, however, that for the time being at least, most low-budget nonlinear editing tools should be thought of as training devices. The quality of the resulting computer video signals is far inferior to even ordinary VHS tape. So the edited movies created as QuickTime or Video for Windows computer files are not generally considered presentable on regular TV screens.

Adobe Premiere

Adobe Premiere is one of several very powerful new computer video editing programs that work with both Quicktime and Video for Windows files. With Adobe Premiere, the editing plan appears as a seven-track storyboard style time line. There are two video tracks (the A and B rolls), and a video effects track in which transi-

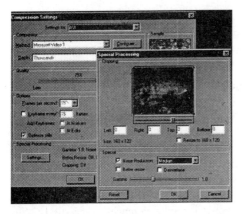
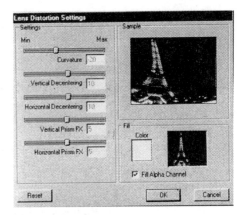

Adobe Premiere offers extensive image manipulation features, in addition to editing.

tions during the overlap periods are specified. There are also three audio tracks, and a video superimpose track for overlaying titles and other graphics.

Video editing is a breeze—and a welcome relief from the tedium of working with VCRs. You can create the electronic equivalent of a "bin", where you keep all the little snippets of video you want to assemble together. Using the mouse to move things around, you cut and paste the video segments to the time lines, and select a transition from the menu (available effects include dissolve, wipes, flips, and about a dozen other options).   If this sounds too good to be true, note that there are several catches:

As mentioned earlier, the picture quality is crude. Although performance will vary from computer to computer, I found that with my reasonably powerful IBM compatible (a 486DX-50 with 20-megabytes of RAM), the most comfortable setup to work with was a 120 (vertical) x 160 (horizontal) pixel image, at a frame rate of 15 frames per second. When I specified higher resolution, the system couldn't generate new images fast enough, so rather than looking better, it took on a stroboscopic quality.

A resolution of 480 x 640 is what's really needed for high quality video—but that's sixteen times as much picture information! And since the standard video rate is 30 frames per second, that means getting a broadcast-quality video signal would require 32 times the information handling capacity of today's typical PC technology. (That's the technological leap needed to make computer video files a no-compromise replacement for today's tape-based video editing techniques.)

The software by itself is inexpensive enough (assuming you've already got a computer), but perhaps the biggest catch is that you'll need additional hardware and software to convert your camcorder footage into compatible QuickTime or Video for Windows files.

A separate plug-in board and software, like VideoSpigot for Windows (from Creative Labs), are needed to capture original video footage. And that's just for the picture—you'll also need an audio board, to capture and playback audio. (Fortunately, most multimedia ready computers already include a sound board.)

A lower-cost way to get your feet wet editing with Adobe Premier (or similar products) is to play around with pre-recorded QuickTime and AVI movies. (AVI is the technical name for Video for Windows files—it stands for audio-video-interleave.) Adobe Premier comes with an excellent set of about a dozen short video clips showing an acrobat jumping and twirling in the air. A number of sound effects, and still frame graphics are also included. Using this kit, someone interested in editing could spend many hours excerpting segments and splicing them together, learning the basics of editing by trying to create a smooth, flowing sequence.

Similarly, you can edit "found footage"—QuickTime and AVI files—contained in many other software products. A CD-ROM drive (standard equipment on multimedia computers) greatly enhances your access to such prerecorded material. One excellent title for this purpose is, "QuickTime The CD," from Sumeria. It's a two-disc collection of winning QuickTime movies from QuickTime Film Festivals. Most of the sixty movies run for three to five minutes, and include synchronized sound (which can also be separately edited).

What do you do when you finish editing your computer-video movie? For most productions, the computer format represents the end of the line. The final file can be copied onto a floppy disk, and distributed to other computer users. With the appropriate hardware, the computer video presentation can be converted back to NTSC (standard American TV), and recorded on a VCR. (Expansion cards that output NTSC video are more expensive than input cards like the Video Spigot—one advantage of Amiga computers is their built-in NTSC outputs.)

But because of the crude picture quality, it's probably not worth the effort. When blown up to fill a TV screen, the image will look like it was filtered through a mosaic special effect.

Big budget video and film producers use nonlinear technology differently—after the computer editing is over, the original videotapes (or film negatives) are edited to conform to the decision list created on the computer. But such technology—such as the Avid video editing system—currently costs upwards of forty thousand dollars.

For video enthusiasts confined to less expensive tools, today's computer video formats offer an exciting educational experience, and a chance to produce materials for the unique new distribution outlet of personal computer screens (as opposed to TV screens). In the not-too-distant future, as raw computing power becomes faster and cheaper, this technology will replace the old tape dubbing techniques for practically all video editing. The only question is how soon.

Digital Video is Not Inherently Better

The era of digital video has arrived. Though the quality of the MiniDV tape format is superb, most of the other new digital video devices are not as stellar. The DSS home satellite dish system, in particular, provides very good but not excellent picture quality. Using MPEG data compression, artifacts (defects in the picture) are clearly evident every few minutes. Unlike the introduction of digital audio over a decade ago, digital video does not always represent a big improvement in quality – especially whenever computers and video games are concerned.

Of course, digital video enhancements—in the form of special effects buttons for VCRs, LaserDisc players, and camcorders—have been around for years. But the essential recording and transmission systems have, until now, been analog. DSS (Digital Satellite System) and Video CD change all that, by actually delivering digital video signals to your home.

DSS first went on sale in 1994. DSS features a very small 18" x 19" (pizza box size) dish antenna that you can install yourself, and receives up to about 150 channels of digital video signals. Programming services are similar to cable-TV offerings, except the over-the-air networks (ABC, CBS, NBC, Fox, PBS) are excluded. Packages of 30 or 40 basic channels (such as MTV, Nickelodeon, ESPN, CNN, C-SPAN, etc.) are available at monthly rates of about $10 to $20 per month; premium channels and many pay per view movies are also available.

Not to be outdone, around the same time DSS hit the show-rooms, Primestar a competing analog satellite broadcasting system, upgraded its 20-channels of analog video to 70-channels of digital video. Primestar dishes are considerably larger than DSS however—38" x 39"—making them less suitable for rooftop or window installation, and thus inherently less appealing to most consumers.

The digital Video CD format never caught on. Up to 72-minutes of digitized video fit onto a standard-size 5" CD—most movies thus require two discs. The format, at least for now, appears to be mainly an extension of Philips' CD-I interactive player system, though stand-alone Video CD players are also available.

Unfortunately, the image quality of these pioneering digital video technologies is spotty. By most accounts, Primestar has the best digital image, followed by DSS, and then Video CD. Thankfully, all systems offer very high quality digital stereo sound.

The newest digital video consumer format—the digital video disc (DVD)—promises better quality. But like the audio CD, this will be a playback-only format.

The MiniDV tape format is clearly the best of all the digital video media introduced to date. It offers superb picture and sound quality, the ability to record, playback, and flexible editing. As explained in the chapter on MiniDV, this high quality comes from using a much higher bitstream rate – lower compression ratios – than most nonlinear systems.

Digitizing Video

The process of digitizing video signals is similar to what happens in digital audio recording, except that it happens a lot faster. Whereas the most rapid changes in an audio signal occur in about one twenty-thousandth of a second, the most rapid changes in a video signal occur in about one six-millionth of a second.

Converting analog signals to digital is done by sampling—the voltage level is periodically converted to a number and stored in computer memory. But while audio CDs have about forty-four thousand samples per second, digital video requires millions of samples per second.

The higher the sampling rate, the finer the detail in the digital video image. But higher sampling rates also mean more data per second—the digital video bottleneck. That's where data compression comes in. Using advanced algorithms, the raw video data is converted into a more efficient compressed form of information, requiring less storage capacity and narrower radio/cable channels.

But even with the most advanced compression schemes commonly used, the quality of the highly compressed digital video image does not generally surpass conventional analog video systems. The only exceptions, among current formats, are MiniDV and the Digital Video Disc.

With DSS the horizontal resolution doesn't stay constant—it varies, depending on the complexity of the image and how rapidly it's changing. DSS and many CD-ROMs use variations on the MPEG-1 compression standards (MPEG is the Motion Picture Experts Group, an industry-wide committee that establishes standards for digital video compression.) MPEG-1 has, at worst, only the same resolution as ordinary VHS videocassettes—about 240-lines, horizontally. (By comparison, the analog LaserDisc format offers 425-line horizontal resolution.)

Highly compressed digital video images, such as MPEG-1, occasionally freeze up for a fraction of a second—something that never happens with a VHS videocassette, and only very rarely with cable-TV channels. The high data rate of MiniDV prevents these freeze-ups from occuring.

The Video Flyer

When the Video Toaster was introduced back in 1991, it offered unprecedented value for creating special effects, animation, and titles. NewTek, the Toaster's manufacturer, had always wanted to offer a more complete editing solution, but it wasn't until 1995 that they introduced the Video Toaster Flyer, a nonlinear editing system.

As explained previously, nonlinear editing is tapeless editing. Instead of copying from one videocassette to another, the video and audio signals are digitized and stored on computer hard disk drives. One big advantage is that you can edit, trim, refine, and revise to your heart's content, with no worry about generation loss. And there's no waiting for tapes to cue. While nonlinear systems such as Avid (professional quality) and Adobe Premier (inexpensive, but low resolution) have been around for several years, what makes the Flyer a breakthrough is its ability to deliver what the company says is D-2 (digital video tape) broadcast quality at a reasonable—though not truly low-budget—price.

Rather than using standard MPEG video data compression, the Flyer incorporates a new proprietary VTASC (Video Toaster Adaptive Statistical Coding) system which, according to NewTek, provides higher quality images with fewer compression artifacts. Besides video, the Flyer can also record and mix four sets of synchronized stereo sound tracks, with CD-quality.

Editing with the Flyer is simplified by a storyboard style interface. Each video clip, audio clip, transition, animation, or graphic element appears as a single box in the storyboard sequence. All of the special effects of the Toaster—including page flips, Star Trek transporter, wipes, venetian blinds, etc.—can be used as scene transitions. Audio and video can run for different time durations, to create split edits.

The Flyer lists for $4,995, but take that price with a grain of salt. You'll also need a Toaster system including a Commodore Amiga computer (the bankrupt Commodore company recently sold its Amiga computer designs to a German manufacturer), a time base corrector, and a couple of hard disk drives with capacity of at least a gigabyte each (the bigger the drives, the more video you can record.) Figure around twelve to fifteen thousand dollars

Control screen of CineWorks nonlinear editor.

for a complete Flyer system. That's not peanuts, but it's less than a tenth what this capability cost using videotape a decade ago, and less than half what broadcast-quality Avid nonlinear video editing systems go for.

CineWorks Nonlinear Editing

I have a love-hate relationship with the D/Vision CineWorks non-linear video editing system. The love stems from the theoretical capability of CineWorks, which, simply put, represents a fantastic price/performance breakthrough. The hate stems from the absolute hell I experienced struggling to get the setup working properly on my IBM-compatible computer.

The promise of D/Vision is the long-anticipated low-budget (just $2395, as an add-on hardware/software package) tapeless computer based video editing "solution". Instead of selectively transferring tape segments from one VCR to another, as in traditional analog video editing, the premise of all nonlinear systems is that first you digitize all the raw videotape and store it on the computer's hard drive; then you edit it on the computer with the same cut-and-paste ease as word processing; then you playback the final edited version out of the computer and record it onto video-tape. Along the way, you can add fully synchronized audio tracks, and all sorts of video special effects such as dissolves, wipes, chroma-key, etc.

Nonlinear Nirvana?

What I've defined so far is commonly available, and readily ac-cessible with today's computers (including both Mac and PCs) using digital video software such as Adobe Premiere. But at best, the resolution with such programs is 320 x 240 pixels—lower than VHS quality—and achieving that resolution at 30 frames per second (the standard video frame rate) is a tough challenge for even powerful computers. Typically, these pro-grams are used at resolutions like 160 x 120 pixels, and/or with a more flickery 15 frames per second rate.

Regardless of resolution, there are two big advantages to non-linear editing systems, compared with tape-based editing: First, the hard drive offers instant access to any part of the recording—there's no waiting for the equipment to search through tapes to find an edit point. Second, you can trim edit points to your heart's content, removing frames and adding them at will, with no worry-ing about generation loss, and no need to organize tapes into A and B rolls for special effects.

It's a tempting convenience; but for most semi-pro video pro-ducers, the sacrifice in resolution is too high a price to pay. A wed-ding videographer, for example, would be embarrassed to offered clients tapes that have lower picture quality than what a $500 camcorder can produce. The main use for programs such as Adobe Premiere has been for the production of computer multi-media video, where crumby resolution and jittery images are the order of the day (for now.)

What makes the D/Vision so extraordinary is its ability—at least its promise—to offer nonlinear editing with 480-line horizon-tal resolution, which is roughly equivalent to broadcast-quality TV (vertical resolution is presumably only 240-pixels—less than broadcast quality—based on an obscure appendix entry I found. The CineWorks literature suspiciously avoids mentioning any reso-lution numbers except for the 480-line "SupeRTV" horizontal specification.) In non-technical terms, this means it's the first low-priced PC-based nonlinear editing system that doesn't severely re-duce picture quality just for the sake of using the computer to edit.

Higher priced high resolution nonlinear editing systems have been around for several years. Avid, the most famous brand in this category, has been dropping prices on its Macintosh-based nonlinear editor, but for broadcast quality output, prices still run upwards of twenty thousand dollars.

But the complete CineWorks kit costs just $2,395, combining a clone of the Intel Action Media 2 audio/video input/output board (with Capture Module), and software. If you've already got the AM2 board—which performs "on the fly" compression of the incoming video and audio data—TouchVision (the publisher of the D/Vision line of editing programs) sells the CineWorks software alone for $995.

A Test Drive

Installation of the complete system is a rather involved process. First you install the Action Media board. Then you install the software for the board (and revise the configuration file to recognize the board when the computer boots.) Then you install the CineWorks software, hook it all up, and test it out.

The computer I tested CineWorks with was a 486 DX - 50 MHz processor, with 20-megabytes of RAM, and a 540-MB Western Digital hard drive (with at least 200-MB free). Though it could be argued that a Pentium processor might have done the trick, ultimately it was my hard drive that proved to be the final, insurmountable stumbling block. But there were many rough starts and detours on the road to learning this.

The highest picture resolution is called "SupeRTV" in the jargon of CineWorks. According to the instructions, SupeRTV requires a hard drive with access speed of less than 12-milliseconds. My IDE hard drive is rated at 11-milliseconds. But according to the final tech support person I spoke with, it is absolutely impossible to get "SupeRTV" mode with an IDE type hard drive, regardless of how fast it works.

So I gave up on SupeRTV, and played with it in the medium resolution RTV mode—which is the quality the Action Media board was intended to produce (RTV stands for Real Time Video—based on some setup info in the appendix, my guess is it's 256 x 240 resolution.) But even in medium resolution, the picture would exhibit odd digitized time artifacts—it would freeze for a few frames, then start moving again.

Nevertheless, I could play around with the available video and audio editing effects. These are indeed impressive. There's dissolve, fade-in/out, freeze frame, and 20 wipe effects available—not nearly as many wipe effects as on the Video Toaster, but all the basic ones, are here. There are four available digital audio sound tracks.

Raw video and audio are stored as AVS files (Audio Video Subsystem). When capture is completed, an AVS file is created, and you can move onto editing.

Editing

The editing screen uses the analogy of tape video. In the top half of the screen there are two boxes on the left and right, representing the "source" and "recorder" of a tape-based editing system. Traditional VCR motion control buttons are located under each screen. To assemble edit, you locate the start point from the raw footage, start the recorder, and then start the player. Edit points are located using a mouse-operated shuttle control that simulates the dial found on editing VCRs; a seek button also lets you locate by entering specific timing information.

The bottom half of the screen consists of time lines, representing the video tracks (including overlaps for transition effects, such as dissolve), audio tracks, and a graphics track. You can also display a traditional-looking edit decision list (EDL), or a screen filled with up to a dozen picture boxes showing opening stills from the selected video clips.

To see a special effect, the computer must calculate the pictures in the transition frames—a process that takes about a minute.

The final step in the editing process is called Complete A Project. When you click on the "Build Movie" button, all the specified transitions and audio mixing are calculated, and placed into one continuous file. The computer must first "de-fragment" the hard disk, creating one continuous blank block of storage area. I attempted to go into this process, but due to the IDE drive problem, my system always crashed. (The tech support people came up with another way to output the completed project in medium resolution, but said it was impossible to do it in high resolution.)

For those who can get SupeRTV mode working, one innovative option helps solve the problem of not enough disk space for all the raw footage. Even with the right hard drive, recording raw footage in SupeRTV mode consumes some 60 megabytes per minute. A 1.2-gigabyte hard drive could only hold 20-minutes at that rate.

The clever solution offered by CineWorks is dependent on the availability of some form of time code—either 8mm RC (or MiniDV), or SMPTE—on the original tapes. The raw footage is first digitized onto the hard disk in low (9 megabytes per minute) or medium (18 mb per min.) resolution, to minimize disk space.

Then, when the editing is completed, CineWorks automatically goes back to the original tapes and re-transfers just the segments that are needed for the final edit, in Super-RTV mode, using time code to find the selected points. (Of course, if the raw footage is on more than one tape, you've got to manually swap tapes.) Effects are calculated, the final edited production is output to tape.

At about the same budget level, the DPS Perception recorder system (about $2000) offers even higher 720x480 resolution at 60 fields per second. It incorporates a SCSI hard disk controller, for use with specified high speed AV hard drives. In conjunction with Adobe Premiere (or similar) software, you've got a very high quality low cost nonlinear system. Assuming, that is, that your tapes are not already digital.

The Hybrid Future

The MiniDV tape format and firewire digital dub connection move the digitizing process from the computer to the camcorder, and make the future of nonlinear editing clear: Hybrid systems that take advantage of the cheap mass storage capabilities of tape-based editing, while enhancing the process with digital effects.

When Sony launched MiniDV they introduced a computer card that can directly input the digitized video signal from MiniDV camcorders equipped with the firewire connection. These cards, and similar third party products that will surely follow, represent the cutting edge of low budget nonlinear editing.

Perception Video Recorder board and software, above, from Digital Processing Systems, plugs into a PC (with PCI slot) and, with appropriate high speed SCSI hard drive and optional daughter-board, records high quality digital video (4 minutes occupies 1 gigabyte) for editing with Adobe Premiere software.

Videonics Media-Motion interface, right, adds automated camcorder and VCR control (compatible with both LANC and Matsushita 5-pin) to Adobe Premiere.

20   Time Base Correctors

Video recordings are all based on very precise timing of the picture information. As each scan line is swept across the screen, it's crucial that these lines perfectly stack up, one atop another, to form the image. If one line should be off by a fraction of a second, the image information will shift slightly to the left or right, creating a minor aberration in the picture. Such timing errors become especially apparent when there's a vertical edge in the shot—when edges of buildings and lampposts look jagged, we know something's wrong.

One of the more obscure technical details that previously divided the world of professional videocassette formats such as Betacam, MII, D-2, and D-3 from the consumer formats such as VHS, Super-VHS, 8mm and Hi8, was in the timing stability. The MiniDV format breaks that barrier, by offering the same timing stability that professional equipment has had for years.

Each horizontal scan line is supposed to occur exactly 1/15,750th of a second after the previous scan line. A millionth of a second early or late, and the image appears noticeably distorted. The professional formats all have better inherent time base stability, and all also incorporate special circuits called time base correctors, or TBCs, to clean up the signal even more. (F.C.C. technical regulations require the timing of broadcast signals to be within very close tolerance—prior to TBCs, portable video formats could not be legally broadcast, except by optically "re-scanning" the picture with a professional camera.)

The time base corrector is essentially a memory device. It creates a very slight delay between the arrival of the input video signal, and the delivery of the TBC's output signal. During this brief interval, the TBC digitizes the incoming video signal (converting the continuous analog stream of picture information into a series of pixels), stores this information in digital memory, and then pumps the information out from memory a fraction of a second later. Because the information coming out of the TBC is being spun out by a digital electronic circuit, and not a mechanical tape playback head (that's spinning around at 60 revolutions per second), its timing is perfectly consistent.

The amount of memory that the TBC has is called the "window". When a VCR has a TBC built in, the window is usually equivalent to a few scan lines of the picture–just enough to compensate for slight error from one scan line to the next. But almost all TBCs sold as separate stand alone units have so-called "infinite" or full-frame windows. The idea is that the TBC has enough memory to store a complete frame of video—525 scan lines.

With a full frame of memory, TBCs can do something remarkable: They can take an asynchronous source, such as any VCR or camcorder, and get it perfectly synchronized with another video device—such as a second VCR. This is what's needed when you want to do A/B-roll editing using a special effects generator (SEG) such as the Video Toaster. A/V image mixers, such as the Videonics MX-1 and Panasonic WJ-AVE7 have built-in time base correction systems—the simpler variations (having less memory) are called "frame synchronizers".

The Personal TBC

TBCs used to cost thousands of dollars, and many professional models still do. But as digital memory prices have dropped, so has the cost of TBCs, and they are now commonly available for under one thousand dollars per channel (you need two channels for use with the Video Toaster). Perhaps the best known of the new crop of low-budget TBCs is the Personal TBC IV, from Digital Processing Systems. This TBC costs less partly because it takes the form of a plug-in computer card, supplied with software. (The costs of building a case, a power supply, and a control panel are all eliminated—the computer provides these functions. An optional RC-2000 control panel accessory can provide more traditional proc-amp knobs and buttons.)

I recently had the opportunity to test out Personal TBC IV. I was curious to see whether passing a video signal through the TBC during ordinary copying—such as occurs in straight-cut video editing, without the use of any special effects—would produce any noticeable difference in picture quality.

The act of digitizing a signal inevitably produces some minor distortion of that signal. Hopefully, if the digitizing system is good enough, these slight drawbacks will be outweighed by the improvements in timing stability. (In technical parlance, the quality of digital conversion, as with audio, is measured by the number of bits recorded in each sample, and the frequency of the sampling. The manufacturer rates Personal TBC IV as having a respectable 58-dB S/N ratio, and frequency response up to 5.5-MHz when the

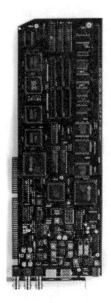

Personal TBC is a plug-in card for Amiga and IBM-compatible computers.

comb filter is used. Residual time base error is rated at less than 15-billionths of a second.)

The card installs in either an IBM compatible or Amiga computer (up to four cards can be installed in a single computer—Video Toaster systems, which are based on the Amiga computer, commonly have two TBC cards.) A single 3.5-inch floppy disk contains software for both IBM and Amiga computers on it.

I installed the Amiga version, almost without a hitch. (The one thing I foolishly overlooked, although the instructions make it quite clear, is that besides plugging into the computer slot, the board must also be connected to the computer's serial port.) The entire installation took less than an hour.

Once installed, the control screen is quite intuitive, at least for anyone who has been around video signals for a while. Besides affecting the signal's timing, the TBC also provides a host of so-called "proc amp" controls. (These get their name from the analog processing amplifier, which existed in broadcast video for many years prior to the digital revolution.) There are slider adjustments for video level, chroma saturation, etc. For color correction, an excellent three-axis graph pops up on the screen (red-green-blue vectors)—you can move the pointer from the center, and observe the tint changes on the output.

You can store ten different sets of these adjustments in memory. Suppose you're editing a dialog between two people, cutting between two different close up shots and a wide shot, and each needs its own set of optimized adjustments. As you edit, you can instantly jump to the settings needed for each.

The card has both S-video and composite video inputs and outputs. An "advanced sync" output connection is provided for use with industrial editing VCRs costing upwards of twenty-five hundred dollars. (The only sacrifice you make using the TBC with a VCR that does not have an advance sync input is that there's a greater likelihood that the TBC will occasionally need to skip a frame, substituting a portion of a frame stored in memory, to "catch up" with the tape.) A genlock input allows the TBC to synchronize with another TBC (as needed for A/B-roll editing), or any other video source.

Multigeneration Testing

Sure, it's fun to play around with color correction, but what about when you're editing good video that was properly exposed, and doesn't need any particular adjustment? Are you better off passing it through a TBC, with all the proc amp adjustments left at normal?

To see just how much difference a TBC could make in the picture quality, I made two sets of copies of copies of the same short (two-minute) video sequence, including a resolution test pattern.

The second generation copies were not much different. The TBC did add a wee bit of noise, visible in the black areas of the picture. By the third generation, however, the TBC copies were emerging as superior. With the fifth and sixth generation copies, the TBC versions looked quite noticeably better, especially whenever a straight vertical line appeared in the picture. Circles (on the test pattern) took on a grotesque out-of-shape distortion in the non-TBC copies, but looked perfectly round in the TBC copies.

Perhaps the most interesting discovery was checking out what would happen if a TBC was applied after making repeated copies without the TBC. This may at first sound absurd, but it's exactly what happens if you edit your videos at home—without a TBC—and then send them off to a professional dubbing facility to make copies, and they have a TBC in the signal chain.

So I played back the non-TBC fifth generation copy through the TBC to see how it looked. It was worse than anything I had previously seen—and considerably worse than the sixth generation copy made without any help from the TBC. The problems with this "no-TBC-until-the-last-step" video were all around the edges of straight lines, which took on a randomly changing staggered quality. The circles did look slightly more circular, but the tradeoff hardly seemed worth it.

It would appear that the accumulated drift of the uncorrected video timing requires the TBC to create a bigger, more noticeable change in the image, and that beyond a certain point, these changes make the image look worse (though the timing may be more stable.) So the conclusion, for low budget producers, is that you shouldn't think of the TBC as a "clean up" device which can simply be inserted at the end of the whole video editing process. It is clearly advantageous to have the TBC inserted in the signal chain every step of the way.

The TBC is not a miracle worker, however. The only thing it really fixes is the timing of the video signal. A lot more can deteriorate. In the camera original resolution test pattern, horizontal resolution of over 300-lines was apparent. But by the third generation, that had dropped to 250, and it was down under 200 by the sixth generation.

The only way to eliminate all the problems of generation loss is with digital video editing – either using digital tape (MiniDV) or nonlinear. Note that if you're shooting with analog tape (Hi8 or S-VHS) most nonlinear systems work much better if the original tape signal is first passed through a TBC before recording on hard disk.

PART III

. . . .

Other Concerns: Audio, Lighting, Graphics, Travel, Etc.

21 Audio Basics

Audio is largely ignored in today's super sophisticated consumer camcorder: With the exception of MiniDV semi-pro models, there is usually no manual level control, no ability to record multiple tracks with good isolation, and sometimes there isn't even a headphone jack to monitor the sound quality while recording.

Audio gave birth to video, and the two technologies have had a strained but productive relationship ever since. From the earliest days of television, the new medium was conceived as a combination of images and sound—radio shows with pictures. There was no golden age of "silent television".

In low budget video production, audio is sometimes an afterthought, if a consideration at all. Only recently have improvements like stereo sound and decent speakers been built into consumer TV sets. Meanwhile, most TVs still have an underpowered, screechy little speaker to accompany the high quality picture.

A critical ear is all it takes to recognize how important sound is for video. If you've ever had a tape ruined (rendered totally unlistenable) by audio problems like wind noise; or weakened (rendered barely listenable) by more subtle audio problems like hum or feedback, then you've probably already been converted to the cause through shock therapy.

Try this experiment: Turn on your TV, but turn the volume all the way down so you can hear nothing. Watch for fifteen minutes, switching channels to try out a variety of different types of programs, getting a sense of how well you can understand what's going on just from the pictures. Next, turn the volume up, and turn the brightness all the way down, so you can only hear the sound but can see no picture. After fifteen minutes of each, I think you'll agree that the basic story line content of most programs is conveyed more through the sound than the picture. For most programs, the picture serves as an embellishment of the sound track, which is really not surprising when you consider that most TV show formats are based on old radio show formats from yesteryear.

It's really not surprising that most beginning videomakers are content to just aim the camcorder at someone who's speaking, and trust the built-in microphone to do the rest. Audio tape recorders are so cheaply available these days, the miracle of audio recording is easily taken for granted.

There's a tendency, on the part of some videomakers, to blame the equipment—or lack thereof—for audio problems. But much of the extra equipment needed for good audio is relatively inexpensive—especially when compared with video accessories that can cost more than the camcorder itself.

Audio quality is largely determined by skill, not budget. After all, practically any camcorder on the market today has the technical capability to record and playback broadcast-quality sound entirely suitable for use by a television network. That's not true of picture quality, where even topnotch camcorders can't match the Betacam and 1" equipment costing tens of thousands of dollars.

Sound and Perception—Psychoacoustics

Psychoacoustics is a field of scientific research and inquiry that deals with how the ear-brain system of sound perception works. A modest understanding of this science can be extremely useful to anyone working with sound—musicians, recording engineers, mixers, sound reinforcement technicians, filmmakers, and videomakers.

Camcorders' technical specifications often include the term "audio fidelity". Fidelity is a way of describing how closely a recorded sound can imitate the original sound as it is reproduced through the sound recording system. In a world of perfect fidelity, listeners would really ask, "Is it live, or is it Memorex?" But factors like location cues (based on complex ear-brain echo analysis) generally give us a good idea of when things are live and when they're recorded.

Psychoacoustics research reveals how human hearing works, and thus defines parameters for high quality audio reproduction. But the ear-brain sonic sensory system has plenty of quirks of its own.

The Nature of Sound

The perception of sound occurs when there are rapid changes in air pressure near the ear. Any disturbance of the air—such as the beating of a drum, the plucking of a guitar string, or the stimulation of human vocal chords—creates alternating areas of slightly compressed and expanded air, which travel in waves from the sound source to the ear at a rate of about 1130-feet per second (about 700 miles per hour).

The number of cycles of compression and expansion per second is called the frequency of a sound, and is expressed by the unit Hertz (Hz). Frequency is one of the three main characteristics of sound waves—amplitude and waveshape are the other two (discussed later).

Psychoacoustic researchers draw a distinction between these three physical qualities—frequency, amplitude, and waveshape—and the terms that are used to describe our *perception* of these qualities. The terms pitch, loudness, and timbre (a French word meaning tone color) are used to describe the perception of frequency, amplitude, and waveshape, respectively.

Although this may seem to be a minor semantic distinction, these differences form the basis of much psychoacoustic research. Frequency, amplitude, and waveshape are physical qualities that can be readily measured using electronic test equipment. But our sense of pitch, loudness, and tone color are more subjective, requiring studies of large sample groups of test listeners stating what they hear during controlled experiments.

Each physical quality is the primary—but not the only—contributor to our perception of its corollary psychoacoustic quality. For example, our sense of "loudness" is determined primarily by the amplitude, or physical intensity, of a sound. But loudness is also affected by frequency and waveshape.

You've probably heard that for good audio fidelity, a piece of equipment should have "flat frequency response"—more or less equal sensitivity to all pitches in the range of 20 to 20,000 cycles per second (that's 20-Hz to 20-kHz in tech jargon).

This 20-Hz to 20-kHz range represents the absolute limits of human hearing perception, although most people don't hear nearly the full range. Young children have the best hearing; as people get older, they tend to lose the ability to hear high frequency sounds.

The high frequency loss problem is worse for men than women. By the age of 60, the average man has lost much of his ability to hear sounds above 5-kHz. (In one psychoacoustic study, for 60- year old men to perceive a 4-kHz tone it had to be some 35- decibels higher in amplitude than for 25-year old men. But 60- year old women required only an 18-dB increase in level.)

The Audio Tracks

Here's a chart summarizing what each video format offers in the audio department, along with some more technical information.

COMPARING CAMCORDER AUDIO

TAPE FORMAT	STANDARD AUDIO TRACK					PREMIUM AUDIO TRACK				
	Name	Frequency Response	Signal-to-Noise Ratio	Mono or Stereo?	Audio-only Dubbing?	Name	Frequency Response	Signal-to-Noise Ratio	Mono or Stereo?	Audio-only Dubbing?
VHS, & VHS-C, S-VHS, S-VHS-C	LINEAR @ SP SPEED	50-12,000 Hz (+/-3dB)	45 dB	Usually mono (some industrial VCRs have stereo)	Yes	VHS Hi-Fi @ SP	20-20,000 Hz (+/-1.5dB)	80 dB	Stereo	No
	LINEAR @ EP SPEED	100-6,000 Hz (+/-3dB)	42 dB			Hi-Fi @ EP				
8mm & Hi8	AFM, AFM-Stereo	20-18,000 Hz (+/-3dB)	75 dB	AFM-Stereo on newer models, mono on older	No	PCM (Pulse Code Modulation)	20-15,000 Hz (+/-1.5dB)	72 dB	Stereo	Yes
Mini-DV & DVC*	12-bit (4-track)	20-15,000 Hz (+/-1.5dB; 32 kHz sampling)	72 dB	Two stereo pairs - one recorded w/picture	Yes - second stereo pair is for audio dubbing	16-bit (2-track)	20-20,000 Hz (+/-1.5dB; 44.1 kHz sampling)	96 dB	Stereo	Yes

* With DV, 12-bit and 16-bit recording are mutually exclusive -- you can have two excellent (16-bit) or four very good (12-bit) tracks.

source: composite estimates by Cliff Roth are averages for each format; actual performance varies from model to model

As mentioned earlier, when you start editing with consumer video equipment, you quickly discover that the format's inherent audio characteristics dictate many of your editing options.

Each of the consumer videocassette formats—VHS, Super-VHS, 8mm, VHS-C, S-VHS-C, Hi8, and MiniDV—offers different audio capabilities. Which is best for you depends largely on what type of productions you want to create, and whose equipment you intend to create it with.

All 8mm and Hi8 tapes are recorded with what amounts to "hi-fi" sound. Technically, the 8mm (and Hi8) audio track is called "AFM"—for "audio frequency modulation"—and is quite similar to the "hi-fi" audio on fancy VHS-format VCRs. The audio signal is combined with the video signal (utilizing the same FM process that makes hi-fi radio possible), and recorded in a mix with the video signal. The system—and quality—is essentially the same for both 8mm family and VHS-family VCRs, except that when it's found on VHS-family equipment, it's always in stereo, whereas some older and lower priced 8mm and Hi8 camcorders have single-channel monaural AFM sound.

Exactly what constitutes "hi-fi" sound quality is a subject of endless debate among audiophiles. Avoiding the esoterica, and boiling it down to the basics, however, there are two main factors which predominate: frequency response, and dynamic range. These are the qualities of both microphones and speakers, which determine how truly a recorded sound can simulate the original.

Truly hi-fi sound equipment must not just have a range of 20-20,000 Hz, to simulate the range of human hearing, but must maintain "flat" frequency response over that range. This means that it should have no tendency to emphasize or de-emphasize any frequencies in that range. The exact measurement of deviation from the ideal "equal response to all frequencies" is made in decibels (dB), a logarithmic unit of the loudness of sound.

The other major aspect of hi-fi sound, dynamic range, is also called "signal-to-noise ratio", or just "S/N" (although there is a very slight technical difference between these terms). Basically, it's a measure of the range in volume, from the quietest possible recorded sound which doesn't get lost in the inherent noise, or hiss, of any recording system, and the loudest possible sound which doesn't cause distortion. Dynamic range and S/N ratio are also measured in decibels.

VHS-family equipment has two types of sound available: linear and hi-fi. The linear track, so-called because the audio is recorded along a straight line on the edge of the tape (rather than in the diagonal video tracks), has audio quality roughly comparable to low-grade audio cassettes. The frequency response is in the ballpark of 50-12,000 Hz (plus or minus 3-decibels, whatever they are!), and the dynamic range is in the ballpark of 50-decibels. That's at the fastest SP tape speed—at the slower EP speed (which you should never use for serious video production, no matter how low your budget is!) the frequency response drops down to 100-5,000 Hz, about the same as a telephone line.

The linear track on all VHS-family camcorders is mono (one-channel), but some VCRs—especially older models—have two-channel stereo linear soundtracks. The fancier VHS and S-VHS editing decks also have stereo linear—in addition to stereo hi-fi.

The Hi-Fi tracks on VHS-family equipment have frequency response of 20-20,000 Hz (+/- 3dB, once again), and have a dynamic range of around 80-dB. The AFM track on 8mm family camcorders has similar hi-fi quality.

The MiniDV format offers the best sound recoring capability of all, with specifications identical to CD audio recordings. Though microphone and preamp circuitry will usually limit it more, at least theoretically it can be 20-20,000 Hz (+/1 1dB). That's when you record in the 16-bit audio mode, which provides just two tracks of sound. Alternatively, it can have four audio tracks, using a lower quality 12-bit mode, in which the high-end frequency response is limited to about 15,000 Hz. The 12-bit mode recordings are theoretically more noisy (lower signal-to-noise ratio), but a non-linear digital-analog conversion scheme compensates for the fewer bits, effectively providing very clean, noise-free sound.

To summarize:

- VHS-family tapes can potentially have four tracks—two linear and two hi-fi—but there aren't any camcorders which offer four tracks. Most VHS camcorders have just a single mono linear track, but some top-of-the-line S-VHS-C camcorders have three—two hi-fi and one linear track. Industrial editing equipment you might inexpensively rent, however, may offer all four.
- In the 8mm camp, most camcorders now have stereo AFM. Some older models have mono. But as described earlier, AFM stereo is not as good as VHS hi-fi stereo when it comes to channel separation—you can't use AFM stereo to record SMPTE audio time code without getting bleed-through to the other channel. You can add two tracks of PCM digital sound, for a total of four. But most consumer equipment limits your ability to get each of the four channels out of a separate jack—they must usually be mixed together.

- With MiniDV, 16-bit recording occupies the full audio track during initial recording, leaving no room to add other audio elements later. The 12-bit recording mode leaves two tracks available for additional dubbing later, such as to add music or narration. The quality of 12-bit is not quite as good as 16-bit. Note that not all camcorders offer all audio recording modes.

Microphones

The microphone starts the audio signal flowing through the camcorder's sound system. With a camcorder's built-in microphone, crossing your fingers and hoping for the best works—sometimes. Understanding the proper use of an external microphone, however, can lead to more consistent audio success.

Every camcorder has a built-in microphone to pick up the sound in front of the lens. For many applications—especially for casual videotaping of family events, travel, etc.—the camcorder's built-in microphone is more than adequate.

Most better camcorders also have a microphone jack that lets you disconnect the built-in microphone, and replace it with an external microphone. The reason why such microphone jacks are so pervasive is because camcorder manufacturers recognize that there are many situations where the built-in microphone simply won't do the job adequately—and it costs just a few cents extra to offer this feature.

Knowing when to plug in an external microphone, and what type to use, can mean the difference between unintelligible, garbled sound, and crisp clear audio.

When To Go External

The human ear is capable of hearing an extremely wide range of listening levels, and, because it works in conjunction with a brain, includes the ability to discriminate between the sound we're interested in hearing and background noise.

The use of external microphones is largely an effort to compensate for the difference between microphones and the human ear. In essence, you will be using microphone location, sensitivity, and pickup pattern to isolate sounds—rather than relying on the human intelligence of the ear-brain system.

When should you use an external microphone? Most often, you'll want to bypass the camcorder's microphone, and plug in an external unit, whenever the sound source is too far away, or too weak to be picked up properly by the camcorder's microphone.

In a lecture hall, for example, where the camcorder may be located twenty feet from the person speaking, you can usually use the zoom lens to get a decently framed medium shot (waist up) of the lecturer. But the audio, from such a back-row position, is likely to be very muddy—filled with reverberations from the walls of the room, noisy sounds of papers ruffling, chairs moving, extraneous speaking, etc.

As an audience member you're mentally able to "tune out" all these other sounds and concentrate on the lecture, but the camcorder's microphone has no such intelligence. Wedding services and bar mitzvahs often present similar recording problems.

The solution is to place a microphone closer to the source. A tie-clip microphone is usually best; a desktop microphone placed on the lectern would be a good second choice.

Third choice would be a highly directional "shot gun" microphone which functions much like an audio "zoom lens".

When recording relatively weak sounds, even though they may be close to the camcorder, external microphones can become necessary. A very soft spoken person standing seven feet away from a camcorder may be audible to careful listeners, but relatively inaudible to the camcorder's built-in microphone. This is especially true on camcorders that have their microphones located *behind* the lens, because such placement tends to pick up the whirring sounds of the zoom and auto-focus motors as they operate.

Similarly, if you're handling the camcorder a lot during a taping session—operating a title generator, fade control, panning, etc.—then the built-in microphone will pick up these sounds to the detriment of what you're trying to record. Remember that whatever's going on closest to the microphone gets recorded louder than what's further away; so even relatively "quiet" sounds of buttons being pressed just a few inches from the microphone may be recorded much louder than someone speaking from a few feet away.

In videotaping theater productions, you may find an external microphone is needed to pick up sound which is not directly in front of the camera. For example, suppose you're shooting a scene where two people are talking, and you want to get "reaction shots" of the person listening. During such shots, the camcorder will be pointing away from the speaker, towards the listener, and the sound will be much weaker than when you point the camcorder at the person speaking.

You'll also need an external microphone outdoors when wind noise makes it almost impossible to get a decent recording. Wind noise sounds nothing like the howling wind you hear in horror movies (if it did, there would be little problem!) On tape, wind sounds like a constant popping or banging as the shifting air pressure overloads the microphone's diaphragm, thrashing it from one extreme to another. You almost never hear this noise with your own ears, since it's created within the microphone itself. You must wear headphones, as you record, to spot it. You can reduce wind noise by putting a foam "wind screen" over an external microphone to absorb some of the wind's energy, and by placing the microphone behind a wind shield such as a piece of cardboard or clothing.

Finally, you'll sometimes need to use an external microphone when the sound you're recording is too loud for the camcorder's built-in microphone. This may occur at a rock concert if you're shooting from right next to the speakers. When the sound level overloads a microphone, distortion results. By plugging in a less sensitive microphone, or one less prone to overload, such as a dynamic type (see below), you can often eliminate this distortion.

Condenser Microphone Technology

Most microphones fall into two general types: "condenser" and "dynamic". (A third, more obscure "ribbon" microphone is found occasionally in professional recording studios, but is rarely used in videomaking.)

Virtually every camcorder's built-in microphone is of the condenser variety. Technically, condenser microphones work on the electronic principle of "capacitance" ("condenser" is an old electrical term for "capacitor"—a basic electronic component). A "capacitor", or "condenser" normally consists of two thin electrical plates which store oppositely charged electrical particles. It functions a bit like a battery, except that it holds much less electrical power.

As the distance between the plates changes, the electrical charge between them changes. A condenser microphone takes advantage of this principle by allowing one of the plates to vibrate with the air. Since sound consists of subtle, rapid changes in air pressure, or vibrations in the air, the condenser microphone responds to those slight changes in air pressure by producing corresponding changes in electrical energy.

Condenser microphones are generally crisper sounding and more sensitive to faint signals, but they also have drawbacks: They are easily overloaded by loud signals (causing annoying distortion), they're more susceptible to wind noises, and they require power for their built-in circuitry.

The best condenser microphones, used in recording studios, get this power from the mixing console, and are called "phantom power" microphones. More common in video applications are condenser microphones that require a small battery, which must be periodically replaced. The least expensive condenser micro-phones are called "electret condenser" types, which have a perma-nent electrical charge (like a tiny battery) that lasts for at least a decade.

Condenser microphones can be built in a smaller size than dy-namic microphones. Consequently, practically all "lavaliere" and "tie-clip" microphones, designed to be worn on a person's chest, are of the condenser variety. Such microphones are a staple of TV talk shows and news anchors, but note that when people move around, these microphones can pick up a lot of unwanted sounds from clothing rubbing up against the microphone. Thus, they're generally best used when people are sitting.

Dynamic Microphone Technology

Dynamic microphones tend to be more ruggedly built than con-denser types. They can usually handle very loud sounds without distorting, and require no batteries. They deliver a warmer sound quality than condensers, and they're less vulnerable to wind noise.

Technically, dynamic microphones take advantage of the rela-tionship between electricity and magnetism, in much the same way as a speaker works, except in reverse. Most people know that when you run electricity through a coil of wire it creates magne-tism. The converse is also true—when you move a magnet through a coil of wire, it creates electricity in the wire. This pro-cess is called "induction" (because electricity is magnetically in-duced), and it is the principle behind practically all electrical power generators, including the "alternator" in your car.

The dynamic microphone works like an extremely low power electrical generator: A diaphragm that responds to subtle vibra-tions in the air is attached to a thin coil of wire, wrapped around a magnet. Sound makes the diaphragm vibrate, creating a very small electrical current in the microphone's coil.

Note that almost all built-in microphones found on camcord-ers and portable cassette recorders are of the condenser variety, not because they're necessarily better, but because they make bet-ter cheap microphones than dynamics. If you only have a dollar or two to spend on the microphone, condenser technology is clearly superior. On the other hand, if you're willing to spend fifty or one hundred dollars on a good microphone, you may find better value in the dynamic types.

Pickup Patterns

The pickup pattern is the area from which a microphone picks up sound. This pattern can be omnidirectional (picking up sound

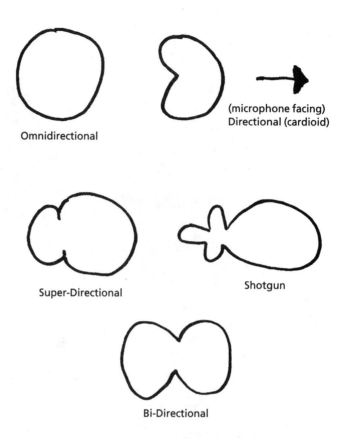

Omnidirectional

(microphone facing)
Directional (cardioid)

Super-Directional

Shotgun

Bi-Directional

from all around the microphone), directional (also called unidi-rectional or "cardioid" — because of the heart-shaped pickup pat-tern), superdirectional ("super cardioid"), hyperdirectional (also called "shotgun" and "hypercardioid"), or bidirectional ("figure eight").

Directional microphones allow you to focus the microphone onto the sound source while rejecting extraneous noises coming from other directions, but you will find that the more directional a microphone is, the more difficult it is to use.

In the most extreme form, hyper-directional shotgun micro-phones require very careful aiming directly at the mouth of the person speaking in order to work properly. Some models even include cross-hair sights. An error of just a degree or two of angle can mean the differ-ence between great sound and garbled sound. The advantage

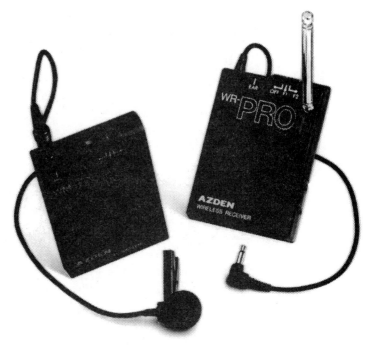

of these microphones, which makes them worth the trouble, is that they allow you to pickup sound from a much further distance (several dozen feet) from the sound source than any other.

Note that each microphone technology (dynamic and condenser) is available in each of the pickup patterns. Some microphones even offer selectable pickup patterns. Bidirectional microphones can occasionally be useful for picking up two sources that are 180 degrees apart from each other—such as two singers, or an interviewer and interviewee. Usually, however, you don't want the bi-directionality, so it's useful to be able to flick a switch and make the mike unidirectional.

Wireless Microphones

The wireless microphone consists of two parts: a transmitter, which is sometimes built into the body of a hand- held microphone; and a receiver, which you locate right next to your camcorder. The advantage is obvious: good sound pickup without the hassle of running long cables.

But because you're using radio signals, you can receive all sorts of interference from CB radio, cordless telephones, etc. This is especially problematic in dense urban areas. You must wear headphones to monitor the sound when you use a wireless microphone.

The most versatile transmitters allow you to plug in any microphone you want, but the less expensive models usually have a permanently connected microphone. A convenient arrangement for videomaking is to connect a tie-clip microphone, by wire, to a transmitter tucked conveniently in a pocket.

The wireless microphone offers creative audio possibilities and quality that would simply be unachievable with the camcorder's built-in microphone, and which would be too cumbersome using a wired external microphone. Wireless microphones have thus become the first accessory microphone that many videomakers buy.

In making travel videos, a wireless microphone can be a lot of fun. The camcorder operator sits comfortably at a cafe, or inside a restaurant, looking out on a scenic street or view. The host walks around this outside area, speaking and moving freely—thanks to the wireless system.

Recording a lecture in an auditorium, or a wedding in a large hall, the wireless microphone lets you setup your camcorder far enough back from the lectern (or alter) to get wide, medium, and close-up shoots of the person speaking. Instead of getting the typical boomy audio—a result of all the reverberations around the auditorium's walls, floor, and ceiling—that the camcorder's built-in microphone would normally pickup from this position ten to fifteen feet away, the wireless microphone lets you record a crisp, clear, more intimate sound track.

On loud city streets, in noisy factories, at a beach or waterfalls, and in a host of other situations where ambient background audio levels are high, the wireless microphone lets you separate the

Azden wireless microphone components

voice of your subject from the din. The louder the background sound, the more important it becomes to get the microphone up close to the source of sound. A camcorder's built-in microphone may work fine for shooting someone speaking five feet away in a suburban back yard, but would be useless picking up the sound of the same person speaking from five feet away while riding on a subway.

The radio frequency used for wireless microphone operation can make a big difference in the overall sound quality. Specifically, there are three bands that are commonly used—the 49-MHz general use consumer band, the 170-216 MHz commercial use band, and the same 900 MHz band that's now available for cordless phones. This is one case where I'll admit up front you might call me a nut, but, despite excellent performance, I am personally afraid of working for extended periods of time with equipment operating in the 900 MHz region – these are microwave frequencies that I believe are potentially more dangerous than the VHF band.

Models operating in the higher 170-216 VHF (very high frequency) band generally perform much better than those in the noisy, overcrowded 49-Mhz band. The 49-Mhz band is also commonly used for cordless telephones, garage door openers, and radio controlled toys—making 49-MHz highly prone to interference, especially in large cities. Videomakers are best off avoiding 49-MHz.

To pick the exact frequency within the 170–216 MHz VHF band, matching crystals are installed in both the transmitter and receiver. Usually these are in the narrower range of 169–172 MHz, which is the portion set aside by the F.C.C. for "travelling" commercial use—meaning that there are no radio stations with permanent antennas operating in this range.

Some VHF wireless systems, like Azden's moderately priced WMS-Pro (about two hundred fifty dollars list price), allow you to choose between two different frequencies, so that if there is heavy interference on one (from another travelling user) you can switch to the other.

When you purchase a VHF wireless microphone system without specifying a frequency, you'll usually get a randomly assigned frequency. In the unlikely event that you are aware of specific interference problems, you can order crystals that avoid the problem frequency. But most of the time interference problems are transient—a cab driving down the street, for example.

Professional audio engineers utilizing multiple wireless microphone systems simultaneously, such as for two singers performing together (each with their own handheld wireless microphone), must worry not only about interference from extraneous sources, but also between the multiple units.

For such multi-channel applications, the Lectrosonics CR185 receiver claims to allow simultaneous operation on four different channels in the 169 –172 MHz range, without interference. But list prices for complete Lectrosonics systems begin at about a thousand dollars.

Other brands, like Samson and Nady, offer a choice of ten different frequencies between 170 and 216-MHz which have been selected to avoid interference with each other. (Nady's lowest priced model 151VR wireless microphone system comes in just one of two frequencies—170.225 MHz, or 170.850 MHz.)

As the person carrying the wireless microphone moves around, the exact path the radio signal takes to get to the receiver changes. The more movement, the more likely it is for obstructions or reflections (such as from a steel framed building) to cause occasional dropouts of the radio signal.

A "diversity" receiver solves this dropout problem by using two different antennae, in two different locations, to receive the radio signal. The strongest signal is selected at any given moment in time, and the switchover from one antenna to the other is noiseless.

Nady's model 201, Samson's Stage 22, and Shure's model L4 are good examples of reasonably priced (under five hundred dollars) diversity systems that should be of interest to event and performance videographers who don't mind spending a bit more money to prevent problems.

Note that with diversity systems, you lose some of the portability on the receiver side. Non-diversity receivers are usually battery operated belt-clip units, but the diversity receivers are larger textbook size units that sometimes require AC power, and have two antennae pointing out in different directions.

All wireless systems incorporate a "squelch" system that silences the receiver when the transmitter is turned off or moves out of range.

Moving beyond that, noise reduction circuitry—such as the dbx processing found in Samson's moderately priced MR-1 system and Lectrosonic's pricier XR-mini-L system —suppresses background hiss during transmission, utilizing techniques similar to the Dolby noise reduction used in audio recording. Similarly, Sennheiser's VHF 1-B has "HyDyn" noise reduction, and Cetec Vega's Pro Plus receivers have Dynex II noise reduction.

Note that in addition to the cost of the wireless microphone system itself, you'll also be incurring ongoing expenses keeping your wireless components supplied with fresh alkaline batteries.

Most videomakers have gotten spoiled by the cheap and abundant AC power that recharges their camcorder and video light batteries, but with wireless microphones the 9-volt alkaline battery is usually the power source—both for the transmitter and the receiver.

Some professional units also accommodate more expensive lithium batteries, which can provide longer life. There are rechargeable 9-volt batteries available, but they usually don't last very long in wireless microphone systems.

Typically, you'll be changing the batteries after every few hours of operation. Sometimes the receiver battery goes out faster, and sometimes it's the transmitter. If you're very concerned about this expense, you can check out the "power consumption" specifications of various brands to see which ones are lightest on the juice.

Microphone Impedances

You'll hear the term "impedance" quite a bit as you begin your exploration of microphone technicalities. Some older camcorders and VCRs have high-impedance inputs (also called "hi-Z"), but most newer models have relatively low-impedance ("low-Z") inputs. There is usually no problem feeding a low-impedance microphone into a high-impedance input. Problems do occur in the other direction—going from a hi-Z microphone to a lo-Z input—but the situation rarely comes up in videomaking. In general, you should avoid hi-Z signal sources—low-Z microphones tend to cost more, but they're worth it—in reduced hum and noise.

"Z" is electronics jargon for impedance, measured in units called ohms. Anything under 1000-ohms (or "1-K") is considered low impedance, while hi-Z microphones are usually in the range of 10,000 to 50,000-ohms. It is usually less expensive to make hi-Z microphones, so they tend to be found on cheaper consumer equipment; whereas lo-Z microphones are almost universally used in professional recording studios.

The advantage of lo-Z microphones is that they generally produce more electrical power, creating stronger signal-to-noise ratio's. When running long microphone cables (more than about ten feet), lo-Z microphones are essential, because there will be less hum (low pitched buzzing) picked up in the cable.

Low impedance microphones almost always have a three-prong "XLR" connector (also known as a "Canon" connector). The three-wire "balanced" system, when used in conjunction with low-impedance microphones, helps further minimize the hum picked up in the microphone cable.

To plug such a microphone into a camcorder, you should use a "matching transformer", also called a direct box, to convert from the three-wire system to the standard two-wire ("unbalanced", in audio engineering jargon) input jacks found on camcorders and VCRs. The lo-Z to hi-Z transformer should be located right next to the camcorder, to get the advantage of the three-wire microphone cable.

Microphone Placement

Picking up sound properly requires experimentation, patience, and practice. A fancy microphone in the wrong hands will not sound nearly as good as a cheap microphone in the hands of a professional boom operator, who has spent years learning to point the microphone in just the right way (getting it as close to the source as possible without entering the frame).

The closer the microphone is to the sound source, the higher the ratio between the desired signal and the unwanted noise (street sounds, air conditioners, refrigerators, office clatter, etc.) which inevitably accompanies the desired sound.

When recording a person talking, it is usually best to point the microphone not towards the mouth, but rather towards the lower neck/upper chest region. This allows the natural resonance of the upper chest cavity to help deliver a fuller, mellower sound quality, and avoids annoying "pops" from percussive consonants like "P's" and "B's", as well as sibilance from "S's" and "Z's". Similarly, when using a handheld microphone, speak *across* it rather than into it, to avoid these problems.

You should always carry a roll of gaffer's tape with you, and neatly tape down long microphone cables. Be especially careful at spots where people may trip over the cords. Avoid running microphone cables alongside electrical wires, because more hum gets induced as these wires get closer. If the microphone cables must cross an AC power cable, it's best to cross the cables at a 90-degree angle, to minimize hum.

The only exception to the "get the microphone as close to the source as possible" rule occurs with very loud sounds that cause distortion when you get too close. This problem occurs more frequently with condenser microphones, because it's harder to overload dynamic types. For this reason, many fancy condenser microphones include built-in "attenuator pads" that can be switched in to reduce the level by 10- or 20-decibels. When such attenuators are available, it is always preferable to get the microphone up close and attenuate it, rather than keeping it further back without attenuation. The only way you can tell whether or not there's distortion occurring is by listening to the signal as you record it.

Some fancier microphones also have "low frequency cutoff" switches that let you attenuate just the bass pitches. Such switches are especially useful to minimize the rumble from the wind, or when setting up microphones in front of amplified speakers, such as when recording a guitar in a rock band (because there tends to be a lot of hum). But unless you specifically need to get rid of the low pitch range (because of a hum or wind problem), these low-cut switches should not be engaged.

Wear Headphones

Finally, to properly monitor the sound you're recording with your spiffy new microphone, you *must* wear headphones as you record. Ideally, you'd also monitor the sound by checking levels on VU meters, but most camcorders – except the semipro models – don't offer this professional luxury.

Most camcorders that have an external microphone jack also have a headphone jack. You'd never think of shooting pictures with your video camera without looking through the viewfinder, would you?

The best headphones for videomaking are the old fashioned "earmuff" type that block out extraneous sounds. The "Walkman" type earphones let a lot of ambient sound to get mixed in with the headphone signal, creating confusion about whether you are hearing the desired audio through the headphones. The cheap single piece earphone that comes supplied with most camcorders should be avoided for this reason as well.

You may find that when you plug in higher quality headphones, though, that the level is quite weak—and a "headphone amplifier" (such as the Koss EQ/30, or many other models available in music stores for guitar practice) is needed. Some wireless microphone receivers incorporate built-in headphone amplifiers for this purpose.

For all those low-budget videomakers who gripe about not having all the fancy equipment of broadcast television, remember that in the audio department, you don't need tons of money to create top-quality recordings. A good microphone, a few other accessories like a microphone stand, wind screen, and a pair of headphones are all you need—combined, of course, with your skill and ingenuity.

Recording Sound on Location

As mentioned, audio is probably the most neglected aspect of amateur video, and nowhere is the problem more acute than when you're shooting on location. In a living room "studio" you can reasonably expect quiet, and you can take control of many potential noise sources such as refrigerators and air conditioners by shutting them off. When you're on location, outdoors or in, you're often faced with much noisier circumstances which you must put up with.

Understanding some of the basic principles of recording sound in the field is as essential as understanding how to frame your shots. Sound recording is a very major part of professional film and video production, where elaborate 64-track sound mixing is not uncommon. In a big-budget Hollywood film, there can easily be a half dozen different sound tracks, just to recreate the background sounds of the beach: two tracks of the ocean, one of the wind, one of birds flying by, and two of families in the background talking. While amateur and semi-pro video soundtracks are not nearly as complex, aspiring moguls with tin-pan budgets do require considerable ingenuity to make do with simple one-and two-track audio-for-video production.

Scouting the Location

If you're feeling more than casual about a location shoot (i.e., getting paid for it) it's best to scout it out at least a day or two in advance, so you have time to borrow or buy any special audio cables, adaptors, etc. which you may need. (If you get really serious, you should put together a kit bag with every conceivable audio adaptor and cable you may ever need. Add two or three types of external microphones, and you'll avoid many of the most frequent headaches.)

The ideal spot to locate your camera for the best shots is usually *not* the ideal spot to pickup the sound from. If, for example, you're shooting people speaking or performing, you almost always want to be at least eight or ten feet back, and often much more if you need to cover an entire stage. But the best audio pickup is usually obtained by placing a microphone within a few feet of the sound source. Except when you are shooting extremely close to a person speaking, this means you'll usually get best results with an external microphone—not the microphone built into the camera. Or, you can go direct (see box).

The universal rule in locating your microphone is to get it as close to the source of the sound as possible. The closer to the source, the higher the ratio between the desired signal and the unwanted noise (street sounds, air conditioners, refrigerators, office clatter, etc.) which inevitably accompanies every location sound recording. (After all that's one of the chief advantages of using a studio rather than shooting on location.)

Most dramatic productions use a directional condenser microphone suspended over the heads of the actors by a pole, commonly called a "fishpole". News interviews commonly use handheld omnidirectional dynamic microphones—although the omni pattern picks up more noise, it's less susceptible to problems when it is held at a slight misalignment with the person's mouth.

Depending upon the sophistication of your production, you may wish to record a minute or two of background "room ambience" at the location. This ambience track, also known as "room tone", comes in handy when you're editing and need blank audio which maintains continuity with the rest of the material you've recorded. Your post-production audio setup may also include a small mixer, and an equalizer to change the tonal characteristics of your field recordings. As you gain experience editing the sound, you'll also gain more skill recording in the field—since you learn from your mistakes.

Going Direct

Whenever you record live music, or a speaker in a large auditorium, you get the choice of picking up the sound acoustically, or "going direct". When you go direct, you bypass the use of your own microphone(s) entirely, and take an electrical feed from the sound mixing console, or sometimes from musical instruments themselves.

Going direct offers numerous advantages, especially when recording live music and panel discussions, but it also has some drawbacks. When you're recording a complicated setup such as a five-piece rock band or a panel discussion with ten participants, you essentially get a free ride off someone else's mixing system.

In a small nightclub, the room's acoustics can be atrocious, and the music can be fed into the nightclub's speakers at high levels which cause considerable distortion. These problems are avoided by taking a direct feed off the mixing board. In the case of a panel discussion, a separate microphone has already been placed in front of each participant—making it unnecessary for you to duplicate the setup.

1/4" phone plug   phono plug (RCA plug)

The potential pitfalls of going direct should be weighed carefully against these advantages however. First, you need permission from whoever is running the sound board. Sometimes this can be tricky, especially if the sponsor of the event who has given you permission to videotape has hired a separate subcontractor to handle the sound.

Second, you must be sure that all the sound you want has been included in the sound board mix. In a small nightclub, for example, it is very common to leave the drums out of the amplifier mix entirely, since the drums are so loud to begin with. If you take a feed from the console, you'll be without drums, except for what may be accidentally picked up by the microphones intended for vocals.

Third, especially when taking direct feeds from musical instruments rather than from mixing boards, you must keep in mind the fact that often the instrument's amplifier is really a part of the instrument, and makes a major contribution to the tonal quality which the musician wants to achieve. Most guitar amplifiers, for example, have reverb and other tone-shaping characteristics, including special effects like flanging, distortion, and the sound of the speaker itself. For this reason, most guitar players prefer that you set up a microphone in front of their amp, rather than taking a direct feed from the guitar's output jack.

Fourth, when you start making direct electrical connections, you enter a nebulous and nerve-wracking electronic world of signal level matching and hum induction. Understanding how to make the right connections can help minimize these problems, but even the most experienced audio engineers know that every situation is unique, there are no sure cures, and sometimes you must simply give up on the direct feed and just place a microphone in front of the PA system's speaker instead. If you can make stereo (two track) recordings, you can go direct on one track and use a microphone for the other, putting off the final decision which to use until later, in the edit.

1/8" stereo mini-plug (3.5mm), commonly used for headphone and microphone jacks.

1/8" mono mini-plug (3.5mm)

The Most Common Audio Connectors

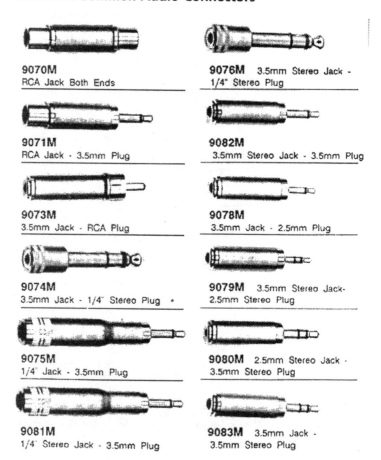

9070M
RCA Jack Both Ends

9076M 3.5mm Stereo Jack -
1/4" Stereo Plug

9071M
RCA Jack - 3.5mm Plug

9082M
3.5mm Stereo Jack - 3.5mm Plug

9073M
3.5mm Jack - RCA Plug

9078M
3.5mm Jack - 2.5mm Plug

9074M
3.5mm Jack - 1/4" Stereo Plug •

9079M 3.5mm Stereo Jack-
2.5mm Stereo Plug

9075M
1/4" Jack - 3.5mm Plug

9080M 2.5mm Stereo Jack -
3.5mm Stereo Plug

Commonly needed
audio adapters.
Courtesy of Mogami.

9081M
1/4" Stereo Jack - 3.5mm Plug

9083M 3.5mm Jack -
3.5mm Stereo Plug

The Right Connections

To take a direct feed, the first and most obvious thing you'll need
is a cable which connects from the mixing board to the audio input of your camcorder or VCR. This sounds easier than it is, because there are literally dozens of different audio connectors
which you may find at the output jack of the board. You must be
prepared, with the appropriate adaptor.

Matching the jacks, however, is just the beginning. You'll often
need to consider matching the levels as well. Most camcorders are
equipped with microphone input jacks; while most VCRs have

"line-level" audio input jacks. A "line-level" signal is much stronger (higher in voltage) than a "mic-level" signal.

If you feed a line-level signal into a microphone input jack, the signal level may be too powerful ("hot") for the sensitive input pre-amplifiers to handle, and will result in distortion. If this is this case, you must reduce the signal level with an "attenuating connection cord", available at most audio stores. You may need to purchase additional adaptors to hook it up, as well. Some camcorders have very wide range input circuitry which can handle low microphone-levels as well as high line-levels: the only way you can be sure, is by listening with headphones.

On the other hand, if you try feeding a mic-level signal into a line-level audio input (such as the standard RCA phono jack inputs found in back of most VCRs), it will usually sound very weak and distant. The only solution is to pre-amplify the mic-level signal up to line level with a small microphone preamplifier or mixer.

Many professional sound consoles include both mic-level and line-level outputs. In general, you always want to use the strongest signal possible, without overloading (distortion). The reason is because any time you run an audio signal through a wire, you pick up a certain amount of hum and other electrical noise in the cable. The higher the signal level, the less noticeable this hum will be.

The XLR Connection

No discussion of "going direct" can be complete without at least a brief explanation of what goes on inside the aforementioned three-wire "balanced" microphone cables, which have three-prong XLR connectors at their ends. The three-wire system, when used in conjunction with low-impedance microphones, helps minimize the hum picked up in the mic cable. However, it is a constant

XLR plug and jack

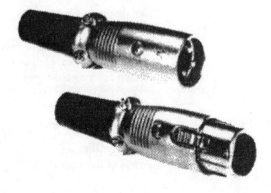

source of frustration when you try to use adaptors to convert from the three-wire system to the standard two-wire input jacks found on camcorders and VCRs. (In technical jargon, three-wire systems are called "balanced lines" and two-wire cables are called "unbalanced lines".) This is because there are different ways that the three wires can be connected to the two. It is desirable to have a "direct box" which has built-in switches to allow you to quickly try various connections until you find the one that has the least amount of hum. They are available at professional audio stores and many music stores. When running long microphone cables, it is always better to use low impedance microphones because there'll be less hum.

A Field Audio Kit

If you're getting serious about the quality of your video productions, here's a list of basic items you'd want to include in your audio kitbag. For a less than a few hundred dollars, you can put together a very complete professional kit of microphones and accessories for use in the field:

• Headphones

You must wear headphones if you want to take audio seriously. It's that simple! Generally, most camcorders and VCRs do not offer a volume control for their headphone jacks—it is therefor desirable to choose headphones which do have a volume control built in. Remember, "earmuff" type headphones will block out ambient noise more effectively that the "Walkman" type. Don't buy new headphones for this purpose without first testing them in the store, using your camcorder or VCR, to be sure the volume is loud enough.

• An Adapter Collection

Basically, you want to convert from any plug or jack to any other plug or jack. You can build up your collection piece by piece, acquiring each new permutation (phono to 1/4", mini to sub-mini, sub-mini to phono, etc.) as you need it; or, you can buy a complete kit such as Comprehensive Video's $100 ADAP-1 Audio Kit, and get it all over at once. (Their number is 1-800-526-0242.)

• A Fishpole Boom

If you intend to do dramatic work in which the microphone must stay out of the frame, you'll need a boom to hang the microphone above the heads of your actors. The basic "fishpole" is cheap and efficient, but can get tiresome for whoever must hold it.

• Microphone Desk Stand

This is the most basic professional touch. Sure, you can just lay the microphone down on the table, or prop it up with some books, but imagine how that will look on the videotape. Whenever a microphone will appear in the picture, you should make it look nice. The desk stand performs this function.

• Microphones

Letting go of your video camera's built-in microphone can be painful, because admittedly it's less convenient to have another wire and piece of equipment to deal with. Unless you've got a rich uncle that's bankrolling your video production startup costs, you'll probably build up your microphone collection one piece at a time. Be sure to get a matching wind screen for each microphone you buy.

Bear in mind that super fancy professional microphones used in recording studios and for big budget films can cost over a thousand dollars each; but even a humble fifteen or twenty dollar microphone can vastly improve the sound quality of your video productions—by allowing you to optimize both the best place to get the picture and the best place to get the sound. If you've got a bit more to spend, here are some suggestions (note that the technical description of each of these mics can be found in the Microphones section).

A Rugged Omnidirectional Dynamic Microphone

This should be your first external microphone, because it is the most general purpose. The Electro-Voice EV-635A is probably the single best value in this category—practically every TV and radio station in America has several of these on hands. They sell new for under $100; but I bought one used for around $15 about fifteen years ago, and it's still working fine. This extremely sturdy microphone is ideal for handheld use, such as in news-style interviews. A second choice in this category is Shure's SM-57, a rugged, directional, dynamic mic which is very popular among musicians.

A Tie-Clip Condenser Microphone

For lengthy interviews (such as reminiscences of family members) the tie-clip microphone is usually the best all around choice for convenience and quality. This is the type of microphone used by newscasters and on public affairs interview programs. When using them, you must listen with headphones to make sure that rustling clothing sounds which occur when people squirm, cross legs, are not objectionable. Sony's ECM-series microphones are excellent for this purpose.

A Shotgun Microphone

This ultra-directional microphone requires very careful aiming, but can also be mounted on the video camera so that it will listen to whatever you look at. It is essential for getting sound from someone who is speaking from a distance of ten or more feet away. The Sennheiser ME 80/K3U system can be pricey (several hundred dollars), but is an excellent choice if you're serious about sound. For starting out, Comprehensive Video's SGM-2, which sells for $65, can give you a less expensive introduction to the world of shotguns.

A Wireless Microphone System

The wireless microphone consists of two parts: a transmitter, which is sometimes built into the body of a hand- held microphone; and a receiver, which you locate right next to your camcorder or VCR. The advantage is obvious: good sound pickup without hassling with wires. However, the disadvantages can be problematic: Because you're using radio signals, you can receive all sorts of interference from CB rigs, mobile phones, etc. You must wear headphones to monitor the sound constantly when you use a wireless mic. Better than the handheld models, the most versatile transmitters allow you to plug in any microphone you want—this is especially useful with the tie- clip mics since you can fit the transmitter conveniently in a pocket. Truly professional wireless mic systems can cost upwards of a thousand dollars, but Nady and Azden make some excellent semi-pro VHF models that cost less than two hundred dollars. Avoid units operating at 49-MHz. And beware of radio interference problems, especially in urban areas, with cheap wireless systems.

Something Sound Funny?

Wearing headphones is as essential to video production as looking through the viewfinder, because it's the only way you can tell if everything's OK with the audio. Here are typical sound problems youshould be listening for:

• Hum

This is probably the most common audio bugaboo. It sounds like
a very low pitched tone mixed in with the signal. Hum can come
from many sources—proximity of the microphone or the camcorder body to electrical equipment such as TV's, motors, and
fluorescent lights is a common low-grade culprit. The hum can be
magnetically "induced" just by placing a mic cable next to electrical power cables, even though there is no connection between the
wires.

The most catastrophic sounding hum is usually attributable to
"open grounds" in which the metal shielding of the audio cable
becomes disconnected from one end of the audio line. This is usually the culprit when you get hum whenever you touch a microphone, or piece of equipment. You can cure "open ground"
problems by attaching a wire from the metal chassis of the VCR
or camcorder to the metal case of the microphone, console, or
whatever else you're using. Try to find a metal screw which you
can loosen slightly from the chassis to make this connection.

• Wind Noise

Wind sounds like a constant popping or sense of banging, as shifting air pressure overloads the microphone's diaphragm. You must
wear headphones to hear this effect. You can reduce it by putting
a foam "wind screen" over the microphone to absorb some of the
wind's energy, and by placing the microphone behind a wind
shield such as a piece of cardboard.

• Distortion

Most people already know what distortion sounds like, but it can
be difficult to describe in words. At its worst, it becomes a buzzing
sound which accompanies the signal whenever it gets loud. Try
listening to a portable cassette player or radio when the batteries
are almost dead, with the volume cranked up all the way, and
you'll have a good taste of what distortion sounds like. Avoid distortion by placing the mic correctly *before* the shoot. Do a mic
check—if at all possible have a speaker or musician talk or play
into the mic while you check the level in your headphones. Adjust
the mic and record level if necessary, and make a note of the mic's
placement relative to the sound source.

• Weak Signal

Surprisingly, it is sometimes difficult to notice a weak signal when
listening with headphones, because you also hear the sound directly through the air, and it can be hard to discern how much

you're hearing through the headphones. Therefore, the best way to check for strong enough levels is to make a short test recording and play it back through the headphones. If the main sound seems garbled, or you hear a lot of background noise mixed in with the signal, then you should get closer to the sound source.

Automatic Gain Control

Every camcorder incorporates an "automatic gain control" system in its audio recording circuitry. For videomakers, the AGC system is both a blessing and a curse. While it eliminates the outright tragedy of gross errors—such as having a manual record level turned all the way down—the AGC system introduces its own distortions.

And with most camcorders, you have no choice in the matter, since no manual audio recording level adjustment is available.

The AGC system averages the sound level over a period of time—usually about one or two seconds. If the average sound level is low, it boosts the recording level accordingly. If there's a loud sound that gets recorded so strongly that it becomes distorted (because it exceeds the maximum possible magnetization level which the tape can handle), then the AGC will lower the recording level.

The key to outsmarting the AGC is understanding that the changes it makes are always delayed by a short period of time.

Try this experiment: Start your camcorder recording in a quiet room, wait fifteen seconds, then say "hello" directly into the camcorder's microphone (from about a foot away). Wait one second, then say "hello" again. Wait fifteen seconds, and say "hello" twice more. Rewind the tape and listen to it.

You'll probably hear a faint background hiss which gets louder for a while, then levels off until the "hello's". The first "hello" will sound distorted, but the second "hello" will probably sound alright. The background hiss will be much quieter again, but then it will gradually get louder, and level off until the next "hello".

What's going on? After the AGC senses a short period of silence, it begins increasing the recording level to compensate. It keeps raising the recording level until one of two things happen: Either it raises the background noise to the point where it becomes "normal" in volume—that is, until the background noise sounds about as loud as someone speaking might sound; or the AGC reaches its maximum amplification level beyond which it can increase no further. Either way, the level stops rising and remains constant.

When the first "hello" occurs, the AGC has cranked up the audio amplification so high that practically anything louder than a pin drop creates distortion. But a moment later, responding to the loud level of this first "hello", the AGC reduces the recording level. Thus the second "hello" sounds a lot cleaner. Over the course of the next fifteen seconds, the AGC again rises to maximum amplification, and the sequence is repeated.

In the jargon of audio engineers, the characteristic sound of increasing background noise levels is called "pumping", and is usually associated with audio compressors. The compressor is like a sophisticated version of an AGC circuit. It's more sophisticated because it lets you control the various parameters of the situation—over how much time the signal is averaged before it responds, how much amplification and signal reduction should take place, and over how wide a "dynamic range" should the volume be allowed to vary before compensation occurs.

It would be great, of course, if such sophisticated audio control could be afforded to camcorder users, but we don't even get a simple audio frill like manual level control!

But you can outsmart the AGC, sometimes:

The most common AGC-related problem is the initial buzz that you often hear when someone begins to speak. Ironically, this problem is at its worst when you have an extremely quiet recording environment—an acoustic environment that would otherwise be ideal.

As you shoot video, consider how the AGC might be behaving at any given moment in time. When you start recording someone speaking, you can avoid the initial audio distortion by having the person say something a moment before the actual material you wish to record. For instance, if Jennifer, the host of your program, is about to introduce herself, have her say, "Hello. (pause) Hello, my name is Jennifer..." Later, when you edit the material together, you'll skip the first "hello" and start the shot with the second.

What if you're editing "in the camera", trying to create a polished production as you go along, without editing later? It's a bit harder, but with some practice, you can determine precisely how long it takes from the instant you push the start/stop "trigger" button till the actual beginning of a recording. Note that on most camcorders, the AGC is active even when you're in the "Record Pause" mode, so that you can establish a reduced AGC level by having Jennifer say "hello" before you start recording, then start the tape rolling with Jennifer's second hello. But perfecting this technique can take some practice, because you're racing against both the AGC's timing, as well as the camcorder's mechanical response time.

Conversely, if you're trying to record a faint signal, such as your daughter's star performance in the school play—as seen (and heard) from the rear balcony—then be sure to keep the camcorder in pause, or running for several seconds before anything important is said, so the AGC has a few moments to raise the level.

Bumping into the camcorder, touching its controls, brushing clothing against it, or any of hundreds of other possible disturbances will not only sound annoying in their own right, but will also make the AGC lower the recording level for the next few seconds.

Note that the AGC is also engaged when you plug in an external microphone, or use an "audio dubbing" cable.

Professional audio mixers for film and big budget video often utilize a separate track of "background ambience" to smoothly glide between varying background noise levels from one shot to another within a scene. But it's hard to do the same thing in low budget video editing, because the audio is generally pieced together shot by shot, rather than "mixed" in one continuous pass. One advantage of hi-fi VHS and S-VHS equipment is that you can retain the hi-fi tracks, and add a new "linear" track through the "audio dub" feature, then mix them all together during playback.

To operate a manual audio level control properly, you really need the aid of a VU-meter, which may have something to do with why manual audio is such a rarity. Not only do the knob and meter add to the cost, they also take up precious space on the miniaturized camcorder case.

Making a Music Video

One of the most challenging—and creative—things you can do with home video equipment is produce your own music video. Whether you're fooling around in your garage, or going into business cooking up video basement tapes to expand a wedding video service, here is a guide to rolling your own MTV-style music videos.

The starting point for a music video is the music—and it should be already recorded, in final form, when you begin. In general, it is usually a bad idea to attempt to record live music as you shoot—unless you know an awful lot about microphones and sound mixing, and have enough crew to both mix sound *and* shoot the picture, all at the same time. (An exception to this would be in a live performance where the band is already fully microphoned and mixed through a professional console, and you can plug into the console's "line output" to take a direct audio feed.)

On a semipro level, a "demo tape" recorded in an 8-track studio is usually the starting point for making a rock video. The eight tracks are mixed together into a 2-track "stereo master", and this stereo master becomes the soundtrack for the video. But even if you just record your band with a simple cassette recorder, you can try various microphone placements and recording levels until you create the best "stereo master" you can.

Depending on your particular video equipment, you may have to mix together the left and right channels of your stereo audio tape into mono. Most inexpensive VCRs have only mono sound. Hi-fi VCRs offer excellent sound reproduction capability, but as explained in a moment, there can be a tradeoff between getting the best sound and getting the best picture when you use them for making low budget rock videos.

The Equipment You'll Need

So what equipment will you need to make a rock video? Well, the ideal setup would be a MiniDV camcorder and DV edit system. But at the absolute simplest level, you could get by with just a VHS or Super-VHS format camcorder, if it has a flying erase head and "video dubbing" capability. You'll probably be able to do a better job of it—and it will be a lot less nerve racking—if you have a camcorder and a VCR, so that you can edit by selectively copying the original footage.

Either the camcorder or the VCR should have a flying erase head, and the ability to do "video insert editing" (also called "video dubbing"). This is vital to producing music videos, because it lets you first record the sound on the videotape, and then insert pictures to go along with it. Note that no 8mm or Hi8 camcorder can do this—as explained earlier, there are some industrial VCRs that can do it, but you're generally better off editing onto another format.

Several inexpensive accessories will prove very helpful in making low-budget music videos: a tripod, an inexpensive audio mixer, a "powered speaker" (such as the type you connect to a Walkman cassette player), a set of photoflood lights and stands, and a good pair of headphones.

Editing in the Camcorder

If you're working with just a camcorder, editing as you go along, you're performing "in camera edits", using the video-only insert feature ("video dub"). First, record the audio for the full length of the song. If you're taking it from a cassette or other audio tape, use appropriate dubbing cables, and don't worry about the picture. You may need to use "attenuating" patch cords (available at any Radio Shack) to plug the output of a cassette deck into the "Microphone" input of a camcorder. In the context of a live performance, record the sound along with a wide shot of the band on stage.

Next, go back to specific points in the song, and use the "video dub" feature to insert lip-synchronized close-ups, of other images which seem relevant. For example, when the lyrics speak of love as a flower, you can show a picture of a tulip.

Shooting to Edit

But in-camera editing is a very tedious way to work. For one thing, if you make a mistake and accidentally let an insert edit run too long, then you'll erase the previously recorded picture in a spot which you might have intended to save. In-camera editing is the quick and dirty method, but you can get greater precision and creative control if you shoot to edit, separately recording all the pieces. Later, after all the shooting is done, you'll edit them together by selectively copying from one VCR (or camcorder) to another.

Let's assume you have a camcorder and a VCR, and the VCR has a flying erase head and video insert capability. Record the sound (and perhaps the live performance picture) onto a blank tape in the VCR. This will become your "edited master" tape. Next, you'll use the video insert feature to edit in pictures which match the sound at various points in the song. If you make a mistake, you always have the option to go back and perform the edits again, since you're leaving the "camera original" tapes intact.

Another advantage of shooting to edit is that you can shoot out of sequence. You can spend months shooting images which, when edited, appear to all occur in a single moment.

Try story boarding your production—sketching a series of cartoon like frames which show each of the shots you want to get—to serve as a visual script. You will notice that some shots—such as entering a house and leaving a house—may occur at different times in the script, but involve basically the same camera position and setup, so you can shoot them at the same time.

The story board also helps you think visually—to tell a story through pictures. For example, if a man is singing about a woman who left him, you can show a series of shots in which we see her packing her bag, ripping up a photo of him, and closing the door behind her.

Special Effects

When you edit video using a simple home brew setup, all of your transitions from one shot to another will be straight cuts—that is, one image simply ends and the next one suddenly pops in. This is by far the most widely used transition from one shot to another, but you're no doubt aware of many other transitions—dissolves, wipes, fading up from and down to black, etc.

The dissolve is the most common special effect: one image gradually replaces another, over the course of a second or two. But dissolves are expensive to creates (see the "A/B Roll Editing" section).

Some camcorders allow you to create a few special effects. The best models, with "digital effects", allow you to end a shot with a freeze frame, and then dissolve from the freeze frame to the next shot. This can be a fantastic tool for making music videos, but you must edit these transitions in-camera.

Lip-synching

When a singer attempts to sing along with his/her own previously recorded voice, for the sake of getting good camera images, it is called "lip sync" recording. Note that it will take quite a bit of practice.

The most accurate way, on a low budget, to lip-sync is by editing in the camera using a camcorder with video insert capability. But this technique can end up accidentally erasing other picture material on the master video tape, so it's usually a good idea to record all the lip synch shots first. Alternatively, to play it safe, you can record the lip-synch shots separately, and then copy that entire tape to the master edit tape, using its soundtrack as the basis for further editing.

The singer needs to hear him or herself in order to sing along, and an amplified speaker is a handy accessory for this. As you record the lip-synched picture, play the recorded sound through the camcorder's headphone jack, into the speaker.

Hi-fi Sound Dilemma

To maintain the best sound and picture quality throughout your editing procedure, you should always work with the fastest possible tape speed. But even at the SP speed, the audio fidelity of standard VHS recordings is not very good—it's roughly comparable to a cheap audio cassette deck, with no Dolby or fancy tape equalization.

The "hi-fi" sound featured on some VCRs and camcorders offers truly superb sound quality—far better than the standard "linear" audio track (the soundtrack used by all non-hi-fi VCRs)—and almost as good as a CD. But for making low-budget music videos, there's a catch:

With most hi-fi VCRs and camcorders, the hi-fi sound must be recorded at the same time as the picture—it is impossible to perform video insert edits and leave the hi-fi sound intact. (JVC recently announced that they will soon offer a new top-of- the-line Super-VHS VCR which allows you to dub hi-fi sound onto previously recorded pictures, but apparently not the reverse.)

If your music video does NOT involve lip synching, then it is possible to take advantage of a hi-fi VCR, but you must sacrifice precise synchronization between picture and sound. Here's how to do it:

Transfer the audio master (the song) to the standard linear audio track of a blank tape, and edit the video to match this sound. When the editing is complete, move the edited tape over to the player side of your player-recorder editing system. Put a blank videocassette on the recorder, and setup the recorder VCR for hi-fi recording. Hook up the hi-fi recording VCR to your audio source—the cassette, CD, turntable, or open reel tape deck where the original audio master is recorded. The hi-fi VCR thus receives the picture from the source VCR or camcorder, and the sound from the audio cassette deck or CD.

Practice synchronizing the sound on the cassette deck to the sound on the source video (the edited tape). It's helpful to have drumstick clicks just before a song begins. When you can get the two almost perfectly synchronized, you're ready to record.

But note that this system is crude. By the end of the song the audio will probably be out of synch by several seconds, and you must go down a generation with the picture to get the better sound. Unfortunately, with hi-fi sound, it's hard to have your cake and eat it too.

Editing Audio

As with video, the main goal in editing audio is to hide the seams—to make the edits as unnoticeable as possible. Experimental video artists often take exception with this philosophy (wanting to bring attention to each edit point), but for the vast majority of commercial and non-commercial projects, the goal is to get listeners to think about the contents—the message—of the production, and not the production methods.

So how do you hide the audio seams?

For spoken words—voices—there are a number of techniques. First, pay careful attention to where sentences begin and end. The safest, most unnoticeable edits are between complete sentences: Let one sentence end completely, then edit to the next, leaving a brief, natural-sounding pause between them. Maintaining consistent background ambience during this brief pause is crucial to keeping the edit sounding smooth.

A beginning editor's first instinct is to put the edit point right smack in the middle of the pause between the two sentences. If the pause is to be one second long, for example, the tendency is to include a half second of silence (ambience) following the end of the first, and a half second preceding the beginning of the second sentence. This is the easiest and safest method, since you have some elbow room around the edit points to compensate for mistakes or tape slippage, but it is not the best.

More experienced editors know that the best place to make the cut is immediately preceding the start of the second sentence. Here's the reason: Inevitably, there will be some unintended audio artifact resulting from the edit—either a click, a change in background ambience level, or a change in the texture of the background ambience. It will probably be subtle, but it's there. In the middle of a second of silence, the listener has nothing else to attend to, so such subtle details become more noticeable.

If this edit artifact occurs just prior to someone speaking, however, the listener will become distracted by what the person is saying, and not notice the click or level-change as much. It is the audio equivalent of the "cut on action" picture editing rule—edits become less noticeable if they occur just as exciting (relatively) things are happening.

What if you need to edit between words, instead of using whole sentences? The same principle applies, but on a finer scale—try to move the edits as close to the beginning of the new word as possible, without clipping off the very beginning, and maintaining a very short pause after the end of the previous word to keep pacing consistent with the way that person speaks.

Editing in mid-sentence is tricky business, however, due to intonation. When people speak, intonation clearly indicates which words are at the beginning of a sentence, and especially which words are at the end. The pitch of the voice tends to go down at the end of a sentence—unless it's a question, in which case it goes up.

I once made a short video that got shown in some major festivals and on network TV in which I edited a speech by Ronald and Nancy Reagan. Originally, their speech had a "Just Say No" anti-drug theme, but as a spoof, I re-arranged things so their message became "Just Say Yes". To pull it off, believably, required very careful listening to the way fragments of sentences could be put together. One cardinal rule was to always begin a sentence with a real beginning (from a sentence from the original speech that began that way), and always end with a real ending from the speech. In the middle, I might put three or four fragments from other sentences.

When editing speech, pay particular attention to the speaker's breathing. Listening with headphones will help you hear this better. Everyone breathes while they speak, and every microphone picks this up. You don't normally notice it much, when listening to interviews, because it sounds natural. But if you cut a breath in half, at the edit point, you'll bring it to the foreground and make it quite noticeable. Either include the entire breath, or leave it entirely out. Don't cut every breath out, however, or you'll make the speaker sound unnatural. No one can say three or four sentences in a row without taking a breath.

Music Editing

Editing music has its own dynamic. The need to edit music comes up often when producing industrial videos and low-budget drama, where you may need music for a scene that lasts thirty seconds, but have selected a piece of music lasting three minutes.

The sloppy, lazy approach is to simply fade the music out at the end of thirty seconds. It works, but it sounds like you faded it out, and the incomplete feeling this evokes (lack of closure) becomes especially noticeable with familiar works of music.

A tighter sounding, more professional approach is to edit the work down to the required time. It's the same principle I described above for editing spoken sentences—you want the piece to begin with a beginning, and end with an end. Don't fade down—cut out the middle.

It sounds easy, but in practice it requires finer precision than editing speech. If your video editing system isn't capable of accuracy within a frame or two, forget it—attempting to edit music will be completely frustrating. This may sound really low-tech, but your best bet may be to transfer the music to an audio tape (ideally open reel running at fast speed, but in a pinch cassettes will do), edit the music on the audio tape using an old-fashioned razor blade and splicing block, and then transfer the edited version back to videotape. Or, if your computer is equipped with an audio input board and digital audio editing software (high quality boards include the Sunrize Studio 16 for the Amiga, and Turtle Beach Pro for IBM), you can do the editing on your computer, and then transfer back to tape.

The key to making music edits sound smooth is to always edit on the beat. You must pay careful attention to where the edit occurs, and to maintaining the timing of the music.

As with speech, the cleanest sounding edits are made just prior to the point where something occurs—in this case, the beat of the music. Rock and disco music is the easiest to work with, for beginners, because the beat is prominent. Most popular music has a time signature of four beats per measure, meaning that if you count out loud, "one, two, three, four, one two, three, four, one..." in sync with the loudest drum beats (usually the kick drum), you'll find that most changes (new verse, new chorus, new instruments, change in tempo, etc.) occur on the beginning of a new measure (on the "one" beat of the count). So the discussion below assumes you're dealing with four-beat music.

Musical edits will sound most natural and unnoticeable if you edit just before the "one" beat. This applies both to finding the cut-out point at the end of the beginning section you want to use (following the "four" beat), and finding the cut-in point at the beginning of the next section you want (prior to the "one").

It is extremely important to maintain the same amount of time between the "four" beat before the edit and the "one" beat after the edit. This maintains the timing of the music. A mistake in this timing is readily noticeable to a listener, and hangs like a big sign that reads "edit". If you cut-out immediately after the "four" beat of the beginning section, you'll ruin this timing. Let the music play all the way to the very end of the measure, and cut at the point immediately before the "one" beat of the next measure.

(Imagine counting half beats: "One and two and three and four and one and two..." If you cut after the fourth beat, without getting close to the beginning of the next measure, your edited music will sound like: "One and two and three and four one and two and three and..." You need the "and" between "four" and "one" to maintain the timing.)

The rules above may sound basic, but follow them diligently and you'll be ninety-percent of the way to professional sound editing. I used to teach twelve-week long classes in audio editing, and these simple rules constituted the lion's share of the curriculum. Most of the class time was devoted to listening and editing. Getting good at audio editing doesn't require the fanciest equipment, but it does require patience and an ear that's willing to listen.

Computer based digital audio facilitates extremely precise editing (top) and the ability to mix multiple tracks (bottom).

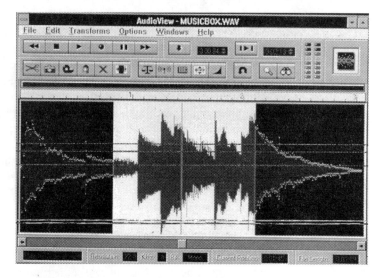

22 Lighting

If audio is the most neglected aspect of low budget video production, then lighting is second most.

Lighting is a language that can convey mood, time of day, and style of production. Speaking in this language means controlling how your subjects are lit—either by manipulating the angles and intensities of the light sources, adjusting the position of the subject to receive light in appropriate ways, or both.

For many videomakers, any concern about lighting is limited to making sure that the low light warning doesn't start flashing in the viewfinder. This attitude may be fine for casual travel and family videomaking, but is problematic with professional work.

Simply put, if you ignore lighting you're playing Russian Roulette with picture quality—as well as missing the opportunity to make your subjects and shots look their best.

When you don't pay attention to lighting, most of the time you'll still end up with reasonably acceptable results, but there will be occasions when the picture is poor. A face may appear completely in shadow, for example, or the light from a window will make the inside of a room entirely dark.

Most camcorders have a backlight compensation button or control to adjust for this specific situation, but the use of such an adjustment should be thought of as a last-ditch effort to be avoided whenever possible. Hitting the backlight button, or opening the iris, represents an acceptance of the lighting the way it is.

This section concerns what you should be doing long before you ever think of hitting the iris control. Rather than merely accepting a given set of circumstances, we'll first set up the ideal lighting situation, and then see how this ideal model can be applied to real world low-budget videomaking situations.

Three Point Lighting

Ideally, from a professional standpoint, you should have as much control as possible over the light. Outdoor lighting has one big advantage—there's plenty of it—but it is largely controlled by nature. Indoor lighting, such as in a studio, can allow for more precise control , as well as consistency over long periods of time.

Although it might at first seem easiest to just bathe the subject in light coming equally from all directions, such lighting tends to look flat and uninteresting. Flat lighting is merely adequate — faces are illuminated, but they are not lit to look their best.

Flat lighting is sometimes necessary when there are many people to be lit — such as at a seminar or conference — but the most careful lighting of an individual subject does not attempt to illuminate the face evenly. Instead, the subject is lit by different lights at different angles and with different intensities. This emphasizes contours, and highlights some facial features.

Key Light by itself creates harsh shadows.

The most common approach to studio lighting is called three point lighting. Three different lights are placed around the subject.

The strongest source of light is called the key light. It is typically placed about 45-degrees off center (horizontally), illuminating one side of the face more than the other. Vertically, the key light is usually also about 45-degrees upwards from the subject (half-way between straight in front and straight above a person's head). However, some experimentation with the height of the key light is recommended—many film and videomakers prefer key lights that are almost at the same height as the subject they illuminate.

The second light in the setup is called the fill light. As its name implies, the fill light is intended to fill in the shadows created by the key light. It is located on the other side of the face— usually at a 45-degree angle (by convention), but other angles, including directly in front of the subject, are recommended for experimentation. Its intensity is usually adjusted to be about half as bright as the keylight—although it's up to you to decide to what extent you want the harshness of the key light's shadows reduced.. This is accomplished by using a lower wattage bulb, or by moving the light further away from the subject than the key light.

(When you move lights further back from the subject, the intensity drops off in proportion to the square of the distance ratio— that is, a light that is twice as far from the subject as another light will produce an intensity of only one fourth the brightness of the closer light. This is called the inverse-square law. If two lights have the same brightness, moving one to a position that is 1.4 times further from the subject than the other will result in half the illumination of the closer light.)

The combined effects of the key and fill lights create a softer set of shadows.

Ideally, different lighting instruments are used for each light. The key light can be a directional spotlight, in which all the light seems to come from a single point. The fill light is typically a more diffuse source of light. Rather than coming from a single point, the fill light comes from a wider area. This can be accomplished by bouncing the light off of a reflector—such as a large white card or a white reflective umbrella—or by passing the light through diffusion material such as spun glass, tracing paper, Dacron, or heat proof opalescent plastic. Such light is commonly called soft light, because it doesn't create the harsh, hard-edged shadows that point-source lights create.

This key-fill arrangement mimics what goes on in nature, outdoors, when the sun acts as a point source of light to illuminate

Fill Light Alone. The fill light fills in shadows created by the key, but is not as strong.

one side of the face, while the sky fills in the shadow areas of the face with a softer, more diffuse light.

The third component of the three-point lighting setup is the back light. It is located behind the subject, and usually high above, pointing down and slightly forward. The purpose of the back light is to highlight the top of the head, creating bright points in the hair, and separating the face from the background.

The back light is typically brighter than the key light—one and a half to two times brighter. Because it is pointing down, most of the this light does not actually illuminate the subject. When work-

Back Light Alone. The back light creates highlights in the hair and separates the subject from the background.

ing with low ceilings, it can sometimes be tricky setting up a back-light so that it cannot be seen in the frame, especially in wide shots.

A barn-door attachment to the lighting instrument can help prevent the light from spilling into areas where it shouldn't go. This becomes particularly important when lighting more than one subject simultaneously—such as in a talk show. Barn doors also prevent lights from creating "hot spots" in the picture—such as the edge of a desk, or a white wall. With barn doors, you can literally sculpt the light to hit only the subjects you want it to illu-minate. If your lighting setup is too low budget to afford profes-

Key + Fill + Back Lights. Subject is illuminated by the complete three-point lighting setup.

sional barn door attachments, improvise by using cardboard to block the light where needed. But be careful to keep the cardboard a safe distance from the light (at least two feet away)—too close, and it's a fire hazard.

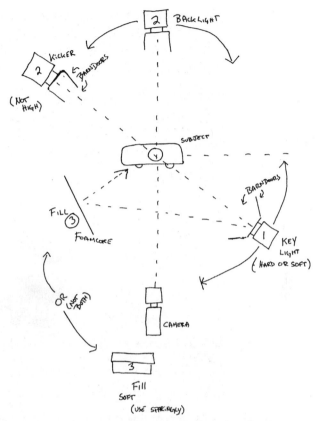

A three-point lighting scheme. A reflector can be used to provide fill light. Back light (#2) is traditionally placed directly behind and above subject, but experimenting with more angled backlights is suggested.

. . . .
Apparent Sources Of Light

The three-point lighting plan is usually the basis for lighting talk shows, news desks, and similar studio productions where there is no pretense of reality. The studio lighting scheme is simply designed to help make people look most attractive to viewers.

In dramatic production, however, another element enters the lighting picture: believability. The lighting scheme is generally designed to make the set look more real, to support the apparent truthfulness of the shot. If there's a window in the room and the scene is taking place during the day, for example, then the key light should be coming from the direction of the window.

If a scene takes place in a bedroom at night, and there's a lamp in the wide shot, then the key light should appear to come from the same direction as the lamp.

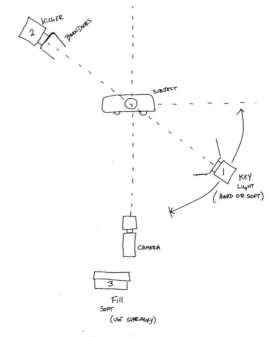

In this three-point lighting scheme, the fill light is placed directly in front of the subject (and behind the camera), rather than off to the side.

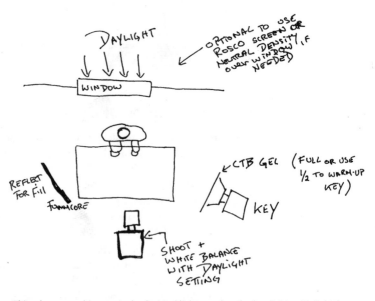

This scheme combines a single electrical light, used as the key light, with light from a window that serves as the backlight. A reflector catches both the key and window light to provide fill light.

Practical Lights

In lighting jargon, whenever a light actually appears within the frame as part of the set—such as the bedroom lamp—it is called a practical light.

In some cases, the practical light is actually being used as one component in the lighting scheme, but more often than not, it simply serves as an apparent source of light.

Usually, if you install a bulb that's really bright enough to illuminate the subject, then the light will appear way too bright in the picture—saturating the camera beyond its maximum white level. A lower wattage bulb makes the light look more normal as part of the set, but then you have to illuminate the face using a different, higher power lighting instrument that is aimed from the same direction as the lamp.

The Light Kit

Many professional video crews carry a three-light kit as a basic setup for field use. Such kits typically consists of three light stands, three light instruments, and attachments to hold accesso-

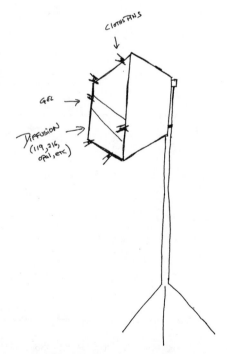

You can build an inexpensive soft light using plywood, foam core, and electrical supplies, for under $50. The diffusion material is available from pro photo and film supply shops.

ries like barn doors that block the light from hitting places where you don't want it to go, and scrims which dim the light and protect against bulb explosions.

Some kits, like Lowell's Tota light set (a workhorse of field production), include reflecting umbrella attachments for the lights, to create diffuse sources of fill light.

A low budget alternative to professional halogen lamps is to use photoflood bulbs in clamp-on reflectors. The bulbs are available in professional photo supply stores, and the clamp-on reflectors (which include the socket and cord) are available in most hardware stores.

When using lights mounted on stands, you can avoid accidents and create the sturdiest setup by adhering to this sequence:

First, assemble the stands in the positions where you want the lights. Extend the legs, using the thickest poles possible. Next, attach the light instruments to the stands, and then add any attach-

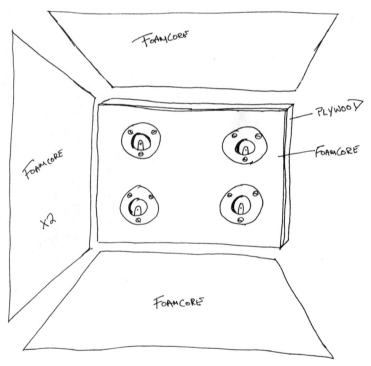

The light consists of four tungsten photoflood bulbs, surrounded by white foam core reflectors. The bilb and ceramic sockets are available from lighting supply stores; buy foam core boards at art supply stores.

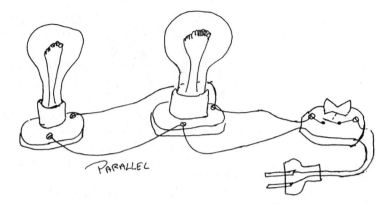

PARALLEL

The electrical wiring is a basic parallel connection of the lamp sockets, with a switch inserted between the lamps and the AC plug. (Two lamps are shown here—continue the wires for four.)

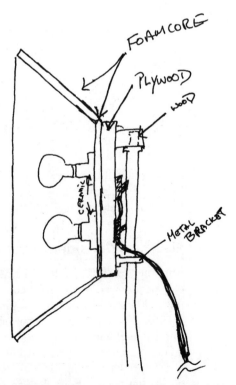

FOAMCORE

PLYWOOD

WOOD

CERAMIC

METAL BRACKET

A side view of the soft light's construction. Use photoflood bulbs balanced for 3200-degrees. Try 100-watt bulbs for starters; go up to 250-watt if needed, but watch the heat!

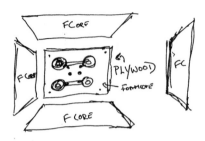

The supporting pole should be securely attached to the back of the light.

ments that will be used. Finally, plug the electrical cord into the light, and use gaffer's tape (or duct tape) to secure electrical wires that people may accidentally trip over.

Electrical Considerations

Running a professional three-point lighting kit requires a lot of electrical power. A typical kit consists of three halogen lamps using 1000-watts of power each—three thousand watts total.

Most home wiring cannot handle such a 3000-watt load on a single branch circuit. Most houses and apartments have several different branch circuits available, usually organized by room.

The trick to getting the high power you need for professional quality lighting, without blowing a fuse or circuit breaker, is to spread the lights out among several different branch circuits. This usually requires heavy duty extension cords, to plug some of the lights into outlets in other rooms than the one you are shooting in.

Each branch circuit has its own circuit breaker or fuse. You can figure out which outlets are part of which branch circuits by individually turning off one circuit breaker (or removing one fuse) at a time, and plugging a lamp into each outlet to see where it doesn't work.

The fuse or circuit breaker for each branch circuit is labelled with a maximum number of amperes, or amps, or just the letter A (such as 15A for 15 amps).

You can convert between amps and watts using the following formula:

$$\# \text{ of watts} = \# \text{ volts} \times \# \text{ of amps}$$

In the U.S., where household voltage is usually around 115-volts, the formula becomes:

$$\# \text{ of watts} = 115 \times \# \text{ of amps}$$

or, expressed to calculate amps,

$$\# \text{ of amps} = (\# \text{ of watts}) / 115$$

Using this formula, it can be seen that to run 3000-watts of lights on one circuit requires that it have a capacity of at least 27-amps, but most household circuits have only a 15-amp capacity.

With 15-amp household wiring and 1000-watt lights, you'll need to put each light on a different branch circuit to prevent fuses from blowing, or circuit breaker trippings.

A basic 3-light kit: The Lowel Elemental Kit (model TO-98) consists of one Lowell Tota light, two Lowel Omni lights, stands, gels, umbrella, barn doors, and other accessories. With 1000-watt bulbs in each light, you'll need electrical circuits capable of carrying 27-amps.

Portable Lighting

The easiest way to avoid electrical problems, of course, is to use battery powered portable lights that don't require hookup to a wall outlet except for recharging.

Portable lights tend to be lower powered, to make the battery last longer, and more limited in controllability. Most units are in the ten to fifty watt ballpark. A built-in rechargeable battery usually supplies the power—except on some low powered five to ten watt lights that come supplied with certain camcorder models. The accessory lights that come supplied with some camcorders operate off of the camcorder battery, and therefor tradeoff a reduction in the overall run time of the camcorder when using the light, to gain the convenience, light weight, and lower cost of a light that doesn't require its own battery.

The amount of time you can run the light on each charge of the battery is typically between fifteen minutes and half an hour. You can calculate the exact amount if you know the milliamp-hour (ma-hr) and voltage rating of the battery, and the wattage rating of the lamp.

First, convert the milliamp-hour rating to an ampere-hour rating by dividing by one thousand. A 1200 mA-hr battery, for example is the same as a 1.2-ampere-hour battery.

Calculate the run time, in hours, with this formula:

$$\text{Run Time} = \frac{\text{battery ampere-hours x volts}}{\text{bulb wattage}}$$

For example, if you have a 7.5-volt battery with a 1000 ma-hr rating, and are running a 15-watt light, then

$$\text{Run Time} = \frac{1 \text{ ampere-hour x } 7.5 \text{ volts}}{15 \text{ watts}}$$

$$= 0.5 \text{ hours}$$

$$= 30 \text{ minutes}$$

All this math may seem very scientific, but in fact, there's a lot of voodoo when it comes to rechargeable batteries—factors like operating temperature and discharge habits can influence actual capabilities. The run time you calculate is approximate—only an actual test run will determine the exact value.

Positioning Portable Lights

Most portable lighting devices are designed to mount directly on top of the camcorder. This location is convenient for one person hand-held operation, but it is far from ideal in terms of the lighting effect.

If you can get the portable light into a similar position to that of the key light in the studio—up and off to one side—it will usually look better. This is especially effective if the other side of the face receives reflected light off a wall or ceiling, to help serve as fill light.

Holding a light several feet above the camcorder, and off to the side, can be a difficult feat for a one-person crew, however.

One compromise which can be very effective is to keep the light mounted on the camcorder, but point it up so that it bounces off the ceiling and illuminates the face from above. This technique is called bounce lighting. To be effective, the ceiling must be white or a light color, it must be reasonably low (under twelve or fifteen feet), and the light must be fairly powerful, since the intensity of the reflected light is much lower than if the light is pointed directly at a face.

White Balance

When you're shooting in the field with a portable light, it is rarely the only source of light. Usually there is some room or outdoor light that is also illuminating the subject. Exactly how significant your supplemental lighting will be in the overall picture will depend on how strong the available light is, and how powerful your own lights are. In some cases the supplemental light may serve as the key light, while in others it will serve as the fill or even the blacklight.

Different types of light, such as outdoor, incandescent, and fluorescent, have different color characteristics that require different white balance settings on the camcorder. As explained earlier, the different types of light are characterized as having different color temperatures. White light consists of a mixture of all the different colors in the spectrum. The color temperature describes which colors are more dominant in this mix, and the white balance adjusts the camcorder to compensate for these differences.

Most lights designed for use in TV and film lighting have a color temperature of 3200-degrees Kelvin. The bulbs are specially designed so that even as they get older, the color temperature does not change much. The 3200-degree color temperature is commonly called the "tungsten" light setting, named after the original filament material in incandescent photoflood lights. However, most professional video lights actually use quartz-halogen bulbs that have the same color temperature as tungsten.

However, when you mix different types of light together, the camcorder can only be adjusted for one type of light—any others will seem extremely wrong.

For example, if a face is illuminated by outdoor light from a window on one side, and by indoor light on the other side, one of two things will usually occur: Either the indoor side will seem normal, while the outdoor side appears blue; or the outdoor side will seem normal, and the indoor side will seem very red. If the camcorder's automatic white balance is on, the decision will be determined by which type of light fills the majority of the picture.

Since most camcorders have black and white viewfinders, casual videomakers generally don't recognize this mixed lighting dilemma while shooting. In black and white, the different light sources blend together harmoniously. But later, when viewed on a color screen, the results can be disappointing.

The best way to avoid problems from using mixed lights is to choose just one type—such as outdoor light coming through a window—and eliminate all other sources (turn the lamps off).

If you must used mixed light sources, working on a low budget, you should select one as the dominant type and manually set the camcorder's white balance to that type of light, so that the camcorder's automatic white balance system doesn't flip back and forth between different color adjustments as you change the shot.

On a big-budget Hollywood level of production, colored translucent filter sheets made of plastic film or gelatin are used to convert one type of light to another. Orange colored sheets taped around windows convert outdoor light to match the color temperature of tungsten. The ideal orange color is called a Wratten 85 filter, available in any professional photo supply store. It's also called CTO—color temperature orange.

Conversely, a blue filter over an electric tungsten light gives it a similar color temperature to outdoor light. The ideal blue color is called a Wratten 80B filter. It's also called CTB—color temperature blue.

You can buy sheets of filter film in professional film supply stores, but a lower budget alternative is to get a sample of the ideal color in the photo store, and then go to an industrial plastic supplier and try to find a roll of similarly colored sheet plastic.

No matter how good a bargain you find, it will still take a lot of time and energy to properly tape up a window with filter film. It may also require a lot of adjusting and changes in camera angle to prevent reflections from the artificial lights from appearing in the window.

Reflectors

One inexpensive tool that can be quite handy when working with available light is a reflector. Professional reflectors use a shiny silver coated plastic to maximize the reflection, but on a lower budget, a reflector can be as simple as a large white oak tag card, or foam core art board (available at any art supply store). Reflectors can make a world of difference when shooting outdoors.

On sunny days, when the sun shines directly on one side of a person's face, the other side can end up looking very dark, or a harsh shadow from the nose may streak across the face.

By holding the reflector just off camera on the dark side of the face, catching the sun to reflect it back, the effect of a fill light can be created.

This technique can be surprisingly effective, and is one of the lowest budget lighting tricks around. Of course, you'll need the help of an assistant to hold the reflector in place.

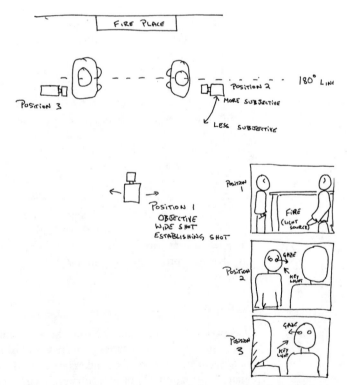

A fireplace can be used for interesting lighting effects. This diagram shows the three camera positions for wide shot and close-ups, observing the 180-degree rule.

Creative Lighting Effects

Beyond the basic three-point lighting scheme, there are a host of creative lighting effects that help create a mood or atmosphere.

Perhaps the most famous of these effects is the venetian-blind lighting technique that characterized film-noir thrillers in the fifties. The stripes of light that result from light passing through venetian blinds creates a feeling of tension. The effect conveys the mood that something isn't quite right.

A single light used without fill light can create a feeling of intensity, as if an actor is on stage with a spotlight. Using a single light from the far side of someone's face, so that most of the face is in shadow, can create a sense of intrigue.

Lighting a face from underneath, rather than above, creates a ghoulish monster movie effect.

A flickering candle or fireplace can create a romantic atmosphere.

Background Lights

So far, we've only discussed lighting the subject. In low budget videomaking this is usually the primary concern, but as productions get more sophisticated the desire to light the setting where the subject is placed becomes important too.

A news show provides a simple example. In addition to using key, fill, and back lights on the news anchor, the background behind the anchor also needs to be lit properly. In the simplest set designs, the background may consist of a nothing more than a blue wall—in which case the goal is to get an even illumination over the entire background so that it does not appear brighter on one side or another. (One or more soft fill lights will probably work best).

A more expensive network news set may have the news writers and editors appearing in the background, and the lighting must be carefully designed so that they are evenly illuminated, but not distracting. If there are TV monitors in the set, care must be taken to avoid reflections from the studio lights on the glass surfaces of the monitors.

Look and See

These tips, of course, are just starting points for your own experimentation and improvisations in the world of lighting. Fortunately, for innovative videomakers who are flexible enough to adapt to situations, lighting is one area where you don't necessarily need a lot of money to get the job done right.

The most important equipment you'll need is your own eye-brain system. Look very carefully at the available light before you start setting up.

If you're shooting in an office, move a chair over by a window so that someone sitting there can be properly illuminated from outside.

If you're shooting in a fluorescent lit kitchen, get your chef to stand behind a light from above, so that it hits his or her face at a forty-five degree angle, and not from directly overhead.

As you approach each shooting situation, you should look upon the lighting as a unique new challenge. Your equipment may be a professional lighting kit, or a simple battery powered portable light attachment, or a piece of white cardboard that you use as a reflector. Whatever your budget and equipment complement, your goal is to make sure your subjects are lit as well as they possibly can be.

If someone is standing in front of a window, so that the face looks too dark, don't reach for the backlight button. Ask the person to move so that the face catches light from the window, or move yourself (and the camcorder) between the person and the window, or close the curtains so that outdoor light stops coming in. Don't just see the light, take control of it.

One big advantage of video, over film, is the ability to see the effects of lighting immediately. The viewfinder doesn't lie. Unlike film, there's no waiting for developing to see results. It's perfect for experimentation—take advantage of this feature.

Lowel's compact Tota lights offer numerous mounting options: with gels or diffusion on stand (1), in multiple arrays using clamps (2), on stands with barn doors (3), with reflective umbrella (4), replacement bulbs (5), stand with flexible shaft flags to block light where needed (6), using frame mount on door frame (7), and by taping frame mount to a brick wall (8).

23 Graphics & Optics

Graphics is the term used to describe any video images that are either created by artwork, or computer generated. In regular TV production, examples of graphics are titles and credits, weather maps on the local news, topical pictures that appear over news anchors' shoulders, logos, etc.

The world of video graphics can be thought of as having three sides—titles, artwork, and animation—though they often blur together in more advanced productions.

Titles

Most camcorders have a built-in titling system. Most models use a digital superimposing technique: the camcorder stores in memory a simple silhouette representation of the title artwork, and then superimposes this image over live video. The color of the superimposed titles can usually be shifted from white to black to yellow, cyan, red, blue, green, or magenta.

Other camcorder models have built-in character generators that superimpose electronically produced titles. These titles are usually limited to one or two lines of text, on one or two pages. (A page is the amount of text that can appear on the screen at any given time).

Both camcorder titling systems offer a lot of power, if you're willing to put in the time and energy. Using editing, you can go way beyond the page limit that is built in to the camcorder. Simply record a page of text for a second, create a new title, and record another page for a second.

This process is tedious and limited, however. You can't superimpose the edited title sequence over a moving video image, and the fast edits are prone to glitch. So once you start adding lengthy title sequences on a regular basis, you'll probably want to begin using a separate electronic character generator system.

There are two basic approaches to adding electronically generated titles. The first, and easiest, is to purchase a dedicated character generator. The CG, as it is commonly called, has a typewriter keyboard and numerous function keys that select font, color, etc.

Most CGs can automatically superimpose the titles over incoming video images, using a device called a keyer.

The second approach to electronic titles is to use a computer. While this may at first seem like the obvious preferable choice—especially if you already own a computer—you may find that it is less costly to buy a dedicated CG. The expense of computer character generated titles stems from the fact that the video signal going to the computer monitor has a different scanning system than regular NTSC video signals. If you have an Amiga computer, you're in luck. All Amiga computers have built-in NTSC video outputs. But with IBM and Mac computers, the purchase of a separate converter board, or box, will usually be required.

A third, though usually inferior approach is to buy a character generator accessory product for your camcorder or image mixer. It's an inferior choice because it locks you into the other piece of equipment it attaches to. If that piece of equipment becomes outdated or breaks, you've lost the utility of the titler along with it.

Which of these approaches makes the most sense for you depends on what equipment you already own, and what you intend to buy. If you've already got a Video Toaster setup, for example, then you've already got an excellent title generating system. And if you've got an IBM 386, or higher end Mac computer with a video converter board (like those made by Targa, Matrox Illuminator, or TrueVision) then all you need is the software.

If all you have is a basic editing system, on the other hand, then a separate character generator, especially a lower priced model like Videonics' might make sense.

And if you've got a Panasonic image mixer, then adding the optional CG accessory may be your least expensive route to titling—though it doesn't provide the same power that a separate stand-alone or computer-based titler would.

In addition to comparing costs and features, you should also consider hassle. A computer-based titling setup will inevitably involve more time and effort to configure, compared with a stand-alone CG. Even if you have a Toaster, remember that it can't be used for other purposes while it is running the character generator program.

Videonics TitleMaker 2000

Videonics' character generator, the TitleMaker 2000, is the logical complement to an A/V mixing system, but it can also be used by itself in the context of a simpler straight-cut editing system. It's useful for adding opening and closing credits, as well as identifying people who are speaking, locations, and providing screens of text for advertising. It provides a really clean looking video signal,

Videonics Titlemaker 2000

with sharp edges, and a good variety of fonts (23 fonts in four sizes each, resulting in about 90 different combinations.) Outline, shadow, and spacing options are also available. International characters are provided.

The memory in the TitleMaker 2000 is organized in pages, just like professional character generator units. There is no limit to the number of pages that can be stored—hundreds are possible—but the overall limit on the number of text characters is 8000. (Text is retained in memory even when power is shut off.) How much text fills each page depends on the fonts and size selected, as well as layout. Each page would normally be a screen full of text, unless you select the crawl or strobe options. With crawl, text moves in a single line along the bottom of the screen; with scroll, the text moves up (or down) the screen continuously, with one page smoothly and unnoticeably connecting to the next.

Besides the characters themselves, the TitleMaker 2000 also generates an impressive variety of backgrounds. Solid colors, speckled patterns (including moving star-like animations), and rainbow effects are available. These can serve as the background sources (you can have a different background for each page), or they can be mixed together with an incoming video signal for even more complex backgrounds. Titles can also be simply superimposed over incoming video, with no additional background pattern.

Colored lines and boxes can be created to add accent to the titles. A special set of symbols offers copyright, registered trademark, open quotes, close quotes, and other typographic characters.

You can fade the titles in or out, or use one of eighteen wipe patterns. Each page can have different in and out effects specified. The titles can last on screen for a programmed duration, or you can manually switch from one to the next, slide-show style. For automated editing, a GPI jack can trigger the title sequences to start.

Overall, the TitleMaker 2000 is a top tool for low-budget character generating. At $599 list, it costs considerably less than even the cheapest computer-based titling systems, and offers stand-alone convenience. Compared to the first model, this new version adds about double the number of fonts, a preview output that lets you prepare a page while displaying no titles on the output (great for sports productions), and better memory organization controls such as the ability to group pages into projects, and to rapidly jump to any page. Compared to the crude little titlers that have been built into camcorders, it's an awful lot of character generator bang for the buck.

Computer Graphics

Besides editing tapes, most desktop video systems can also add titles, graphics, and computer animation. The Video-Toaster has all these capabilities built-in—the Toaster software includes Toaster CG, a character generator system, ToasterPaint, for graphics creation and paintbox style image manipulation, LightWave 3D, for computer animation, and ChromaFX, for color filtering and effects.

Practically any IBM-compatible or Macintosh computer with an NTSC output board can convert graphics created by standard desktop publishing software (such as Aldus Pagemaker, Corel Draw, Adobe Illustrator, etc.) for use with video productions. Simpler video output boards will produce the graphics as images unto themselves; while more sophisticated input/output boards, such as the Matrox Illuminator, can superimpose these graphics over videotape images.

As mentioned earlier, Amiga computers are without question the best low budget computer value for creating titles, graphics, paintbox effects, and animations—because they have the NTSC conversion built in (for output). Programs like Deluxe Paint IV (animation), Art Department Pro (graphics and paintbox), and

The dotted line represents the "TV safe area" which guarantees that titles wil be seen, even on funky old TVs.

Broadcast Titler (character generator) offer powerful graphics capabilities at a much lower cost than the Toaster system—because they require no additional hardware (except perhaps a genlock for superimposing) and can run on simpler and older Amiga models, such as the A500, A1000, A2000, and A2500.

Artwork

In the early days of TV, all graphics were created using standard mechanical artwork techniques. In other words, paper was the medium of choice—graphics were created by drawing, transfer lettering, paste-up, etc.

Nowadays, of course, computers are commonly used to create video graphics. The most complex animation sequences utilize computers costing hundreds of thousands of dollars.

On a lower budget, the Amiga computer can be a fantastic tool for creating animated title sequences. IBM and Mac are also useful for this, at a slightly higher budget level (remember, you need a special converter to create the video signal).

But for low budget video production, the old fashioned mechanical artwork techniques are often the best choice. You can create a complete title sequence on sketch pad, for example, and your hand-lettered titles can be adorned by simple line drawings.

You can create humorous and clever paste-ups, combining photographs, lettering, and drawing in a single graphic.

To get some ideas, try visiting a local art supply store. Look for dry transfer letters, clip art, and poster boards. Multi-color marker pens are always useful too.

When you create graphics, remember that there is a generally accepted rule that all letters and numbers should fit within the "TV safe" (or "title safe") area in the middle of the screen (see diagram).

The reasoning behind this "TV safe" area is that many television sets are adjusted to cut off a bit from the four sides of the picture. To ensure that all viewers can see the information, the extreme edges are avoided.

Animation

Animation has been explored by practically every bored elementary school student who has ever taken a corner of a notebook, and doodled a series of stick figures in the same spot on each page, to create an animated flipbook.

The idea of drawing a series of similar pictures, which can create the illusion of motion when displayed in rapid succession, actually predates motion picture films. In fact, the discovery of the "persistence of vision" effect, in the nineteenth century, which seduces viewers into believing that a sequence of still images actually portrays just a single image in motion, is what prompted researchers like America's Thomas Edison and France's Lumiere brothers to invent machines that photograph a series of still pictures very quickly, thus giving birth to cinema, and its offspring, video.

If you have access to a video camcorder, you can begin experimenting with animation using no additional equipment. Just mount the camcorder on a tripod, or on a table top, and shoot a few seconds of the scene in your living room. Pause the camcorder and move an object—a pillow on the couch, for instance—ever so slightly. Record a very short bit of this—less than a second, if possible—and move it a bit more. And so on.

Similarly, rather than working with real life imagery (your living room), you can create original animation artwork using a sketch pad. Be sure to leave the pages attached to the pad, so that they all line up properly. If you draw the last page first, you can easily redraw the preceding images by tracing each one over the one underneath. Make changes from one page to the next very slight.

To minimize your need to keep redrawing similar images, you can create an animation "mechanical": Draw (or cut out of a magazine) a full picture of a person (from head to toe) standing or walking in profile. Next, carefully cut off the legs at the knees, and reattach them using paper fasteners so that they can bend into different positions. Similarly, you can separate the thighs from the hips and swivel them, as well as the forearms, elbows, and hands.

Sound complicated? Animation is admittedly not for everyone—it can be very tedious, and requires very careful attention to fine detail. But its rewards can be exhilarating. Through animation, you can literally make inanimate objects spring to life. As art, animation has been gaining favor in film festivals and on television in recent years. And increasingly, pure animation is giving way to techniques which combine both animated and real life images, as exemplified by the film *Who Framed Roger Rabbit?* and numerous TV commercials.

Video's Animation Limitations

Technically, the exact meaning of the term animation varies; and is itself in flux. In the world of film, animation usually refers to images which are created through a series of drawings, or through the use of miniatures—scale models. In video circles, the term animation has come to be applied to several other film-style techniques which involve manipulation of the frame rate at which recordings are made, such as slow-motion and time-lapse effects, like those shown extensively in the film *Koyaanisqatsi*. And animation also refers to computer-generated effects and drawings that change over a period of time (like spinning logos).

One reason why video has expanded the definition of animation may be because in the strictest interpretation of this term, video technology is considerably inferior to film technology—at least at this point in time, and on a low budget.

That's because true animation requires an ability to record just one frame at a time—something that's a cinch for practically any movie camera, but as of yet no consumer video camcorder is capable of. At best, some camcorder models are capable of recording about seven or eight frames at a time, producing a jerky but acceptable looking animated image. If you don't own such a camcorder, you'll need to experiment to see how quickly you can stop and start the camcorder to create the shortest possible recording.

Note that some camcorders, and VCRs, do not start recording the instant you press the pause (or stop/start) button, and that some back-up a bit each time you stop them. A good way to experiment is to shoot pictures of a clock with a big seconds hand, or a digital seconds display, for specific periods of time. Then, by replaying the clock sequence in slow motion, you can measure the discrepancy between the start/stop times and the actual recorded times.

The shortest possible interval you can record will depend on your camcorder or VCR. In general, the flying erase head feature will vastly improve your ability to create video animation. But even the best equipment must record several frames at time. Panasonic's AG-1970 industrial Super-VHS editing recorder, for example, can record seven frames at a time; Sony's computer controlled Hi8 Vdeck can record four frame intervals.

In video, the term animation has become blurred with film's special effects, and a precise dividing line is almost impossible to pin down. For example is the computer-assisted colorization technique (which has used computer and video technology to add color on a frame-by-frame basis, to black and white film classics like *It's A Wonderful Life*) animation or special effect?

If your video camera or VCR can effectively record short bursts lasting a fraction of a second without creating a lot of picture instability (rolling, color noise, scrambled pictures, etc.), then it offers a great way to inexpensively experiment with animation. If you don't have this capability, or if you wish to get more serious about creating really smooth looking animated effects, then working with film is probably the most accessible, inexpensive route. A few years ago, it was common to hear film people griping about how they'd have to learn how to operate video equipment; ironically, many of today's new videomakers have never even considered working with film.

Regardless of which technology—or combination thereof—which you choose to work with, many of the techniques for creating animation are essentially the same. Here's a rundown of some of the most common types of animation.

Cel Animation

The Walt Disney classic cartoon films, Bugs Bunny, the Saturday morning TV cartoons, and *Roger Rabbit* were all created by drawings on clear plastic sheets called cels. By using clear sheets, it is possible to layer together several different cels—one for the main character, others for the background and other characters.

A complex animated cartoon can involve literally dozens of cels. The main characters, for example, may have their bodies on one cel, and the arms and legs on other cels. A set of eight or ten arm and leg positions can create a "cycle" for walking, which can be repeated over and over. Thus, it is possible to make the arms and legs appear to be constantly moving without having to redraw hundreds and hundreds of pictures.

Similarly, the background can be moved while the main character appears to be walking. But for truly three-dimensional effects, the background can be drawn in many layers—and this was a characteristic which gave Disney cartoons like *Bambi* considerably more quality than the relatively cheap Hanna-Barbera cartoons like *The Flintstones* and *The Jetsons*, which are characterized by simple, flat backgrounds that are highly repetitive.

The cels are photographed using an animation stand. The animation stand is a vertically mounted camera which looks much like a darkroom enlarger (though it works in reverse). A film camera sits at the top of the stand, and the artwork is placed on the table beneath it. Lights on either side of the table illuminate the artwork, or, for working with cels, a light underneath the table illuminates the translucent white table surface in much the same way that a dentist's lightbox allows him/her to examine X-rays.

You can mount a video camera on an animation stand, or you can create a crude imitation by mounting the camera on a tripod, and setting up an easel a few feet in front of it with photo flood lights on both sides.

A professional animation stand includes special metal pegs which are designed to fit specially cut holes along the edges of the cels, for extremely precise registration. The table top can be moved left and right, and forward and back (in animators' jargon, such movements are termed "west/east" and "south/north", respectively). Similarly, the camera on the top of the stand can be moved closer or farther from the table top, to zoom in or out.

The fancier the animation stand, the more capability it will have to independently move different cels in different directions. To create the three-dimensional Disney effects, cels are placed as much as a foot or more apart from each other, so that to the camera, some are in focus while others are not, and different background elements move at different speeds.

Clay Animation and Models

Another animation technique which has gained favor in recent years is the use of models. The 'California Raisins' commercial used clay models singing *Heard It Through The Grapevine* to promote dried fruit, and brought the claymation technique into millions of living rooms.

Cheap monster movies made in the fifties frequently used miniature models of terrifying beasts, and more recently, science fiction films like *Star Wars* have used highly detailed realistic looking models to render artists' visions of space ships. In fact,

George Lucas created a separate studio, called Industrial Light and Magic, which specializes in creating models and other animation techniques.

Multiple Exposures

Film cameras excel in one other area where consumer video equipment is technologically deficient—the ability to double expose film to two or more different images. This can be exemplified by a standard technique for creating the illusion that you are moving through outer space, passing stars—such as in the old Star Trek series:

Take a black card, and use a small pin to prick several dozen holes in it, in random positions. Then, place this card over a white background, and put it on an animation stand. (An alternative technique is to put small drops of white paint on it.) Light it so that the white holes are reasonably bright, but so that the black background looks pitch black—with no detectable texture or reflections (try to find a truly unreflective, matte black in an art supply store, and/or use polarizing filters to prevent reflections). On the animation stand, shoot one frame of this card, then zoom in ever so slightly, shoot another frame, and continue the zoom.

So far, what you'll end up with is a very phony-looking effect, which gives itself away by the fact that you seem to be passing through all the stars at the same rate. The effect can be made much more striking by utilizing film's ability to be multiply exposed: Take a second black card, create a different set of randomly placed holes in it, rewind and re-expose the movie film to this set of white dots—but this time, zoom in at a different rate—faster or slower. Finally, create a third such card, but this time, try to concentrate more of the dots near the center, so that as you zoom in, the center dots move out towards the edges of the frame. Develop the film, and you'll see some very three-dimensional looking star travel effects.

Multi-image Effects

But another aspect of the star-travel effect—super-imposing the space ship (a la U.S.S. Enterprise) over the stars—is actually easier to do in video, at least with some extra equipment. The ability to create split-screens and other multi-image effects can be achieved in video using a relatively inexpensive (under $1000) device called a special effects generator (see the section on A/B Roll Editing). In conjunction with a special genlock video camera, an SEG lets you create split screens, and keyed effects. The key effect lets you take a model of a plastic space ship, dangle it on black thread in front of a pitch black background, and superimpose it over the moving-star deep space animation sequence.

In this case, the keying effect is preferable to multiple exposures, because it prevents any of the stars from appearing in front of the space ship. If the space ship is entirely white, then stars in front would become invisible with a multiple exposure, but if there are any dark spots on the space ship—window, shadows, etc.—then a filmed multiple exposure would look chintzy.

Creating film's equivalent of video's key effect is a tedious and often costly technique called matting. On an animation stand, you can create a matte by cutting black paper to the exact shape of the image you wish to superimpose—such as the space ship. Then, when you shoot the stars, place this matte exactly where the ship will appear.

It's complex and tedious to get it in the exact spot where you'll position the model space ship, and gets even more complicated if the space ship will be moving around within the frame. That technique is called travelling matte, and requires the preparation of a third film, in addition to the two images being combined, which incorporates a moving high-contrast silhouette of the space ship. The stars are thus blocked where the space ship image will projected. Each frame must be prepared to precisely match the outline of one of the images (such as the space ship). Then, the three films are combined (usually by a film laboratory) using a device called an optical printer, creating a single combined film. The creation of travelling matte film effects is expensive and laborious, but that's how practically all feature films superimpose their high quality animated effects.

Incidentally, this is the reason why low budget film credits most typically appear over a plain black background, and are rarely superimposed over a picture. Practically all low-budget video's, on the other hand, can incorporate titles superimposed over an image, thanks to reasonably priced character generators (some camcorders even have them built in) which, in effect, are capable of keying the titles to combine them in an overlay with the live video image (see the chapter on Titles).

Time-lapse Photography

An intervalometer, or interval timer, for time lapse recording, is available on many of the more advanced consumer camcorder models. You have undoubtedly seen this effect used in a nature film showing flowers opening and closing, and it is used each evening by many local TV station to show a series of radar pictures of cloud movements over the area.

Time-lapse photography condenses action which takes along amount of time into a short time. It can be used for comedic and dramatic purposes. Ideally, a time-lapse movie camera will shoot one frame at a given interval—such as one frame per second, one frame every ten seconds, etc. At the rate of one frame every minute, an entire day gets condensed into sixty seconds.

Video camcorders cannot record a frame at a time, so they suffer from the same general jerkiness as with other animation techniques. But, especially when used for comedic effect, the jerkiness is often not as bothersome when used for time-lapse. Perhaps its because viewers recognize and understand the concept of time-lapse sequences, and can accept the notion of a series of short "samples". Many camcorders—especially Canon's models —have an interval timer feature that can be set to record a half second (or second) every ten seconds, every twenty seconds, every minute, or every five minutes.

Smith-Victor (known for their video lights) has a camcorder accessory product which offers quite a bit of versatility in creating time-lapse video sequences. The 'Video Interval Timer' can automatically make your camcorder record anywhere from one to twelve seconds at a time, at intervals from once a second to every eight minutes. It costs about $100, and requires that the camcorder (or a VCR) have a remote pause jack.

The time-lapse effect can be quite funny if, for example, you set up the camcorder to record a Thanksgiving dinner, or a big project like painting the house. The key to using time-lapse effectively is to keep the camcorder perfectly Still, Mounted On A Tripod or other support.

Sound Advice

Animation is a visual technique, but for it to be effective, you will usually want to combine it with sound. Obviously, the creative ways you can incorporate sound into an animated production are innumerable—you can combine music, narration, sound effects, dramatic character voices (remember *Saturday Night Live's* Mr. Bill?), etc.

You'll need a camcorder or VCR with the audio dub feature, to be able to add sound after the animated sequence has been recorded. You'll find that the sound which gets recorded when you animate by stopping and starting your camcorder is extremely annoying, and you'll almost always want to replace it.

If you or someone you know plays music, try recording live music which is synchronized (by having the musician watch the screen and rehearse several times) to the action of your animated sequence. Note that with video equipment, it will be very difficult to attempt the reverse—to get the picture to synchronize with previously recorded music (such as a pop song). Such synching of the picture to the sound requires the video dub feature (recording new picture, leaving old sound—available only in the VHS family), and careful attention to the timing of your animated movements.

The Bottom Line

Being able to draw from both the worlds of video and film production can give low budget producers the best of both worlds. Using Super-8 film, you can shoot about three-minutes' worth of animation for under fifteen dollars, including processing. That may sound like a lot more than video (five dollars of tape for two hours!), but for a short animated sequence, it may be well worth it. An inexpensive Super-8 camera, with single-frame shooting capability, can cost less than two hundred dollars. Then, to convert the film to video, you can purchase your own "film chain" system to project the film into your video camcorder—or, what might be even cheaper, and yields better results—is to not even buy a film projector, but simply use an inexpensive film editing viewer to verify and edit film sequences, then pay to have them transferred to video professionally. Such transfers typically cost from thirty to one hundred fifty dollars per hour.

Another route, which can yield more professional looking results, is to gain access to 16-mm film production equipment, rather than buying your own Super-8 gear. Many cities have film arts organizations—such as Millennium in New York, and Film Arts Foundation in San Francisco—which rent out 16-mm equipment at very low, subsidized rates (ten or twenty dollars per day). Similarly, you can get to use a professional quality 16-mm animation stand through such organizations, or by signing up for a class in animation at a local college. Rates for using an animation stand can be as low as a few dollars per hour, if you live in a big city and shop around carefully. Using 16-mm film, it costs about forty-five dollars for about three minutes of film and developing. Video transfers cost about the same as for Super-8 film.

Note that the quality of a film to video transfer is usually seen in the amount of flicker that appears in the film image. 16-mm film typically runs at twenty-four frames per second, while video equipment all runs at thirty frames per second. Special projectors manage to get around this problem by showing each frame of the film for one-thirtieth of a second, but by repeating one frame periodically the effective speed is twenty-four frames per second. Such projectors are vital for a high quality film-to-tape transfer.

The Future

These rates may seem outrageously expensive, compared with video tape, (and you can't erase it!), but if you think about it, using film for animation can be the cheapest route available—especially when compared with buying a whole new video camcorder just to do animation.

Animation created with low budget video equipment is fun to experiment with, but will look quite jerky when compared with single frame film animation. That's because at a rate of four images per second—today's state of the art in consumer video animation—the human eye will see four separate images. Research has shown that it takes a rate of at least fifteen or twenty images per second to create the "persistence of vision" illusion of motion. Thus film, at twenty-four frames per second, and video, at thirty-frames per second easily exceed the minimum and create smooth looking motion.

Film has sprocket holes, and it is therefor very easy to move it very precisely by one frame at a time. Videotape has no sprocket holes, and relies on electronic signals to mark the beginning and end of each frame. The tape moves very slowly, and the amount which it moves for a single frame is so small, that it's extremely difficult to create a mechanism which can move the tape by just one frame. The whole video recording system is really designed for smooth continuous recording.

It may be possible to create VCRs or camcorders which move by one frame's worth of tape at a time—someday. But a more promising approach might be to digitally record a sequence of eight images, and then play them out in sequence into a VCR which can record in eight-frame bursts.

The newest version of the Video Toaster is capable of storing several seconds of animation, using the Light Wave Toaster facility, for more precise animation effects.

Blurring the Film—Video Line

The extent to which you can utilize techniques from numerous disciplines, as well as improvising to suit your needs, will determine the boundaries of your production capabilities. With an open mind and imagination, those boundaries can be virtually limitless.

It's no secret that the line between video and film is eroding. Whereas a few years ago, the two industries—at least on the production side—were like enemy camps, today they act more like suspicious friends.

Regardless of how the big boys fight amongst themselves, today's technology offers low-budget video and filmmakers unprecedented opportunity to create, experiment, and explore. To adhere dogmatically to a single moving image technology—film or video—with almost religious fervor (as we've seen many people do in both camps!) is politically naive and artistically suicidal.

After all—when the film industry says film is better, and the video industry says video is better, what are they really saying? It's obviously in their business interests to take the stand each takes. But as a low budget video/film producer, what is your business interest? Keeping the budget low!

If this makes sense, then it should be obvious that strict adherence to either film or video technology is not in the business interests of low budget producers, because there are some things which are dirt cheap to produce in video, but very expensive in film; and there are other things that are very cheap in film, but quite expensive in video.

Frame by frame animation is a good example of the latter. As we enter the mid-1990s, there are no consumer camcorders on the market which are capable of shooting a single frame of video at a time. (Though this may change by the year 2000.) Computer video techniques, which allow you to store up a series of frames, and then record them in sequence on a VCR, are at the cutting edge of low-cost video animation.

To really take advantage of today's moving image technology, you should be able to pick and choose from amongst the various offerings. Film, video, and computer systems are like a bazaar of processes available for our use.

Personal Animation Recorder control screen, from Digital Processing Systems.

Even though you essentially may be making a video, there may be times when you'd like to incorporate animated film sequences within it. Similarly, filmmakers may incorporate video sequences within their films—and ultimately, most films get transferred onto videotape for mass distribution.

Digital image recording can be very memory-intensive game. To record just a single live video frame, uncompressed, with reasonably good quality (640 x 480 pixels, with 256 steps each of red, green, and blue), requires 768-K of computer memory. To record one-second's worth of full animation (each frame is different), uncompressed, requires 23-Megabytes, and a half-minute sequence would need 6,191-Megabytes! Data compression such as MPEG and JPEG can reduce these numbers by a factor of 100 or more, but at high compression ratios picture quality suffers.

The Personal Animation Recorder, from Digital Processing Systems, is at the cutting edge of offering top quality hard disk-based animation at a reasonable price.

But, although it is truly amazing what today's computers can do, in many cases, a simple $100 film camera with a single frame shutter can be much more versatile for experimenting with animation.

Lens Filters and Adapters

Electronically manipulating video images using high-tech digital toys may seem like the most sexy and dazzling way to achieve special effects, but working on a much lower budget, you can also alter video images quite effectively using the wide variety of optical filters and adapters that are available for camcorders.

Star Filter. Courtesy of Tiffen.

Long the domain of still photographers and cinematographers, filters alter the image at the source—before they ever got recorded onto tape, and before the light even enters the camcorder's lens. They're screwed into the front of the camcorder's lens—just about all "traditional" camcorder designs (those with a round lens extending forward) include such threads at the very front of the lens barrel. The size of these threads vary from

Contrast filters. From top to bottom: Unfiltered, Tiffen Low Contrast 3, Soft Contrast 3, Ultra Contrast 5.

model to model—ranging from about 45mm to 60mm in diameter.

Perhaps the most fun I have ever had with a filter was shooting a home shopping comedy segment in which a rhinestone studded porcelain "collectable" was spinning around on a slow turntable I had built. This cliche situation called for a star filter, to make the sparkling faux diamonds shoot out rays of light as the figurine spun about.

Besides jewelry ads, you also see star filters used commonly in high gloss TV specials—such as awards ceremonies, beauty pageants, and variety shows—in which stage lights are visible in the frame (typically in the context of an extreme wide angle shot showing the full stage as well as the audience, used as a transition to and from commercials). They're also used for romantic candlelight dinners in soap operas and dramatic productions, so that rays of light beam out from the candle. Star filters are measured by how many rays of light emanate from each point—the most common are 4-point, 6-point, and 8-point filters.

Steamy romance scenes can also be enhanced—optically speaking—by the addition of a fog filter in front of the lens. If you're shooting at the docks on a clear sunny day, but wish you had a more misty, mysterious underworld look, this filter is just the ticket. For maximum effect try a double fog filter, which doubles the effect.

A polarizing filter can help make clouds appear more visible, and can reduce reflected glare from windows, lakes, chrome, and other shiny surfaces. Many still photographers leave polarizing filters on their cameras all the time, because of the slight improvement that is consistently gained. Rotating the filter in front of the lens will vary the effect—especially for glare problems—so some experimentation is needed to find the best setting.

Speaking of glare, one of the most useful lens accessories you can add—and one which technically doesn't even go in front of the lens, but rather, around it—is called a lens hood. It's a tube that extends an inch or more in front of the lens surface, and its purpose is to reduce or eliminate the entrance of stray light that causes glare and flare problems. Lens flare, sometimes a desirable effect—such as when shooting a car driving off into the sunset—is the repetition of ghost images of the camera's iris—appearing usually as series of hexagon shaped white spots. Flare is caused by direct light—usually from the sun—while glare is caused by more subtle reflected light, from the sky, ground, nearby walls, etc. A professional cinematographer once told me that 90% of all outdoor images can be improved just by adding a lens hood. The hood should extend out as far as possible, without encroaching on the edges of the picture.

Outdoor shots may also be improved sometimes with sky and haze filters—also called UV filters. These reduce the blue haze that appears in the distance on clear days.

A neutral density (ND) filter darkens the image, without otherwise changing it. It's useful for two reasons—when shooting outdoors in bright light, it can help give you better control over the camcorder's aperture setting (even though the iris is automatic), and thus the depth of focus (a.k.a. depth of field). Plus, the filter protects the surface of your camcorder's lens—better a $10 throwaway filter gets scratched, rather than a permanently mounted lens that would cost hundreds of dollars to replace. ND filters are calibrated in f-stops' worth of light reduction (an ND-1 filter requires the aperture to open up by one f-stop, for example.)

Color filters—particularly in the orange/yellow/red range—can give videos a warmer look, such as for shooting sunsets. Sepia filters can give the video the look of an old movie. (You can also play with the camcorder's white balance adjustment to achieve similar effects.)

Gradient filters, which vary the effect the way gradient sunglasses darken the sky more than the ground, are useful when you wish to alter just part of the picture—such as adding orange to a sunset (top part) without affecting the bottom as much. Fog filters with clear centers are also available, as are more zany filter attachments, like kaleidoscope multi-images and rainbow effects.

To get a sense of what various filters look like, Tiffen sells a videocassette titled, "Which Filter Should I Use?" ($24.95 list) that shows examples of many different filter products. It's available through their dealers (call 800-645-2522 to find the nearest one.)

Camcorder wide-angle and tele-extender conversion lenses. Courtesy of Sima.

Lens Adapters

If there's one thing that almost always distinguishes consumer camcorders from professional models, it's the permanent attachment of the lens. The only consumer models with interchangeable lenses are Canón's L1 and L2—and price wise, they're clearly in the semi-pro / industrial camp.

Professional video and film camera all offer a standard mounting system that accepts a wide variety of lenses—from 70:1 super-telephoto zooms used in sports coverage, to 180-degree panoramic "fish-eye" super-wide angle lenses.

But camcorders users are usually stuck with more mid-range 8:1, 10:1, or 12:1 zooms. And most of that range, unfortunately,

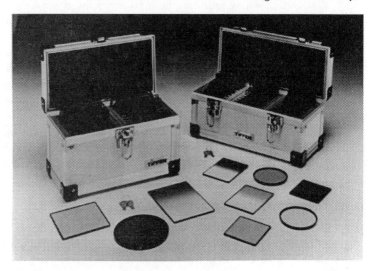

Tiffen professional filters for use with large professional format cameras.

is usually devoted to the telephoto side—even at full wide angle setting, most camcorder zoom lenses provide an image that's barely wider than the photographically "normal" field of view ("normal" is what it looks like if you put a piece of clear glass in front of your eye, with no apparent magnification or reduction in image size.) So what do you do when you've got seven people sitting across a couch and love seat, but you can only step far enough back to fit five of them in the picture? Put on a wide angle adaptor, and they will all fit. Wide angle adapters are rated according to their magnification factor—a 0.6x adaptor will produce a wider field of view, on a given lens, than a 0.7x or 0.8x adaptor.

Alternatively, a telephoto extender adaptor can help make faraway subjects appear even closer, by increasing the effective telephoto reach. The most common magnification factors are 2x and 3x. Ambico offers lens adaptor units with more than 5x magnification, including a "Super Spy" model for those deep telephoto assignments. (There are also infra-red night vision adaptors, like the ones the TV networks used to cover the Gulf War.)

When using telephoto and wide angle adapters, you'll generally keep the lens all the way at the appropriate extreme—zoomed in or zoomed out all the way. Don't expect zooming to work normally—it won't.

Finding the right lens adaptor for your camcorder may take a bit of searching. If at all possible, get one made by the manufacturer of the camcorder, so you'll be assured of a perfect fit. Some adapters are sold with numerous rings that can fit different lens thread diameters, but you're probably better off with one designed specifically for your lens' threads. (The more things you have to screw together, the more opportunity for optical distortions.)

All lenses have aberrations—optical imperfections that produce undesirable distortion. Fortunately for low budget video producers, the crude detail of video images (compared with photographic or 35mm cinematic images) tends to hide these problems. But note for the record that professional cinematographers wouldn't get caught dead using such adapters—instead, they'd insist on renting the exact lens they wanted. Of course, since most low-priced camcorders don't have interchangeable lenses, the question of using "prime lenses" (non-zoom, more optically perfect) is moot. In this context, optical adapters are a godsend.

24 Producing and Directing

Read the credits on a feature film or network TV program, and you'll usually see the names of an executive producer, one or more producers, associate producers, a director, assistant director, and perhaps directors of cinematography, sound design, and lighting. In low budget video production, often you alone must fill all these shoes. You might work with one or two other people, and have the luxury of dividing this work up. This chapter is about what's involved in producing and directing a video production—who does what?

Casual video projects, of course, don't require much thought about producing and directing—as the ads say, to take video snapshots of family vacations, barbecues, and baby's first steps all you need do is just point and shoot. But more serious, professional work, like shooting weddings, documentaries, drama, and public access talk shows can usually benefit from some thought about the differences between producing and directing.

When two or more people are involved as the major players in a project, this discussion can be especially helpful up front, before the project gets underway, to avoid painful fights down the road. Just as music groups tend to form in harmonious enthusiasm, and then break up in bitter disputes, video and film productions can become plagued by personality conflicts and differences in aesthetic and financial judgement. Clarifying responsibilities beforehand can eliminate much of the potential for conflict.

I must admit that in my earliest college days of videomaking, I was bothered by the non-egalitarian spirit of these clearly defined roles. Why couldn't producing video be a communal activity? Well, after numerous hippie-like attempts at working in video collectives, I came to the same conclusion that the traditional Hollywood industry came to years ago—these roles make sense, because they define clear paths of communication and control that lead to the overall efficiency of the production. In a dramatic production, while an actor is trying to give his or her best performance, you don't want to have a fight break out between two co-directors, arguing about how the scene should be played.

Overall, two people will probably get more enjoyment by switching roles—being the producer of one production, and the director of the next—than by trying to share these roles constantly. If you can't decide how to start, flip a coin.

The Producer

The producer is responsible for the overall management and administration of the project. In the big budget world of Hollywood film and videomaking, a project typically begins when a producer reads a novel and decides to option it for the creation of a screenplay or teleplay. Next the producer might hire a scriptwriter, and after the script is written, a director is hired. The producer seeks investments to cover the costs of production, and might set up a separate corporation to produce the project, and sell shares in it.

When casting time comes, the producer consults with the director to choose actors and actresses. Similarly, the crew and production staff are hired. The producer makes arrangements to rent camera and sound equipment, lighting, and arranges for meals and locations outside of the studio.

The producer is in charge of all contract negotiations, determining how much it is worth to get top-name talent and crew. This is largely why investors trust a particular producer or production company with their money—presumably, the producer has a track record of handling money responsibly, holding the line on inflated salaries and shares of the profits.

The producer arranges for renting facility time for post-production, and sets the schedule and deadlines. In consultation with the director, the producer makes arrangements to get any music that's needed—either by hiring musicians to create original compositions, or by clearing the rights to use previously recorded music.

After the production is completed, the producer arranges for distribution of the program. This may involve simply shipping the edited master to a cable system or network for airing, or it may involve running off hundreds or thousands of copies for distribution. In the case of feature films, a separate distribution company, called appropriately enough the distributor, is contracted to handle the promotion and distribution. With films, the distributor delivers prints to theaters, and accounts for revenues received from theaters. A big budget film producer will typically sign separate deals to handle the distribution of the film in theaters, on pay-cable-TV, and for home video.

The Director

The director's role is generally more creative, and more focused on the actual production of the film. In the realm of big budget production, a director is typically hired while a script is in development, or after it is completed and committed to production. The director may comment on and influence the rewriting of the script, and of course, many big name film directors also end up sharing writing credits.

Once the script is settled on, the director analyzes it for specific shooting concerns. The director will draw up storyboards, or oversee having them created by an art department. The storyboard looks like a cartoon strip that shows how the film will be shot—what the camera angles will be, how major background elements should be placed, etc.—on a scene-by-scene basis.

At the highest budget level, the director works in conjunction with several sub-directors who take over creative responsibility for major elements of the production: cinematography, lighting, and sound. Ultimately, when any conflicts arise, the director has final say, but in general, deferring to these experts for most decisionmaking helps free the director to concentrate on working with the actors during the shoot.

In theory the director has creative control while the producer has management control, but there is obviously a lot of room for interaction and conflict. A director may feel that he or she absolutely needs to show a building blowing up, for example, while the producer insists that shooting such a scene is too expensive.

During the actual shooting, the director is the person who is in charge. Everyone—including camera (cinematography) personnel, lighting personnel, sound crew, actors, and production assistants—ultimately reports to the director. What the director says goes, and producers traditionally defer all on-the-spot decision making to the director to keep this chain of command intact. (Of course, Hollywood lore is also filled with horror stories of directors who have been fired on the spot by producers who did not think they were doing their job right, so it is indeed the one who controls the purse who has the ultimate say.)

It is the director's responsibility to keep the production proceeding on schedule. The producer typically rents production equipment, and has hired crew, for a certain number of days or weeks of production. Any extension of this schedule costs more. A director's track record in the industry is not just based on the quality of the completed work, but as the saying goes, on the director's ability to get the project finished on time and under budget.

In multi-camera studio television production, the director has a unique role as the person who chooses which camera to record on tape, or send live to the transmitter, at each given moment in time. In effect, the director of a multi-camera studio shoot is functioning like the editor of a single camera production. In the multi-camera studio environment, where the goal is to have a virtually completed tape at the end of the shooting (or in the case of live TV, the production process *is* the final step), the atmosphere can be so frenzied that the director's role seems to shift from creative to technical. The director gets so involved with barking orders to camera operators to change framing, and to audio personnel to cue music and sound effects as needed, that he or she scarcely has time to work with the actors on their performances.

In theory, much of this creative stuff is worked out beforehand during rehearsal (just as the director of a stage play puts most of his or her energy into the rehearsal process, so that by opening night everyone has internalized the instructions they've received from the director). In practice, the producer may be on hand in the studio, or a floor manager may step in and work with the cast, while the director remains in the control room.

After the shooting is over, the editor steps in. With multi-camera studio shoots, practically no editing may be needed. But with most productions shot with a single camera, much of the creative control of the finished project rests in the editing. Like the cinematographer and lighting director, the editor ultimately reports to the director, who has final say over editing. Some big name directors edit their own work, but most prefer to leave this tedious and time consuming process to others. (Most feature films take just two or three months to shoot, but over a year to edit.)

Three Step Production Process

No matter how big or small, all video productions can be generally thought of as having three distinct phases: pre-production, production, and post-production. Analyzing your own video projects, and the differing responsibilities of producer and director during each of these phases, can go a long way towards organizing the effort and avoiding ego conflicts.

Pre-production includes everything that happens before the shooting begins. While the producer might be concerned with such questions as camera rental rates and catering trucks, the director might be scouting locations and working on storyboards. Casting is typically a joint activity.

Even on a low budget, dividing responsibilities during pre-production can be helpful. Let the producer handle negotiations with the sponsor or client (the father of the bride in a wedding shoot, the marketing director for a corporate video, etc.) The director can determine the schedule for shooting, figuring out how much setup time will be needed, where lights and microphones should be placed, etc. After the director determines lighting and electrical needs for the shoot, he or she may then ask the producer to secure the use of the actual equipment—lights, extension cords, etc.

For dramatic shoots, storyboards and/or shooting scripts are highly recommended, and the director should prepare these in advance. A shooting script is a list of shots organized around setups, so that all scenes to be shot in the same setup are done at the same time, out-of-sequence from the original script.

Production

On the day of the shoot, the producer should generally defer to the director for most creative decision making, and provide more of a support role—being there for any last-minute needs that arise. In a low budget production, this may mean that even though the producer appears to be "Mr. Big," he or she is the one who ends up running out for sandwiches, going to the store to buy more blank tape, finding the superintendent or custodian of a building to get help with fuses or circuit breakers, etc. Adopting this attitude—the director is in charge, and the producer is there to take care of contingencies—will help two people to work as a team and not like a couple on the verge of divorce.

When everything goes according to plan, the producer may have the luxury of laying back and watching a perfectly organized production process unfold. But usually, hectic changes and an overly ambitious shooting schedule will leave the production with only half of what was expected to be done at the end of the day. What do you do then? Go into overtime? Plan another day of shooting? Give up and try to make do with what you've got?

These are the stressful times when the producer-director relationship can become the most strained, and the lines of decision making become most blurry. The director should try to concentrate on saying things like, "Well this is what it will look like with what we've got in the can (already shot)," or, "I need four more hours of shooting time to finish the script."

If a client is going to be billed for overtime, the producer should act as the buffer, saying things like, "Well, for five hundred dollars more it could be perfect, but if we quit now we'll have a reasonably decent version and it will be within the original budget. The director wants it perfect, but the decision is up to you."

Editing

When it comes time to edit the videotape (post-production), the roles of producer and director are not always clear in low budget videomaking. In professional film and video production, the director usually oversees the editing, but leaves much of the decision making to an editor who has been hired by the producer, in consultation with the director. Some directors, however, make every editing decision themselves, while others practically walk away from the project after it's shot, leaving it entirely in the hands of the editor. (Big name directors jumping from one film to another might say to an editor, "Show me something in six months.")

In low budget video production, the producer or director often acts as editor as well. There are advantages and disadvantages to choosing each for this role, but just as with the shooting itself, it is important that the chain of command be established and adhered to early on, so conflicts don't arise. If you're renting editing facilities by the hour, you don't want to be fighting about which take looks best while the meter is running.

The advantage of having the producer edit the footage is that he or she has some distance from what's on the tape. Often when someone shoots and edits himself (or herself), he tends to remember what he was trying to get in a particular shot, rather than objectively assessing the quality of what actually got captured on tape. An editor who did not personally spend two hours trying to achieve a particular effect will be more inclined to cut it out if doesn't seem to fit right. The director who toiled so hard will be more inclined to try to use it.

Alternatively, having the same person shoot and edit will require less communication. If an editor is brought in, handed a script and raw footage, and told to go at it, he or she will probably have a zillion questions about why certain shots exist, what cutaways were intended for what scenes, etc. The director is already juggling all this information in his or her head.

An excellent way to divide work among three relatively co-equal participants in a small video production company is to have one person be producer, another director, and the third as editor.

Whichever way you choose to assign editing responsibility, the producer will be in charge of arranging and negotiating for use of editing or special effects equipment that is needed. Just as with the production itself, conflicts can easily arise when things don't quite work out as planned. What happens when the producer has arranged for twenty hours of editing time, but after twenty hours the editor reports than an additional forty hours will be needed? Again, the producer should act as the buffer between the editor and the client—offering options and apologies as needed. (This is one good reason why the producer should not edit the project him or herself, so he or she can act as an intermediary.)

With very low budget projects where you're doing all the editing in-house, post-production time overruns may not actually cost more money, but may simply delay other projects from being worked on, by tying up the facility. These ramifications should still be carefully considered, to prevent egos from clashing. No one likes to hear someone say, "Your project will have to wait because mine is taking longer than expected."

Big budget projects generally have a post-production supervisor who is in charge of making sure that every element of the editing process comes in on-time and within the budget. This includes picture editing, adding sound effects, recording music, preparing titles, optical and electronic special effects like slow motion, etc. The post production supervisor manages the project as it works its way through editing and sound mixing

Distribution

After post-production is completed and you have a final edited master, the producer generally takes over, handling all aspects of distribution. On a low budget public access cable TV show, this may just mean driving over to the cable company and dropping off the tape. Making wedding videos and industrials, this may mean arranging to have dubs made, printing up labels for them, addressing envelopes to mail them in, etc.

Producers of low budget video should take care to give a properly labelled dub of the completed project to every important person in the production. Actors and actresses thrive on their ability to show off their talents through demo reels, as do camera crew, sound technicians, lighting crew, and editors. It is the producer's responsibility to give each a copy—especially when these people have worked for little or no pay.

On a larger budget, the producer may negotiate for distribution through a professional distributor, or may independently print up posters, press releases, and other items to help promote the project. While the producer is handling these mundane tasks, the director might go on tour, working the talk-show circuit on TV and radio to promote the project. During this phase, the director acts like the front man (or woman) for the project, while the producer is the behind-the-scenes person pulling all the strings.

At the highest Hollywood budget levels, much of the distribution has been arranged before production begins. An executive producer typically owns a large production company that simultaneously creates several or even dozens of programs. By virtue of his track record (unfortunately, most top studio bosses are men) he can secure investments in new projects, and hire top talent to execute them. Once a deal is put together, the executive producer leaves most of the nitty gritty work to the producer.

Often a deal will be presented to a production company by an agency that represents directors, scriptwriters, and actors—the agency has essentially taken over the primary role of putting the creative elements together, and is offering a take-it-or-leave-it package deal to the production company. When big name stars and directors are involved, the production company usually takes it. Such deals typically include distribution companies as investors—the cable-TV and home-video distribution rights have been pre-sold as a way of raising money for production.

This may sound like a great way to raise millions of dollars for a production, but it also carries the curse of creativity by committee. The worst thing for a director is to have representatives from the home video distribution company and cable-TV network appear on the set while shooting is taking place, putting their two-cents in about how things should be done. One of the jobs of the producer is to help insulate the director from such interference.

Staying Friends

This advice is intended to help small production companies get started organizing tasks and avoiding duplicate efforts and conflict. Two people who have worked together for years, intuitively filling in for each other whenever needed, may find the strict division of roles outlined here absurd. On the other hand, two people who meet at a trade show and decide to go into business together may find this invaluable as a way of organizing their small video production business.

Organization will impress clients: Even if both of you attend meetings together, the client will probably be more impressed if one of your business cards says, "Producer," on it while the other says, "Director," rather than having both cards say "Co-producer." In a small video production company, where union contracts and work rules are not a factor, there is of course a limit to how seriously you should take these roles. In a professional level network shoot, for example, union work rules may forbid a camera operator from touching a piece of sound equipment, but such constraints don't apply to low-budget productions. If you find yourself, acting as director, screaming at the top of your lungs to the producer things like, "I am the director and what I say goes!" then you know you have gone too far. Don't over-do it.

In the final analysis, both of you will have a relatively similar understanding of the circumstances, and you should recognize this in your conversations. Don't be pompous. Either of you could do either job. Don't act like you are the director because you are more talented at if (even in you think you are!)—act and speak like you are the director because it provided an efficient way to divvy up the work.

The most important skills in any working relationship are listening and compromise.

25   Travelling with a Camcorder

Low budget video producers travel with their camcorders. What better way could there be to incorporate exotic backgrounds in your productions? After all, when you're shooting low budget, practically all shooting is "on location".

Whether you're schlepping the kids to Disney World, or shooting a documentary about trekking through Nepal, a camcorder also adds fun and captures memories in exciting ways that still photographs can't match. But you'll have to work a bit harder, and take a few precautions to ensure success and prevent thievery.

In addition to the tapes you bring back home, the camcorder will also become part of the travel experience. From getting friends and family to play "host" in travelogues, to keeping batteries charged, to getting the cooperation of locals while you shoot, to worrying about the camcorder getting stolen, there's no question that the act of carrying a camcorder changes the way you travel.

My favorite camcorder travel story took place in northern Thailand a couple of years ago. My friend and I had taken a cab to the outskirts of town to check on some train schedules, and were trying to explain to a different cab driver that we needed to go to the post office next. The driver spoke no English, French, or Spanish, we spoke no Thai, and we were reverting to hand signals when I remembered that I had shot some footage of the big radio tower at the post office earlier in the day. I found the spot on the tape and convinced the driver to look in the viewfinder as it played back. "Of course!" he must have said in Thai—a big smile came across his face, and there were lots of laughs all around. In a small yet meaningful way, video had brought us together, and it certainly got us to back to the post office.

What To Bring

We all know the nerdy image of the guy with five cameras strapped around his neck, his belt bursting with lights, meters, and other accessory gadgets, and carrying a bag or two of tripods, light stands, and other larger accoutrements.

How close you're willing to come to this extreme depends on what kind of shooting you're doing, as well as how much you're willing to carry the extra stuff that can improve your production.

If you're shooting a documentary, making an independent film/video, for example, then you will indeed need to bring a full set of professional accessories—lights, microphones, tripod, etc.

Most vacationers bring none of this—just the camcorder, charger, and perhaps an extra blank tape. For those who are willing to carry a bit more than just the minimum, here is a list of recommended accessories to bring along:

- An extra battery for the camcorder.
- A low power accessory light.
- A wireless lapel microphone system; extra batteries for it.
- A pack of lens cleaning tissues and lens cleaning fluid.
- Lightweight in-the-ear type headphones.
- An electrical extension cord with 3-way outlet.
- A 220 to 110 voltage converter, adapters, for foreign travel.
- A lightweight, very small tripod, such as the Culman Magic I or II; or the Steadicam JR support system.
- At least twice as much blank tape as you intend to shoot.
- A bag to carry all this stuff in; foam for shock protection.

Of all these accessories, the one I have found most useful in shooting travel tapes is, oddly enough, the wireless microphone. This may seem a bit advanced for casual travelogues, but it can really add a lot of fun and excitement to the tape.

Suppose you're in Paris at the Eiffel Tower, for example. The most boring thing to do is shoot the Eiffel Tower by itself, so most people get their travel companions to stand in front of the Eiffel Tower and wave, proving that they were there. This can be funny for about two seconds, after which time it wears thin. Generally, you have to stand ten or twenty feet back from your companions to get them properly framed in a wide shot with the Eiffel Tower. They can't speak, because they're too far from the camcorder's built-in microphone, which picks up only wind noise. That's where the wireless microphone system comes in.

Instead of recording wind during all those scenic wide shots, the wireless microphone lets you record people talking. This in turn gives you the opportunity to cut from the scenic wide shot to close-ups of the people talking, creating more variety in the shots and a more interesting tape.

Similarly, you can sit in a sidewalk cafe, with camcorder resting on the table (an improvised tripod), while your friend across the street roams about and narrates, using the wireless microphone.

What type of tape should you bring? The best available for your camcorder. It's true that in many cases the same tape is packaged in different boxes and sold as different grades, and there's a lot of blank tape voodoo out there. But when you're travelling, a minor difference like having a more environmentally sealed box, or having stronger backing material, can matter. As always, stick to name brands—3M, Fuji, TDK, Maxell, Sony, JVC, Panasonic, Canon, etc. A cheap tape by one of these name brands is usually a better bet than a top of the line tape by an unknown manufacturer. Note also that blank videocassettes are probably less expensive in the U.S. than anywhere else on the planet. You may pay through the nose for a blank tape in a tourist trap shop, or in a foreign country, so bring enough with you.

How to Shoot

Before you start shooting the stewardess' entire presentation on emergency aircraft procedures, or half an hour of ocean waves splashing up against your hotel room's balcony, you should at least have some idea of who you expect to watch this tape, and how much work you intend to put into making it.

The vast majority of camcorder users want to record home movies—the video equivalent of snapshots—without a lot of fuss and bother. The intended audience is family and friends.

More ambitious projects may be to shoot a program for public access, or to make a low budget independent film or rock video on location. In these cases, you're shooting to edit—gathering raw footage that will be pieced together after you get back.

But for most casual camcorder users, such post-production editing is too involved, and creates an unnecessary obligation to labor for tedious hours long after the travel is over. There's nothing worse than coming back with hours of rambling footage, requiring weeks of work to edit down to something interesting.

The best strategy, for casual travel taping, is to edit in the camcorder, as you shoot. Be aggressive about going back over boring parts and recording new material (assuming you have a flying erase head). Keep each shot short. When in doubt, pause the tape. Err on the side of recording too little, not too much.

If you're travelling with others, make them the stars. Get them to introduce things and structure the tape—record a beginning and end to the whole travelogue. Get your travel companions to ham it up and explain where you are and what you are doing at each point in the trip. Have them do this quickly.

Look for visual cues to shoot that will indicate where you are, and what time it is—like road signs and sunsets. Spice up the production with "on the way" footage—such as a shot of the driver of the car followed by a shot through the windshield of the road ahead. Keep these shots short, and you'll have some slick connecting sequences that help break up and liven the finished tape.

Most tapes end up structured chronologically—beginning at the beginning of the trip, and ending at the end. This may seem natural and easy, but it is by no means necessary. Especially with the 8mm and Hi8 formats, it is very easy to record over sections of a tape, or jump ahead to a spot in the middle and later fill in the beginning. Bringing headphones along makes it much easier to review footage that you've shot and decide where to record over parts that are boring.

One discipline that I have used with varying success, and recommend purely as an experiment, is to purchase a 30-minute tape (or 15 or 20 minutes) for the travel video. I convince myself that I will absolutely limit all recording to this amount of time. If the tape fills up, I must go back and find spots to record over. Of course, I always have a spare blank tape in my accessory bag just in case, but barring some incredible photo opportunity (Castro flees to Key West while I'm shooting the sunset, for instance) I'll try to keep the faith and limit my running time.

. . . .

Security

Even the cheapest camcorders are expensive, and inevitably the fear that your camcorder will be stolen rears its ugly head in your travels. Suppose you're at the beach with your friend or spouse, and both of you want to go in the water at the same time. Can you leave your camcorder in a bag on the beach? Should you have left it in the hotel room—even though a maid comes in to clean?

There are no clear answers to these questions—the more you travel with a camcorder, the more you develop a "feel" for each situation. Here are some general tips to guide your security precautions, but there is a lot of subjectivity here.

Most importantly, exercise "street smarts"—even in remote locations. If you're at the beach as described above, for example, and you're going to leave the camcorder to go for a swim, keep the camcorder in the bag until after you've gone swimming—don't announce that you have it and you're abandoning it to everyone on the beach!

Whenever possible, find someone to keep an eye on it. Take turns swimming. Travel with large groups makes this easier. But with large groups, ask one specific person to keep a watchful eye—don't assume the entire crowd will somehow prevent theft.

Many hotels offer "safe deposit box" service for valuables at the front desk, and implore guests not to leave valuables in the rooms. But unfortunately, these boxes are often too small to hold a camcorder. When you check in, ask to see how big such boxes are.

There are many tricks for hiding valuables in a hotel room, but unfortunately, experienced hotel thieves know most of them too. You're looking for spots where the maids shouldn't be poking around—deep in drawers filled with clothes, in obscure closet cubby holes, etc. If you get into this kind of hide-and-go-seek mind game, remember: to a thief, an empty 8mm videocassette box means there's a camcorder too. Hide everything.

One "failsafe" tip for protecting your most valuable footage: take the tape out of the camcorder, and store it separately, as soon as it has something recorded on it that you'd be devastated by if lost. Keep the tape where you keep your absolutely most valuable travel items—with your air tickets, passport, and wallet.

International Travel

When you travel internationally, there are several other concerns you should consider. Voltage, of course, is at the top of the list—will you be able to plug in your camcorder's recharger in the country you're visiting?

Most European countries have 220-volt household outlets—double the standard American line voltage. Some camcorder battery chargers can accommodate a range of voltages from 110 to 240, but most operate strictly on 110. If you don't have a multivoltage charger, then by all means visit Radio Shack or any other electronics store before you leave and purchase a 220 to 110 volt transformer.

In addition to the voltage variations, note there are also outlet variations. Not all 220-volt outlets are the same. Again, with a visit to Radio Shack or a well stocked electronics store you can find a kit of a half-dozen or so adapters that cover most outlet types. Fortunately, these plastic adapters are lightweight and inexpensive, making it easy to carry the whole kit whenever you travel abroad.

Some countries—especially poorer countries—are very concerned that you are not illegally importing a camcorder for the purpose of selling it. In Nepal, for example, a customs official once wrote the serial number of my camcorder right next to the passport stamp. If I did not have the camcorder when I left the country, there would be an import duty to pay. In extreme circumstances, it can be helpful to carry a photocopy of your sales slip from the camcorder purchase—to prove when and where you bought it.

Pack and Shoot

If you are traveling by air you will inevitably encounter luggage checks. It is recommended that you never pack either camcorder or recorded tapes with your checked luggage—always carry these items with your hand luggage, so they don't get lost. Inevitably, this will mean that your equipment and tapes get X-rayed. Fortunately, X-rays don't pose the danger to magnetic tapes that they do to film. It is certainly better to X-ray tapes than to walk through the metal detector with tapes in your pockets—the metal detectors use magnetic waves that can partially erase videotapes. (Also, the magnetic tapes can trip the alarm.) So the rule of thumb is: Carry photographic film in your pockets as you walk through the metal detector, but send the videotapes through the X-ray machine.

If you are carrying several accessories, like a light and wireless microphone, you may find it handy to also have several different bags that you can use to carry the equipment. The smallest bag might just hold the camcorder only—for short trips, while a larger "day pack" bag might hold the full complement of accessories.

Remember to use your camcorder but don't abuse it. Be polite with others too. Being "on camera" is work—and though most people like to ham it up on occasion, there will also be times when your spouse/travel companion is sick and tired of being in front of the camcorder. Know when to shut it off.

Don't forget to get yourself into the picture, too. Try to share the control of the camcorder with your travel companion, or at least get him or her to shoot some footage of you doing something—driving, getting dressed, asking directions, shopping, etc.

This philosophy should be applied to all your shots. Don't just shoot video postcards—shots of your travel companion(s) standing in front of famous monuments or buildings. Try to have them doing things, saying things, just to make the moving video interesting. Instead of standing statically in front of a statue, have your companion purchase a soda from a sidewalk vendor next to the statue, and shoot the exchange with the statue in the background. Then cut to a nicely framed shot of the statue.

Loosen up! If you're making home movies, and not shooting an episode for National Geographic, you can be goofy and spotty in your coverage. You don't have to capture everything on tape.

Take time to smell the flowers after you spend six hours shooting time lapse footage of them.

. . . .

International Video Standards

Although the basic principles of scanning remain the same for just about all video systems, the specific details vary from one country to another. There are three main sets of scanning standards used throughout the world—NTSC, PAL, and SECAM.

The technical differences between the three systems have served as electronic borders that insulated one culture from another. The selection of which standard is used in each country tends to follow the patterns of old colonial and geo-political borderlines. Converting a television program produced with one video standard to play on another system used to be a very expensive proposition, but thanks to low-cost digital video technology, VCRs that do the conversion have become quite inexpensive.

NTSC stands for National Television Standards Committee, a U.S. government panel that was convened in the 1950s to update the original black-and-white TV standard so that it would be compatible with color television. As mentioned earlier, the American NTSC system (also used in Japan and elsewhere) creates each frame with 525 horizontal scan lines, and approximately 30 frames are presented each second. Because of interlacing, as explained earlier, approximately 60 fields (half-frames) are thus displayed each second. (Note that in the old days of black-and-white, the field rate was precisely 60 per second. When color was added, this rated shifted slightly, to 59.94 fields per second. This slight difference is at the heart of the "drop frame" counting system, explained later in the section on "SMPTE Time Code and VITC".)

PAL is the system used throughout most of Western Europe, except for France. It offers better vertical resolution than NTSC, but there's more visible screen flicker. Each frame consists of 625 scan lines. But there are only 25 frames per second. (This is very close to the standard frame rate used in 35mm and 16mm films, which is 24 frames per second.) The interlace technique is also used in PAL, to reduce the perception of flicker—there are thus 50 fields (half frames) per seconds. PAL stands for Phase Alternate each Line—an acronym describing the technical process by which the color information is encoded in the video signal.

SECAM is used in France and most of the countries of the old Soviet Union—including Russia and Eastern Europe. It has the same number of scan lines per frame, and the same number of fields per second as PAL—625/50. What's different about SECAM is the way the color picture information gets encoded into the video signal. SECAM stands for Sequential Colors with Memory (in French), which describes the color encoding scheme. Without getting into the technicalities of what it means, suffice it to say that it makes PAL and SECAM incompatible for color, but compatible for black-and-white.

These differences in scanning rates and color encoding describe only the picture (video) part of the TV signal. Internationally, there are also differences in the way the audio signal gets mixed with the video, and broadcast over the air (or on cable-TV). The differences in broadcasting standards help explain why a PAL TV from one country may not properly receive sound when used in another country. But for the purpose of video editing—in which the sound is recorded separately (as explained in the next sections)—a PAL videocassette recording made in one country should be able to playback on a PAL VCR in another country.

You can mix and match the three international video standards with the various videocassette tape formats described in the following sections. Each of the major videocassette formats (VHS, 8mm, Betamax, etc.) is capable of recording NTSC, PAL, or SECAM. To playback a tape successfully, you need to match both tape format, and recording system. It's a confusing situation.

To help simplify playback of recordings made in other countries, several companies offer "multi-standard" VCRs and TV sets, which are capable of operating at two or all three of the international standards. Note that a multi-standard VCR is still limited to just a single tape format, however (such as VHS).

With most older multi-standard VCRs, no conversion takes place—the signal remains in its original scanning system, and a multi-standard TV is also needed to display it. However, some of the newest multi-standard VCRs incorporate digital video conversion systems, so that a PAL or SECAM tape can be displayed on an American NTSC TV—and can also be edited onto another NTSC-compatible videocassette.

The following list shows which countries use each of the three video scanning systems, and what sort of electricity is available:

Country	Video	Voltage/Frequency(Hz)
Abu Dhabi	PAL	240/50
Afghanistan	PAL	220/50
Alaska(USA)	NTSC	110/60
Albania	SECAM	220/50
Algeria	PAL	220/50
Andorra	PAL	220/50

Country	Video	Voltage/Frequency(Hz)
Angola	PAL	210/50
Antigua	NTSC	230/60
Antilles	NTSC	120/60
Argentina	PAL	220/50
Australia	PAL	240/50
Austria	PAL	220/50
Azores	PAL	220/50
(US Forces)	NTSC	
Bahamas	NTSC	110/60
Bahrain	PAL	230/50
Bangladesh	PAL	210/50
Barbados	NTSC	110/50
Belgium	PAL	220/50
Bermuda	NTSC	110/60
Bolivia	NTSC	120/50
Botswana	PAL	220/50
Brazil	PAL	110/50
Brunei	PAL	230/50
Bulgaria	SECAM	220/50
Burma	NTSC	230/50
Burundi		220/50
Cambodia		120/50
Cameroon		127/50
Canada	NTSC	110/60
Canary Is.	PAL	220/50
Central African Republic		220/50
Chad		220/50
Chile	NTSC	210/50
China	PAL	210/50
Colombia	SECAM	110/60
Congo	SECAM	120/50
Costa Rica	NTSC	120/60
Cuba	NTSC	120/60
Cyprus	SECAM	240/50
Czechoslovakia	SECAM	220/50
Denmark	PAL	220/50
Diego Garcia	NTSC	

Country	Video	Voltage/Frequency(Hz)
Dominican Rep.	NTSC	110/60
Dubai	PAL	220/50
Ecuador	NTSC	110/60
Egypt	SECAM	220/50
El Salvador	NTSC	115/60
Ethiopia	PAL	220/50
Fiji	PAL	240/50
Finland	PAL	220/50
France	SECAM	220/50
Gabon	SECAM	220/50
Gambia		
Germany, East	SECAM	220/50
Germany, West	PAL	220/50
(US Forces)	NTSC	220/50
Ghana	PAL	220/50
Gibraltar	PAL	240/50
Greece	PAL	220/50
Greenland	NTSC	220/50
Guadeloupe	SECAM	220/60
Guam	NTSC	110/60
Guatemala	NTSC	120/60
Guyana (French)	SECAM	220/50
Haiti	SECAM	115/60
Hawaii	NTSC	115/60
Honduras	NTSC	110/60
Hong Kong	PAL	200/50
Hungary	SECAM	220/50
Iceland	PAL	220/50
India	PAL	230/50
Indonesia	PAL	220/50
Iran	SECAM	220/50
Iraq	SECAM	220/50
Ireland	PAL	220/50
Israel	PAL	230/50
Italy	PAL	220/50
Ivory Coast	SECAM	220/50
Jamaica	NTSC	110/50

Country	Video	Voltage/Frequency(Hz)
Japan	NTSC	100/60
Jordan	PAL	220/50
Kenya	PAL	240/50
Korea, North	SECAM	110/60
Korea, South	NTSC	110/60
Kuwait	PAL	240/50
Lebanon	SECAM	220/50
Liberia	PAL	120/60
Libya	SECAM	230/50
Luxembourg	PAL/SECAM	220/50
Madagascar	SECAM	220/50
Madeira	PAL	220/50
Malawi		230/50
Malaysia	PAL	230/50
Malta	PAL	240/50
Martinique	SECAM	220/50
Mauritania		
Mauritius	SECAM	230/50
Mexico	NTSC	120/60
Midway Is.	NTSC	
Monaco	SECAM	220/50
Mongolia		
Morocco	SECAM	220/50
Mozambique		220/50
Netherlands	PAL	220/50
New Caledonia	SECAM	220/50
New Zealand	PAL	230/50
Nicaragua	NTSC	120/60
Niger		220/50
Nigeria	PAL	230/50
Norway	PAL	230/50
Okinawa	NTSC	
Oman	PAL	220/50
Pakistan	PAL	230/50
Panama	NTSC	120/60
Paraguay	NTSC	220/50
Peru	NTSC	220/60

Country	Video	Voltage/Frequency(Hz)
Philippines	NTSC	110/60
Poland	SECAM	220/50
Portugal	PAL	220/50
Puerto Rico	NTSC	110/60
Qatar	PAL	240/50
Reunion	SECAM	220/50
Rumania	SECAM	220/50
Russia	SECAM	220/50
Rwanda		220/50
Sabah/Sarawak	PAL	240/50
Samoa	NTSC	230/50
Saudi Arabia	SECAM	220/50
Senegal	SECAM	220/50
Sierra Leone	PAL	230/50
Singapore	PAL	230/50
Somalia		230/50
South Africa	PAL	220/50
Soviet Union	SECAM	220/50
Spain	PAL	220/50
Sri Lanka	PAL	230/50
St.Kitts	NTSC	220/60
St.Pierre	SECAM	115/50
Sudan	PAL	240/50
Surinam	NTSC	115/60
Swaziland	PAL	230/50
Sweden	PAL	220/50
Switzerland	PAL	220/50
Syria	SECAM	220/50
Tahiti	SECAM	240/60
Taiwan	NTSC	110/60
Tanzania	PAL	230/50
Thailand	PAL	220/50
Tibet		120/50
Togo	SECAM	220/50
Trinidad/Tobago	NTSC	115/60
Trust Islands (Micronesia)	NTSC	

Country	Video	Voltage/Frequency(Hz)
Tunisia	SECAM	220/50
Turkey	PAL	220/50
Ukraine	SECAM	220/50
United Arab Emirates	PAL	220/50
Uganda	PAL	240/50
United Kingdom	PAL	240/50
Uruguay	PAL	220/50
USA	NTSC	120/60
USSR (former)	SECAM	220/50
Venezuela	NTSC	
Vietnam	NTSC	230/50
Virgin Is.	NTSC	110/60
Yugoslavia	PAL	220/50
Zaire	SECAM	220/50
Zambia	PAL	230/50
Zanzibar	PAL	220/50
Zimbabwe	PAL	230/50

PART IV

. . . .

New Media and Opportunities

26   Cable TV

Cable TV is losing its high-tech luster, and America's communications infrastructure could well use an overhaul. The federal government deregulated the cable industry in 1984, re-regulated rates in 1992, and then deregulated the entire communications industry in 1996. But despite all the hype of the information superhighway, cable companies appear to be going very slow towards building any sort of video dial tone service on a large scale. As in the early days of cable-TV, a few small-scale experimental two-way systems get maximum press coverage for a minimal investment in infrastructure.

Democracy is fragile, and dependent on free speech — yet criticism of the cable industry usually ignores this broader context of telecommunications policy, and turns into a gripe session about high rates and bad reception.

In the 1970s, there was a lot of hype about the "community programming" possibilities of cable-TV, promising dozens of local special interest channels. But the reality, in the early 1990s, is that public access, leased access, and college or city-run channels are generally too local, and low budget, to attract much interest. Saturday Night Live's "Wayne's World" reflects the current state of cable's "community programming", and the cynical mockery of free speech it represents.

Americans are woven into a national fabric of special interests that transcend municipal boundaries. Sure, some issues are local — like installing traffic lights, and school board elections — but most people's interests are shared by others all across the country — interests like being entertained, informed about world and national events, hobbies, etc.

The bottleneck of programming flow is at the local cable-TV systems. There are currently about ninety national cable-TV networks offering round-the-clock programming, but most local cable systems can't possibly carry all these channels. Most systems have just 54 channels, and that number must include local TV stations. The cost of producing 24-hour a day television is getting cheaper (just look at all the home shopping channels), yet it gets ever harder to get a new channel onto cable.

What does the cable industry do to alleviate this? Instead of expanding capacity, they fight F.C.C. "must carry" rules that require them to carry local TV stations (and thus open up a few channels). "Rebuilding" and upgrading of cable systems is usually delayed until there are outcries of public pressure at franchise (license) renewal time, and channel capacity usually goes up to just 54 or 75 channels.

America needs a far more radical cable-TV rebuild: We need a system that can "switch". Cable technology should be structured more like the phone system—a "switched network" that can connect from any point to any other point.

The mail offers such point to point connections for thousands of magazines, newsletters, and journals; the telephone system offers instant audio communications anywhere.

Imagine if a new magazine was told by the U.S. Postal Service, "Sorry, we can't deliver it—we don't have the capacity." Yet that's exactly what local cable companies tell new TV networks. Other elements of our communications infrastructure—the postal service and the phone system—increase capacity to keep up with demand.

But cable-TV plays by its own rules. Each new network must negotiate to get onto local cable systems, and in most cities that will mean some other channel gets dropped. The "marketplace" of programming a local cable TV system is a corrupt, sleazy backroom world where executives declare themselves to be in the best position to decide which networks each community should see. They refuse to give their customers the full choice of available cable channels.

After all, why should local cable systems expand capacity, when they're in cahoots with the very same companies—the big networks—that want to maintain their current audience shares by leaving things alone? HBO, Cinemax, and USA, for example, are owned by Time Warner, which also owns hundreds of big city cable systems. The big cable networks are owned by the same companies that determine how many channels there will be in each local community—so there's little incentive to expand capacity and bring newcomers in.

These cable conglomerates also limit access to premium channel "scrambling" technology—allowing just a handful of "pay" cable networks to coexist on each local system. New cable networks cannot "sell" directly to the public—they must raise money through advertising.

There's a natural limit to how many channels can be carried by a single cable—even using fiber optic cable. There's also obvious inefficiency, bringing dozens of channels into the home that no one watches. You can only watch one at a time.

The technical solution to the local cable bottleneck, as embodied in our national phone system, is to bring in just the desired signal — through electronic switching. With switched cable, you'd request a channel from the central office, and instantly see it on your TV. Hundreds if not thousands of channels could thus be available.

A switched, national cable-TV system would offer benefits beyond more television programming choices. High speed communication between computers, videophone service, access to video libraries (request a film and see it a few seconds later), are among the many new services made possible. (Imagine what will become of phone sex!)

Despite all the grumbling about how America is falling behind Japan and Germany, we still excel in our information industries — Hollywood films, TV, the music business, publishing, computer software, etc. Switched cable would serve as a highway for all these information industries. We need a national communications highway for video and other electronic signals — one that is accessible and democratic.

America's cable-TV is rapidly looking like a technological dinosaur. In Japan and Europe, development of switched, two-way cable systems have been underway for years, with the national telephone companies leading the way.

In America, phone companies are barred from offering phone and cable-TV service in the same community. The cable industry says the phone companies, with their large size and guaranteed profits, would have an unfair competitive advantage. But consumers might benefit from cable-TV via telephone companies.

The phone system has a long history of operating as a "common carrier" — carrying anyone's message for a fee, and constantly upgrading and expanding capacity to meet demand. This is something that cable operators have steadfastly refused to do — insisting that each local cable company is like an "electronic publisher" whose free speech rights entitle them to pick and choose which networks to show to their communities.

For two centuries Americans have persevered to keep information flowing freely. Few Americans support book-burning, yet most seem perfectly complacent about local censorship of cable TV programming.

If DBS — Direct Broadcast Satellites — catch on in the next decade, then cable may be forced to upgrade to switching technology, just to survive. To bring a television channel into forty or fifty million homes, cable is an expensive delivery system. A single antenna in space (DBS) can beam dozens of channels into every home much more efficiently.

For the networks, DBS offers another opportunity to distribute programming, but for local TV stations and cable systems, DBS threatens to bypass them entirely. If people can watch NBC, or HBO, directly from DBS, then why should they tune into their local NBC or ESPN affiliate—especially if it has inferior picture and sound quality?

Local broadcasters may become relegated to second-rate status, perhaps spinning rock video's, and mimicking radio formats like all-news and talk. Regular TV may become like the AM radio of video, as better technologies become available.

If DBS becomes more widely accessible, cable must offer something better - technologically—than carrying the same networks with local ads. That technical edge is available through a switchednetwork: cable could finally deliver on its promise of freedom of choice. Let us, as a matter of national policy, create a real marketplace for video programming—whether it be built by the cable industry, or the phone companies.

27   Public Access

Wayne's World may be the most famous public access cable-TV program, but of course, it isn't real. The variety of zany and serious programs it is based on is staggering, however. They're produced largely by ordinary people and organizations. In New York City, where public access is probably more active than anywhere in the country, the programs fill up the better part of the day on two public access channels. There are talk shows where people sit around and discuss housing, health, social services, education, investing, exercise, newspapers, and dozens of other "serious" topics. There are entertainment programs galore—mostly *Tonight Show* style variety shows, which sometimes degenerate into a bunch of guys sitting around with cans of beer, cracking jokes with one another. Then there are the more abstract "art" shows, and shows about how easy it is for anyone to walk into the studio and make their own TV programs.

If the pen is mightier than the sword, then the video camera may prove to be mightier than the machine gun. Television is such a powerful influence in our society that it almost seems trite to repeat all the statistics—the number of people who rely on TV news for their view of world events, the number of hours children spend watching, etc.

America has more than two-hundred million people who watch TV every day, but less than one percent of that population is capable of creating their own messages through television. Like "literacy workers" in third-world countries who teach the population how to write as well as read, there are groups of "video literacy workers" in America who feel that learning how to use the TV medium on a grassroots level has similar political urgency. The name of their movement is "Public Access".

You don't need a political message to utilize public access— you can use video to communicate about all sorts of ideas— drama, information, emotions, poetry, sports, art, natural beauty, music, etc.

Public access is a way to show your video productions to other people in your community, via the local cable TV system. The rules of public access usually require the cable system to show just about anything you care to put on, for free (although some censor-ship regarding nudity and/or obscenity often occurs). The time is generally available on a first come, first served basis. Depending on your local situation, you may also be able to get free or low cost use of a TV studio, editing facilities, and industrial quality video equipment.

Although your neighbors may not be all that interested in see-ing your children's birthday parties, other common home-video camera applications, such as making travelogues of your summer vacations, or local Little League games, can be quite appealing for people to watch. Remember the documentary "An American Family" which appeared on PBS in the seventies? (Albert Brooks directed a brilliant spoof on this idea with his film *Real Life.*) People love to see other people caught up in day to day stress, ex-posing their personalities before the camera. The goal of public access is to de-mystify television in Order To Democratize It, And Simple, Personal Productions are encouraged.

History of Public Access

Public access got started in the early 1970s, during a time of great social upheaval, student unrest, community organizing, musical experimentation, and all the other things we've come to think of as "The Sixties". The first low-cost black and white video equip-ment had just become available from Sony, and New York's cable TV system, like most around the country, had lots of empty chan-nels to fill. After all, it would be another five to ten years before satellites came into vogue for distributing national cable TV net-works. Public access was heralded as a forum which could em-power voices in the community who felt their ideas were being denied expressive outlet on conventional broadcast television. New York's TV stations reach some twenty million people, and small issues like the need for a street light on a particular corner, can get glossed over by TV stations trying to cover a sprawling megalopolis.

Additionally, minority voices often felt that mainstream media cov-ered their issues with the bias of "the establishment", and that if the tools and training were made available for people to present their own messages, greater understanding and political empowerment could be achieved. The City of New York pioneered the creation of rules and structure which would allow any citizen to air their views over the cable TV system, and the Federal Communications Commission (F.C.C.) soon created similar regulations nationwide.

In the late seventies and early eighties, public access usually meant that cable companies had to offer up not just time on their channels, but also studios and portable video equipment, as well as training to use this equipment properly. In many cities, independent organizations not affiliated with the local cable company received grants to operate public access production facilities, thus removing the taint of cable company control and censorship.

Since the advent of the camcorder, it has become commonplace for ordinary citizens to own their own production equipment. Although a well-lit studio with live phone-in capability and electronic editing systems are still beyond the means of most home video users (and therefore necessitates shared facilities), it is increasingly common for public access producers to put together their own programs using a simple camcorder and VCR at home. But many cable companies still discriminate against the consumer tape formats, and demand that public access producers transfer everything to $3\frac{1}{4}$" before they'll air it.

Public Access and the First Amendment

The First Amendment to the U.S. Constitution guarantees freedom of speech and freedom of the press, but applying these concepts to the era of electronic communications can be tricky. After all, freedom of the press offers liberty only to those who own a press. Although most newspapers voluntarily print "Letters to the Editor", the paper's publisher has full control over the content of the paper. Broadcasters—TV and radio stations—do not enjoy similar freedom, because the limited number of broadcast frequencies requires that the government pick and choose who it awards licenses to, and thus obligates them to serve "the public interest" by providing fair, balanced programming.

Cable television is in a category all by itself. Cable systems don't receive licenses from the federal government, but are franchised by the local government to operate as local monopolies. Each municipal government negotiates its own franchise agreement, creating thousands of different sets of rules across the country regarding cable regulation. Meanwhile, the owners of cable television systems claim that, despite their government granted monopolies, cable systems are the electronic equivalent of printing presses, and the government has no right to say what they must carry on their channels. Thus, the issue of public access pits the "free speech" of individual producers against the "free speech" of the cable system owner.

Public access is a unique accommodation which attempts to balance this conflict between the free speech of individuals and the free press of giant media corporations. No other mass medium—not print, radio, broadcast TV, or film—guarantees people the right to say whatever they want using someone else's facilities. Understandably, most cable companies don't particular like this idea, but begrudgingly go along with it, when forced to, as the price of doing business. The battle for public access has a long history of public hearings, legal maneuvering, backroom deals, and judicial challenges.

The Cable Communications Act

After years of court wrangling, Congress passed the Cable Communications Policy Act of 1984. Previously, the F.C.C. had created its own rules regarding cable, but without a clear mandate from Congress to regulate cable, the F.C.C. was losing many courtroom cases. In a nutshell, the Cable Act makes no specific rules about public access, but gives local governments the authority to require public access channels as part of the franchise agreement (previous court decisions had denied this authority), and the muscle of the F.C.C. to enforce the local provisions.

More significantly, the Cable Act does set aside specific channel capacity for commercial use by "persons unaffiliated with the operator"—that is, independent program suppliers. If the cable system has between 36 and 54 channels, 10 percent must be set aside for such use. With 55 or more channels, 15 percent must be set aside, and with fewer than 36 channels, only the local franchise agreement applies.

Leased Access: Pay for What You Get

The concept of making channel time available on a rental basis, rather than for free, is called "leased access". A cable operator can lease time by the hour (in which case it's just like public access except that you pay a fee, usually under $100 per hour), by the month, or year. The Cable Act's requirement of leased access may, in the long run, prove more important for the democratization of television than local public access regulations. The reason for this is economic: A public access producer is by definition a non-commercial entity. There is no opportunity to ever make money with a public access program, because most local franchises forbid advertising or other commercial activity on public access channels.

With a leased access program the potential exists to develop revenue, which, if pumped back into the program, can lead to better, more professional production values which might ultimately become competitive with slick Hollywood programs. For example, suppose you're interested in photography and start a leased access program about your hobby. You can go to a local camera store and ask them to sponsor your program, at say, fifty dollars per half-hour show. As the show develops an audience you can charge more for the sponsorship, and get other people, such as a local photo club, to kick in money as well. Then you can expand into other communities, leasing time, selling ads to other local merchants, and so on.

Ultimately you create your own network of cable systems. As more money flows, you can hire people to help produce and edit the program, and rent satellite time to distribute the program more efficiently than mailing tapes from one system to another. It may lose its grassroots quality, but its success means that the television medium is opening up to a wider diversity of program producers than the traditional Hollywood mills. It is the video equivalent of someone who opens a small grocery store, and ends up owning a chain of supermarkets.

Satellite Access and Nationwide Programs

Public access is inherently low budget and local. It fosters video literacy, serves as a binding community force, informs people about local issues, and most importantly, it serves as an outlet for the creative expression of people who are sick and tired of being couch potatoes. But most of the politically motivated people who get involved with public access really wish they could reach bigger audiences than a single cable system can provide. After all, most of the controversial issues today—defense, abortion, pollution, energy, civil rights, etc.—are really national, or at least regional in scope.

The next frontier for access is not at the local cable headquarters, but 22,000 miles up in space: the satellites which feed network programming to thousands of cable systems nationwide. Satellite time can be purchased for about five hundred dollars an hour—more than most ragtag producers can afford on a weekly basis, but affordable to some public access organizations. Deep Dish TV, in New York, is one organization of public access producers which has rented satellite time to present excerpts of public access programs from across the country. These efforts may eventually lead to the creation of a nationwide public access network.

Alliance for Community Media

The Alliance for Community Media (formerly The National Federation of Local Cable Programmers is an organization which has been consistently promoting public access: to federal state and local governments, cable companies, and independent producers. They can help you organize public access in your own community, help you resolve disputes regarding access with your local cable company, and they also organize an annual competition of locally produced programs to help motivate would-be producers.

The Alliance also publishes The Cable Programming Resources Directory, which includes listings of hundreds of public access centers across the country. This book can help you locate a public access facility near to where you live, and has information about cable networks and how independent producers can sell their programs to national networks.

How to Get Public Access on Your Local Cable System

- 1 Study your local cable system. Figure out how many channels it has, and what's on each. Pay careful attention to any "cable classified" channels—these will often give information about how to obtain public access time on the system. If no info is given, proceed as follows:
- 2 Call the cable company's executive offices for your local cable system (not their national headquarters, but their local administrative offices). Do not call the billing department. Ask to speak with the Director of Programming, or if no such person exists, ask for the General Manager. Be polite, but firm. Explain that you would like to present a program over their cable system and are inquiring about the procedures for obtaining public access time.

    Find out if anyone else is presenting public access programs on the cable system. (Get their phone numbers and make contact.) Find out if the cable system operates a production center, or if there is an independent public access production center in your community.

    If the cable company accepts videocassettes for playback on their system, what format(s) do they accept? If they only take $3/_4$" U-matic, ask if you can dub a copy of your $1/_2$" VHS or Beta tape up to $3/_4$" if you bring your own VCR or camcorder in. (If not, you'll have to find a facility which will make the transfer for you, usually for about $25 per hour tape.)

- **3** If the cable company officials say they offer no provisions for public access, ask about leased access, and if the answer is no, ask if they produce any local programming at all. Rather than taking an adversarial posture (trying to use legal pressure to get them to open up their channels), you may find a more successful and educational route by offering to volunteer to help them with local productions. This can be particularly effective if they are cable casting city council meetings (the most common local programming cable systems produce), because you will be rubbing elbows with the local power brokers who can help you get your own shows onto cable later.

- **4** If you get a complete brush-off from the cable company, then fighting for your rights is the only way to go. DO NOT GIVE UP! Many others, including myself, have gone down the same road. However, do not start fighting with company officials just yet. Get off the phone politely, tell them you'll be getting back in touch with them in the near future, and start doing some research.

  Contact City Hall, and ask for the department which is in charge of franchising. Tell them you want to see a copy of the cable television franchise, and that you are specifically interested in those provisions which relate to public access, community programming, leased access, local programming, government access, and educational access. Make photocopies. If such provisions exist (they usually do, even when no public access is going on) ask the city official in charge of franchise enforcement whether anyone has ever tried to get the company to live up to its agreement with the city before. You may find that you have a strong ally at City Hall, or you may get the names of other citizens who have inquired about public access.

  If there are no public access or leased access provisions, find out when the franchise will be up for renewal. Most franchises last fifteen years. Often, just the threat of making a big stink about public access at renewal time will get cable companies to concede the point now. Call Congress at (202)-224-3121, ask for the office of your Congressperson, and have them send you a copy (it's free) of public law 98-549, the Cable Communications Policy Act of 1984.

- **5** Call the cable system's General Manager or Program Director back, and make an appointment to see them. When you meet, be polite but firm. Remember that you are basically asking them to give you, for free, a piece of their money-making business. Try to stress the idea that they will be better serving the local community, living up to promises previously made, and generally bolstering their image. Don't threaten them with legal action unless there appears to be no other choice.

- 6 If all else fails, cite the provisions of the local franchise, sections 611 and 612 of the Cable Act, and explain that you are prepared to pursue this issue through legal action. Ask them to think it over.

- 7 Call the F.C.C. at (202) 632-7000, ask to speak with the Cable TV Bureau, and tell them you think that your local cable company is in violation of its franchise and the Cable Act, and you'd like to file a complaint.

- 8 Keep nagging the cable company. Be cordial about it, but let them know that you are not giving up. Try to find a few other people in your community who are also interested in public access, and form an impromptu group—The Hooterville Public Access Producers' Organization, for example. Have each person in the group call the cable company every week, creating the impression that there is a groundswell of activity and that this wave will not be stopped. Nine out of ten times no legal action is required—a bit of pestering is usually all it takes.

28   Finding Funding

Practically anyone who has ever played around with a video camcorder for an afternoon has fantasized about shooting a big production, with lots of fancy equipment, talented people, and with plenty of money thrown at you for sitting in the director's throne.

But are these delusions of grandeur, or could you ever possibly get funding for your pet video project? To get someone else to pay for your production sounds ideal, doesn't it? Unfortunately, it can also be a real burn, for those who are not prepared for the "real world" of TV and video art financing.

You *can* get video projects funded, but they're not always the exact same fantasy projects you'd love to produce, direct, and star in! This basic fact of life about "the industry" is practically a Hollywood cliche. Martin Mull's recent film *Rented Lips* spoofed on this principle: a dedicated, idealistic documentary filmmaker made a package deal to produce his own film along with a pornography film. Woody Allen's *Crimes and Misdemeanors* similarly portrays a documentary filmmaker who is almost corrupted by his brother-in-law, a successful Hollywood producer.

Before you start diverting all your time and energy into fundraising for your video project, make a realistic assessment of its appeal to potential funding sources. That appeal is based not just on the merits of the project, but on your personal track record as well.

When it comes to funding, experience counts. Like the old chicken and egg dilemma: You must have a reasonably impressive track record to get some funding, but in order to build up that track record, you need funding to make tapes that establish the track record. How do you get around this Catch-22?

Usually, it's through personal circumstances. Many beginning video and filmmakers—particularly those in college or grad school—will "self-finance" some fairly elaborate productions, in order to both learn the crafts and establish a reputation. Similarly, many people get started using "other people's money" (or "OPM", as it's sometimes affectionately called), after a friend or business acquaintance offers to help finance a project. (This lofty-sounding world of money and contacts, realistically, can be as plain as having a friend of a friend offer to pay you to videotape a wedding.)

For the more ambitious projects—narrative fictions, documentaries, video art, etc.—you must ask yourself, and your associates, a series of obvious, yet easily overlooked questions: Who is the intended audience? Why would anyone want to reach them through your program? Will the technical quality of your program be suitable for the intended audience? Will funding this project risk embarrassment for the sponsors, if poor technical quality, sloppy production values, or inept creative work plague it?

Keep in mind that what constitutes good quality for one market can be completely different for another. For example, if you set up a business videotaping "family portraits" in your community—interviewing family members and distributing copies to the family—the acceptable production values would not have to be as slick as if you were trying to make a documentary about American families for network television.

Proposals

A written proposal is almost always used to describe a film or video project to potential funding sources. Depending on the nature of your particular project, certain potential funding sources will obviously be more likely than others. But to maximize your chances of getting money from practically any source, try to strengthen the proposal by incorporating as many of these selling points as possible:

- **An Identified Audience**. Even if you intend to make an obscure work of video art, for the obscure video art audience, identify it in your proposal. Research galleries, museums, and other places where such work is shown. Explain who will want to see your project and why.
- **Bankable Names**. If you're unknown, perhaps you could get someone more famous to associate with your project—such as having a local celebrity serve as the "host" or narrator of your production. Similarly, the more experienced people in your production team—camera operator, sound recordist, editor, etc.—the better it looks on paper.
- **A Distribution Plan**. If your only plan for the completed videotape is to show it to friends and family, then it's unlikely that anyone—besides your friends and family—will want to fund it. If you intend to reach a larger audience, you must be prepared to tell potential funders exactly how you will reach that audience—be it through public access cable television, mass duplication and mailing, a professional distribution company, a television station, network, or whatever else you might realistically expect.

In some cases, the funding source implies built-in distribution—such as when the Corporation for Public Broadcasting offers grants for individual episodes of programs like "Frontlines".

* **A Realistic Budget.** If someone likes your idea, the budget can make or break its success in getting funding, because it reflects your seriousness and competence. The budget should be divided into such categories as Talent (producer, director, writer, actors), Production Personnel (camera, sound, and make-up people), Equipment Rental, Tape Stock and inter-format transfers, Editing Equipment Rental, Music, and Office expenses. Be sure to figure in the costs of meals and other expenses for your talent and crew.

Be realistic in your budget. Make phone calls to see what things cost. Don't promise what you can't deliver—remember that in video, there are special effects that require very sophisticated equipment, and rental costs for one-inch editing suites run upwards of one hundred dollars per hour. Decide what level you're working at—home brew, semipro "industrial" (using 3/4" or S-VHS editing systems), or broadcast quality (Betacam and one-inch). The corresponding budgets vary tremendously.

Remember to include "in kind contributions" in your budget. These are non-cash contributions, and they add up quickly. For example, if you're in school and can borrow a camera for a weekend, you can list the equivalent market value for renting the camera for a weekend as an in kind contribution. Similarly, if you're getting professional actors to work for free, you can list their services as an in kind contribution.

One of the benefits of listing these in kind contributions is that it creates the appearance that many investors have already jumped on the bandwagon. For example, if you're trying to raise ten thousand dollars for a project with a total budget of seventeen thousand dollars (including seven thousand dollars' worth of in kind contributions), it seems like you're already well on the way toward your goal.

Commercial Television

Television, as an extension of radio, was conceived from the start as a commercial medium, so in a way, trying to find commercial sponsors for your video project can seem the most natural approach.

A local cable-television public access program about photography, for example, could be supported by a local photo shop—either with direct advertising, or through a "softer" PBS-style "thank you" at the beginning and end. Similarly, you might be able to find a local garden supply store that will fund a gardening program, or a hardware store that will contribute to your own version of *This Old House*. Remember that stores like these may be a lot more generous if you ask for donations in the form of merchandise, rather than cash.

Many cable systems offer "leased access" channel time, allowing you to rent a half hour or hour per week, and sell advertising. This is perhaps the most grass roots method of breaking into the business of television, because the commercial environment mimics the bigger budget world of broadcast television; but you can get away with lower "public-access style" production values, so that it's easy to experiment with the marketplace on a low budget.

The business of television may be fascinating, but many video and film artists prefer to do their own thing, without structuring a program around an advertising market. For such projects, the ideal source of funding is a grant.

Grants

Financing video and film projects through grants is literally a dream come true—especially for arts grants that give you almost total creative freedom (though the limits of this freedom with grants from the National Endowment for the Arts has been challenged by some right-wing members of Congress).

But getting a grant can be very difficult—especially since government funding for the arts has been drying up. And even when the money was flowing more freely, it wasn't that easy. In his book, *The Independent Film and Videomakers Guide*, written in the 1970s, author Michael Wiese (who went on to become a top executive at Vestron Video) notes that he got his first grant after applying to the American Film Institute for nine years.

I myself have never received any grant money whatsoever, though I've tried perhaps a half dozen times, and—like many independent film and videomakers—got frustrated with the expenditure of time and energy required just to apply. I have been paid small sums (very small!) to have my work exhibited here and there, but I've never received a grant to make a film or video.

It's not impossible to break into the grants scene, but be forewarned that it's usually more difficult than it may appear from the application forms. Once you achieve a certain level of success in the film and video world, your name becomes known to the decision-making committees which award these grants. Thus, for the most part, the serious contenders for grant money are not anonymous strangers to the committee, but people whose works they're already familiar with.

Critics of the grants scene frequently complain of an atmosphere of cronyism. The grants seem limited to a circle of people who generally know each other: sometimes people who receive grants one year sit on committees to award grants the next year. It's natural, however, that people who begin receiving grants get better and better at it each time they apply.

For a beginning grant seeker, the more you learn about the grant committee—who the decision makers are, what their concerns are, which projects they've supported previously, etc.—the better qualified you'll be to meet their criteria in your proposal.

ITVS

A new alternative television service—funded by the Corporation for Public Broadcasting—and dedicated to financing projects by independent film and videomakers was specifically set up in the late 1980s to address all the problems that indpendent producers complained about regarding public TV. It was originally called the Independent Production Service, but has since been renamed ITVS, for Independent Television Service.

ITVS was created specifically to fund independent productions which have not had access to more mainstream PBS and CPB funding. It is the result of years of wrangling between independent producers, the Public Broadcasting System, the Corporation for Public Broadcasting, and the U.S. Congress.

In a nutshell, the independent film and video community has complained that the so-called "independent" programs created for the PBS network are actually the productions of local PBS-affiliates (note that many PBS shows are the productions of a few key PBS stations, in big cities like New York, Washington D.C., Boston, L.A., etc.) Although Congress, in funding CPB and PBS, previously encouraged funding of independent productions, it was not enough to satisfy the independent film and video community's outspoken advocates. After lots of political struggle, the birth of ITVS has taken place—but at least so far, it hasn't changed public broadcasting much.

Besides public broadcasting, there are literally thousands of government agencies and foundations that distribute grant money for video and film projects, with varying degrees of narrowness regarding topics. Many advocacy groups will fund projects that promote a cause (political, environmental, industrial, etc.) or special interest group (youth, the disabled, racial and ethnic minorities, the aged, etc.) Practically every state and city has an arts council that distributes grant money. Regional educational broadcast networks, city cable-TV commissions, libraries, and educational offices are other common government agencies that offer grants.

Private corporations are a very rich source for grant money, too. Though some ardent independents will argue that taking corporate money automatically corrupts a project, it is sometimes surprising to see just how much leeway corporate sponsors will allow—even on controversial issues.

The reasoning behind this may be as simple as a corporation wanting to appear "concerned" about an issue, or as cynical as funding low-budget "opposition" projects to assure that contrary views will be relegated to the relatively obscure world of documentary film festivals (or public access cable channels). Either way, it is common for oil and chemical companies to give money to pro-environmental media, and documentaries about alternative fuels projects like solar-powered car.

Investors and Limited Partnerships

A very common way for independent filmmakers to raise money for moderate budget films (say, ten thousand dollars and up) is through the investments of individuals. The investments are usually made in the form of "limited partnerships". In a "limited partnership", a legal arrangement is made between investors (the "limited partners") and the "general partner" (you). A legal agreement specifies how partners can invest, how profits will be determined and divided, etc.

Limited partnerships are sold through a prospectus, or sales offering. Typically, you invite a group of potential investors to a meeting, where you screen a short sample of the work you're trying to create, and/or present whatever talent you have working for you, and make your sales pitch. In addition to your spiel, you give these people free food, booze, and a copy of the official legal prospectus, along with promotional literature.

One word of warning on seeking investors: You may find that with your own enthusiasm and naive belief that your project will make tons of money, you can convince a small group of friends and relatives to invest in your project, basically on faith. But you can only "burn" such people once—if it ends up a big money loser, you'll not only never get another nickel out of them, but you may end up losing some friends and estranging some relatives.

So be realistic, and honest, in your assessment of the project's money-making capabilities. If you're basically looking for "gifts", don't disguise it as an "investment opportunity"!

Artistic Purity (and Your Career)

In the final analysis, only you can decide whether fundraising is the logical next step for your videomaking career, or whether it requires too much compromise in time and sacrifice of artistic purity. Fundraising is often a more difficult, and time consuming project than the actual production of a film or tape. It is not something you can do casually—unless you have a lot of rich friends and relatives willing to give you money for anything!

Beginning videomakers generally have a difficult time getting funded, and might be best advised to spend their time learning the craft, rather than trying to drum up business right away. Remember that everything you do will ultimately feed into your future fundraising efforts, because track records are so important.

If you have a great idea for a documentary, but have never produced such a program before, you'd probably be best off first producing a super low budget, rough version with your camcorder. It will help you hone down your idea, practice for the future, and if the quality of your rough version turns out good enough, it will become something you can show to potential funders.

Many videos would never be made if they weren't financed from the word go. Videographers would certainly never show up at strangers' weddings without the promise of financial remuneration! The range of video activity is so tremendous—from recording peoples' most personal moments, to the creation of network programs seen globally by hundreds of millions of people—that just deciding where you fit into this spectrum can be a continual question.

Some videomakers are perfectly content producing self-financed low budget works as a hobby or artistic pursuit; while others are only looking to do work for hire. Most videomakers try to achieve some balance between these extremes—working on their own projects when they can, and doing other people's projects for pay. Going for the grant money, or other funding sources, usually reflects an effort to reconcile this dilemma—to get paid to produce something reasonably close to what you want to do anyway. It's a great trick if you can pull it off. Good luck!

29 HDTV and Wide Screen TV

For manufacturers, HDTV promises to be the next "big thing" to catch on and keep the flames of consumption burning brightly into the next century—now that sales of VCRs, CD-players, and even camcorders have leveled off. For America's aging baby boomers, HDTV promises to make cocooning even more appealing, by bringing film-like picture clarity into the home. With HDTV, television will not only be more convenient than going to a theater, but almost identical in quality too (minus, of course, the audience reactions and social experience).

Yet the odd interplay between technology and politics has already delayed the introduction of HDTV in the United States for several years.

Technically, HDTV simply adds more detail to the screen. Television images, as explained earlier, are created by a series of horizontal scan lines. From the top of the screen to the bottom, there are about 500 scan lines. (The complete TV frame consists of 525 scan lines, but you only see about 480 of these—the scan lines at the extreme top of the screen are set aside for non-image information, such as closed captioning for the hearing impaired, and time-code for video editing.)

HDTV improves television's ability to portray fine detail by doubling the number of scan lines, to over one thousand. (The exact number is still a subject of heated debate, with 1125 and 1050 being the main contenders for "true HDTV".)

Additionally, HDTV changes the "aspect ratio"—the width to height proportions—of the TV screen, to better match the wide-screen format of most feature films. Today's TVs, regulated by NTSC standards, are one third wider than they are high (regardless of the exact screen size.) This ratio can be stated as 1.33 : 1, or 4 : 3.

Ordinary TV is a third wider than it is high.

Old films from the forties and earlier are generally in the same proportions, but most movies made since the fifties have been shot in "Cinemascope", "Panavision", or "Vista-Vision"—"wide screen" formats. The most extreme versions have an aspect ratio of 2.33:1, but most of today's Panavision films settle for a more modest 1.833:1 format. The generally agreed HDTV aspect ratio is about 1.8:1 (that's also expressed as 16:9), with slight variations between proposals.

The basic HDTV video screen thus defined—wider, with more detail—is a relatively simple engineering feat that was accomplished years ago. The difficult part, both technically and conceptually, revolves around "squeezing" the new high definition signal into the same "bandwidth" that ordinary over-the-air TV stations occupy.

What is "bandwidth"? In a nutshell, it's the electronic version of real estate—each radio and TV station has been given so much space, by the F.C.C., to transmit their signal. One reason why FM radio stations sound so much better than AM is because each FM station is given twenty times more bandwidth than AM stations. (You could fit twenty AM-type stations in the space allotted to a single FM broadcaster.)

Now, along comes HDTV, and the signal has essentially six times as much electronic information as conventional NTSC. (That's because the number of scan lines is doubled, and the information in the horizontal dimension is almost tripled, due to increasing fine-detail resolution, and the wider-screen format. Plus digital stereo sound, to boot.)

Without using any "compression" techniques, the bandwidth of five or six of today's TV stations would be required to transmit a single HDTV signal. Thus, for example, Channels 2, 3, 4, 5, and 6 could all be converted into one HDTV channel!

This scenario is obviously unacceptable to today's turf conscious broadcasters, so the challenge in engineering HDTV revolves around data compression. In 1993, the F.C.C. decided to

HDTV (bottom) is wider and has about twice as many scan lines as regular TV (top).

allow a consortium of U.S. companies to cooperate in creating a compression scheme for HDTV. That compression system, MPEG-2, became available around 1995. But as this book was going to press, the broadcast industry was arguing that it didn't really want to jump into HDTV broadcasting just yet, and that it would prefer to use the new digital video compression techniques to broadcast multiple new channels (with inferior MPEG-1 quality) rather than a single high quality HDTV channel.

NHK, the Japanese state-run broadcasting company (with close ties to Japan's vast consumer electronics empire), began HDTV transmissions in 1992. But NHK's "MUSE" system of compression is analog. With MUSE TV sets selling for upwards of five thousand dollars in Japan, it hasn't caught on. That's what American broadcasters are fearful of—investing in new HDTV transmitting that only a very small number of consumers will by sets to see.

All compression techniques utilize computer intelligence to analyze the video images. Rather than transmitting a complete new frame every thirtieth of a second, as today's TV stations do, the idea is to only transmit information that changes from one frame to the next. If the background stays the same, there's no need to send a whole new picture of it. But in practice, this is easier said than done, and most compression schemes sacrifice some picture quality, especially for fast moving objects.

Top: Letterbox presentation on TV. Bottom: Original wide screen film.

Some camcorders offer a "cinema mode" shooting option that electronically squishes the picture. But unlike the letterbox mode (which can be viewed on any TV), a 16 x 9 TV set is needed.

16 x 9

Meanwhile, many industry observers wonder how important the improved picture quality will be to the consumer. After all, most Americans watch TV on 13" or 20" screens. Full appreciation of HDTV quality requires larger screens—27" and up. If HDTV will only be of interest to the "video connoisseurs" who currently make up the small (but highly profitable) "home theater" market— along with sports bars that currently feature the comparatively crude looking NTSC projection TVs—then it is hardly worth re-vamping our entire national broadcasting system for it.

What most people probably would appreciate, however, even in a small screen size, is the wider aspect ratio. That, in a nutshell, is the logic behind the 16 x 9 wide screen television sets that have recently been introduced.

Viewers know that movies on today's TVs usually have their sides chopped off, except for a few that are "letterboxed" (with black borders along the top and bottom of the screen). 16 x 9 sim-ply widens the screen, without increasing resolution. In fact, when playing letterbox format recordings, the resolution is actually re-duced, since the scan lines at the top and bottom of the frame go unused.

HDTV Politics

The F.C.C. is looking to develop HDTV standards for the next century, utilizing digital transmission techniques and new TV channels. Each existing broadcaster will probably get a second, new HDTV channel. But there are plenty of other worthy recipients for these scarce public airwaves—after all, why not just have more regular-quality TV stations?

In Japan, direct broadcast satellites (DBS) transmit the programs as a premium service directly into Japanese homes. A small window-mounted satellite dish antenna is required. Muse VCRs, laser disc players, and possibly even camcorders will soon be available.

DBS is unacceptable to American broadcasters, because it challenges the system of distributing network television through local affiliates. DBS renders the "middlemen"—local TV stations and local cable systems—unnecessary. If the major networks—CBS, NBC, ABC, PBS—and the pay-cable services—HBO, Showtime, etc.—attempted to begin their own new DBS services, they would be opposed by their own affiliates—hundreds of local TV stations, thousands of cable systems, and their powerful Washington lobbying arms—the National Association of Broadcasters (NAB) and the National Cable TV Association (NCTA). (Politics makes strange bedfellows—normally, NAB and NCTA are at each other's throats!)

The safest policy for the F.C.C., which has long supported localism in American TV, is to try to find a way to just add the new HDTV signal to regular TV transmissions—the way color and stereo sound have been added. But HDTV has too much picture information to "fit" into the established channel slots for TV stations, at least with today's MPEG compression technology.

This technical debate revolves around *broadcast* standards. HDTV is already an established fact as a *production* format—there are video cameras, tape systems, laser disc players, and video monitors already available for rental to the professional film production industry (using the 1125 scan line format). Such equipment is used for shooting and editing; the production can then be transferred to 35-mm film or to standard NTSC video. (Kodak has even proposed a super duper HDTV format with 2160 scan lines, to replace photographic film.)

Two distinct sets of HDTV standard are thus emerging—a super high quality "production standard", and a consumer quality "broadcast standard"—probably MPEG-2—with heavy compression.

Additionally, as this book was going to press we were about to see the introduction of one or two new Digital Video Disc (DVD) formats, to replace the two-decade old analog LaserDisc as the playback movie medium of choice.

But for all of today's TV "alternatives"—cable, VCR, video disc, camcorder, etc.—the vast majority of viewers are still watching over-the-air broadcast television, and it would presumably be very difficult to sell expensive new TVs that only improve the alternatives.

A single digital HDTV channel, without compression, would require almost one hundred regular TV channels to broadcast! Compressing what amounts to the entire TV band (channels 2 through 83) into the bandwidth of a single TV station may sound like a tall order, but look at how far the rest of the electronics world has progressed since the 1930s, when the basic parameters of today's TV system were developed. So it should come as no surprise that the endless delays in adopting HDTV standards have allowed technology to march on, and highly compressed digital HDTV is now very close to reality.

If all goes according to the original plan, beginning in the late 1990s, each broadcaster will get a second, new channel, for an HDTV signal. Then, sometime around 2010, the old VHF and UHF bands will be converted to other uses, assuming by that time everyone has made the transition to HDTV.

But as this book was going to press, a controversy was raging about whether broadcasters should have to pay for the new spectrum space, and whether they would have to use it for HDTV only, of for other purposes. In the same spectrum space as a single HDTV signal, a broadcaster (TV station) could fit between four and six regular quality channels. This tanatalizing prospect to TV station owners makes them want to maintain maximum flexibility with any new spectrum space they receive.

30 Direct Broadcast Satellites

Direct Broadcast Satellites use more transmitting power than current satellites, dosing the entire continent with more microwave radiation. But the advantage of this increased power is that only a small antenna is required for good reception. Thus DBS will allow you to tune in to satellites without the need for a big dish antenna. Exactly how big an antenna is required depends on whose DBS you are talking about—since each satellite has a different transmission power level.

DBS finally came to the United States in a big way in 1994, when RCA (owned by Thomson) introduced the DSS Digital Satellite System. It has been the most successful new product introduction in consumer electronics history, with over a million units reportedly sold in the first year. DSS utilizes a small 18" dish antenna, and MPEG digital video compression that allows the unit to receive over 150 channels, though the picture quality is not quite as good as a traditional big dish antenna.

Courtesy of PrimeStar.

PrimeStar, a competing DBS service introduced around the same time, uses slightly larger (about 30") dishes and has fewer channels available.

These smaller dishes are replacing the big five and ten foot dishes that many people think of when they hear the word "satellite." Although the big dishes ultimately evolved into a legitimate DBS economy, they started in the late 1970s as an outlaw movement that was accused of stealing cable-TV network signals. After arguing for years that they were only "stealing" these signals because they lived in remote areas where cable-TV companies refused to provide service, the satellite owners were finally given legal status and an organized system of descrambling boxes, called VideoCipher, was established to allow satellite dish owners to properly pay for the channels they receive.

But the big dishes require motor mounts that move from satellite to satellite to pick up all the channels. DBS—in other words, satellite signals intended specifically for consumers, and not cable companies, to receive—is more convenient. The dish has a fixed position, yet receives all channels.

The introduction of true DBS (such as DSS and PrimeStar) in America was delayed, compared with Japan and Western Europe, for a variety of reasons: First and probably foremost, it threatens very powerful established interests—all the local TV stations and cable systems in America! (Remember the "fight pay TV" campaign of the 1960s? Now both terrestrial TV and cable TV have a common enemy.) Second, during the 1980s, a number of other new video technologies became available. Third, in the late 1980s, the Space Shuttle blew up, preventing the launch of many new satellites.

Sony DSS receiver system

For conspiracy theorists, ponder this: The catastrophe of the Space Shuttle Challenger in 1987 had a direct benefit for the American broadcast and cable industries, by delaying the introduction of DBS in America for several years. No other major American industry benefited so greatly from this disaster. (Perhaps that's why everyone in TV news replayed the explosion so many times.)

In Europe, DBS service has been around for the better part of a decade. Rupert Murdoch, the billionaire media baron who created the Fox television network, has been underwriting the "Sky Channel" direct broadcast satellite service in Britain for years. A competing five-channel "British Satellite Broadcasting" service has also been created..

In Japan, DBS service was introduced in the late 1980s by NHK, the huge Japanese state-run broadcasting conglomerate that owns TV networks and local stations. In the early 1990s, NHK (Nippon Hoso Kyokai) used DBS to introduce Japanese consumers to the pleasures of HDTV—high definition television.

Back in America, in 1982, the F.C.C. set aside large chunks of radio frequencies, in the microwave band, for direct broadcast satellites. Sixteen satellites with sixteen TV channels each were planned. The permits to launch were gobbled up by big companies like RCA, Hughes, CBS, and Western Union, but then they sat on their spectrum allocations like real estate speculators waiting for value to go up. Several permits expired in the interim, but now eight satellite companies split up America's 256-channel DBS franchise.

Numerous DBS plans have come and gone over the past decade, and several are still on the drawing board. A consortium of Rupert Murdoch (Fox TV), NBC, Cablevision Systems, and Hughes Communications announced plans for a billion-dollar "Sky Cable" DBS service many years ago, and then it fizzled out. Another consortium combining General Electric and nine large cable-TV companies once announced plans for a DBS service called "K-Prime". And a service called "SkyPix" offering 80-channels of DBS programming was announced in the early 90s, endlessly delayed, and then went bankrupt.

But by 1995, two DBS offerings became reality in the US: DSS, and PrimeStar. Both used digital video compression to offer more channels from a single satellite. DSS offers far more channels, including a zillion pay-per-view movie channels.

Ultimately, DBS is limited in the marketplace to people who have homes where a satellite dish can have an unobstructed view of the southern sky. This includes many, but far from all apartment dwellers. The initial success of DSS may be more a reflection of how reluctant cable-TV companies have been in wiring rural areas, rather than a mass rebellion against cable-TV.

DBS technology directly threatens the concept of localism in the electronic media—a concept that has been around since the earliest days of the F.C.C. Instead of receiving the big networks like ABC, CBS, and NBC via local stations, who tack on their own local commercials as well as local news and public affairs broadcasts, DBS gives you the opportunity to take the feed direct from the national network, essentially bypassing the local middleman. (With DSS, you must take an oath stating that you live in a fringe area to get broadcast networks, and local stations have the right to challenge your ability to receive network TV via DSS if they think their signal isn't so fringey.)

For people devoted to even more local forms of television — such as public access, leased access, and local origination on cable-TV — DBS means there will be fewer people to watch their cable-only programs.

For those concerned with community broadcasting, these are distinct negatives. But taking a broader view, DBS may ultimately lead to more varied voices existing nationally. DBS theoretically makes it easier for the entrepreneur to get access to a national market, bypassing the bottlenecks of broadcasters and local cable systems.

PrimeStar satellite dish.

31 The Internet

Imagine turning on your TV set, and instead of choosing from some fifty to one hundred channels on cable-TV or satellite, having literally tens of thousands of choices — equivalent to a well stocked video store, except that many of the choices are live or network style TV, rather than just individually selected prerecorded movie titles. Imagine, as the producer of a low budget TV show, having the absolute right to distribute your program (or network) without having to negotiate (or get the approval of) TV stations, networks, or cable systems — your right to "publish" a TV program would be as secure as your right to make a telephone call.

That scenario, which currently goes by the names "video on demand" or "video dial tone", is an elusive technological dream that I have been writing about in various forms for more than fifteen years. Back in the early 1980s, when most homes in the U.S. were first being wired for cable-TV, the cable industry decided to build a "tree-and-branch" system architecture, based on the principle of programs (TV channels) originating from a single, central location (the cable system headquarters).

Alternatively, I and others argued back then, they could have built an inherently more democratic, and more costly "star" architecture, similar to the way the phone system is built, in which any point can have its own unique connection to any other point. Such a system would operate as a "common carrier" — willing to carry anyone's signal for a fee.

What I have just described now represents the dream of the Internet to come. Talk to any Internet visionary, or wannabe, and they'll tell you that being able to see video over the Internet is on the horizon.

The Internet, of course, is the global meeting place of computers. Built originally by scientists working on defense projects for the U.S. military, the Internet has become the town square of planet earth. Anyone with a computer practically anywhere in the world can get access to it (in the U.S. it's usually for a monthly fee of about $15 to $25 per month), and thus can get access to practically any other computer.

In his book, "Being Digital," Nicholas Negroponte, a Founding Director of MIT's prestigious Media Lab, said, "The set-top box will be a credit-card-size insert that turns your PC into an electronic gateway for cable, television, or satellite. In other words, there is no TV-set industry in the future. It is nothing more or less than a computer industry: displays filled with tons of memory and lots of processing power."

But the reality of today's Internet is a far cry from that dream. Especially with respect to bandwidth — the amount of data that can be transmitted each second. Talk to someone in the trenches, who is actually implementing Internet access from a hardware and networks standpoint, and they'll tell you that the prospects of being able to distribute video over the Internet are real, but hardly on the horizon. Major upgrades in the Internet's infrastructure will be needed.

Bandwidth and Modem Speed

Today's fastest modems — the devices that connect your computer to the Internet over the telephone line — run at 28,800 bits per second; ISDN telephone connections (which cost about $40 to $60 per month in most of the U.S.) can increase this rate to 128,000 bits per second. By comparison, good quality compressed video signals, such as the MPEG-1 signals used in DSS satellite broadcasts, require about 1.5-megabits per second (mbps). Pro-quality digital video, such as used in the new Mini-DV camcorder format, records onto tape at a rate of 25-mbps, and raw uncompressed digital video — at broadcast quality levels — runs at 150-mbps.

This is the reason why, until recently, if you wanted to send video or audio over the Internet, you couldn't do it in "real time". Instead, you must download a file, and then view or hear it. It might take as much as an hour to download a five minute video. Audio has just recently become manageable in real time — that's how the Internet telephone systems (such as Quarterdeck's WebTalk and VocalTec) and the RealAudio Internet broadcasting system work (see below).

Considering that MPEG video is already compressed by a factor of 100:1 (from 150-mbps to 1.5-mbps), it seems like a pretty tall order to squeeze it down by another factor of 10 to 50, which is what's needed to run on ISDN or ordinary phone lines, respectively.

But even if breakthroughs in data compression do produce the 1500:1 ratio needed to send broadcast-type video using 28.8 modems, bandwidth isn't the only problem with sending video over the net. There's also the way the net itself works.

I recently met with executives from a company that specializes in setting up servers for Internet publishers. They have designed and implemented systems capable of handling hundreds of simultaneous Internet "hits" (visitors), and are specialists in integrating web pages with vast data bases. They explained that on the Internet, all communications between any point and any other point are broken down into packets of data, and each of these packets travel independently. In fact, depending on traffic patterns, a connection to a particular Internet site might start out taking one route, and then take a different route. Each packet is like a little boat making its way across a lake in its own unique path.

The beauty of packet data is that your information gets intermingled with lots of other people's information — essentially you're all sharing the same line. producing economies of scale. Packet data works fine for accessing text and graphics — which is pretty much the state of the Internet as it exists today.

But audio and video information do not lend themselves readily to packet data transmissions. These signals, which are commonly called "data stream" or "bit stream" sources in digital parlance, really require continuous connections to work properly. It is possible, like all digital signals, to send them in packets, but it requires precise timing and even more bandwidth.

For example, let's assume that advances in compression produce a decent quality Internet video signal that requires just 100-kbps. If that signal gets sent in packets, and the receiving computer gets these bursts just 10% of the time, then the bandwidth must be 1-mbps — in other words, short bursts of even higher speed data.

Online And Off The Hook

Beyond the packet switching problem, there's also the matter of the continuous connection. Current telephone switching office technology, and the interconnecting regional and long-distance trunk connections, are based on the premise that at any given time of day, only a fraction of the installed telephone numbers (subscribers) will actually be in use. If everyone in the country picked up their telephones simultaneously and attempted to dial, very few would get through.

Today's telephone rates are based on this premise, too — that everyone in the pool is sharing the switching system at different times. Building a phone system designed for continuous use by virtually all households during prime-time viewing hours would require considerable additional investment in the telephone infrastructure.

Without such upgrading, trying to watch TV over the Internet during prime-time viewing hours could be like driving on the San Gabriel Freeway, or the Brooklyn-Queens Expressway at rush hour. Heavy traffic could bring things to a standstill. Forget about the ghosts and static buzzes of yesteryear — watching TV in the future could be a glitchy series of spurts — packets of a few seconds of program, followed by an hourglass icon, then more spurts, etc.

Multimedia On the Net: Today and Tomorrow

If you have a computer and want to play around with audio and video on the World Wide Web (which is the section of the Internet that most people are interested in, because you can access everything via "browser" software such as Mosaic or Netscape), there are numerous home page sites that specialize in these areas. Of course, this technology changes constantly, but two spots that were interesting as this edition was going to press:

RealAudio (htttp://www.realaudio.com) provides a system for listening to live and prerecorded audio over the Internet. The home page site includes broadcasts you tune into like a radio; the software is also catching on at various other home pages as a way of extending the World Wide Web to include audio clips.

VDOnet (http:\\www.vdolive.com), offers a download of VDO Player. According to the company, it can accommodate practically any modem speed — at 14.4 kbps you'll see what amounts to a slide show with sound; while at ISDN speeds (56, 64, or 128 kbps) you'll actually see moving video of varying quality. (Even with ISDN, it's still not capable of the 30-frames-per-second rate of normal TV).

With all this software available for free download on the net, you may wonder how these companies actually make money. Like most Internet software, the players, viewers, and browsers are given away free in the hopes that a standard will be established, and the software publisher will make money selling authoring tools to Internet publishers. With VDOLive, for example, a software package enabling five simultaneous streams of video on a server costs $1,199; while generating up to 100 streams costs $9,999.

Both these products do indeed appear likely to become industry-wide standards, as they've been incorporated into Netscape's popular Navigator browser software. (Depending on whose estimate you believe, Netscape Navigator is used in some 50 to 75% of all Internet enabled computers.)

Despite the hype of TV news reports, today's Internet is anything but an "information superhighway" — it's more like an unpaved road, with lots of potholes and dead ends. If you want to amuse yourself with a taste of things to come, you can try downloading some of these players yourself — presumably, as more web pages adopt these audio and video standards, they'll become more useful.

Today's Internet multimedia pioneers are somewhat reminiscent of an earlier era, in the 1920s and 30s, of ham radios, cat's whiskers and vacuum tubes. Just take a look at a modern digitally tuned cable-ready TV, compare it to those pioneering models of the 1950s (with the picture always rolling), and imagine what multimedia on the Internet will look like in ten or twenty years. I have no doubt that someday the dream of a truly unlimited "magazine stand" of video programming — video on demand — will come true. But it won't be next year.

32 Conclusion

Well that's it in a nutshell—the world of low budget video, and a glimpse at things to come. Now it's time for you to go out and do it—create your own video programs on a low budget.

Do it fast though, because this stuff is changing rapidly. In a few years, the tape formats described here may be surpassed by newer and better technology. Perhaps by the year 2000 there will even be a digital HDTV consumer camcorder.

As technology advances, distinctions between the quality of consumer and professional equipment will get smaller. That's what has already happened with audio—the raw quality of consumer recording equipment is now superior to the professional standards for radio broadcasting.

As the years go by, remember too that not just video technology advances, but also the language of visual storytelling. Be on the lookout for new editing techniques and effects that imply new meanings.

If you've got some ideas for your own original productions, try putting them in writing as a first step towards making them. Enlist the help of friends, family, or other interested parties. Remember: You don't need a lot of money, but you do need to devote your time and energy. Edit in the camcorder as a quick and easy technique. Avoid the trap of having tapes piled up for years, waiting to be edited.

If you're excited about this technology but are unclear about your own projects, then by all means visit a local cable-TV public access center, or school media center, and volunteer your time. You'll learn how to operate equipment, and will develop contacts with others interested in low budget video production.

A visit to such a center is also a good idea if you're planning to purchase a camcorder or editing system. In my experience reviewing camcorders and video equipment for a number of magazines, I have found many excellent pieces of equipment through hands-on testing. I've also noticed that most people who have not played with so many different makes and models tend to be more—not less—opinionated about which brands and formats they prefer. So take opinions you hear with a grain of salt. People can only love or hate what they are familiar with. An access center can be an extremely valuable resource—exposing you to new equipment, and giving you the opportunity to rent a particular type of camcorder before buying it. There's also a lot of logic to choosing a format to work in based on what the access center has available.

In the appendix of this book I've listed some resources that you may find useful in your pursuits of low budget videomaking.

Finally, remember: No matter how sophisticated and endlessly complex this technology gets—with the merging of video, computer, and audio technologies—there will always be a gap between what professionals can do and what low budget producers can do. And there will always be a gap between people who are absolute wizards with the equipment but haven't the faintest idea what to do with it, and people who don't understand most of the technology but manage to get competent at a few basics of the medium, and manage to create simple, elegant low budget masterpieces.

I of course advocate your pursuit of both types of expertise, creative and technical. The lower your budget, the more you'll need to understand the technical stuff to achieve your artistic goals (after all, at a higher budget you can just hire people to take care of those details).

Whatever your take on the low budget video scene, these are exciting times in the Information Age. Welcome to the club.

APPENDIX

Low Budget Video Resources

. . . .

A: DVS Video Editing Service

The publisher of this book, Desktop Video Systems, offers a unique low-budget editing service designed specifically to meet the needs of low budget video producers who want top quality editing of their tapes, without the expense and hassle of buying their own editing systems or renting time on a semi-pro system to do it manually.

The service DVS offers is highly accurate and flexible, utilizing advanced time code technology to correlate edit points on your camera original tapes. It is the best quality, lowest cost service that's available today.

For more information, there's a coupon at the back of this book that you can send in—DVS will mail you a starter kit with complete instructions and price information. Most tapes end up costing less than $150 to edit using this service.

At some point you may outgrow the Editing Service and feel that it's time to buy your own editing equipment, and/or upgrade to more expensive tape formats. DVS also offers, for more advanced videomakers, a desktop video editing consulting/buying service. If you're interested in putting together your own editing system, DVS offers one stop shopping and systems integration, as well as reasonably priced advice.

B: Support and Access Organizations

Alliance for Community Media
666–11th Street
Washington, DC 20001.
(formerly the National Federation of Local Cable Programmers,
they can help you locate a public access center in your area, and
help you in obtaining public access time on cable-TV)

East Bay Media Center
2054 University Avenue, Suite 203
Berkeley, CA 94704
415-843-3699

EZTV
8547 Santa Monica Blvd.
West Hollywood, CA 90069
213-657-1532

Film Arts Foundation
346 Ninth Street
San Francisco, CA 94103
415-552-8760

Film/Video Arts
817 Broadway
New York, NY 10003
212-673-9361

Foundation for Independent Video and Film
625 Broadway 9th floor
New York, NY 10012
212-473-3400

Media Alliance
356 West 58th Street
New York, NY 10019
212-560-2919

Millennium Film Workshop
66 East 4th Street
New York, NY 10002
212-673-0090

(We're interested in hearing from other media/public-access organizations for inclusion in future editions.)

. . . .
C: Manufacturers

Adobe (Premiere software)
1585 Charleston Rd.
Mountain View, CA 94039
408-944-0100

Azden (wireless microphones, accessories)
147 New Hyde Park Rd.
Franklin Square, NY 11010
516-328-7500

Avid (non-linear editing systems)
800-949-AVID

Bogen (tripods)
17-20 Willow Street
Fair Lawn, NJ 07410
201-794-6500

Canon
One Canon Plaza
Lake Success, NY 11042
516-488-6700

Cinema Products (Steadicam JR)
3211 S. La Cienaga Blvd.
Los Angeles, CA 90016
213-836-7991

Digital Processing Systems (TBCs, video capture/record boards)
606-371-5533
800-455-8525 product info

D-Vision Systems (non-linear editing)
800-838-4746

Fast Electronics (nonlinear editing)
393 Vintage Park Dr.
Foster City, CA 94404
800-684-MOVIE

Future Video (edit controllers)
28 Argonaut, Suite 150
Laguna Hills, CA 92656
714-7704416

Hitachi
401 W. Artesia Blvd.
Compton, CA 90220
213-537-8383

Lowel Lights
(they publish an excellent newsletter, available for free)
475 Tenth Avenue
New York, NY 10018
212-947-0950

JVC
41 Slater Dr.
Elmwood Park, NJ 07407
201-794-3900

Matrox (video capture boards)
1025 St. Regis Blvd. Dorval
Quebec, Canada H(P 2T4
800-361-4903
514-685-2630

Media 100 (nonlinear editing.
(Data Translation)
800-832-8188

Miro (nonlinear editing)
955 Commercial St.
Palo Alto, CA 94303
800-249-MIRO

Mitsubishi
800 Biermann Court
Mt. Prospect, IL 60056
708-298-9223

Nady Systems (wireless microphones)
6701 Bay St.
Emeryville, CA 94608
510-652-2411

Netscape Communications
501 East Middlefield Road
Mountain View, CA 94043
415-254-1900

NewTek (Video Toaster, LightWave 3D)
1200 S.W. Executive Dr.
Topeka, KS 66615
913-228-8000

Panasonic
One Panasonic Way
Secaucus, NJ 07094
201-348-7000

Philips (Magnavox)
One Philips Drive
Knoxville, TN 37914
423-521-4316

Play (video capture, mixing)
2880 Kilgore Road
Rancho Cordova, CA 95670
916-851-0800

Power Express (camcorder batteries)
3 Portola Rd. Unit A
Portola Valley, CA 94028
800-POWER-EX

Progressive Networks (RealAudio)
616 First Ave. Suite 701
Seattle, WA 98104
800-230-5975

Radius (video capture cards)
215 Moffet Park Dr.
Sunnyvale, CA 94089
408-541-6100

Sharp
Sharp Plaza
Mahwah, NJ 07430
201-529-8200

Shure (microphones and mixers)
222 Hartrey Avenue
Evanston, IL 60202
708-866-2200

Sony
Sony Drive
Park Ridge, NJ 07656
201-930-1000

TDK (tape)
12 Harbor Park Dr.
Port Washington, NY 11050
800-TDK-TAPE

Thomson Cons. Electr. (RCA and GE)
10330 N. Meridian
Indianapolis, IN 46290
317-587-3000

Tiffen (optical filters)
90 Osar Ave.
Hauppauge, NY 11788
516-273-2500

Toshiba
82 Totowa Rd.
Wayne, NJ 07470
201-628-8000

VDOnet Corp. (video on Internet)
4009 Miranda Ave. Suite 250
Palo Alto, CA 94394
415-846-7700

Videonics (edit controllers, mixers, titlers)
1370 Dell Ave.
Campbell, CA 95008
408-866-8300

Vinten (pro grade tripods)
709 Executive Blvd.
Valley Cottage, NY 10989
914-268-0100

. . . .

D: Funding Sources

California Arts Council
2411 Alhambra Boulevard
Sacramento, CA 95817
916-739-3186

The Canada Council
99 Metcalfe Street
PO Box 1047
Ottawa, Ontario, Canada K1P5V8
613-598-4365

Corporation for Public Broadcasting
901 E Street, NW
Washington, DC 20004
202-879-9740

Independent Television Service
190 Fifth St. East, suite 200
Saint Paul, MN 55101
612-225-9035

Illinois Arts Council
100 West Randolph
Chicago, IL 60601
800-237-6994
312-814-6750

National Endowment for the Arts (NEA)
1100 Pennsylvania Avenue, NW
Washington DC 20506
202-682-5448

National Endowment for the Humanities (NEH)
1100 Penssylvania Avenue, NW
Washington, DC 20505
202-786-0278

New York State Council on the Arts
915 Broadway
New York, NY 10010
212-614-2900

Texas Commission on the Arts
920 Colorado Strett
Austin, TX 78711
512-463-5535

Women In Film Foundation
6464 Sunset Boulevard
Los Angeles, CA 90028
213-463-6040

For more detailed listings of state arts councils and other organizations offering funding for low budget independent video projects,
get a copy of *MONEY FOR FILM & VIDEO ARTISTS,* by the
American Council for the Arts. It's available from Consortium
Book Sales, 287 East Sixth Street, Saint Paul, MN 55101.

. . . .

E: Recommended Reading

Books

The Independent Film & Videomakers Guide, by Michael Wiese,
available from Focal Press.
Independent Filmmaking, by Lennie Lipton.
Grammar of the Edit, by Roy Thompson. Focal Press.
Grammar of the Film Language, by Daniel Arijon. Silman-James
Press.
Marketing with Video, by Hal Landen. Oak Tree Press.
The Recording Studio Handbook, by John M. Woram. ELAR
Publishing.
When the Shooting Stops, The Cutting Begins, by Ralph
Rosenblum. Viking Press.

Magazines

DV
600 Townsend St.
San Francisco, CA 94103
800-998-0806

The Independent (published by FIVF)
304 Hudson St. 6th flr.
New York, NY 10013
212-807-1400

New Media
901 Mariner's Island Blvd.
San Mateo, CA 94404
609-786-4430 (subscriptions)

Video
1633 Broadway - 45th flr.
New York, NY 10019
815-734-1283 (subscriptions)

Videography
2 Park Ave. Suite 1802
New York, NY 10016
subscriptions:
PO Box 0513
Baldwin, NY 11510

Videomaker
PO Box 4591
Chico, CA 95927
619-745-2809 (subscriptions)

. . . .
F: Frequently Asked Questions

Which format is best?
Without question, it's MiniDV, for both picture and sound quality. But other factors you may be juggling, besides quality (Hi8
and Super-VHS are second best) are compact size (DVC, Hi8,
8mm, VHS-C, and S-VHS-C are best), compatibility (VHS and
VHS-C are best), recording time (8mm, Hi8, and VHS are best),
and cost (8mm, VHS-C, and VHS are the cheapest).

Why not just leave the camcorder set on automatic all the time?
Most of the time you'll get perfectly good results from auto-focus,
auto exposure, and auto white-balance. But "most" means perhaps
70 to 95% of the time, depending on the type of shooting you do
(wide angle zoom settings and bright outdoor light are the easiest
shooting conditions). The manual controls ensure proper settings
for the exceptional times — the tricky situations that auto modes
can't handle. Examples: Subjects standing in front of windows,

subjects not centered in the frame, mixed lighting environments such as a living room illuminated by both incandescent lights and sunlight, and shooting in low light.

Do I need to use a light when shooting indoors?

Hopefully, no. Lights are annoying to your subjects, and they tend to create a severe exposure imbalance — only the person or thing located a few feet in front of the camcorder is illuminated, everyone and everything else appears black. And lights create harsh shadows. With that said, lights are useful in situations where there just isn't enough light. In a typical living room you'll probably have enough ambient light, but note that most rooms are very unevenly lit — there are bright spots and dark spots. Most camcorders produce very recognizable images in very low light, but the pictures tend to be very noisy —choose a model with a very low lux rating for best results. Adding a light (such as a built-in one) eliminates the noise, but suffers from the aforementioned problems.

If I have image stabilization I don't need a tripod, right?

If you agree to always keep the zoom lens set at the widest wide angle position, and to hold the camcorder with two hands, holding it as steady as humanly possible, then the camcorder's image stabilization can indeed make a handheld shot look like it was shot on a tripod. But don't think this is license to be sloppy —image stabilizers can only compensate for the most minor forms of camera shake. And if you zoom in, you'll still need a tripod, or some other improvised support, to keep the picture from shaking.

Does blank tape make any difference in picture or sound quality?

Yes it does, but it's subtle. Differences in blank videotape are not at all like differences in film, where the blank media determines all kinds of attributes like light sensitivity (ASA speed), color sensitivity (indoor/outdoor), color or black-and-white, graininess, etc. With video, all those attributes are essentially determined by the image sensor(s) and recording format. Ditto for sound quality, which is primarily determined by the camcorder itself (exception: VHS-C and VHS camcorders that don't have Hi-fi sound). The main difference you can see between tapes are dropouts, which appear as short-occurring streaks. This is the main advantage of Hi8's EP tapes over the MP tapes — fewer dropouts.

How can I shoot in Black and White?

The tape itself makes no difference whatsoever. Some camcorders offer a black and white recording mode that makes it easy. You can also record initially in color and then convert to black and white when you make a copy (such as during editing). An S-video Y-C splitter cable, in conjunction with a Hi8 or S-VHS camcorder, can be used to feed just the black-and-white luminance (Y) signal to a VCR's video input jack. Or you can use a video effects processor and turn the color all the way down.

Why can't I just splice tape to edit?

The helical recording system used in all video camcorder formats makes splicing an absolute taboo. The video heads spin around so fast that any aberration in the tape surface, such as from a splice, could cause severe damage. Further, the tracks themselves are at an extreme diagonal slant, making cuts along the frame line very difficult, and the tracks are so thin it would be impossible to cut between them without damaging the information. You must therefor edit by copying to another tape, or to a computer's hard disk.

Can I overlap or double-expose images, like with film?

No, but some camcorders that have digital picture effects offer something that comes close: A digital still frame dissolve that lets you end one shot with a freeze frame, and then dissolve (or wipe) from that frame into the beginning of the next shot.

How can I shoot animation?

Both film and computer-based animation are better than camcorder animation, because they offer true single-frame recording. Some camcorders offer an animation mode, but unfortunately, most record about 4 to 7 frames of video at a time. Video runs at 30 frames per second (in the U.S.), so animation recorded at 4 frames per second (the effect of 7-frame bursts) looks jittery. The DVC format may allow individual frame recording in video.

How can I eliminate a scene in the camcorder?

It depends on whether the item you want to eliminate is the last thing that was recorded on the tape — in which case it's easy — or is in the middle of other stuff you want to save. Most camcorders have a "record search" feature to look through the tape in the camera mode. Some have a "scene re-shoot" that takes you back to the beginning of the last shot you recorded (erasing everything since the last time you released the pause button.) But if you want to eliminate something that's followed by a scene you want to save, you'll have to record over that spot, for the same amount of time. With 8mm, Hi8, and DVC such an insert takes place automatically by shooting in the normal way; with VHS and VHS-C you must usually press a special "insert edit" button.

Why do manual controls cost more than automatic?

It is indeed ironic that professional video cameras costing upwards of $20,000 don't have the automatic focus and white balance features commonly found on $600 camcorders. Consumers expect point-and-shoot simplicity, so this is the baseline for all camcorders. Adding manual controls does add expense for the knobs, software or circuitry, and readouts — especially for providing ergonomically comfortable adjustments, such as a rotating lens ring for focus (as opposed to cheaper pushbutton or dial controls). Beyond that, as with most products, intense competition for low-priced models keeps them cheap, while manufacturers can build more profit into the pricing for pro-sumer type equipment, knowing the more limited audience is willing to pay a premium.

What's the difference between Hi8 and 8mm?

Picture detail. Hi8 tapes can record horizontal resolution up to 400-lines, while regular 8mm tapes only have 240-line horizontal resolution. Note that all video formats have the same vertical resolution (roughly 330 effective-lines, or 490-scan lines), so the differences between formats show up only in the horizontal resolution.

What's the difference between Super-VHS and VHS?

Picture detail. See above — Super-VHS has 400-line resolution (as does S-VHS-C), while VHS and VHS-C have 240-line horizontal resolution.

Should I buy an extended warranty?

No, in most cases. Most camcorder repairs are needed because of damage that isn't covered by extended service contracts, due to drops or other physical damage that's readily evident. The pricing of these plans, by actuarial statistics (comparing the likelihood of needing repair and typical repair costs), are exorbitant — some deep-discount dealers lose money on the camcorder but make it back on the service plan. Best advice: Purchase the camcorder with a gold credit card or American Express — your warranty period will be automatically doubled, by up to a year.

What's macro focus?

Most zoom lenses have a minimum focus distance, in the ballpark of 3 to 5 feet. Subjects closer than this can't normally be focused on. But through clever manipulation of the lens elements, the camcorder can switch to a macro mode, which is a lens for physically close objects (up to an inch in front of the lens, or even closer!) Most camcorders today go into macro mode automatically (when autofocus is on), but you must keep the zoom set all the way back at wide angle for it to work. Also, when in macro mode the zoom won't work normally — it usually adjusts focus, and you can't zoom).

Which type of viewfinder should I get?

It's a trade-off: The plain old black and white viewfinders are the cheapest and have the most finely detailed picture (for checking focus); but color viewfinders are more fun to look at, and can help you spot white balance problems. The big 3" and 4" viewing screens are a lot of fun to shoot with, but they can be very difficult to see in bright sunlight. They're also more expensive. Sony's Vision series offer both a big screen and a small black and white viewfinder.

How long does the battery last between charges?

Most camcorders claim something like an hour of continuous recording per charge, but take that with a grain of salt. First, there's no industry-wide standard for measuring battery run time. Second, unless you're recording a concert or other event, it's very unlikely that you'll be making a continuous recording. More likely, you'll be starting and stopping the camcorder, operating the zoom and auto-focus motors every time you set up a new shot. This eats up juice at a faster rate. Beyond that, it varies from model to model, and with battery technology (ni-cad, ni-MH, and lithium-ion, respectively in order of increasing energy density efficiency). Most camcorders will run around 40 to 50 minutes under ordinary use, but it may vary from as little as 30-minutes to as much as 70 or 80 minutes.

How much zoom power do I need?

You're almost always better off getting yourself physically closer to a subject, rather than having to rely on a powerful zoom ratio. But if you're in the balcony of an auditorium shooting a play, a powerful zoom (such as 20x) may indeed get you close-ups where a less powerful lens (such as 8x) would only provide a medium shot (from the waist up). Beware, though, that the higher the zoom ratio the more visible camera shake becomes, and the more critical the focus adjustment gets.

What's the difference between digital zoom and optical zoom?

Optical zoom has been around for decades, using the spacing between lenses to vary how close things appear. Digital zoom is comparatively new, and is based on expanding a subset of all the pixels in a camcorder's image sensor to fill the full screen. By definition, picture detail (resolution) gets sacrificed as you blow up fewer and fewer pixels to fill the screen. Most people find a digital zoom extension of about 2x to 3x (taking an 8x optical zoom to 16x or 24x) to be the limit, before the picture becomes unacceptably grainy. Nevertheless, a veritable digital zoom war has broken out, with some contenders offering 64x, 100x and even 140x combined (digital + optical) zoom ratios.

How long can I expect a camcorder to last for?

Considering how delicate and precise the internal components are, camcorders are surprisingly hardy. When they go out of whack, it's usually because of physical damage, such as accidental drops or rough handling during transit. Of course, some models do occasionally just break down on their own — for this reason, it's a good idea to use a camcorder extensively at first, during the first week or two, when a store's guarantee is still in effect, so as to uncover any problems in manufacturing. Beyond that, figure that after about five years your camcorder will probably still work, but may seem outdated when compared with new features that will be available by then.

Won't I get better value if I wait until next year to buy a camcorder?

Certainly. When it comes to camcorders, perhaps nothing is more certain than the fact that next year, there will be even more features available for even less money. The problem is, when next year arrives, the following year will begin to seem very attractive, and so on. Camcorder technology just keeps getting better, and if you're waiting for some kind of levelling off, forget it. If you can use a camcorder today, go buy one. And if you're looking for an excuse to wait, there will always be one.

. . . .

G: Glossary

Accessory Light: A snap on low power (usually 3 to 5-watt) light, useful for illuminating subjects located a few feet from the camcorder, in low-light situations.

Accessory Shoe: A small slot on top of a camcorder, useful for attaching a light, a wireless microphone receiver, or other accessory devices (see HOT SHOE).

AC/DC: Camcorder operation from either AC line power or battery.

Adjustable Diopter: A viewfinder lens adjustment that can compensate for moderate nearsightedness or farsightedness, so that eyeglass wearers can see clearly without their glasses.

Adjustable Viewfinder: Viewfinder can move from the left to right side of the camcorder, or can tilt up and down and rotate.

AFM: The standard method of recording audio in 8mm and Hi8 camcorders. (Stands for Audio Frequency Modulation. See also STEREO, HI-FI.)

Age: A TIME/DATE feature that keeps track of children's ages. Itconverts the current date to the child's age, and superimposes this information over recordings.

AGC (Automatic Gain Control): Maintains a constant video luminance level by boosting weak (low light) picture signals electronically.

ALC (Automatic Level Control): Audio recording level is adjusted automatically, maintaining consistent sound level.

Amorphous: A metal alloy with high magnetic saturation flux density and permeability, and low friction noise. Used primarily in Hi8 or S-VHS applications.

Aperture: See IRIS.

Audio Dub: Replaces the sound track on a previously recorded tape with a new one, without disturbing the video material.

Authorized Repair Center: Independently owned service facilities that have been authorized by manufacturer to perform repairs and honor manufacturer's warranty coverage.

Automatic Exposure (AE): Feature which sets iris (aperture) automatically, so that the amount of light hitting the image sensor provides a proper average exposure level. Automatically re-adjusts exposure when electronic shutter speed is changed.

Automatic Exposure Lock: Holds the exposure setting while you re-compose the scene or pan the camcorder.

Automatic Focus: System that automatically senses distance between camcorder and subject, and adjusts the lens focus accordingly. (See INFRARED and TTL FOCUS.)

Automatic Macro Focus: Camcorder automatically flips lens into close-up mode when subject is less than two or three feet away. Zoom may automatically shift to wide angle. See MACRO FOCUS.

Automatic White Balance: Establishes the tint, or color shading, of the picture by automatically adjusting sensitivity to red, blue, and green light. Adjustment depends primarily on the COLOR TEMPERATURE (see also) of the light—such as sunlight, incandescent light, or fluorescent light. When properly adjusted, white objects will appear as white—rather than with a purple or green tint.

Backlight Compensation Switch: When the background is brighter than the subject—such as when the sun is behind a person's face—activating the backlight compensation (BLC) will increase the exposure level, allowing more light to reach the image sensor, so that faces will appear brighter.

Battery Charger: The AC adaptor that recharges the battery.

Battery Discharge: See BATTERY REFRESH.

Battery Life: The length of time a battery will keep a camcorder recording for. Battery life is affected by ambient temperature, and by the amount of power consuming camcorder features that are used (such as zooming). Also called "run time".

Battery Memory: Problem where battery lasts for shorter and shorter times between charges, caused by failure to fully discharge before recharging. (That is, it "remembers" that it only gets used for ten minutes between charges, and then only lasts for ten minutes). Also called "voltage depression" and "cell depression."

Battery Refresh: A charger feature that first "empties out" all remaining battery power before recharging begins. Helps eliminate BATTERY MEMORY and prolongs battery life.

Betamax: The first popular home VCR videocassette format.

Camcorder: A combination camera-recorder—Video Camera and Videocassette Recorder (VCR)—in one compact unit. Prior to the early 1980s, cameras and recorders were separate pieces of equipment.

Capstan: Rotating shaft that drives tape at a constant speed during record and playback.

Car Adaptor: Powers camcorder from cigarette lighter jack.

Cassette: A plastic magnetic tape container. Eliminates the need to manually thread open-reels of tape.

Cassette Housing: The mechanical arrangement for lowering the video cassette into position for playing or recording.

CCD (Charge Couple Device): The most commonly found type of image sensor in consumer camcorders. The CCD is a semiconductordevice (an integrated circuit) consisting of hundreds of thousands of PIXELS that individually sense red, green, and blue light. Typically $\frac{1}{4}$" to $\frac{1}{2}$" diagonal measurement (see IMAGE SENSOR).

Character Generator: Electronically creates alphabet letters and numeric type, which can be superimposed as captions or titles across the picture.

Chrominance: The color portion of the video signal, representing the saturation and tint at a particular point of the image.

Color Viewfinder: A small, solid state LCD (liquid crystal) display panel using thousands of red, green, and blue dots (pixels) creates a color image in the viewfinder. (Replaces the black and white CRT.)

Color Temperature: The proportions of colors that are mixed together to make white are measured in degrees Kelvin, and called color temperature. Tungsten bulbs are around 3200-degrees; fluorescent light is about 4500-degrees; and sunlight varies from 5600-degrees to about 10,000-degrees.

CRT: Cathode Ray Tube. An ordinary television picture tube. A highly miniaturized CRT, with a screen measuring from $\frac{1}{3}$" to 1" diagonally, is generally used as the black and white viewfinder in camcorders.

Data Screen: A display of current camcorder status information, such as shutter speed setting, date/time, index counter position, tape remaining, current function, etc.

Date/Time: Lets user superimpose the date and/or time on the tape, as it is being recorded, so that it will show in the picture on playback.

Decibels: A system used for measuring audio and video signals, and amplification factors, based on logarithmic comparisons. Abbreviated dB. A boost of 6-dB usually represents a doubling in signal strength.

Depth Of Field: The range of what's in reasonably good focus, in front of and behind the main subject. Generally, depth of field is much wider in strong light (outdoors), due to reduced IRIS setting. Also called depth of focus.

Digital 6: see DV

Digital Special Effects: Video circuitry that creates one or more of the following effects: Freeze frame dissolve into live action; freeze frame wipes to live action; solarization; mosaic; and/or mosaic dissolve. Digital memory is used to store the last frame of each recording, so that the freeze frame can be mixed with the beginning of the next segment.

Digital Titler: Camcorder feature that snaps a silhouette freeze frame image, and superimposes it. Useful with original title artwork created on paper.

Digital Zoom: Video circuitry that extends the optical (lens) zoom range by expanding the central portion of the image sensor to fill the entire screen. At extreme magnification, there aren't enough pixels to create a detailed image, so a coarse mosaic effect is created.

Diopter: See ADJUSTABLE DIOPTER.

Display: A visual indicator of various camcorder functions, via text superimposed over the viewfinder image, separate indicator lights, and or a separate liquid crystal display (LCD) panel. Also called readout.

Dropout: A momentary loss of the playback signal, which appears as a white horizontal streak flashing for an instant across the screen. Usually caused by tape erosion, sometimes by dirty tape or tape heads.

Dual Automatic Exposure: An exposure system that combines spot metering and center-averaged light metering to give user the correct exposure for backlit subjects.

Dubbing: Playing a tape on one camcorder (or VCR), and recording (copying) it to a tape in another VCR or camcorder.

DV: (Digital Video) The highest quality consumer video format. Tape is 1/4" wide (6mm); MiniDV tapes are the smallest of all camcorder tapes. Recordings are digital for both picture and sound. Format introduced in 1995, agreed to by dozens of manufacturers. Tapes come in two cassette sizes, for VCR and camcorder use. Also called Digital 6, DVC.

8mm Video: A compact videocassette tape format. The tape is eight millimeters wide. It is a worldwide standard established in 1983 by the 8mm Video Conference. Allows high quality video and audio recording. (This is a magnetic video tape format—not photographic movie film—and therefor 8mm video is not the same as 8mm or Super-8 film.)

Elapsed Time Counter: See REAL TIME COUNTER.

Electronic Viewfinder: A small TV monitor on the top or side of the camcorder lets user see what will be recorded through the lens. Information displays are also shown on this screen. May be black and white (CRT) or color (LCD).

Exposure: The combination of the amount of light the IRIS lets through to the IMAGE SENSOR, and the length of time the HIGH SPEED SHUTTER sensitizes the image sensor for.

Factory Service Center: Service facilities owned and operated by consumer electronics product manufacturers.

Field: Half a video frame. See INTERLACE.

Firewire: Nickname for high speed serial port used for digital dubbing with DV and MiniDV format equipment. Officially known as IEEE 1394, the system supports data transfer at rates of over 200 megabits/second.

Flying Erase Head: Facilitates smooth, seamless edits whenever the camcorder is paused. Without a flying erase head, a video "glitch" may occur at scene transitions. The erase head is mounted on the spinning (flying) video head drum.

Focal Length: Optical term measuring how close or far away a lens makes things appear. See ZOOM LENS.

Focus Lock: Useful when the subject is not positioned in the center of the frame. Lets user maintain (or lock onto) a certain focus setting while re-composing the scene.

F-stop: Measurement of what proportion of light the IRIS will allow to reach the image sensor. In standard f-stop series—f/2.8, f/4, f/5.6, f/8, f/11, f/16, f/22—each successive number represents a halving of the light intensity.

Frame: Video signals consist of a rapid series of still images. Each still image is called a frame. In the American NTSC television system, each frame consists of 525 scan lines, and there are 30 frames per second (fps).

Gain-up Switch: Boosts the video signal, when activated, to compensate for low-light conditions, such as a dimly lit room. Also called Video Gain switch. The degree of boost is measured in DECIBELS.

Head: The electronic component that makes contact with magnetic tape, to convert electricity to magnetism (for recording), or magnetism to electrical signals (for playback). Most camcorders have at least two heads for video recording, and one for erasing; some have more video heads, as well as an additional audio head.

Helical Recording: System of rapidly recording diagonal TRACKS along the videotape, using a spinning (rotary) video head cylinder (drum).

Hi8: An improved version of the 8mm format capable of recording better picture resolution (detail). Hi8 cassettes look the same as 8mm cassettes, but use different types of tape inside, and require a different recording and playback process. The high-density metal tape provides a wider luminance bandwidth, resulting in sharper picture quality, with horizontal resolution of over 400-lines (compared with 250-lines for regular 8mm). Also called "high-band 8mm." Hi8 camcorders feature S-video jacks, which separate the luminance and chrominance signals, for improved monitoring (on a TV receiver/monitor) and dubbing.

Hi-fi: Audio recordings which exhibit very good to excellent fidelity, in terms of frequency response (tonal range) and dynamic range (freedom from noise and hiss). (See VHS HI-FI.)

High Band: A recording method in which the carrier frequency is shifted higher, in order to get higher resolution.

High Speed Shutter: Electronic system that speeds up the rate at which the IMAGE SENSOR scans out each FIELD. Normal speed is 1/60th of a second. Note that tape recording speed remains the same. Used primarily for playing back sports recordings in slow motion—the high speed shutter eliminates picture blur in individual frames.

Horizontal Resolution: A rating of the fine detail of a TV picture, measured in lines. The more lines, the higher the resolution and the better the picture. A standard VHS format VCR produces 240 lines of horizontal resolution, while over 400 lines are possible with Super-VHS, S-VHS-C, and Hi8 camcorders. (Not to be confused with vertical resolution, which is the same for all formats.)

Hot Shoe: An ACCESSORY SHOE that also provides power to the attached device, such as an ACCESSORY LIGHT.

IEEE 1394: Standard for high speed digital data transmission used to carry DV format video and audio signals. See Firewire.

Image Mix: This feature allows user to hold an image in memory so it can be superimposed on another image later. (See DIGITAL SPECIAL EFFECTS.)

Image Sensor: Located behind the lens on most camcorders, the image sensor receives the focused image. It functions like an electronic retina, converting various levels and colors of lightinto electronic signals that make up the TV image. CCD indicates the camcorder has a charge-coupled sensor. MOS means the camcorder has a metal oxide/semiconductor sensor. Tube means that the camcorder uses an old-fashioned vacuum tube-type sensor. CCD and MOS image sensors are solid-state integrated circuits that consist of hundreds of thousands of PIXELS.

Image Stabilization: Takes out minor picture shakiness, either optically or electronically. Electronic digital systems usually cause slight picture degradation (loss of detail), whereas optical image stabilization systems have no degradation.

In-camera Battery: The battery slips inside the camera and does not have to be attached to the back.

Index Counter: An arbitrary 4-digit display of how much tape has elapsed. It's arbitrary because the numbers themselves have no meaning (see REAL TIME COUNTER).

Infrared Focus: An automatic focusing system that involves bouncing a narrow beam of infrared light off the subject. A sensor measures the angle at which the beam is reflected back; electronics inside the camcorder use that angle to calculate the distance and adjust the lens accordingly. Infrared focusing can be foiled by black or angled shiny surfaces that reflect little or no light back to the camera, by subjects too tiny to reflect the entire beam, by glass windows that you're trying to shoot through, and by off-center subjects that the beam misses entirely.

Insert Editing: Allows user to insert new audio/video segments into the middle of a previously recorded tape. (Some camcorders insert both audio and video simultaneously; others can insert — or dub — audio and/or video separately.)

Instant Review: Lets user playback through the viewfinder the last few seconds that were shot. Also called "quick review".

Integrated Circuit (IC): An electronic circuit in the form of a microminiature silicon chip, consisting of thousands or even millions of transistors (and other components). Usually about the size of a fingernail or smaller.

Interlaced Scanning System: There are 525 scan lines in each video frame. But each frame consists of two half-frames, consisting of the odd (1, 3, 5... 525) and even (2, 4, 6...)numbered scan lines. Each half-frame is called a "field", and thus consists of every other scan line. This system of alternating the display of every other scan line is called interlace—it reduces the perception of screen flicker.

Internal Focus: Mechanism by which the power lens is electro-mechanically moved forward or backward by a motor mounted inside the camcorder. In conventional focus systems, a ring in the front of the lens is moved to adjust focus.

Interval Timer: See TIME LAPSE.

IPS: Inches per second. Used for measuring tape speed.

Iris: A circular opening inside a lens that adjusts in size to allow more or less light through to the image sensor. Also called APERTURE. The size of the iris opening is measured in F-STOPS. The iris setting, combined with the HIGH-SPEED SHUTTER setting, determines the EXPOSURE.

LANC: Advanced remote control jack offering two-way communication between camcorder or VCR and computerized edit controller.

Lens Aperture: See IRIS.

Lens Speed: Important for low-light operation, lens speed is the widest aperture setting. Measured as an F-STOP number—the lower the number, the "faster" the lens and the more light it can let in. "Slower" lenses require more light. Low light sensitivity also depends on the type and size of sensor used and on the associated electronics.

Linear Track: The standard VHS (and VHS-C, S-VHS, and S-VHS-C) audio track. Usually monaural (see VHS HI-FI).

Loading: The threading of tape to the VCR's video heads.

Loading Motor: The motor that powers the camcorder's mechanism for load/unload of tape with respect to the heads.

Low-light Sensitivity: A camcorder's ability to produce decent images in low light. Depends mostly on IMAGE SENSOR and LENS SPEED. See LUX.

Luminance: The degree of brightness at any given point in the video image. (Technically, measured in "IRE-units".)

Lux: A metric unit of light, similar to the foot candle (10 lux equals approximately 1 foot candle). Used for measuring camcorder low light sensitivity, but different manufacturers may use slightly different standards for establishing camcorder lux ratings. Although ratings are typically given in the 1 to 7-lux range, most video camcorders require over 100 lux to produce a bright, high-quality picture.

Macro Focus: A close-up focusing range that lets user get very close to the subject—less than two or three feet. Newer camcorders may have an electronic button, or AUTOMATIC MACRO FOCUS. Older camcorders require pressing a button on the lens, and using the zoom as a focus control. Macro focus usually requires first setting the zoom to wide angle.

Manual Focus: Adjusts focus manually—either by rotating a focus control ring, or by pressing "near-far" focus pushbuttons.

Manual White Balance: Useful in mixed light situations, so that tint doesn't vary wildly as camera points towards a window. Usually offers fixed settings for indoor and outdoor light. (See COLOR TEMPERATURE, WHITE BALANCE LOCK.)

Memory Counter: Helps users locate specific passages on a tape by numeric counter. User manually sets the counter back to zero before starting to record. Upon rewinding, the camcorder will stop at this tape position.

MiniDV: Small cassette version of DV format for camcorders. See DV.

Neutral Density Filter (ND Filter): An optical filter that reduces the amount of light entering a camera without influencing the color reproduction. Useful when very bright sunlight illuminates snow or sand; or to adjust depth of focus.

Newvicon Tube: An image sensor tube found in older camcorders.

Ni-cad: Standard nickel cadmium rechargeable battery.

Nickel Metal Hydride: A lighter weight rechargeable battery.

Non-Linear Editing: Tapeless editing in which raw video and audio are stored on disk and edited via computer.

Optical Viewfinder: A simple non-electronic viewfinder system consisting of a tube with lenses and markings that show approximately the same field of view that the camcorder's image sensor sees.

PCM Audio: An additional pair of audio tracks available on 8mmand Hi8 videocassettes; can be dubbed later. PCM stands for pulse code modulation—a digital recording process.

Pinpoint Focus: See ZONE FOCUS.

Pixel: A picture element—the tiniest point in a TV picture. An image sensor chip consists of hundreds of thousands of pixels—the more pixels, the higher the HORIZONTAL RESOLUTION.

Plug-in Power: Microphone jack system that provides power to accessory microphones.

Power Zoom: A motorized zoom lens. The speed of power zooming may be fixed or adjustable. See ZOOM RATIO.

Program Auto Exposure: System that simultaneously adjusts both IRIS and HIGH SPEED SHUTTER to achieve a desired effect—sports mode will maintain the fastest possible shutter speed, for example, while the panorama mode will maintain the widest possible range of what's in good focus (DEPTH OF FIELD).

Quick Review: See INSTANT REVIEW.

RC Time Code: Identifies each frame on the videotape with a unique number, to improve editing accuracy. Available on HI8 and 8mm only, RC stands for rewriteable consumer, because it can be added later or re-recorded without affecting video or audio.

Real Time Counter: A display showing hours-minutes-seconds of tape that has been recorded (elapsed time), or how much tape remains.

Refresh: See BATTERY REFRESH.

Remote Control Jack: Useful for editing, to synchronize camcorder with VCR.

RF Adaptor: Allows camcorder to playback tapes into any TV on Channel 3 or 4.

ROM Graphics: A system utilizing "Read Only Memory" (ROM) chips to superimpose color graphics over a video image.

Scanning: The process whereby each video frame is created from a rapid sequence of horizontal scan lines.

Self-timer: The self-timer allows the user to set the camcorder to start after a delay of about 10 seconds, so that she or he can get into the picture.

Sensitivity: See LUX.

Special Effects Playback: Camcorder (or VCR) can playback pictures at other than normal speed—still frame, slow motion, or forward/reverse scan with good picture quality. Also called Tricks Mode.

Stereo: Two channel audio. Separate left-channel and right-channel audio signals are recorded, instead of a single monaural (one channel) signal. Creates more realistic sound when played on stereo TV or through headphones.

Still Frame Playback: When the tape is paused, a good quality still frame image can be seen, free of video noise glitches.

Super Betamax: An improved version of the Betamax videocassette format featuring 290-line horizontal resolution.

Super VHS (S-VHS): An improved version of the VHS format capable of recording better picture resolution (detail). Super-VHS videocassettes look the same as VHS cassettes, but use a different type of high-density tape inside, and require a different recording and playback process. The tape provides a wider luminance bandwidth, resulting in sharper picture quality, with horizontal resolution of over 400-lines (compared with 240-lines for regular VHS). Also called "high-band" recording. Super-VHS and S-VHS-C camcorders feature S-video jacks, which separate the luminance and chrominance signals, for improved monitoring (on a TV receiver/monitor) and dubbing.

S-VHS-C (Super-VHS-compact): A miniature version of the Super-VHS format, utilizing smaller cassettes that also play in full-size Super-VHS VCRs (see also VHS-C).

S-video (Separated Video) Connectors: A system of plugs and jacks that interconnect camcorders, VCRs, and TV monitors in such a way that the luminance (brightness) and chrominance (color) are kept separate. Improves picture quality. In tech jargon, luminance is called Y, and chrominance is C, hence S-video connectors are also called Y/C connectors.

Synchro Edit: Remote control camcorder jack that hooks up tocompatible VCRs and allows for semi-automated editing control.

Time Code: System of identifying each frame of a videotape, useful for editing.

Time Lapse: A system that automatically records a few frames of video periodically, to compress time. A time-lapse recording of one second every minute, for example, will compress an hour into a one minute video recording. Also called interval recording.

Track: A magnetic recording along the surface of the tape. A videotape is divided into invisible tracks, representing individual video FIELDS and audio signals. (See HELICAL RECORD-ING.)

TTL Autofocus: (Through The Lens.) Focus is adjusted by the camcorder's efforts to create the sharpest possible edges around the subject.

Vectorscope: Electronic test instrument used for checking the color portion of the video signal.

VHS (Video Home System): The most common home VCR videocassette tape format used in the U.S.

VHS Hi-Fi: Improved stereo audio recording and playback system found on some camcorders and VCRs. VHS Hi-Fi tracks must always be recording at same time as video—dubbing is not possible.

Video Cassette: See CASSETTE.

Video Dub: Ability to record new video pictures over a previously recorded tape, without erasing previously recorded sound. Also called video insert editing.

Vidicon: A type of image sensor tube used in older camcorders.

Viewfinder Indicators: Information that can be seen in the viewfinder, such as low battery warning, end of tape warning, high-speed shutter, low light warning, moisture condensation, operating mode, time remaining on tape, index counter, and pinpoint focus zone.

VITC: Vertical Interval Time Code—system where each video frame is numbered in the unseen scan lines at top of frame.

Waveform Monitor: Electronic test equipment used for analyzing video signals.

White Balance: The adjustment for sensitivity to different COLOR TEMPERATURES. (See AUTOMATIC WHITE BALANCE, WHITE BALANCE LOCK.)

White Balance Lock: An advanced form of MANUAL WHITE BALANCE that uses the automatic white balance system on a one-shot basis to lock onto a color setting.

Wireless Remote: Camcorder remote control for playback and recording. Some remotes offer zoom control.

Y/C Connections: See S-VIDEO.

Zone Focus: Automatic focus adjustment that varies the size of the area of the picture that the lens tries to focus on. Also called pinpoint focus.

Zoom Lens: A lens that makes objects appear closer or farther away, thus offering a variety of framing options while keeping the camcorder a fixed distance from the subject. Technically, a zoom lens is called a "variable focal length" lens.

Zoom Ratio: The amount of variation a zoom lens offers for making things appear closer or further away. Technically, the zoom ratio is a comparison of the lens' longest FOCAL LENGTH to its shortest. A zoom lens whose focal length varies from 6mm to 48mm would thus have an 8:1 zoom ratio.

(portions courtesy of the Electronics Industry Association.)

H: Acronym Glossary

Video technology is an alphabet soup of acronyms. Here's some help decoding the babble.

AFM Audio Frequency Modulation, the system used for recording audio on standard 8mm and Hi8 audio tracks

AGC Automatic Gain Control, a system used to set levels; used for both picture and sound

BNC A type of video connector used in professional video equipment. (To use with consumer gear, you usually need a BNC to phono adaptor.)

CATV Cable TV

CMX A company which set the standard for high-end computer controlled editing; professional Edit Decision Lists conform to this standard.

dB Decibel, a logarithmic method of comparing levels commonly used for describing both audio and video signals

DBS Direct Broadcast Satellite

DCT Discrete Cosine Transform. System of data compression used in DV cassettes.

DV Digital video tape format.

EDL Edit Decision List, a list of the start and stop points that define an edited sequence.

EIS Electronic Image Stabilization, a digital technique to eliminate minor camera shake

F.C.C. Federal Communications Commission (regulates broadcasting)

HDTV High Definition Television (high resolution video with over 1,000 scan lines)

Hi8 A better quality camcorder videocassette format

HP Headphones

JPEG System for compressing digital data in still photographs and moving images (Motion JPEG).

LANC A sophisticated remote control jack found on Sony camcorders, VCRs, and other equipment (also called Control-L, stands for Local Applications Network Control)

MiniDV Compact camcorder version of DV digital videocassette format.

MPEG Motion Picture Experts Group. Widely used system for compressing data in digitized video.

N.T.S.C. The American TV scanning system (525 lines per frame, 30 frames per second). Stands for National Television Standards Committee

P.A.L. The European TV scanning system

RF Radio Frequency. When a video signal is put onto Channel 3 or 4 on a TV set, it becomes an RF signal.

RG-6 A thick coaxial cable used for carrying video and cable-TV

RG-59 A slightly less thick coaxial cable used for carrying video and cable-TV

SC Subcarrier. Usually provides a color tint adjustment, same as phase adjustment.

S.E.C.A.M. The French and former East Bloc TV scanning system.

Super-VHS (S-VHS) A higher quality consumer videocassette format

VCR Videocassette recorder

VF Viewfinder

VHS The standard US videocassette format (Video Home System)

VHS-C A smaller camcorder version of VHS

VU Volume units (audio level)

Z Impedance, usually expressed in ohms. Better quality low impedance microphones are usually about 600-ohms, cheaper high impedance microphones are around 10,000-ohms (10K); video signals usually require 75-ohm inputs and outputs.

Index

Symbols

16 x 9 406
16mm 12
180-degree rule 107, 175
220 to 110 368
3-chip 33
3/4 SP 158
3/4" U-matic 13, 157
35-mm film 4
4:1:1 148
4:2:2 148
8-track studio 311
8mm format 137

A

A/B roll editing 202, 236, 260
A/V insert editing 222
A/V mixer 243
A/X editing 240
Acquisition format 233
Action 168
Adobe Premiere 153, 264
Advance sync 255
AFM audio 138
AG-1980 36, 187
AGC 66, 308
Aiwa 22
Alliance for Community Media
    392
American Express 28
Amiga 238, 260
Amps 331
Analog signals 268
Analog video recordings 232
Animation 344
Animation stand 347
Aperture 57
Apple 264
ASA 62

Aspect ratio 403
Assemble editing 221
Associate producer 359
Audio 80, 281
Audio dub 222
Audio dubbing 225
Audio fidelity 160
Audio master 315
Audio tracks 135, 159
Authorized dealers 31
Automatic focus 52
Automatic gain control 66
AVI 266
Avid 261

B

Back light 322
Back light compensation 59, 319
Balanced lines 303
Barn doors 323
Batteries 32
Beats per measure 318
Betacam 162
Big budget 5
Blackburst 224
Blackened 160
Blank areas 111
Blank Tape 24
Blank tape 127
Blank videocassettes 128
Blue filter 334
Bogen 116
Brand names 22
Broadcast quality 3, 13
Broadcast-quality 74

C

Cable Act 394
Cable TV 383

Camcorder 47
Camera burns 159
Camera movements 115
Camera moves 113
Camera operator 167
Camera original 203
Canon's L-2 34
Carrying cases 33
CCD 62
CDR-VX1000 33
Cels 347
Character generator 84
Character generators 339
Chroma 76
Chroma key 88
Chroma saturation 254
Cinematographer 6
Circuit breaker 331
Clapboard 184
CMX-compatibility 206
Color temperature 70, 333
Color viewfinder 82
Commercial 4
Commercial sponsors 397
Commodore 238
Common carrier 385
Component recording 13, 162
Component video 78
Composite video 78
Compression ratio 153
Compression ratios 263
Condenser Microphone 289
Conflict 104
Control track 135, 214, 221
Control-L 208
Corporation for Public Broadcast-
    ing 399
Counter 214
Cut 100, 172
Cutaway shot 173, 174

D

D-2 13, 162
D/Vision CineWorks 270
DAT 30
Data compression 147
Data rates 263
Date 84
DCT compression 148

Decibels 75
Deep Dish TV 391
Depth of field 60
Digital Betacam 13, 149, 162
Digital dubbing 143
Digital effects 88
Digital Processing Systems 276
Digital superimpose 84
Digital tape 263
Digital video 200, 267
Digital Video Cassette 141
Digital video effects 237
Digital video recording 262
Direct Broadcast Satellites 409
Direct broadcast satellites 407
Directional microphones 291
Director 361
Discrete Cosine Transfer 150
Dissolve 179, 236
Distribution copies 233
Diversity receiver 295
Docked 47
Dollying 115
Downstream keyer 251
Drop frame 216
Dropouts 129
DSS 409
Dubbing 199
DV 13, 142
DVC 141
DVCPro 153, 222
DVD 268
Dynamic microphones 290
Dynamic range 286

E

Edit controller 36
Edit controllers 203, 204
Edit decision list 204, 216
Edit master 152
Edit points 206
Editing 152, 167
Editing accuracy 213
Editing audio 316
Editing systems 159
Editing Technology 199
Editing VCR 187
EditLink 260
Editors 169

Electrical power 330
Elevator column 116
EP/SLP speed 79, 134
Erase head 80, 163
Error correction 151
Establishment shot 170
EV-635A 305
EVF 81
Executive producer 359
Experimental 167
Extended warranty 27
External microphone 287

F

F-stop 58
F-stop number 61
F.C.C. 275, 388
Fade in 101, 168
Fader 68
Fades 178
Field 73
Fill light 321
Film 63
Film style 182
Filters 354
Fine cut 153, 218
Firewire 144, 209
First Amendment 389
Fishpole 304
Fluid head 114
Fluorescent 69
Flying erase head
    80, 164, 201
Focal length 49
Focus 50, 52
Focus motor 54
Fog filter 355
Fonts 341
Foreign television 231
Found footage 200
Frame 73
Frame grab 86
Frame numbers 215
Frame synchronizer 237
Frame-by-frame 189
Framing 49
Franchise 384
Freeze frame 246
Full frame 276

Fundraising 395
FutureVideo Products 208, 259

G

Gain 67
General purpose interface
    210, 229, 237
Generation loss 151, 232, 233
Genlock 240
Glitch 163
Glitches 187
Going direct 300
Gold Card 28
Gold Disk 260
Grants 398
Graphics 339
Gray market 29
Grip equipment 117

H

HDTV 155, 263, 403
Head drum 71
Head, tripod 114
Headphone amplifier 298
Headphone jack 281
Headphones 103, 298
Helical recording 71
Helical tracks 146, 163
Helical video 164
Hi-fi tracks 134
Hi8 233
Hi8 format 138
High speed shutter 61, 85, 86
High-impedance 296
Horizontal resolution 74
Hum 307
Hybrid systems 274

I

IBM 260
IDE drive 273
IEEE 1394 209
Image sensor 62
Image stabilization 89
Imaging device 56
Impedance 296
In kind contributions 397

In-camera editing
102, 110, 179, 180
Incandescent 69
Independent Television Service
399
Index/address 135
Industrial VCR 196
Industrial video 24
Infrared 52
Infrared remote 204
Inner-focus 57
Insert editing 220
Intercut 168, 172
Interformat editing 233
Interlace 73
Interlacing 85
International standards 374
Internet 413
Interval timer 349
Intervalometer 87
Interview 180
Iris 57
ISDN 414
ISO 62
ITVS 399

J

Japanese 21
Jog/shuttle control 188
Jump cut 167, 173

K

Key light 321
Keyer 254
Koyaanisqatsi 345
Kuchar, George 6

L

LANC 207, 234, 257, 259
Language 101
LaserDisc 267
LCD 82
LCD screens 82
Leased access 390
Lecture hall 287
Lens 48
Lens speed 61
Light 103
Light kit 32

Lighting 319
Lightwave 3-D 242
Line voltage 371
Line-level signal 303
Linear audio track 134
Lip-sync 314
Logging tapes 186
Long-playing speed 79
Low light 53, 60
Low-impedance 296
Luminance 76, 161
Luminance keyer 248, 254
Lux 66

M

Macintosh 260
Macro range 56
Manual focus 54
Manual iris control 58
Manufacturers 22
Mastercard 28
Matsushita (Panasonic) 5-pin 207,
208, 259
Media Logic 261
Medium shots 172
Metal Evaporated 130
Metal Particle 130
Mic-level signal 303
Microphone 287
Microphone jack 287
Microsoft 264
MIDI 186
MII 162
MiniDV
141, 165, 209, 233, 287
Minority voices 388
Mix switch 165
Model numbers 26
Modems 414
Modes 78
Modify VCRs 166
Montage 178
MOS image sensor 62
Mosaic fade 88
Mount Rushmore 105
MPEG 147, 267, 414
MPEG-1 263
Multi-camera 106, 183
Multi-camera shooting 182

Multi-image effects 348
Municipal government 389
MUSE 405
Music Editing 317
Music videos 159, 310

N

NAB 407
NCTA 407
Neutral density (ND) filter 356
NewTek 238
Noise 299
Noise levels 76
Nonlinear editing 17, 261
Normal 51
Normal focal length 56

O

Obie 120
Off-line 76
Off-line edit 206
On-line edit 206
One-shot focusing 54
Optical filter 354
Orthochromatic 85
Out-of-sequence 110
Outdoor light 70
Override 53

P

PAL 147, 232, 373
Panasonic AG-1980 189
Panasonic WJ-AVE7 247
Panasonic WJ-MX30 254
PCM audio tracks 139
Pedestal mounts 113
Personal Animation Recorder 354
Personal TBC 276
Philips 22
Photoflood lights 70, 333
Piezo electric 52
Pinpoint focus 55
Pixels 64, 75, 82
Playback speed 86
Polarizing filter 355
Porta-packs 159
Portable lights 332

Post-production 181
Post-production editing 110, 180
Power zoom 51
Practical light 327
Pre-production 181
Pre-roll 206
Pre-roll time 111
Price fixing 28
Prime lenses 358
Producer 360
Production 181
Proposal 396
Prosumer 22
Pseudo-dissolve 88
Psychoacoustics 282
Public access 387
Public Broadcasting System 399
PV-DV1000 33

Q

Quasar 22
Quasi-S-VHS 133
Quick review 79
QuickTime 19, 264

R

RC time code 140
RCA 22
Reaction shot 167, 173
Reflector 335
Registration cards 31
Rent 16
Resolution 65, 74
RGB 148
Rodney King 3, 91
Rough cut 152, 217
RS-232C 212, 255

S

S-video 77
S/N ratio 75
Sampling 268
Saturation 76
Scan lines 63, 73, 275
Scouting location 107
Screen continuity 168, 174
Screen direction 176
Script 184

Scriptwriter 360
SECAM 232, 373
Self-timers 87
Shake 99
Shooting to edit 312
Shot list 184
Shotgun microphone 291
Shoulder-mount 113
Shutter speeds 85
Shuttle 188
Simultaneous action 176
Sitcom 3
Slow motion 196
SMPTE 215
SMPTE time code
       160, 166, 185, 186
Sony DHR-1000 191
Sony XV-D1000 252
Sound bytes 104
SP speed 79, 134
Special effects generator 236
Spectrum space 408
Splice 199
Splicing videotapes 199
Sprocket holes 352
Squelch 295
Star filter 355
Stationary erase head 163
Stationary head 71
Steadicam JR 117
Steady Shot 90
Storyboard 184
Straight cut 178, 236
Studio television 182
Subcarrier 148
Super-Bowl 4
Super-VHS 233
Synchro-edit 201, 209
Synchronization 76

T

T-120 79
Tape 24
Tape speed 79
TBC 11
Telephone 415
Telephoto 50
Telephoto extender 358
Thomson 22

Three Point Lighting 319
Three-chip 17, 64
Thumbs Up 256
Time base corrector 77, 236, 275
Time code 16, 183, 208, 215
Time code editing 227
Time code generators 216
Time-lapse 87, 350
Titlemaker 256
ToasterCG 242
Tota light 328
Tracks 116
Transfer 231
Travel 369
Tripod 32, 101
Tripods 113
Trucking 115
Tubes 159
Tungsten light 70
TV commercials 4
TV safe 344
TwinCam 21
Two-way cable 385

U

U-matic 157
Ultra-directional microphone 306
User bits 215

V

VCR mode 78
VGA 263
VHF 294
VHS format 133
VIASS 135
Video camera 47
Video dial tone 413
Video Director 36, 260
Video disc 18
Video dub 226
Video editing 169, 231
Video Flyer 269
Video for Windows 264
Video format 124
Video head 71
Video Toaster 238
Videonics 256
Videonics MX-1 243
Videonics Thumbs Up 256

Videonics TitleMaker 340
VideoSpigot 266
ViewCam (Sharp) 35, 82
Viewfinder 81
Visa 28
VISCA 210, 255
Visible spectrum 69
Visual storytelling 168
VITC 216, 257
VU meters 298

W

Warranties 27
Watts 331
White balance 69, 333
White balance lock 70
Wide angle 50, 99
Wide angle adapter 358
Window 276
Wireless microphone 292
WJ-AVE5 252
WJ-MX30 254
Workprints 140, 219
World Wide Web 416

X

X-ray 372
XLR connectors 296, 303
XLR microphone jack 26
XV-D1000 253

Y

YUV 148

Z

Zapruder 3
Zoom lens 100, 172
Zoom ratio 48
Zoom Speeds 51
Zooming 172

Desktop Video Systems

Send in this coupon for more information on:

☐ D.V.S. At-Home Video Editing Service

☐ D.V.S. Newsletter

☐ D.V.S. Video Consulting Service

Name _____

Address _____

_____

City _____ State _____ ZIP_____

Please answer the following questions to help us evaluate your needs and offer additional services in the future:

Do you own a camcorder?   ☐ Yes (What kind?) ☐ NO

Do you own an editing VCR? ☐ Yes (What kind?) ☐ NO

Do you own a computer ☐ Yes (What kind?) ☐ No
        ☐ IBM Compatible ☐ Macintosh ☐ Amiga ☐ Other

Does it have a CD-ROM drive? ☐ Yes ☐ No

How did you obtain this book?
        ☐ Bookstore ☐ Mail order ☐ Telephone order ☐ Other

Mail to:
Desktop Video Systems
Box 668, Peck Slip Station, New York, NY 10272

Comments

We're interested in reader feedback. If you have any comments, gripes, or suggestions for future editions of this book, please write us.

Desktop Video Systems

Send in this coupon for more information on:

☐ D.V.S. At-Home Video Editing Service

☐ D.V.S. Newsletter

☐ D.V.S. Video Consulting Service

Name _____

Address _____

_____

City _____ State _____ ZIP____

Please answer the following questions to help us evaluate your needs and offer additional services in the future:

Do you own a camcorder?   ☐ Yes (What kind?)   ☐ NO

Do you own an editing VCR?   ☐ Yes (What kind?)   ☐ NO

Do you own a computer   ☐ Yes (What kind?)   ☐ No

☐ IBM Compatible   ☐ Macintosh   ☐ Amiga   ☐ Other

Does it have a CD-ROM drive?   ☐ Yes   ☐ No

How did you obtain this book?

☐ Bookstore   ☐ Mail order   ☐ Telephone order   ☐ Other

Mail to:

Desktop Video Systems

Box 668, Peck Slip Station, New York, NY 10272

Comments

We're interested in reader feedback. If you have any comments, gripes, or suggestions for future editions of this book, please write us.

Save $5 With This Special Offer!

The Low Budget AUDIO Bible

by Cliff Roth

Everything you need to know to get professional audio quality on a low budget. Publication date: Feb. 1998. Cover price: $32.95. Save $5 with this special offer. Mail in the coupon below. Send no money – we'll bill you upon publication – 30-day no risk free trial basis.

Name _____

Address _____

_____

City _____ State _____ ZIP _____

☐ Please send me THE LOW BUDGET AUDIO BIBLE at the special price of $27.95 (plus $4 shipping and handling and sales tax, where appropriate), for which I will be billed. If not completely satisfied I can return the book within 30 days and owe nothing.

Signature _____

Mail to:
Desktop Video Systems
Box 668, Peck Slip Station, New York, NY 10272